The Changing Geography of
AFRICA

The Changing Geography of
AFRICA

A. T. GROVE

EMERITUS FELLOW, DOWNING COLLEGE,
AND SENIOR RESEARCH ASSOCIATE,
DEPARTMENT OF GEOGRAPHY,
UNIVERSITY OF CAMBRIDGE

OXFORD UNIVERSITY PRESS

Oxford University Press, Walton St., Oxford OX2 6DP

Oxford   New York   Toronto
Delhi   Bombay   Calcutta   Madras   Karachi
Kuala Lumpur   Singapore   Hong Kong   Tokyo
Nairobi   Dar es Salaam   Cape Town
Melbourne   Auckland   Madrid

and associated companies in
Berlin   Ibadan

Oxford is a trademark of Oxford University Press

ISBN 0 19 913386 7
Editorial and design by Hart McLeod, Cambridge
Typeset by Goodfellow & Egan, Cambridge
Printed and bound in Great Britain by
Butler & Tanner Ltd., Frome and London

PREFACE

In the course of the late 1970s the economies of many African countries were shored up by loans from Western countries. Expenditure on oil products and imported food was increasing, industries were suffering from the high prices of imported inputs and, nearly every African country carried a heavy burden of debt. Populations were continuing to rise faster than in any other large part of the world, doubling every twenty years. Towns were rapidly expanding with people seeking wage labour and security in times of famine and conflict. It seemed possible that by the end of the century a minority of Africa's population would be rural. Industrial growth, except in South Africa was making slow progress, and in the rural areas there was still little sign of a Green Revolution producing a surplus to feed the urban dwellers.

Drought returned to both the Sahel/Sudan and southern Africa in the early 1980s. Not only was the gap widening between standards of living in Africa and the industrial countries, but levels of income per head in many African countries had fallen since the 1960s. The economies of southern Africa ceased to grow as the ethnic struggle for power in South Africa moved towards a climax. Indications of a crisis in the continent's affairs were only too evident in the form of armed conflicts, poverty, famine, and disease.

The first eight chapters of *The Changing Geography of Africa*, which appeared in 1989, considered the continent's physical and ecological patterns and outlined the ethnic situation, historical development and population trends. Four chapters were devoted to the various fields of economic activity which make use of the continent's resources: mining, water resource development, industry and commercial agriculture. Finally, in a concluding chapter, some of the main features of the crisis were outlined—notably drought, desertification, famine, conflict, aid, and indebtedness. The same scheme has been followed in this updated edition.

The outlook continues to be gloomy. Rainfall values in the Sahel/Sudan have remained lower than they were in the 1950s and 1960s; in 1992, the worst drought in living memory was afflicting southern Africa. Commodity prices have been falling. There are, however, some hopeful signs. The end of the conflict between communism and capitalism, signalled by the departure of Cuban forces from Angola and the independence of Namibia, has somewhat relieved political stresses in the continent, though the long-term consequences of the contest between the super-powers continue to reverberate. The civil war in Ethiopia has been concluded. The end of white domination in South Africa seems certain, but that struggle has yet to be finally resolved. Indebtedness attracts less attention than it did a few years ago; some debts which are evidently not going to be repaid have been written off by the lenders; the fall in oil prices to levels not very different from those of the early 1970s and a weaker American dollar have helped matters a little, at least in the countries that have no oil resources. Governments are becoming somewhat less dictatorial than they have been in the past, and under pressure from international agencies and realizing that their effectiveness depends on the support they receive from the mass of people, are more ready to submit themselves to the electorate. The rate of population increase remains alarming but the possibility that growth may slacken as a result of the continued spread of AIDS provides no comfort, only a deeper foreboding.

A.T.G.
Cambridge, November 1993

CONTENTS

Preface   v
List of figures   ix
Acknowledgements   x

1   The physical environment   1
1.1   Introduction.   1
1.2   Relief and rocks—evolution of the   3
structure and relief; rock
weathering, residual crusts and
stripped landscapes; coastlines
1.3   Climate—atmospheric pressure,   15
wind systems and the pattern of
precipitation; tropical cyclones;
evaporation; climatic variability
1.4   Lakes and rivers   29

2   Ecology   35
2.1   Biomes—tropical forest; tropical   35
savanna; steppe and desert; high
montane vegetation; north Africa's
vegetation
2.2   Soils—arid zone soils; soils of sub-   46
humid and humid regions; plants
as soil indicators; soils and
topography
2.3   Fauna—mammals; birds; fish   50

3   Pests and Diseases   53
3.1   Locusts   53
3.2   Termites   55
3.3   The mosquito, malaria, and other   56
mosquito-borne diseases
3.4   The tsetse-fly, trypanosomiasis,   57
and sleeping sickness
3.5   Parasitic worms   59
3.6   Onchocerciasis or river blindness   59
3.7   Schistosomiasis or bilharzia   60
3.8   Rinderpest   61

4   Ethnicity   62
4.1   Race—racial tension   62
4.2   Culture—language; society;   65
religion

5   Traditional ways of life   69
5.1   Hunting and collecting   69
5.2   Pastoralism   69
5.3   Cultivation—forest cultivators;   73
savanna cultivators; oasis
cultivators
5.4   Fishing   82

6   Africa before the colonial period   86
6.1   Prehistory   86
6.2   Ancient history   87
6.3   Medieval times—the western   90
Sudan zone; north and east Africa
6.4   Expansion of Europe into Africa—   92
Portuguese exploration; the slave
trade; the settlement of South
Africa; nineteenth-century
penetration

7   The colonial era and the coming of   104
independence
7.1   The partition of Africa   104
7.2   The beginning of the colonial era   107
7.3   Railway construction   107
7.4   The First World War and its   111
aftermath
7.5   The inter-war years   112
7.6   The coming of independence—the   114
Second World War and its sequel;
white settlers and strife
7.7   Development—the growth of   118
commodity exports; the
development decades
7.8   Crisis conditions   122

8 Population, migration, and urbanization 124

8.1 Numbers of people and population growth 124

8.2 Distribution of population—regions of sparse settlement; regions of dense settlement 127

8.3 Migration—migrant labour 134

8.4 Urbanization 136

9 Mineral extraction and oil production 145

9.1 The mining industry in High Africa—South Africa; Zimbabwe; Zambia; Zaire; mining elsewhere in High Africa 145

9.2 Mining and the petroleum industry in Low Africa—oil 152

10 Water resource development 157

10.1 Hydroelectric schemes—the Zambezi; the Akosombo dam on the Volta river, Ghana; the Niger; the Tana; other hydroelectricity schemes 157

10.2 Irrigation schemes—the Inland Niger Delta; the Kano river scheme; the Bakolori scheme; the South Chad Irrigation Project; Senegal river schemes 163

10.3 Integrated river control projects—development of the Nile waters; the Orange river scheme 169

10.4 Small-scale irrigation 173

11 Industrialization in Africa 175

11.1 Industrialization in mineral-rich countries—South Africa; Zimbabwe 177

11.2 Industrialization in oil-producing countries—Egypt; Algeria; Nigeria 181

11.3 Industrialization in countries with economies based on agriculture—Kenya; Tanzania; Ghana; Ivory Coast 184

12 Modernizing agriculture 189

12.1 Land tenure—traditional tenure systems; introduced tenure systems; villagization; changes in land tenure in pastoral areas 192

12.2 The scale and management of modern farming systems—large-scale farmers; smallholder schemes 199

12.3 The indigenous contribution 204

13 Crisis in Africa 206

13.1 Famine—food aid; the geographical distribution of famine hazard and disasters 206

13.2 Drought 211

13.3 Desertification—north Africa; Sudan–Sahel region; the rift valley region of east Africa; southern Africa 215

13.4 Conflict within states 221

13.5 Relations between African states—regional groupings 223

13.6 Aid and indebtedness 225

13.7 The way ahead 227

Guide to further reading 228

Statistical table 235

Index 236

LIST OF FIGURES

Fig.

1.1 Major physical features
1.2 Africa as part of Gondwanaland
1.3 Simplified geological map
1.4 Geological table
1.5 Development of a landscape by weathering
1.6 Lagos
1.7 Mean temperatures and mean night/day ranges
1.8 Atmospheric circulation and air mass interaction
1.9 Mean annual number of thunderstorms
1.10 Mean annual precipitation
1.11 Diurnal and seasonal variation in relative humidity
1.12 Mean monthly values of precipitation and temperature
1.13 Climatic transect across west Africa
1.14 Annual rainfall, Banjul and Nyala
1.15 Annual rainfall, Sahel zone stations
1.16 The Roda Gauge
1.17 West–east profile of the Ruwenzori range
1.18 Past and present extent of blown sand
1.19 Inter-tropical lakes in the early Holocene
1.20 The Chad basin
1.21 Longitudinal sections of the Nile, Senegal–Niger–Benue–Chad, and Zaire rivers
1.22 Levels of the Great Lakes and Lake Chad, and discharge of Niger, Nile, and Zambezi
1.23 Seasonal and annual discharge of the Nile
1.24 Discharge of the Niger and the Benue
1.25 Lake Chad in 1973
2.1 Vegetation in relation to rainfall
2.2 (*a*) Limits of the Sahel
2.2 (*b*) Biomes of west Africa

2.3 Altitudinal zoning of vegetation on Mt Kenya
2.4 (*a*) Soil catena in the forest zone of south-west Nigeria
2.4 (*b*) Catenal arrangement of soils in southern Ghana
3.1 Desert Locusts
3.2 Breeding areas of *Simulium damnosum*
3.3 Life cycle of *Schistosoma haematobium*
4.1 The main races in Africa
4.2 States, tribes, and languages
4.3 Widely spoken languages
5.1 Cattle and fisheries about 1984
5.2 Distribution of some important crops
5.3 The heavily settled area of south-east Nigeria
5.4 (*a*) Nigeria: main crops and minerals
5.4 (*b*) Nigeria: the States
5.5 The Volta delta
5.6 The Inland Niger Delta
6.1 The Cape
6.2 Southern Africa
6.3 The Nile valley
6.4 The Maghreb
7.1 (*a*) Africa after the Berlin Conference
7.1 (*b*) Africa at the outbreak of the First World War
7.2 Railways in 1987
7.3 West equatorial Africa
7.4 (*a*) Africa at the outbreak of the Second World War
7.4 (*b*) Africa in 1987
8.1 Population of Egypt, 1840–1980
8.2 Population increase in Africa, 1920–85
8.3 Population growth rates in African countries, 1980–85
8.4 Rural and urban settlement patterns
8.5 The industrial heartland of southern Africa

8.6   The Nile delta
8.7   Rwanda and Burundi
8.8   Ethiopia
8.9   Agricultural land resources
8.10 Migratory movements
8.11 Nigeria: main centres of population
8.12 Yoruba town
8.13 Urban population growth
9.1   Values of main African commodities, mid-1970s and mid-1980s
9.2   Zimbabwe, Zambia, Malawi, Mozambique: mineral resources
9.3   Rail, road, and river routes to ports from Copperbelt
9.4   Origin of Copperbelt ores
9.5   The Zambian Copperbelt
9.6   The western triangle of west Africa
9.7   Oilfields and pipelines of Libya
9.8   Oil wells and pipelines in southern Nigeria
9.9   Oil production, 1970s and 1980s
10.1 Hydroelectricity schemes
10.2 Settlements around the Volta lake

10.3 Dams on the upper Tana, Kenya
10.4 North-eastern Nigeria
10.5 The Bakolori scheme
10.6 Irrigation near Lake Chad
10.7 (a) Lower Senegal irrigation schemes
10.7 (b) The Diama barrage
10.8 Irrigation schemes in the Sudan Republic
10.9 The Gezira irrigation scheme
10.10 The Orange river scheme
11.1 East Africa: economically productive areas
11.2 Ivory Coast, Ghana, Togo, and Benin
12.1 Villagization in Tanzania
13.1 Countries with a decrease in national output 1960–82
13.2 National output by country, 1983
13.3 The famine syndrome
13.4 Zones of political friction
13.5 Zones of desertification risk
13.6 Annual rates of soil erosion
13.7 Sedimentation in a Tanzanian reservoir
13.8 Oil price rises and African commodity price fluctuations

ACKNOWLEDGEMENTS

We are grateful to the following for permission to reproduce photographs:

H. Chazini and FAO – p40 (bottom); FAO – p169, p200; W. Gartung and FAO – p40 (top), p41; W.J.E. Grove – p7, p121, p136, p140, p196; B.E. Harrell-Bond – p144; R.M. McIntosh – p213 (bottom); F. Mattioli and FAO – p227; N. Munro – p14 (bottom), p39; D. Scott and the Durham University Kilimanjaro Expedition 1987 – p37, p50, p51, p79 (left), p117, p141 (top), p186 (both), p189, p190, p194, p204 (bottom); Crew of the Space Shuttle, NASA and Gordon Wells – p85, p118, p167, p172.
All other photographs are by the author.

We also wish to thank Mott MacDonald (Lake Victoria levels and Nile discharge), Hunting Technical Services (Nyala rainfall), Sir Alexander Gibb (Zambezi discharge), the Institute of Hydrology and the Malawi National Resources Master Plan (Lake Malawi levels), the Meteorological Office (Bathurst/Banjul rainfall), Dr Mike Hulme of the Climatic Research Centre, University of East Anglia (African rainfall) and Professor H. Faure, CNRS, Luminy, Marseille (Sahelian river discharges), for hydrological and climatic data to update Figures 1.14, 1.15 and 1.22.

THE PHYSICAL ENVIRONMENT

1.1 Introduction

Africa is the second largest of the continents, with a total area of 19 million km² (11.8 million mls²). Lying across the equator with its southern tip, at Cape Agulhas near the Cape of Good Hope, at 35°S and the northern coast between the Straits of Gibraltar and Tunis at about 35°–37°N, it is the most tropical of the continents. The Sinai peninsula at the northern end of the Red Sea, though cut off by the Suez Canal, is conventionally regarded as part of the continent. Madagascar, one of the world's largest islands, and the relatively small islands of Mauritius, Reunion, and the Seychelles are also parts of Africa.

African landscapes and resources vary regionally on account of contrasts in relief, geology, and climate. The south-east is largely high plateau country, the north-west mainly plains and shallow river basins. The Sahara occupies about half of the continent north of the equator. The extreme north and south have Mediterranean types of climate, with winter rain and summer drought; between the tropics, the rains are concentrated in the summer months or, near the equator, occur in two seasons of the year. Rain forest survives in the Congo/Zaire basin and in shrinking areas elsewhere. These environmental contrasts have an important bearing on the opportunities available for development, especially agricultural development. Costs depend on soil and weather conditions; where they are unfavourable projects are unlikely to succeed.

Industrial development is also related to the availability of resources, notably water, energy, and economic minerals. Water supplies depend on natural hydrographic conditions; not only rainfall but also the volume, quality, and accessibility of surface and sub-surface water. Availability of energy depends on the existence of suitable sites for generating hydroelectric power and on the location of geological formations containing oil or coal. Economic minerals are widely distributed but there are strong concentrations in particular areas, especially in southern Africa (Fig. 1.1).

The relief, rocks, and climate have largely controlled the soils and vegetation that have developed. The resulting assemblages of natural resources have in some areas been attractive to people; in others, the harshlands, people have been deterred from settling. As contacts between African peoples and the rest of the world have become closer over the last few centuries and new technologies have been adopted in the course of the colonial and post-independence periods, Africa's developing economies have become more and more integrated with those of the rest of the world. The pattern of population distribution has changed accordingly, but the environment continues to exert a strong influence on economic activity.

The physical and biological features of the environment are not unchanging. The continents themselves are mobile; the Great Rift Valley of east Africa and the volcanoes in its vicinity are testimonies of this. Ice sheets have covered large parts of Africa in remote geological times; the deserts were more extensive 15 000 years ago, and, while people have become herders and cultivators within the last 10 000 years, lakes have occupied wide areas of the Sahara and have disappeared again. In recent years we have been reminded of the fact that climate is not constant by the diminution of rainfall in the Sahel zone on the south side of the Sahara while, at the same time, some equatorial lakes have risen to their highest levels this century.

In the modern world we are learning how people influence the environment as well as how the environment influences people. It is possible that some of the climatic changes occurring in Africa are related to changes in the

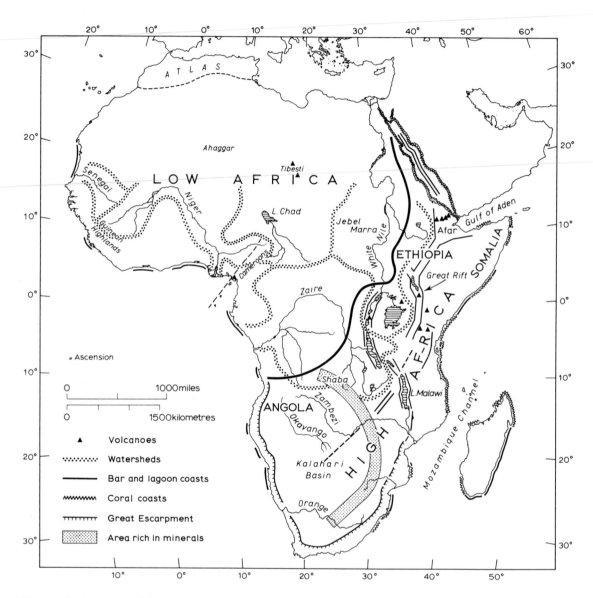

Fig. 1.1 *Major physical features. A line from Angola to Ethiopia divides the continent into High and Low Africa. High Africa is mainly above 1000 m (3300 ft), except for Somalia, lowlands either side of the Mozambique Channel, and narrow coastal plains and river valleys elsewhere. Even the Kalahari Basin is at more than 1000 m, and the surface of Lake Victoria, between the two arms of the east African rift valley, stands at 1130 m (3700 ft). Low Africa is largely made up of sedimentary basins and upland plains 150 to 600 m (500 to 2000 ft) above sea-level, with land above 1000 m confined mainly to the Atlas Mountains in the Maghreb, Ahaggar and Tibesti in the Sahara, Jebel Marra in the Sudan Republic, the highlands between the Cameroon Republic and Nigeria, and the Guinean Highlands in the headwaters of the Niger.*

composition of the atmosphere caused by the burning of fossil fuel. Smoke from grass fires in tropical Africa and dust from the deserts and their margins are also atmospheric pollutants which may be having an effect on climate. Certainly the plant cover of Africa is being drastically changed by burning, grazing, and cultivation. There are fears of soil erosion, desertification, and other forms of environmental degradation which could have long-lasting consequences for the habitability of the continent. Such matters are discussed in the final chapter. Clearly there is good reason to begin a study of the geography of change in Africa by distinguishing the main features of the environmental patterns and their development through time.

1.2 Relief and rocks

The pattern of the relief and the distribution of the various kinds of rocks help to explain the spatial variation in Africa's resource endowment. In regions with high relief, such as the Rift Valley region of Ethiopia, access is difficult and transport costs are high. The possession of oil, gold, and phosphates has been of much benefit to certain African countries. The presence of such valuable minerals may allow one country to prosper while its neighbour without such resources remains impoverished.

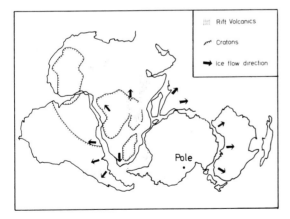

Fig. 1.2. *Africa as part of Gondwanaland, and showing the regions of very ancient rocks, the old cratons. The flow patterns of a polar ice-cap are shown by arrows; it existed 230 million years ago when the southern continents were grouped in this kind of arrangement near the South Pole.*

1.2.1 Evolution of the structure and relief

The explanation for the regional patterns of relief and the distribution of mineral wealth lies in the succession of events in the continent's geological history. This history can be divided into two ages (1) the Pre-Cambrian lasting from the earliest times until about 600 million years ago, (2) Cambrian and later times, from 600 million years ago to the present day.

1.2.1.1 Early earth history The Pre-Cambrian began with the origin of the earth, which geologists currently place about 7000 million years ago. Rocks have been found in Africa which are about half this age. Such very old rocks, intensely folded in mountain building over 1500 million years ago, form three 'older cratons' (Fig. 1.2). They occupy much of the western lobe of Africa, Zaire–Angola and the Zimbabwe–Transvaal–Orange Free State region. Within these older cratons are found most of Africa's gold, diamonds, chromium, asbestos, and iron-rich minerals. Bordering them are the 'younger orogens', regions where folding has taken place within the last 1200 million years. They contain most of the continent's copper, lead, zinc, cobalt, beryl, tin, tungsten, and niobium-tantalite ores (Fig. 1.3).

The Pre-Cambrian rocks have commonly been mineralized in the vicinity of granite or quartzite igneous intrusions and it is mainly in such restricted areas, within the cratons and orogens, that metallic minerals are present in sufficient concentrations and quantities to be worth mining. The ore bodies of economic value are often quite small at the surface. Some were recognized and worked long before Europeans arrived on the scene. Others have been discovered as a result of surveys using satellite imagery, air photographs, and airborne sensing equipment. Surface mapping and prospecting of promising structures are still required; the geologist with a hammer, laboriously sampling and mapping the rocks in the field, still plays an essential role. Finally drilling is necessary to locate the optimum sites for mining. A heavily mineralized zone at Tsumeb in Namibia, south-west Africa, for instance, is only 120 m by 15 m (400 ft by 50 ft) at the surface; there must be many others of similar size underlying the forests and deep weathered layers in many parts of the continent. A kimberlite pipe containing diamonds was discovered beneath the Kalahari sands in Botswana in 1967 and nickel was found in the north-east of the country about the same time, thereby transforming the country's economic prospects.

It requires skilled operators and large sums of money to make such finds, and these are scarce in Africa. The technicians, funds, mining equipment, and business organization are usually provided by multinational companies. They expect to benefit from the profits and as

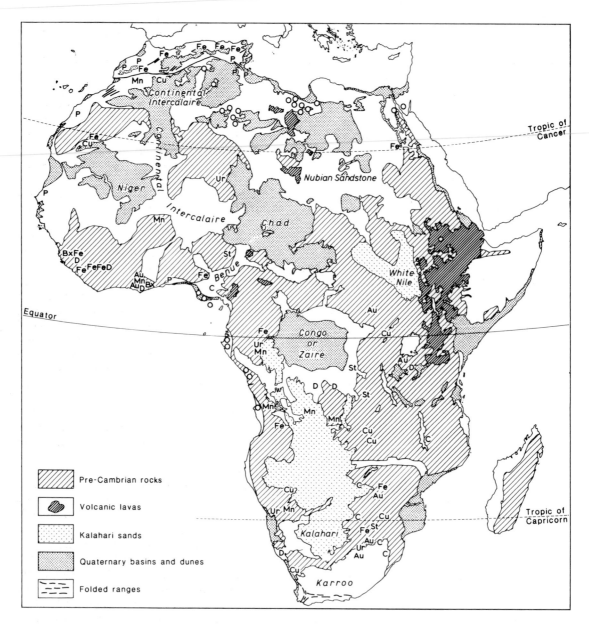

Fig. 1.3. *Simplified geological map. The unshaded areas are underlain by sedimentary rocks—sandstones, shales, and limestones. Such rocks, and also volcanics, occur in the rift valley troughs of East Africa. Au—gold, Bx—bauxite, C—coal, Cu—copper, D—diamonds, Fe—iron, Mn—manganese, O—oil, P—phosphates, Sn—tin, Ur—uranium.*

a result control of the enterprises remains effectively in their hands rather than in those of the national governments concerned.

In some cases the high-density ores released by weathering have been successively concentrated over thousands of years in hillslope deposits, river alluvium, and river terraces. Such ores can be won by relatively simple techniques. In contrast, there are very hard Pre-Cambrian sedimentary formations in which metallic ores have accumulated. Amongst them are the gold-bearing quartzites of the Rand in South Africa, derived from the nearby older craton. To extract the gold and uranium, large volumes of rock have to be extracted from a great depth, crushed, and processed; again costs are high.

Most of the old rocks are intensely folded schists and banded gneisses, resistant to erosion but commonly less resistant than the granites and quartzites intruded into them. Over wide areas these old rocks are characterized by extensive, gently sloping surfaces, the solid rock being concealed beneath a deep weathered layer. Vast bodies of ore in such weathered material, not necessarily of high grade, are capable of yielding, after concentration, high-content ores that can be evacuated by heavy-load transport.

1.2.1.2 Later earth history Rocks of Cambrian and later age commonly contain the fossilized remains of plants and animals. The earliest fossils are of invertebrates, creatures without backbones, then in turn fishlike creatures appear, followed by reptiles and forest plants, dinosaurs, birds, and mammals.

For the first two-thirds of Cambrian and later times, in the Palaeozoic era, Africa was part of a supercontinent called Gondwanaland. Madagascar and India lay alongside Somalia and east Africa; Antarctica and Australia extended east from southern Africa; South America was on the west, with the corner of Brazil fitting neatly into the Gulf of Guinea. Around Gondwanaland great thicknesses of sediment accumulated, derived in part from the erosion of the surface of the supercontinent. They now form sandstones, shales, limestones, and dolomites in the Maghreb of north-west Africa, the western Sahara and at the Cape. Some of these rocks are very resistant to erosion, notably the tough

sandstones of the Cape Series building Table Mountain behind Cape Town (Fig. 1.4).

In Ordovician times, seas spread over what is now north-west Africa. Resting on the marine shales and sandstones dating from this time are tillites, the lithified glacial boulder clays deposited by continental glaciers that occupied much of what is now the western Sahara some 450 million years ago, when it was located not far from the South Pole. The ice sheets left behind roches moutonnées and such typical glacial features as eskers. They were buried under Silurian sediments, lithified, and subsequently uncovered by erosion. Now the glacial lineations can be recognized on satellite imagery.

The Lower Palaeozoic rocks were tilted and fractured by earth movements about the time of the Caledonian Orogeny, but folding was less intense than in Europe and North America. Later, while the coal measures of north-west Europe were accumulating, about 230 million years ago, it was the turn of southern Gondwanaland to be glaciated (Fig. 1.2). The supercontinent had shifted across the surface of the globe until Argentina, southern Africa, Australia, and Antarctica were clustered around the South Pole and covered by an enormous ice-cap (Fig. 1.2). In parts of southern Africa the lithified boulder clays are several hundreds of metres thick. Where the tillites and overlying sedimentary rocks have been removed by natural erosion or stripped off in quarries, scratched rocks and roches moutonnées can still be distinguished and in Namibia deep glaciated valleys can be recognized, but the exhumed glaciated landscapes are not as extensive as those dating from Ordovician times in the north-west Sahara.

While the Carboniferous ice-caps still persisted, the southern tip of the continent was convulsed by violent earth movements comparable in age to the Hercynian in Europe. The rocks of the Cape were strongly folded and subsequent erosion has given highland ranges running parallel to the coast, south of the interior plateau known as the Great Karoo. The Karoo gives its name to a system of rocks that accumulated over much of southern and central Africa in the ages known as Upper Carboniferous, Permian, Triassic, and Lower Jurassic in Europe (Mississippian in North America). The system includes the glacial tillites already mentioned, marine clays, coal-bearing continental

5

deposits, debris eroded from the Hercynian fold mountains, sandstones that accumulated in lakes and deltas, and enormous sheets of volcanic lavas. In Lesotho the lavas rise to nearly 3500 m (11 400 ft) and are as much as 1800 m (6000 ft) thick. In north Africa, the Continental Intercalaire, a system of rocks varying to a similar degree but much thinner than the Karoo, accumulated at a somewhat later stage. It includes the Nubian Sandstones and other water-bearing beds that underlie much of the Sahara and are tapped by deep boreholes.

Gondwanaland was torn apart in the Mesozoic era by currents in the molten interior of the earth and newly independent continents moved away, first from the east and then from

Geological table

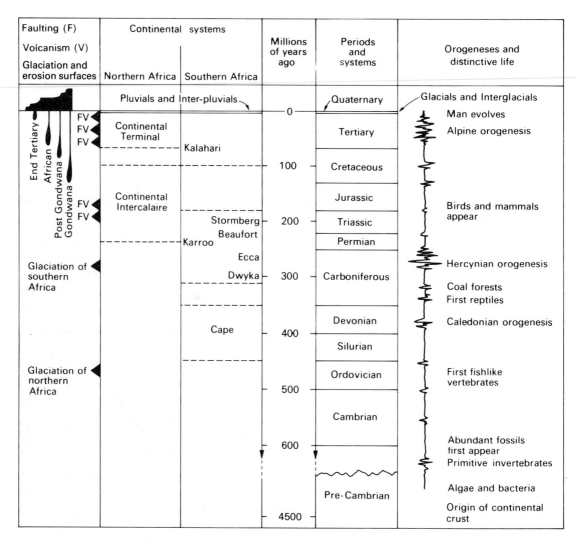

Fig. 1.4. *Geological table. Caledonian earth movements affected mainly the Cape in the extreme south-west, Hercynian and Alpine movements mainly the Atlas region in the north-west. Faulting and volcanism, especially marked in the Tertiary and Quaternary (together called the Cainozoic), affected mainly eastern Africa. Much of the continent consists of upland plains, in the southern part of the continent eroded across old rocks, in the north underlain by sedimentary rocks.*

the west, great fracture systems were generated in the adjacent parts of Africa (Fig. 1.2). Rocks belonging to the Karoo system, let down in rift fractures in the Jurassic, subsequently guided the evolution of the relief and drainage in the south-east. Later, as the South Atlantic widened in the Late Cretaceous, the Benue fault trough opened from the Gulf of Guinea and penetrated far to the north-east into the Saharan region (Fig. 1.3).

From Jurassic times onwards the geological history of the southern half of the continent is quite different from that of the north. The south was left high and dry, only its margins being covered with marine sediments. Further north, Jurassic seas spread over what is now northern Kenya and Ethiopia from the widening Indian Ocean. In Cretaceous times the Saharan region was flooded by seas advancing south from Tethys, a geosyncline in which thick layers of limy and sandy sediments accumulated, and

seas also flooded the Benue rift valley and what is now the lower Niger valley, advancing north to link up with the shallow Saharan seas.

India moved quite rapidly northwards in the Cretaceous and Cainozoic, compressing the sediments that had accumulated in the eastern part of the Tethys geosyncline to form island arcs and folds now forming the Himalaya. Africa moved north more slowly, deforming the western part of the Tethys geosyncline and its contents to produce an island arc where volcanism was widespread and granites were intruded. From these rocks and structures the Atlas ranges have been derived by long-continued erosion and intermittent uplift. The southern boundary of the Atlas, shown on Fig. 1.3, is clear-cut, a series of faults separating the folded rocks from the rigid Saharan block.

About half-way through the Cainozoic era, some 35 million years ago, the Ethiopian–Arabian region was elevated into an immense

Kilimanjaro; the glacier-capped Kibo crater seen from the southern slopes of the mountain at a height of about 4000 m (13 000 ft).

dome which eventually split, giving three rifts arranged in a Y. The two northern arms of the Y grew wider as Arabia drifted away to the north to produce the Red Sea and the Gulf of Aden and enormous volumes of lava poured out over the Ethiopian region. The Afar Depression forming the stem of the Y extended south across Ethiopia as a trough that was prolonged across another somewhat smaller lava-capped updoming in south-west Kenya. Faulting also took place further west and south, rejuvenating the rift faulting that had originated in the Jurassic period and giving troughs that came to be occupied by Lakes Albert (Mobutu), Edward, Kivu, Tanganyika, and Malawi (Nyasa).

In the course of the early Cainozoic (the Tertiary and Quaternary) era, the shallow seas of the Saharan region gradually retreated and the Mediterranean acquired something like its present form. About 15 million years ago, towards the end of the Miocene, its connection with the Atlantic was broken, possibly as a result of the continued northward movement of Africa or, it has been suggested, because of a fall in sea-level associated with the buildup of an ice-cap in Antarctica. Evaporation from the Mediterranean was at that time high, as it is now, and its supply of water from rain and rivers was low. Eventually the great lake it had become dried up and the Mediterranean was converted into an immense desert basin with Crete, Sicily, and Malta rising as mountain ranges thousands of metres above its floor. The lower Rhone and the Nile cut deep canyons and constructed great alluvial fans on the floor of the basin. Then in the Pliocene, about 6 million years ago, the waters of the Atlantic began to pour over the sill at Gibraltar, filling up the Mediterranean basin, which acquired a completely new marine fauna.

Many of the islands in the Indian Ocean and Atlantic are the fragments of old volcanoes that originated on the crests of mid-ocean ridges and were carried away from the crests as the sea-floor continued to spread. The oldest are the furthest from the ridge crests. A volcano on Reunion is still active and so are Mount Cameroon and a number of volcanoes in the vicinity of the East African Rift Valley. The highest point in Africa is a glacier on the rim of Kibo, the active crater forming the summit of Mt Kilimanjaro. Mt Kenya is the core of an extinct volcano. Many other volcanoes, such as

Rungwa at the northern end of Lake Malawi, and Tousside and Emi Koussi in Tibesti, southern Sahara, are dormant at present but might spring into life at some time in the future.

1.2.2 Rock weathering, residual crusts, and stripped landscapes

Most of the earth's surface is mantled by a layer of weathered rock and debris; solid rock comes to the surface only where the products of breakdown have been removed suddenly, or as quickly as they formed, for example on steep slopes or in arid areas where breakdown is slow and removal may be fast. The debris and drift mantle, sometimes called the regolith, is the parent material from which soils are derived, and so an understanding of its nature is of some importance in attempting to appreciate the interaction of the elements of the environment and the nature of African soils.

Chemical weathering is more active in Africa than in higher latitudes because the high temperatures speed up chemical reactions and biological activity, causing rock minerals to decay rapidly, especially if there is plenty of moisture present. Weathered rock was not removed by glaciers as it was in North America and northwest Europe. In the humid areas a plant cover persisted even in the drier periods of the Quaternary era and consequently we find the rocks in the wetter parts of the continent are commonly decomposed to depths of 15 m (50 ft) or more. In some places it is difficult to find fresh rock and hard gravel for building such things as roads and harbour works, and then rocky inselbergs become useful as well as being scenically attractive.

In the wetter regions, under natural conditions, the thick regolith and soil are protected from the impact of raindrops by a leaf canopy and the decaying leaves and branches on the ground beneath form an absorbent layer that soaks up the rain so that it can percolate down without running over the surface. When forests are cleared, the leaf litter soon oxidizes, less water filters down into the soil, and much more of it runs over the surface. Within a few years the topsoil can be washed off hill slopes or they are gashed by gullies and landslips. The debris is carried into stream channels, reducing their capacity, and the higher floods spread sedi-

Deep weathering of crystalline rocks in east Africa, with an inselberg in the background resulting from stripping away of the weathered layer.

weathering processes, at work over thousands or even millions of years, have resulted in the accumulation of certain distinctive layers in the regolith. Where these layers have been exposed by erosion of the overlying soil (as a result of climatic changes or human interference) they are revealed as thick, hard, surface crusts, sometimes called duricrusts. Three main kinds can be distinguished, called ferricrete, calcrete, and silcrete.

1.2.2.1 Surface ironstone Ferricrete is rich in iron and alumina, so rich that some types have been used as iron ore by African iron-smelters. It covers quite extensive areas in the savanna lands and is typical of old upland plains developed over many kinds of rock. The original enrichment of the soil layer with oxides of iron and alumina was probably the result of long-continued leaching away of silicates and the more soluble products of weathering in areas of low relief where erosion by running water had practically ceased. The hardening of the iron-rich layer may have taken place either as a result of the soil layer being dried out following uplift and rejuvenation of the streams, or in consequence of the climate getting drier.

When streams cut into a ferricrete-covered plain, steep slopes are formed, mantled with bouldery ferricrete debris. This moves slowly down to the new erosion surface and is incorporated in the soils developing on it to form what is sometimes called secondary laterite. The sequence of iron enrichment, induration, and dissection may be repeated a number of times, giving flat residual surfaces with stepped bounding slopes.

ments over floodplains. In time, pleasant meandering rivers bordered by woodland and cultivable land may be converted to braided streams which are either dry or in flood, spreading over the land alongside and greatly reducing its usefulness. Such has been the case in northern Madagascar, for example, where hurricanes are accompanied by torrential rain and erosion has produced sediments that have been washed down to choke river estuaries.

In the drier parts of the continent, where the rainfall is too low to give much percolating water, chemical weathering is limited and solid rock is usually near the surface, except in structural basins filled with thick layers of Tertiary sediments or where the products of weathering of a past humid period persist, or where blown sand has accumulated. In dry areas, clearing the woodland for fuel and cultivation, or reducing the grass cover by burning and grazing may lead to the soils being eroded by rain and wind.

In many regions, the soil-forming and

1.2.2.2 Surface quartzite Silcrete, which has a very high content of silica, underlies wide tracts of country in the Kalahari region in Botswana and in Cape Province, South Africa. Silica is one of the main dissolved constituents of river water in Africa, as in other parts of the world, being derived from the breakdown of silicate minerals and also from decaying vegetable matter. In many cases it seems that the silcrete has been formed as the result of silica replacing the calcium carbonate in calcrete or other limy material formed at an earlier stage.

1.2.2.3 *Surface limestone* Calcrete is very widespread in North Africa, especially in areas underlain by the extensively developed marine limestones that accumulated in Saharan seas millions of years ago. It also occurs very widely in the Kalahari, outcropping on the higher ground, at the crests of steep slopes, and on the floors of the circular dry lake floors called pans, of which there are hundreds in southern Botswana and the Orange Free State.

Where duricrusts are the parent materials, soils are shallow and usually of little value for cultivation because the lower layers of the soil profiles are too dense to allow satisfactory root development and nutrients are inadequate to support good crops or pasture. They are sometimes useful for building roads and for other constructional purposes.

Geomorphologists visualize the development of the relief in many parts of Africa as being essentially discontinuous, with long periods of deep weathering being followed by relatively short periods of rapid erosion result-

ing from either rapid uplift or a change in climate. Inselbergs and koppies are then seen not as monadnocks, or the final remnants of a rock mass reduced by the parallel retreat of slope units, but as the rock cores resistant to deep weathering, revealed when the regolith has been stripped away (Fig. 1.5).

Stripping away of the weathered layer, if it is repeated time after time in the same area, will eventually result in the emergence of high residual hills overlooking extensive plains. Some inselberg landscapes seem to have an extraordinarily remote origin. We have already noted the preservation of ancient glacial features dating from Palaeozoic times, then buried beneath sediments and exposed when these are eroded away. It seems that some inselberg landscapes have passed through a similar history, having been formed originally by landscape stripping, then buried by sediments in Mesozoic times and, lately, exhumed. Alongside such ancient landforms one may find, in places like northern Nigeria, dunes and

Calcrete (surface limestone) near a pan (a wind-deflated depression) in the Kalahari 'thirstland' of southern Botswana.

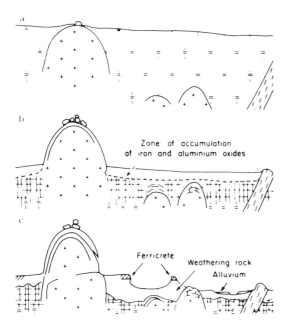

Fig. 1.5. *The development of a landscape by weathering and stripping. The three diagrams show how inselberg landscapes of the savanna lands may have developed, over periods of millions of years. (a) Crystalline rocks are planed off and deeply weathered. (b) Stripping of the weathered layer reveals masses of resistant rock; renewed weathering on the plains leads to the formation of lateritic soils rich in aluminium and iron oxides. (c) Renewed downcutting in the Quaternary period leads to the formation of ferricrete, new valleys, and the exposure of slightly weathered rock. The inselberg residual is split along joint planes parallel to the surface but remains resistant to further weathering.*

lakeshore features that originated as a result of climatic changes only a few thousand years ago in the Late Quaternary.

1.2.3 Coastlines

The coastline of Africa, like that of the other Gondwanaland continents, Australia, Antarctica, and South America, is remarkably free of indentations. This is probably to be explained by its faulted character, by the lack of folding in late geological times, by continental uplift being dominant, and by the deposition of river-borne sediments along the coast as sandbars and deltas during and since the rise in sea-level that took place at the end of the Last Glaciation in high latitudes.

Partly because of the lack of indentations, natural harbours are few and far between. The tropical coasts of the Indian Ocean and Red Sea are fringed with coral reefs that can tear the bottom off a ship driven inshore by the easterly winds. Heavy swell generated by steady onshore winds with a long fetch over the open ocean gives heavy breakers along all the exposed coasts. In the days of sail, African coasts were especially dangerous for shipping. Vessels used to have to anchor well offshore at 'surf ports', where both cargo and passengers had to be carried to and from the shore by small boats specially designed to cope with the difficult conditions. Artificial harbours constructed in this century have greatly reduced the risks; at the same time they have taken away the traffic through the surf ports. The absence of

Coral shore north of Dar es Salaam, Tanzania.

natural harbours no longer hampers development seriously, though congestion at some of the busiest ports presents problems from time to time.

Alongshore drift of beach material is very strong in many areas where the prevailing winds and waves approach the coast at an angle to the perpendicular, and under such conditions harbour works built to keep shipping channels clear of sandbanks have been difficult to construct and expensive to maintain. Commonly they have caused coast erosion on the downdrift side. Lagos in south-west Nigeria has suffered in this way; a million tons of sand are pumped annually on to Victoria beach in an effort to stop erosion east of the harbour (Fig. 1.6). The construction of dams across large rivers has held up the transport of sediment to river mouths and has resulted in coast erosion nearby. The High Dam at Aswan is believed to be responsible for erosion of the Nile delta and in Ghana the Akosombo dam across the Volta river has been blamed for erosion of the Volta delta near Keta and the nearby coast of Togo, though it must be added that erosion had begun there several years before the dam was built. Harbour works at Tema, constructed about 1955, ten years before the dam was complete may be responsible, but

nearly all the coast from Accra to the Niger delta is suffering from erosion.

Low alluvial shores have been shaped by powerful breakers. Barrier beaches sprinkled with coconut palms stretch along the Gulf of Guinea and the east coasts of Madagascar and

Coral sand beach with coral island offshore. Such coasts are very attractive to tourists and are therefore valuable economic assets.

Coast erosion at Keta in south-east Ghana, where the sea has destroyed a large part of a castle built by the Danes in the eighteenth century.

Fig. 1.6. Lagos, until 1991 the capital of Nigeria, is the largest city and the leading port in the country with a population of more than 6 millions. Its harbour, situated on a creek leading into an extensive lagoon, was made accessible to large vessels by dredging the mouth and constructing a breakwater on the western side to divert seawards the sand transported from west to east by longshore drift. One result has been coastal accretion on the west side of the breakwater and erosion of Victoria Island on the east side of the harbour entrance. In recent years the city has grown rapidly northwards towards the airport, and the old central area on Lagos Island is severely congested; the bridges crossing creeks separating Lagos Island from the mainland form bottlenecks which restrict the flow of traffic. A new capital still under construction has been established near the centre of Nigeria at Abuja, but its completion has been hindered by the country's financial problems.

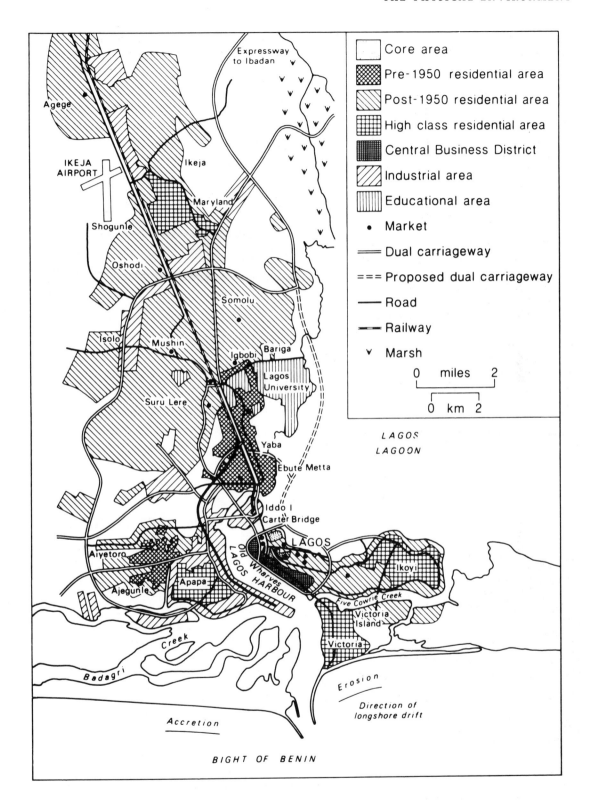

Mozambique, and very long sandspits directed towards the equator are characteristic of Senegal and Angola. Such bars and spits seal off river mouths and prevent easy access to them from the sea. But the lagoons behind provide useful waterways for small boats; they are often well stocked with fish and if they should dry out or are carefully controlled they can provide sea salt on a large scale.

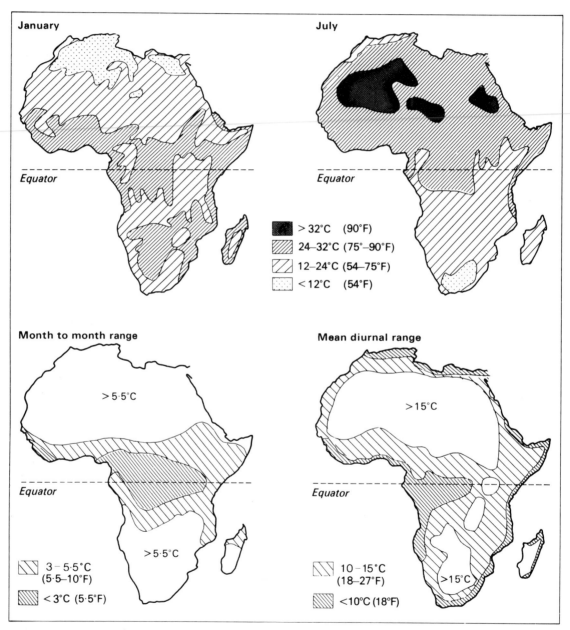

Fig. 1.7. *Mean temperatures (as if at sea-level) in January and July and mean ranges between warmest and coldest months and between night and day.*

1.3 Climate

Because it lies within 35° of the equator, temperatures are high everywhere in Africa except at high altitudes and during the winter in the extreme north and south. The Sahara and the belt of country to the south are hotter than any other part of the world of comparable size. The south-eastern part of the continent is considerably cooler on account of its greater altitude (Fig. 1.7).

Differences in the environment from one region to another are mainly to be explained in terms of spatial variation in the amount and seasonal distribution of the rainfall. This variation depends on position in relation to the pattern of the atmospheric circulation over the continent, distance from the coast, and local topography.

1.3.1 Atmospheric pressure, wind systems, and the pattern of precipitation

The circulation of the atmosphere over Africa is dominated by cells of high pressure centred over the adjacent oceans about the tropics of Cancer and Capricorn. The high pressure cells give winds between east and north-east, over the Sahara and the Kalahari; these regions are arid because they are occupied by dry, subsiding air for most of the year (Fig. 1.8).

Northern and southernmost Africa, like western Europe and much of North America, receive most of their rain from mid-latitude depressions moving from west to east. They follow tracks near enough to the tropics to bring rain to the Cape and to the Maghreb and Cyrenaica, mainly in the winter half of the year, and such depressions moving down the Red Sea are rather unreliable sources of rain for northern Ethiopia in April/May.

Moist air moving into Africa south of the Sahara, mainly from the South Atlantic and also from the Indian Ocean, is monsoonal in character. The humid, unstable air moves inland in the summer, its front wedging beneath the drier, subsiding air at what is called the Intertropical Convergence Zone or ITCZ. The moist air is unstable and, where it is deep enough, it rises and is chilled to the point where condensation takes place, clouds form and develop vertically, and rain falls.

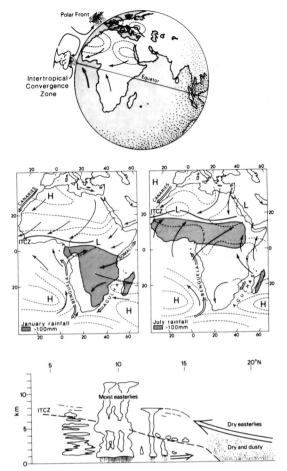

Fig. 1.8. *Atmospheric circulation and air mass interaction over Africa. Low-level flows of air converge in the Intertropical Convergence Zone (ITCZ). This moves north with the sun in the first half of the year and south in the second half. Convectional activity and precipitation are concentrated within the humid air masses on the equator side of the ITCZ. The lowermost part of the diagram is a north–south cross-section of the troposphere over west Africa in May.*

The moist air rises where it flows across highlands in its path, the windward slopes receiving more rain than the lowlands, especially those in the lee of the high ground. The highlands of Ethiopia and Kenya consequently receive much more rain than the Afar depression and the floor of the rift valley.

Weather systems involving convergence of air at low altitudes and upward spiral movements (vortices) also give precipitation. The most violent of these weather systems are tropical cyclones (or hurricanes); they are infrequent and confined to the Indian Ocean and the east coast of Africa. Much more widespread are Easterly Waves, disturbances that move from east to west on the equator side of the ITCZ and bring outbreaks of rain to a broad zone south of the Sahara.

Surface heating produces vertical convectional movements, the up-currents in moist air masses being accompanied by condensation and the release of latent heat, promoting greater instability and thunderstorms. Near stretches of water such as Lake Victoria, breezes from the land develop during the night and generate thunderstorms over the water, and most of the rain falls on occasions such as this (Fig. 1.9).

In all three cases the amount of rain falling increases with the strength of the inflow of the moist air mass and its depth. Consequently, rainfall is usually greater near the coast than further inland, as can be seen from the mean annual rainfall distribution over Nigeria or Sierra Leone in west Africa (Fig. 1.10). On the other hand, near the tropics, where the winds blow parallel to the coast, ocean surface water is impelled to move offshore, bringing cool water to the surface from deeper down. This cool water chills any air moving inland, air which in any case is likely to be stable and subsiding. The cold Benguela, Somali, and Canaries currents thus help to explain the aridity of coastal Namibia, Somalia, and Mauritania. The Namibian coast rarely experiences high temperatures and on half the days in the year it is shrouded in fog in the mornings and dewfall is quite heavy.

The seasonality of the rainfall is an extremely important characteristic of the climate almost everywhere in Africa (Fig. 1.8). In January inflows of unstable moist air from the South Atlantic bring rain to the Congo/Zaire basin while the Indian Ocean is the source of rain for the countries stretching from Natal to Tanzania. As the sun moves north, so the ITCZ follows. By March the rainy season is over in Botswana and Zimbabwe and is beginning in a zone stretching across the continent from Kenya to Sierra Leone. By July/August the ITCZ

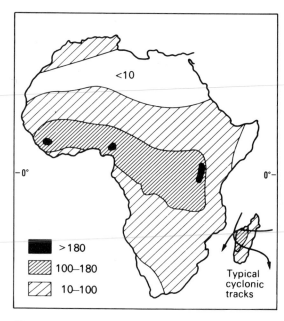

Fig. 1.9. *Mean annual number of thunderstorms and the region affected by tropical cyclones (hurricanes).*

has reached its furthest north and Atlantic air occupies much of the continent between a few degrees north of the equator and the tropic of Cancer; rain falls over most of west Africa and Ethiopia with occasional showers even on the Tibesti mountains in the Sahara. In September and October the rain belt moves rapidly south again, bringing a second rainy season to the equatorial zone. Then the cycle starts again.

The prediction of rain only a few hours ahead is no easy matter in tropical Africa. Convectional rain comes from cloud masses only a few kilometres in diameter, and while one place may receive several centimetres in an hour another place only a kilometre or two away from the track of the storm may record no rain whatsoever. This helps to explain the variations in crop yield that one may find in a particular year over quite short distances. One village may have received rain at a vital time when the seeds had just germinated, while its neighbour had been unlucky and the crops failed.

1.3.2 Tropical cyclones

Between November and April, when the equatorial westerlies swing south, violent revolving

16

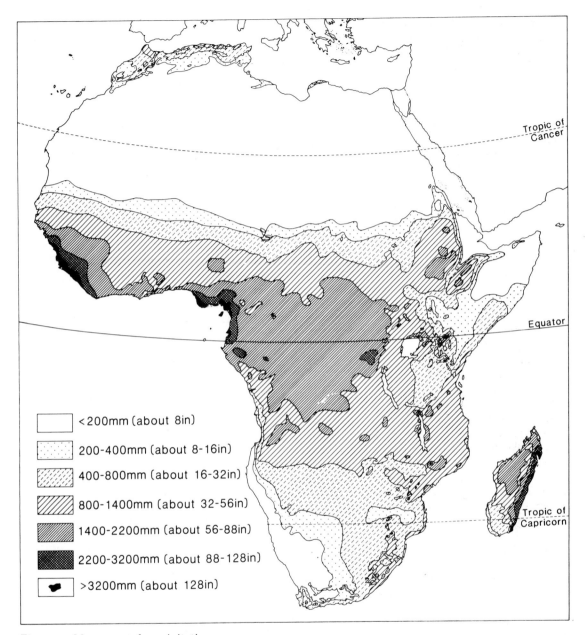

Fig. 1.10. *Mean annual precipitation.*

storms are generated from time to time in the south-west of the Indian ocean and move in a westerly direction towards east Africa (Fig. 1.9). Small cyclones, or hurricanes as they are called in many other parts of the world, occasionally cross Zanzibar and the extreme southern coast of mainland Tanzania, causing severe damage over small areas. Mozambique, Swaziland, and Natal are liable to be affected but the risks of damage are greatest on the islands of Madagascar, Mauritius, and Reunion, the storms usually curving away to the south and dissipating without reaching the African mainland. Damage is inflicted not only by the very high winds, which may exceed 200 km (120 mls) per hour round the central eye of the storm, but

17

also by a temporary rise in sea-level and great waves that run well ahead of the slow-moving storm. Coastal areas are therefore at greatest risk, and destruction may be increased by torrential storms, with hundreds of millimetres of rain falling in a few hours.

1.3.3 Evaporation

The high temperatures result in high rates of evaporation from the soil and from water sur-

faces, annual rates varying from about 750 mm (about 30 in) in the more humid and cooler regions to over 2000 mm (80 in) in the Sahara, rates four times those in the British Isles. Evaporation losses from the surfaces of lakes and reservoirs and from the leaves of growing plants are greatest in the dry season when the relative humidity of the air is lowest (Fig. 1.11). Although the evaporating power is greatest during the dry season, actual evaporation losses from the soil are restricted at that time of year by the lack of available water in the surface layers. Grasses dry up not long after the end of the rains; trees continue to transpire so long as they retain their leaves.

Rainwater is protected from direct evaporation once it has penetrated into the ground to a depth of a metre or two, and from transpiration when it sinks down below the level of roots. If geological conditions are favourable and the regolith and rocks are pervious, water percolates downwards to feed the groundwater held in the joint and pore spaces at depth. The surface between the deep rock saturated with water and the unsaturated rock above is called the water-table. If a well should be dug, it will strike water when it penetrates the water-table. Such water slowly moves sideways through the ground in the direction of the slope of the water-table and eventually emerges in springs, river-beds or swamps fed by seepage. So although the beds of many rivers are dry for much of the year, water can still be obtained from most of them by digging pits a few metres deep into their sandy beds. Away from rivers, deeper wells and boreholes allow people to obtain water from greater depths where geological structures are favourable. Unless the water is under pressure much energy has to be expended in lifting it to the surface, and in many places this still means ropes and manpower. In the last half century the exploitation of underground water, some under pressure and some lifted by pumps, has opened up many thousands of square kilometres for herding, notably in the Kalahari in Botswana.

Because of the great evaporation losses and the high demand for water by plants, land in Africa receiving less than 500 mm (20 in) of rain annually is likely to be of little value for cultivation unless it is irrigated. Unless the rain falling in a month exceeds 50 mm (2 in) it is not enough for growing crops. At the height of the

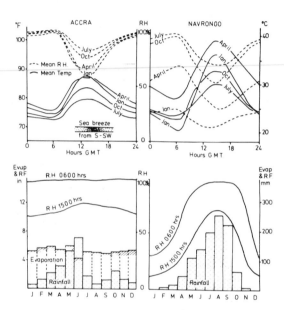

Fig. 1.11. Diurnal and seasonal variations in relative humidity and other climatic elements at two stations in Ghana: Accra and Navrongo. At both Navrongo in the north of Ghana and Accra in the south the relative humidity (R.H.) reaches a maximum at dawn and a minimum in the early afternoon, but the seasonal variation in relative humidity is much greater in the interior than at the coast. Navrongo's climate is typical of the Sudan zone. Accra's climate differs from that of Lagos in Nigeria and has rather a special character. A coastal dry zone stretches from west of Lagos to west of Accra, the second peak of the rainy season, experienced in Lagos, being very subdued in Accra. A sea breeze setting in about midday and reaching its maximum strength a few hours later helps to keep the temperature down in the mid-afternoon. Except in June the mean monthly values for evaporation from a free-water surface exceed the mean monthly rainfall and the climate is semi-arid.

Cattle at river-bed waterholes in the south-east Sudan. Tall acacias are able to obtain water from deep down in the alluvial material bordering and underlying the channel.

rainy season, on the other hand, when humidity is high and skies are cloudy, over 600 mm (24 in) of rain may fall in a month, much more than can be evaporated, and there is consequently a surplus not only to supply plants abundantly but also to fill river channels and feed aquifers, the water-bearing rocks underground. In the diagrams of Fig. 1.12, the monthly temperatures are plotted in such a way as to give some indication of the potential evaporation losses in comparison with the rainfall. In months where the temperature line runs well above the rainfall line, water is deficient for many purposes.

At the beginning of the growing season, soil moisture conditions in intertropical Africa are quite the opposite to those in middle latitudes. The soil is desiccated after the long dry season and so if there are gaps of several days between

storms at the time of planting and sowing there is no supply of water stored in the soil for the young plants to fall back on. They quickly wilt and die. In the semi-arid and sub-humid regions the crop season proceeds as a running battle between evaporation and transpiration on the one hand and rainfall on the other, with evaporation gaining the upper hand as the rains come to an end. Agriculture in Africa is in consequence more precarious, at least in this respect, than in higher latitudes.

1.3.4 Climatic variability

Climatic conditions vary from year to year and on longer timescales. Fluctuations lasting a decade or a century or two are superimposed on the longer-period oscillations of the Quaternary period.

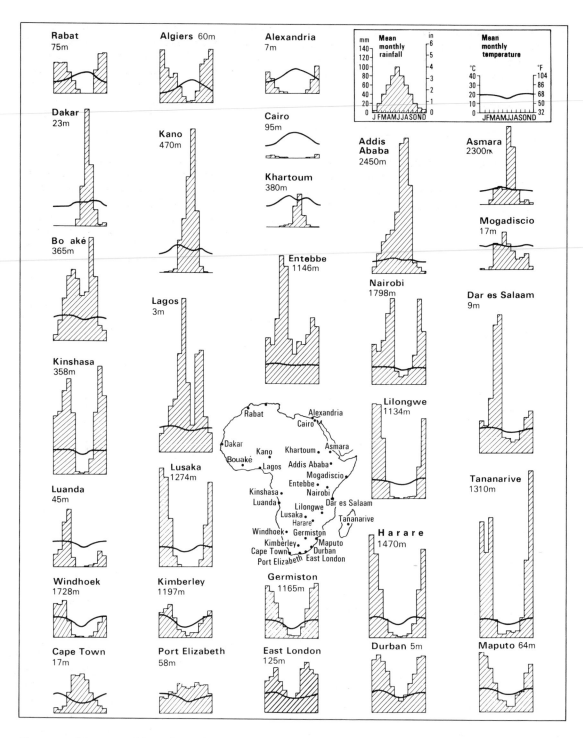

Fig. 1.12. *Mean monthly values of precipitation and temperature. The temperature values have been plotted so as to give some indication of the potential evaporation losses associated with them, thereby giving some impression of seasonal variations in water surplus and water deficit. Heights above sea-level are given in metres.*

1.3.4.1 Interannual variability in rainfall Year-to-year variations in rainfall are very marked, with extreme values 50 per cent more or less than the long-term mean (Fig. 1.13). Over most parts of the continent the probability of the rainfall being within 10 per cent of the mean in any particular year is less than 40 per cent, the percentage diminishing and the rainfall becoming less reliable towards the desert margins. Individual years with very high rainfall totals bring damaging floods and high lake levels. In November 1961, heavy rains in east Africa brought to an end a severe drought in Kenya, at the same time giving the highest river discharges ever recorded there and a rise in the level of Lake Victoria of about a metre (see Fig. 1.22). The years 1913, 1972 and 1973, 1983 and 1984 were remarkably dry years across Africa between Senegal and Ethiopia. There were droughts in south-central Africa in the early 1980s and a very severe drought affected most of southern Africa in 1992.

1.3.4.2 Decadal fluctuations in rainfall There is a tendency for rainy or dry years to cluster together. This is particularly marked in the semi-arid lands on the south side of the Sahara and also in the Kalahari region in southern Africa. In general, the last quarter of the nineteenth century was much wetter than the first fifteen years of this century.

On the south side of the Sahara the 1940s were dry and the 1950s were wet (Figs. 1.14 and 1.15). Then came a group of years, 1968 and 1970–73, when the rainfall was unprecedently

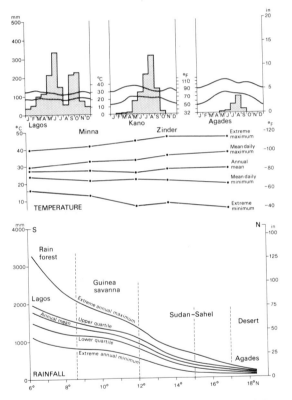

Fig. 1.13. *Climatic transect across west Africa. From the humid coast of southern Nigeria at Lagos to the Saharan interior of the Niger Republic at Agades, mean annual rainfall diminishes northwards. In half the years the rainfall amount is between the upper and lower quartiles. Towards the interior, temperature ranges increase and the length of the rainy season diminishes. The diagrams for Lagos, Kano, and Agades show mean monthly maximum and minimum temperatures and mean monthly rainfall (shaded).*

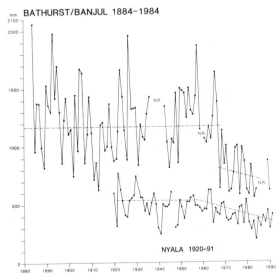

Fig. 1.14. *Annual rainfall records for Banjul (formerly Bathurst), Gambia, and Nyala, Sudan Republic. The Banjul record, though incomplete, is one of the longest for a station in tropical Africa. Until the 1960s the normal rainfall might have been taken to be about 1200 mm, but between 1967 and 1984 values never reached that figure. The record for Nyala in the Sudan Republic shows a strong downward trend since the early 1960s: values for 1986–8 have been interpolated from nearby rainfall stations. N.R. – no record.*

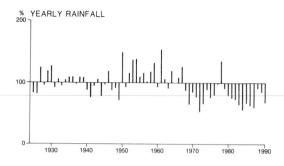

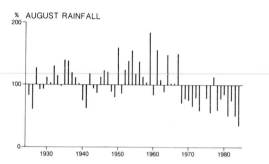

Fig. 1.15a. *The annual rainfall for stations across the Sahel zone shows rainfall deficiencies in the early 1970s and early 1980s after a relatively wet period in the 1950s and early 1960s. Monthly deficiencies have been especially marked in August, usually the wettest month.*

Fig. 1.15b. *Seven year running means of Senegal river discharge at Bakel displayed a remarkably regular oscillation between 1903 and 1979: the contrast between the wet 1950s and the dry 1970s is clear. On this basis it was suggested that the river discharge (and by implication the rainfall of the western Sahel/Sudan zone) might be restored to the long-term mean 1985, as indicated by the dashed line. In fact, after 1976 the seven-year means of annual discharge plunged even lower, to less than half the long-term mean value, as drought deepened in the early 1980s. Desiccation here has coincided with global warming in the 1970s and 1980s but there is no certainty that the warming has caused the droughts. (The rainfall part of the diagram is from M. Hulme, Climatic Research Unit, University of East Anglia).*

low. Year after year the local people and international agencies supposed that the drought must break, but it was 1974 before long-term mean values were reached. For the next few years the rainfall was not much below the mean and then, from 1979 until 1984, each year was drier than the preceding one and the situation became even worse than it had been in the early 1970s.

Without any warning, in 1988, there were heavy downpours and flooding; in many parts of the Sahel–Sudan it was one of the wettest years on record. In the Khartoum region of the Sudan Republic, over 50 mm of rain fell in a single day, causing widespread flooding and the collapse of mud-built houses. More than 400 mm of rain fell in August in the Kano region of northern Nigeria, and a large dam failed when river discharges reached values not experienced for several decades. However, when the rainfall values for the whole Sahel-Sudan zone over the entire year were put together, the annual total was seen to have been less than the longterm annual mean. The drier conditions of the 1970s and 1980s seem to have persisted into the early 1990s.

In southern Africa the rainfall has oscillated over the last century in a fairly regular manner, the period of the oscillation varying from one rainfall region to another. In the summer rainfall region extending from Natal into Botswana the periodicity has been about 18 years. There

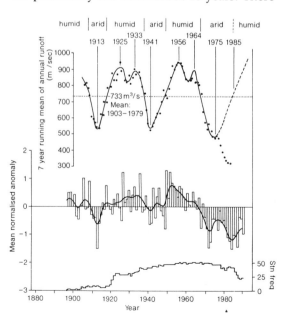

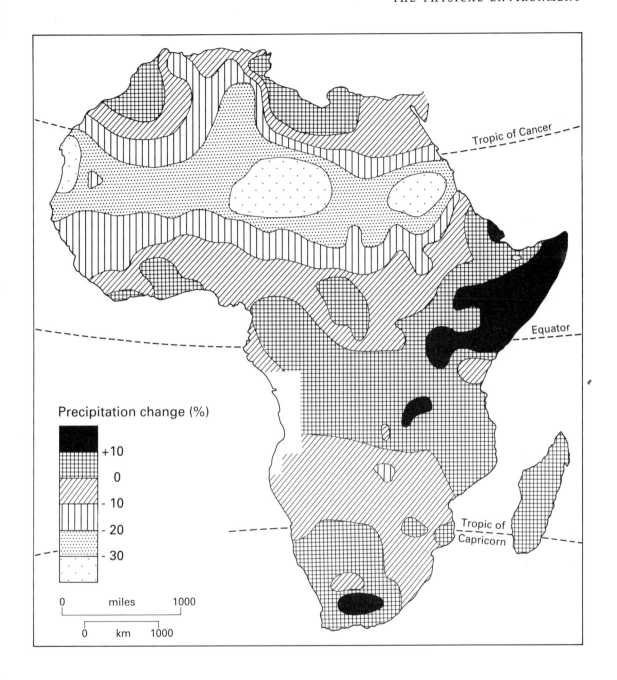

Fig. 1.15c. *The percentage change in mean annual precipitation, 1960–89 as compared with 1930–59. Since 1960 the mean annual rainfall in the Sahel/Sudan zone and northern Ethiopia has diminished by between 20 and 30 per cent, about 100 mm. The reduction over the same period in the Natal-Kalahari region of southern Africa has been between 10 and 20 per cent, also about 100 mm. In the Horn of Africa and equatorial Africa the rainfall has increased by about 10 per cent, again very roughly about 100 mm. (Diagram from M. Hulme, Climatic Research Unit, University of East Anglia)*

Precipitation change (%)

+10
0
- 10
- 20
- 30

0   miles   1000

0   km   1000

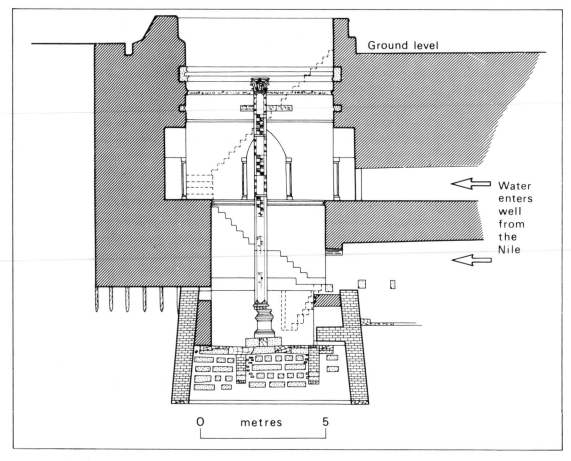

Fig. 1.16. *The Roda Gauge on an island in the Nile at Cairo where the levels of the river at the peak of the flood and at its lowest annual levels were read and recorded over a period of several centuries. The record is most complete for the period between about AD 860 and 1520, but its interpretation in terms of historical changes in Nile discharge is uncertain. The water entered the well in which the graduated pillar stands from the right, through two tunnels.*

were groups of dry years in the mid-1960s and early 1980s. It might therefore have been expected that the early 1990s would on the whole be relatively wet, so the occurrence in 1992 of the worst drought in living memory, extending north from South Africa into Mozambique, Zimbabwe, Zambia and Malawi, came as an unwelcome surprise.

1.3.4.3 Centennial variations in rainfall Variations lasting a few hundred years are difficult to detect because of the lack of instrumental records further back than this century. Records have been preserved of the height of the Nile as it was measured on the Roda Gauge in Cairo (Fig. 1.16) over much of the period from the

ninth century AD to the present day. There are many problems in ensuring the consistency of the record but it seems likely that there were several periods of 40 to 150 years when the river discharge was distinctly higher than it has been on average in this century. It has sometimes been supposed that the rainfall in North Africa in Roman times was greater than that of today. It is possible, but not certain, that it was somewhat higher for a century or so, making agricultural development and penetration of the Sahara at that time somewhat easier than it would otherwise have been.

1.3.4.4 African climatic change in the Late Quaternary Studies by geomorphologists of ancient

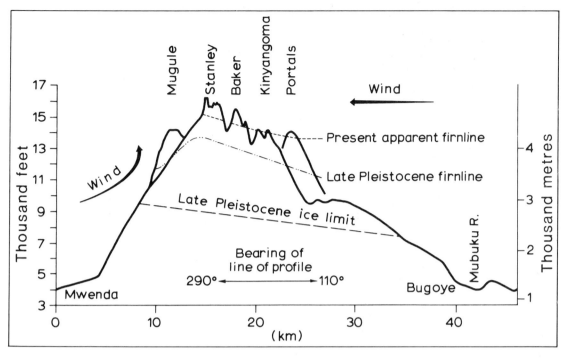

Fig. 1.17. *A west–east profile of the Ruwenzori range, showing the height of the firnline at the present day and about 15 000 years ago. The lowest level reached by the glacier tongues is shown as having been about 2300–3000 m (7000–10 000 ft). (From H. Osmaston in* Processes in Physical Geography, *1975, edited by Peel, Chisholm, and Haggett.)*

lake shorelines and vegetated desert dunes have provided information concerning the sequence and scale of climatic changes in Africa during the Late Quaternary (the last 130 000 years or so) including the Holocene (the last 10 000 years).

It now seems that at the height of the Last Glaciation, about 20 000 to 13 000 years ago, when the accumulation of continental ice sheets caused sea-level to be lowered as much as 130 m (425 ft) below its present level, temperatures in Africa were lower than they are now by at least 5 °C (9 °F) and possibly as much as 8 °C (14 °F). On the slopes of Ruwenzori and the other high mountains of east Africa (Kenya, Kilimanjaro, and Elgon), old glacial moraines, some now overgrown with forest, indicate that glaciers descended a thousand metres and more below their present limits (Fig. 1.17). Freezing and thawing of soils took place at lower altitudes and mountain vegetation belts shifted down 1000 m (3300 ft).

During the last glacial maximum, Africa between the tropics was drier than it is now.

Lake Victoria was reduced to a shallow pool and ceased to overflow and feed the White Nile. Desert dunes extended as much as 500 km (300 mls) south of the present limit of mobile Saharan dunes and the vegetation belts shifted accordingly towards the equator, rain forests being much reduced in size (Fig. 1.18). In southern Africa, the dunes of the northern Kalahari seem to have been active at this time in northern Botswana, western Zimbabwe, and southern Angola and Zambia.

Wetter conditions returned about 12 000 years ago; Lake Victoria filled up and began to supply water to the Nile again, and, especially in the period about 9500 to 4500 years ago, lakes formed in closed basins well into the driest parts of the Sahara. Lake Chad, which has had an area of no more than 26 000 km² (10 000 mls²) in this century, spilled north to fill the Bodélé depression and expanded over about 320 000 km² (123 000 mls²), overflowing to the Atlantic via the Mayo Kebbi, Benue, and Lower Niger (Fig. 1.19). The Niger itself was fed from rivers rising in the Air mountains which now

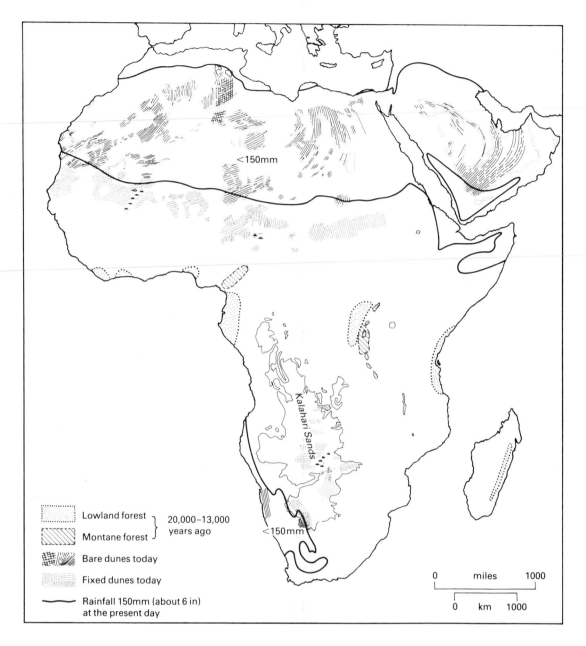

Fig. 1.18. *The past and present extent of blown sand. Bare dunes (moving sand) are mainly confined to the very gentle slopes of basin-shaped areas with mean annual rainfall totals of less than 150 mm (6 in). Old fixed dunes extending into more humid areas indicate that the deserts have been much more extensive, especially about 20 000 to 13 000 years ago. Lowland rain forests were restricted to much more limited areas than at the present day and montane forests had to contend with greater aridity. In the south of the continent the sands of the coastal Namib desert are still mobile while those of the Kalahari are mainly fixed by vegetation. The directions of the fixed dunes as well as the bare dunes correspond broadly with those of the prevailing winds of the present day.*

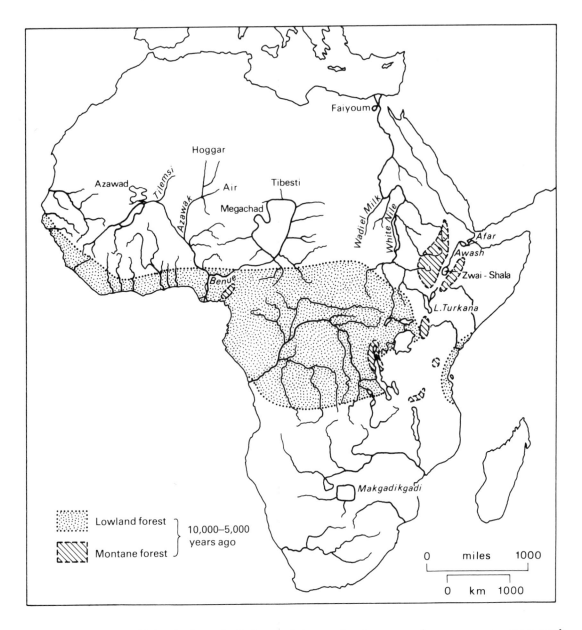

Fig. 1.19. *Inter-tropical lakes in the early Holocene, between about 10 000 and 5000 years ago, were much enlarged owing to higher rainfall than at the present day. Wadis such as Azawak and Tilemsi, which are now usually dry, were then occupied by perennial rivers, and existing rivers had much higher discharges. The rain forests, which had been restricted to refuge areas about 20 000 to 13 000 years ago, expanded over a larger area than they occupy today. The flow of the Senegal was several times greater than now. The Upper Niger overflowed to form an extensive shallow lake in what is now desert north of the Niger bend; a greatly enlarged Lake Chad, Megachad, overflowed to the Atlantic via the Benue river; Lakes Ziway and Shala in the Ethiopian rift valley united and overflowed via the Awash river to the Afar depression; rift valley lakes further south overflowed to Lake Turkana, which spilled into the Nile system. The discharge of the Nile was several times that of the present day; its water spread over the surface of the south-east Mediterranean, preventing the saltwater at depth from reaching the surface and causing deoxygenated black muds, called saprolites, to be deposited on the sea floor.*

Fig. 1.20. *The soils of the Chad basin reflect the climatic changes that have taken place in the basin over the last few thousand years. Light sandy soils occupy much of the area between (1) the southern limit of moving sand of the present day and (2) the southern limit of fixed dunes. The soils below 320 m are derived from the sediments that accumulated on the floor of Megachad, though in some places old dune sands and deltaic sediments rise above the level of the lake clays. The cross-section from the Jos Plateau to Tibesti on page 29 shows the artesian basin of Borno. The artesian water seems to have no connection with the lake.*

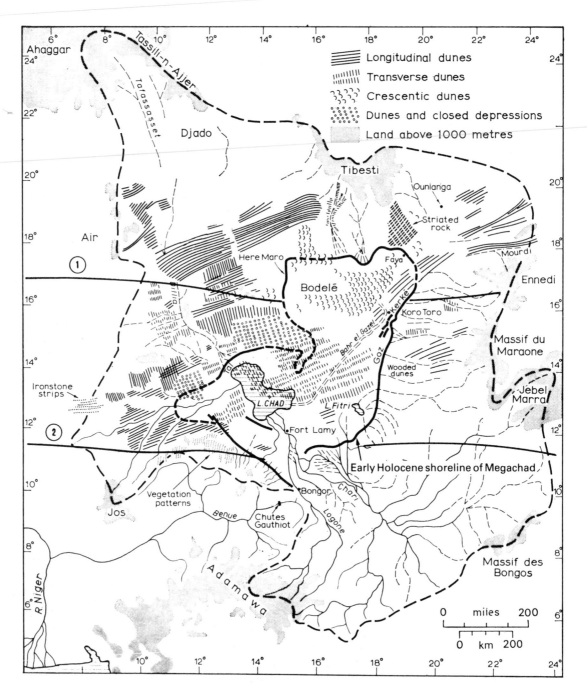

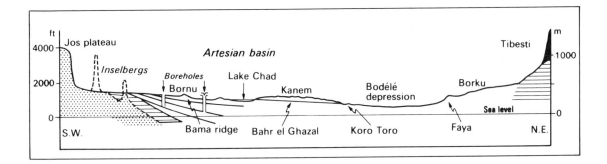

scarcely ever carry water, and the Senegal broke through dunefields to reach the sea. Lakes in the rift valley rose by as much as 100 m (330 ft) and some of those in southern Ethiopia rose until they spilled northwards to the Awash river which runs down into the Afar Depression, while others overflowed into Lake Turkana, which in turn spilled over to the White Nile. Savanna animals roamed regions that are now desert, pastoralists grazed their flocks and herds all over the Sahara; harpoons and pottery found today on long-deserted lakeshores tell of a much greener Africa (Fig 1.20).

Early in the third millennium BC, that is between 4500 and 5000 years ago, a final major climatic shift took place. The lakes between the tropics shrank and many of them dried up completely. The discharge of the main rivers diminished markedly and within a few centuries aridity returned to wide areas. Pastoralists had to evacuate regions where they had migrated with their flocks and herds for centuries. It is possible that the difficulties experienced by the Saharan people at this time may have induced them to congregate in the Nile valley and, on the south side of the desert, encouraged them to domesticate several kinds of cereals that are now widely cultivated in the Sahel and Sudan zones.

Over the last 4500 years the amplitude of climatic changes has probably not been very great, though there is no doubt that there have been centuries and decades when the climate has differed significantly from the means that we calculate from our meteorological records for this century. Excavations and borings made by engineers reveal layers of sediments that provide clues to the nature of past climates. Engineers themselves need to learn more about past temperature and rainfall in order to gain a greater understanding of the nature and reliability of the sources of water they are tapping. Such studies involve the collaboration of scientists and technicians, including geographers, engaged in several different fields; the findings are of practical importance as well as providing a fascinating field of study.

1.4 Lakes and rivers

Most African rivers are dry for half the year and in flood during the rains; variations in precipitation from season to season dominate river regimes. In middle latitudes, where precipitation is more evenly distributed through the year, seasonal variations in evaporation from winter to summer have a greater influence on discharge. In the winter rainfall areas of the

Chew Bahir, the dry bed of a lake in south-west Ethiopia that was 25 m (80 ft) deep about 5400 years ago.

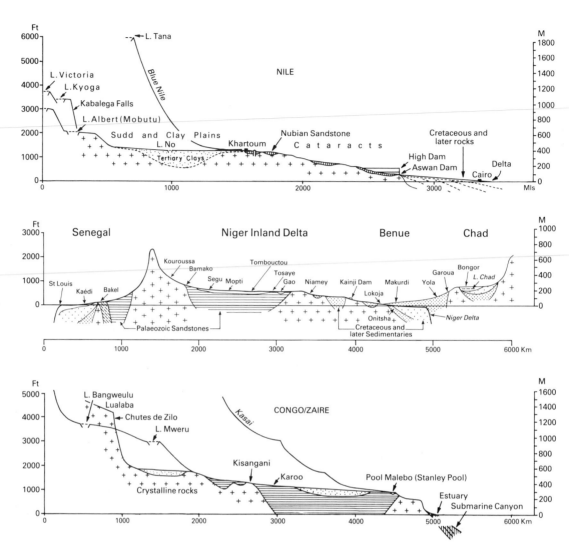

Fig. 1.21. *Longitudinal sections of the Nile, Senegal–Niger–Benue–Chad, and the Zaire (or Congo) rivers. The profiles of the big African rivers, except for the Benue, are very irregular, with rapids upstream and downstream of long reaches at altitudes between about 300 and 450 m (1000 and 1500 ft) above sea-level. The steep course of the Zaire below Pool Malebo is especially marked.*

Maghreb and the Cape, seasonal variations in evaporation reinforce the effects of the seasonal occurrence of the rainfall.

Except for a few streams rising near the crest of the Drakensberg and some high mountain torrents in east Africa and the Atlas mountains, melting ice and snow are not important sources of supply and do nothing to even out discharge through the year. Consequently artificial water storage schemes are needed for agriculture and urban use, especially in the drier parts of the continent.

The levels of most of the bigger rivers, including the lower Niger, rise and fall from season to season through several metres, greatly reducing their value for many purposes. Bridges are very expensive to construct when they must include long approaches across marshy tracks liable to be flooded for several weeks at a time. Navigation is impeded in the dry season by sandbanks and rocks, and during the rains strong currents impede boats moving upstream.

Rapids and waterfalls interrupt the courses of

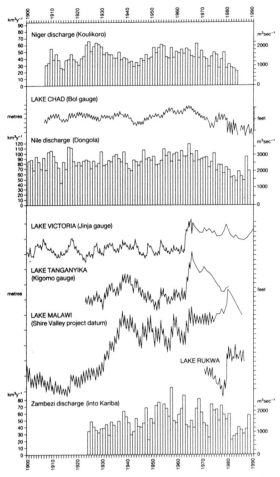

Fig. 1.22. *The levels of the Great Lakes and Lake Chad and the discharge of the Niger, Nile, and Zambezi. The levels of the lakes are controlled firstly by the levels of their outfalls and secondly by the difference between precipitation and evaporation over their catchments. Levels normally rise a metre or two in the rainy season and fall a similar amount in the following dry season. Here the annual, not the seasonal, rise and fall of Victoria, Tanganyika, and Malawi are shown after 1966. Unusually heavy and prolonged rains in late 1961–62 caused all the lakes to rise. They reached their highest levels this century about 1964, with Malawi going on to rise still higher in the years around 1980. Silting at the Lukuga outlet of Lake Tanganyika and subsequent dredging may have affected its level in recent years. The Shire river outlet from Lake Malawi was blocked by sediment when the lake was very low in 1915 and outflow ceased until 1935. The large fluctuations of Malawi afflict shipping, fishing, and lakeshore cultivators*

and residents. The discharge of the Niger fell to its lowest values this century in April 1985 and about the same time Lake Chad was reduced to about one-tenth its 1960s area. In south-central Africa, Lake Rukwa was high in the early 1980s. The Zambezi's annual discharge from 1946 to 1979 was markedly higher than in the preceding 24 years, but in the early 1980s there was a sharp decline which was still more accentuated in 1992. The mean levels of nearly all the rivers and lakes declined in the 1980s and early 1990s.

nearly every big river on the continent except for the Senegal, Gambia, and Benue in west Africa. A prime example is the Congo or Zaire; between Pool Malebo (formerly known as Stanley Pool), where the river is nearly 20 km (12 mls) broad, and Matadi at the head of the estuary, the river falls nearly 270 m (900 ft) by a series of great cataracts over a distance of 240 km (150 mls). These and other falls are the outcome of the break-up of Gondwanaland, followed by intermittent uplift of the continent in Tertiary and later times (Fig. 1.21).

The rivers with the steadiest discharge through the year are in the equatorial zone. The Zaire's vast basin lies across the equator so that the river is supplied for one half of the year mainly from the southern hemisphere and in the other half from the northern. As a result, the ratio between its mean maximum discharge of 70 000 m³ per second (2.5 million ft³ per second) and mean minimum discharge of 23 000 m³ per second (0.8 million ft³ per second) is remarkably low for an African river.

The flow of some rivers varies quite markedly for several years at a time. The discharge of the Zambezi, for instance, was 40 per cent greater on average in the 24 years after 1946 than it had been in the 20 years preceding that date (Fig. 1.22).

The regime of the Nile in northern Sudan and Egypt was dominated, until the construction of the High Dam at Aswan, by summer floodwaters brought down from the Ethiopian highlands by the Sobat, the Blue Nile, and the Atbara. In winter, flow was maintained by the White Nile, the flow of which varies little from season to season, partly because of its equatorial source with two rainy seasons. However,

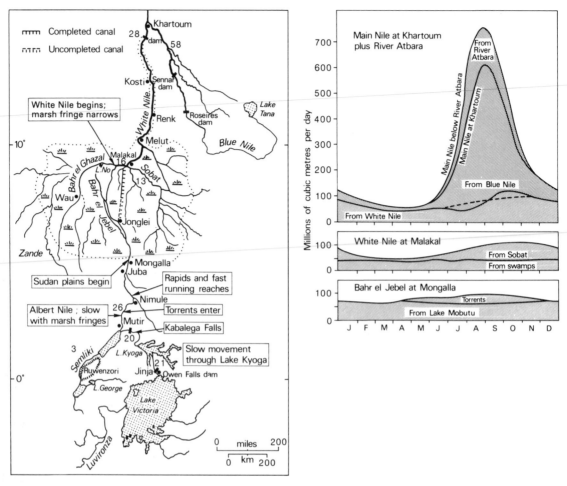

Fig. 1.23. *The seasonal and annual discharge of the Nile. The numbers alongside the rivers give the approximate mean annual discharges in units of cubic kilometres as they were for the first half of this century. They show that about half of the White Nile's water entering the Sudd swamps of the southern Sudan was lost by evaporation between Mongalla and Malakal. In 1980 work was begun on a canal to take a part of the flow of the river direct from Jonglei to Malakal to reduce these losses. Only the northern part had been completed when southern dissidents forced work to be abandoned. From 1961 to 1980, the high level of Lake Victoria, caused by more rain falling on the lake and its catchment, was accompanied by a doubling of its discharge to the Bahr el Jebel. The increase in the discharge of the White Nile caused by this natural event was greater than the increase expected from the Jonglei Canal.*

the discharge of the White Nile has varied considerably over the last hundred years or so; in the score of years after 1961 (when Lake Victoria was a metre or two higher than it had been earlier in the century) its mean discharge was double what it had been between 1900 and 1960, about 40 km³ a year instead of about 20 km³. Its discharge was also high in the last quarter of the nineteenth century. The first Europeans to see the lake, in the 1870's, repor-

ted Lake Victoria as standing at a level which it was not to reach again until the early 1960's.

The flow of the river between Lake Victoria and its confluence with the Sobat is diminished by evaporation from the Sudd, an extensive area of flooding land of a kind that is a feature of other large African river basins. As a result of the river flooding over extensive plains upstream of Malakal and consequent heavy losses by evaporation well in excess of the rain

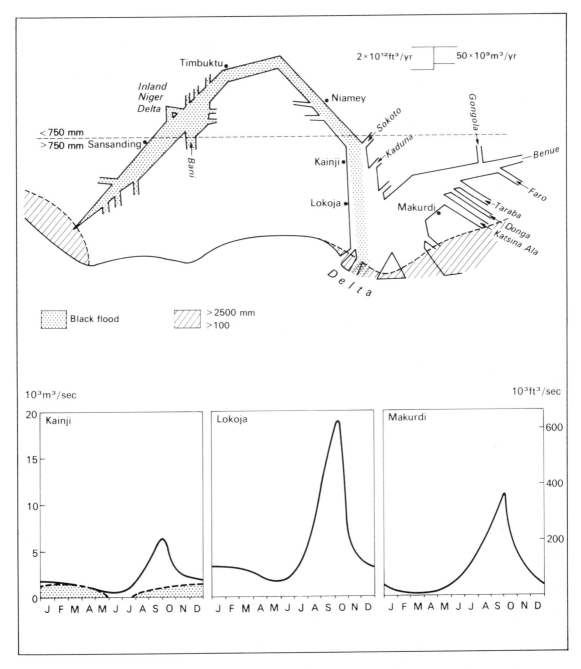

Fig. 1.24. *The discharge of the Niger and the Benue. The flow of the river in Nigeria is maintained in the first quarter of the year by the Black Flood, water which fell as rain on the highlands of Guinea several months earlier and has made its way slowly through the Inland Delta (Fig. 5.7). Little water is received by the river from regions where the annual rainfall totals are less than 750 mm (30 in). The width of the diagrammatic river is proportional to the mean discharge (according to the scale in the top right-hand corner) as it was in the first half of the century. Since 1967 the discharge of the Niger has been reduced as a result of the diminution of the rainfall and a southward movement of the 750 mm isohyet through about 100 km.*

falling on the Sudd, the White Nile's discharge at Malakal is reduced to about one-half that entering the Sudd at Mongalla (Fig. 1.23).

Similarly, the upper Niger loses much of its discharge as it traverses its 'Inland Delta' between Segu and Timbuktu (or Tombouctou). During the dry period of 20 000 to 13 000 years ago the river was diminished in volume and held back above Mopti by dunes formed by easterly winds (Fig. 1.24). When wetter conditions returned, the Niger broke through the lines of dunes and spread out to form several diverging distributary channels which came together again near Timbuktu, below which the river followed an old course running towards the east and out of the inland basin. With the reduction in discharge some 5000 years ago, many of the old distributary channels were abandoned by the river, but today much of its floodwater collects in lakes and swamps in the inland basin. The clear water that eventually escapes, well after the end of the rainy season, moves downstream to enter the Niger Republic and Nigeria in the early months of the year as the 'Black Flood'. This is in contrast to the silty 'White Flood', fed by local rains, which has subsided several months earlier.

Lake Chad is maintained very largely by the Chari and Logone rivers, which rise far to the south in a wide arc from northern Cameroon to the Jebel Marra in the Sudan Republic. The rivers and their tributaries flow across the gently sloping plains of north-central Africa for several hundreds of kilometres, losing much water by evaporation and depositing fine sediments en route and eventually joining together to enter Lake Chad. The water in the southern part of the lake, where the Chari–Logone enters, is quite fresh but as the water gradually moves north, amongst islands which are the remnants of ancient sand dunes, it evaporates and its salinity increases (Fig. 1.25). Some constituents of the solute load are removed by plants and snails and algae in the lake, but the water which eventually seeps away through the sandy northern shores still has quite a high soda content. Much of this is eventually precipitated as sodium carbonate on the floors of hollows between old dune ridges where the seepage water evaporates. The salt is scraped up by the local people for sale as a condiment and cattle-lick.

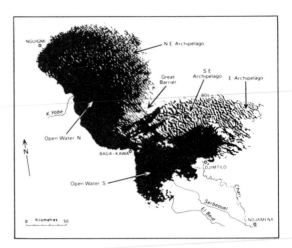

Fig. 1.25. *Lake Chad in 1973 when it was beginning to shrink from the high level it had reached in the 1950s and 1960s. The main source of water for the lake is the Chari–Logone, which brings water which fell as rain far to the south. The lake is only a few metres deep; the water drifts slowly north and east, evaporating and becoming more saline until it seeps away through the ancient dunes which form the linear islands shaped by north-easterly winds between 20 000 and 13 000 years ago (see also Fig. 10.8).*

A similar hydrographic situation exists at the northern margins of the Kalahari, where the Cubango and Cuando rivers join together and then break up into distributaries occupying an ancient dunefield to form the Okavango delta of northern Botswana, which is similar in size to the Nile delta (Fig. 6.2). Most of the incoming water is evaporated from the delta swamps and only a small amount in most years remains to sustain Lake Ngami and feed the Boteti river. The Boteti eventually reaches, in some years, a small terminal lake amongst the salt pans of the Makgadikgadi Depression. In the Late Quaternary, this depression held a lake which was about the size of Lake Victoria and may have overflowed to the Zambezi.

The present-day appearance and behaviour of African lakes and rivers is to be understood in terms of Late Quaternary as well as current climates. Their value to the people and countries within their catchments is very great in view of the critical importance of water supplies for so many purposes.

ECOLOGY

2.1 Biomes

The patterns of the plant cover and the animal life of the continent basically depend on the availability of water in the soil. This depends primarily on the amount of rain that falls and its seasonal distribution and secondly on the relief of the ground surface and the nature of the underlying rocks and soils. Increasingly, the activities of people as cultivators, graziers, woodcutters, and incendiarists modify the natural pattern.

The rainfall varies from place to place and season to season (Figs. 1.8 and 1.10) and the plant/animal systems, or biomes, vary accordingly (Fig. 2.1). The wettest parts of the continent, notably in the Zaire or Congo basin, are covered with rain forest. The driest parts are entirely barren, like the central Sahara and the Namib desert, or semi-desert only sparsely covered with tussocky grasses, shrubs, and small trees, like the Kalahari and northern Somalia. Between the two extremes are vast areas of grassland with fire-tolerant or fire-resistant trees that can survive burning of the grasses annually or at intervals of a few years. On the poleward sides of the deserts are winter rainfall areas with a shrubby vegetation cover.

The forest, savanna, steppe, desert, and winter rainfall biomes are modified on highlands and in the vicinity of large bodies of water. On the highlands, mean temperatures are lower than on the lowlands and there is more wind and cloud. On river floodplains and deltas, seasonal flooding creates swamplands where tall reeds and grasses thrive. In such areas, if the rainfall is low, trees are usually confined to elevated sites with better drainage, river terraces for instance. But in higher rainfall

areas, trees adapted to flooding form swamp forests.

Over extensive areas the biomes have been greatly modified by human activity. Judging from the evidence provided by abundant charcoal in dated archaeological horizons, people have been burning the woodland for tens of thousand of years. In some places hunters still use fires to drive animals into places where they can be killed. Graziers find that burning the grassland when it has died down towards the end of the dry season encourages a fresh growth of grass for their flocks and herds. Iron smelting, which was taking place south of the Sahara over 2000 years ago and until the colonial period, required large amounts of charcoal made by felling large numbers of trees and burning them in heaps covered with earth to restrict the supply of oxygen. Extensive areas of woodland and forest have also been cleared to allow cultivation and to provide timber for construction purposes and firewood for cooking.

The vegetation has been most severely modified where population densities are greatest, and especially in the vicinity of large towns. The modification has usually but not always involved degradation of the environment and a reduction in biological productivity. Especially in areas that have long been settled, the natural vegetation has been replaced by plant species, including trees, that are useful as sources of food. But with the rapid growth of population in recent decades, many areas have become seriously degraded and less productive than they were, with soil being eroded and runoff accelerating. In the drier areas this process of degradation is referred to as desertification (see p. 215).

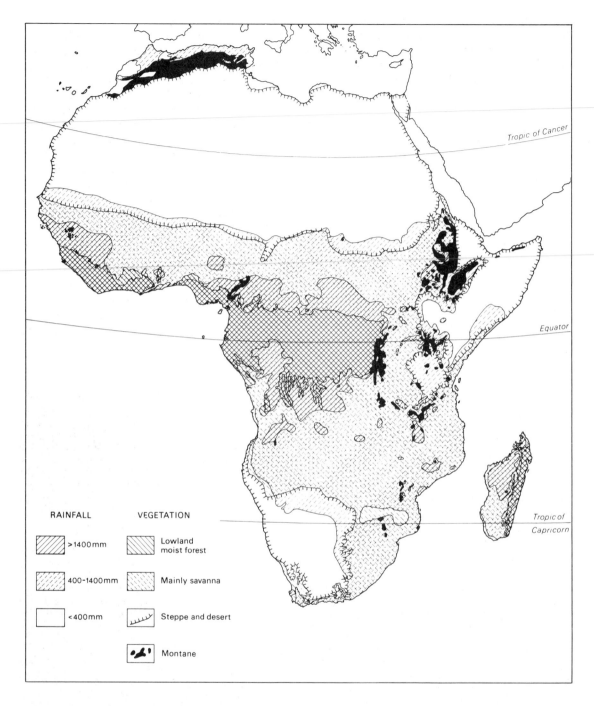

Fig. 2.1. *Vegetation in relation to rainfall. Lowland moist forest is confined to areas with a mean annual rainfall of more than 1400 mm (56 in), though wide areas receiving more than this amount lack moist forest because of the intensity of the dry season or because the forest has been cleared. Steppe and desert areas receive less than 400 mm (16 in) of rain, but some wetter areas have been desertified. Between the 1400 mm and 400 mm isohyets most of the country is savanna, wooded grassland, with montane high forest surviving at levels between about 1500 and 3000 m (5000 and 10 000 ft).*

Few extensive tracts of Africa remain where the plant cover has not been affected by man. Pictures taken from satellites, each image covering about 25 000² km (10 000 mls²), give a general impression of the surviving vegetation over wide tracts of country. One of the most striking features of the landscape they reveal is the contrast in the density of the plant cover on the two sides of international frontiers. Densely settled Malawi appears from space as a pale-toned country, the bare ground surfaces reflecting much more light than the darker, better vegetated country in adjacent parts of Mozambique and separated from it by a clear linear boundary. Similarly, Lesotho and the Black Homelands of the Republic of South Africa, with their dense rural populations, are more degraded and appear paler than adjacent parts of the Orange Free State and Natal with large farms run by Whites.

The floristic composition of the vegetation varies with distance from the Euro-Asian land mass. Broadly speaking, the plants of north-west Africa are comparable with those of the Mediterranean area as a whole; those of the Sudan zone and the Sahara resemble plants from similar climatic regions in south-west Asia, while the species characteristic of southern Africa, and particularly those of the Namib desert and the macchia (shrubby vegetation) in the south-western Cape, have evolved in greater isolation and are much more distinctive. The flora of Madagascar, separated from the rest of Africa since mid-Tertiary times, has its own particular features and shows some similarities to the flora of south-east Asia.

Remnants of the primeval plant cover allow some impression to be gained of the pattern of the vegetation as it would have been had there been no human interference, and so maps of what is called the 'natural vegetation' can be prepared. The distribution of the hypothetical natural vegetation, as might be expected, corresponds fairly well with the climatic zonation, but is modified both in detail and over considerable areas by local soil and drainage conditions.

Montane forest on the southern slopes of Kilimanjaro, at a height of about 3000 m (10 000 ft).

2.1.1 Tropical forest

Tropical moist forest, or rain forest, is the most imposing structure in the plant world. It still covers large parts of the Congo/Zaire basin in central Africa, but in west Africa it is rapidly disappearing and is in need of care and protection if any sizeable area is to survive into the twenty-first century.

The forest is made up of a large number of species of trees of different heights and ages, related only distantly to species in the forests of India and Malaya. In virgin forest, or a near approach to that rare state, the forest floor is fairly open with a shallow layer of decomposing leaves and rotting branches covering the mineral soil. Wherever a large tree has fallen, lianas, vines, and young trees crowd together in dense tangles. Elsewhere, leaves and branches form canopies or layers at two levels, one at a height of about 15 m (50 ft) above the ground and the other at about 30 m (100 ft); the tallest trees, called emergents, push through the top canopy to heights of about 45 m (150 ft) or more.

Rain forest is confined to lowland areas where the rainfall is well distributed through the year and annual rainfall totals exceed 1400 mm (about 56 in). In these humid areas, temperatures fluctuate between about 21 °C and 32 °C (70 °F and 90 °F) and are very seldom outside that range. Towards the drier margins the number of evergreen species diminishes and the proportion of deciduous trees increases, and soil differences have a greater effect on the floral composition.

The composition of the forest also varies with altitude, forests above about 1000 m (3300 ft) including only one-tenth the number of species found in the lowland forest. Such montane forests are scattered across Africa at wide intervals from Mount Cameroon to the highlands bordering the rift valleys and beyond to the slopes of the east African volcanoes and the Usumbaras in eastern Tanzania; yet the assemblages of plant and animal species found in all of them show striking similarities. It is possible that in cooler periods of the Quaternary, forest of the montane type may have reached down to lower elevations so as to occupy a more contin-

Montane forest in cloud; Marsabit in northern Kenya is surrounded by arid desert plains.

Rain forest cleared for cultivation, near the Akosombo dam, southern Ghana.

uous belt across the watersheds of central Africa, the present patches being merely remnants. However, on the last occasion when the climate in tropical Africa was much cooler it was also much drier (see p. 5) and if there has been a more continuous spread of montane forest it must have been at a more remote period still. At the height of the last glaciation, rain forest was probably confined to four main refuge areas, one in the north-eastern part of the Zaire basin, a second in Gabon, southern Cameroon, and Fernando Po, a third in Liberia and Sierra Leone, and a fourth in eastern Madagascar (Fig. 1.18). Then, about 12 000 to 8000 years ago, as conditions became as warm as and considerably wetter than they are today, forest spread over much wider areas than it covers at present (Fig. 1.19). Eventually, 7000 to 4500 years ago, its margins began to retreat as rainfall diminished and people began to clear land for cultivation.

On low-lying, swampy areas near the Niger delta and on the floor of the Zaire basin where rivers flood widely for months at a time, the forest trees are adapted to life in freshwater swamps and stand high on stilt roots. On the coasts of east and west Africa, especially in the Niger delta where alluvium is inundated for much of the time with fresh or brackish water, the mangroves *Rhizophora* and *Avicennia* have colonized the muds and overhang winding creeks and pools.

Now the rain forest is being depleted rapidly, for the tall trees and enriched soils can be very profitably exploited. Montane forests have suffered from cultivators clearing the hillsides and transforming them into open woodland or coffee plantations. The soils of the deciduous forests have been particularly attractive to cultivators, who have cleared very wide areas. Everywhere the rate of encroachment on high forest has accelerated in the last few decades to such an extent that, except in the Zaire basin, little will remain by the end of this century unless it is deliberately protected.

Man's activities have not been entirely destructive; trees that produce fruit or are valuable for their timber have been preserved and continue to regenerate when the rest have gone. Forest transformed by this artificial selection has an enhanced economic value and has been the main source of palm-oil and kola nuts.

Clearing land for a new oil-palm plantation at Butaw in Liberia, an EEC project to assist the development of the palm-oil industry.

Heavy equipment being used to remove debris remaining from unlawful clearing in Ivory Coast preparatory to reafforestation.

Modern equipment used in log handling in a teak forest in Benin.

But the costs of harvesting wild forest produce are high, and in suitable areas extensive plantations of high-yielding oil-palms have been established.

Of the high forest remaining, large blocks are now conserved in forest reserves where indiscriminate clearing is prohibited and lumbering is organized in such a way that natural regrowth can keep pace with felling. Much depends on a government being in a position to take a long-term view and being able to resist pressure from local communities and businessmen wanting to make use of the trees and land with an eye to short-term gains. Once forest has been cleared, it is both costly and technically difficult to re-establish it by planting; for the rain forest is a complex association of plants, appearing at the climax of a long sequence of developments in the formation of the soil and the establishment of larger and more specialized plants, a natural resource to be used with care and deliberation.

The protection of forests on the main watersheds of the continent is essential to prevent erosion and reduce the risk of destructive flooding. The preservation of at least some large blocks of forest is also important to scientists. As Richards has written in *The Tropical Rain Forest*, 1952:

The rain forest flora with its immense wealth of species belonging to thousands of genera and scores of families has acted in the past as a reservoir of genetic diversity and potential variability. During at least the more recent epochs in the earth's history it has been a centre of evolutionary activity from which the rest of the world's flora has been recruited.

2.1.2 Tropical savanna

Savanna is the sub-humid tropical grassland, usually with trees, that occupies the plateau country of south-central and east Africa, and extends westward along the northern margins of the Congo/Zaire basin to the Atlantic coast south of the Gambia River. Many of the species in the north are closely related to those of India;

41

Sparsely populated savanna seen from the crest of an inselberg alongside the Nairobi to Juba road in south-east Sudan Republic.

others are more typical of south-central Africa. The savanna flora south of the equator is very rich and a remarkable number of plants there are able to resist fire and drought. *Brachystegia*, which is amongst the tree species most typical of south and east Africa, is absent from west Africa.

Some of the tall woodlands, such as the *Chipya* and *Marquesia* woodland of Zambia are similar in appearance to rain forest. The savannas of the more humid areas of west Africa include many high forest species and are sometimes called derived savannas because they are believed to have replaced rain forest as a result of human interference. There are other formations dominated by evergreen trees which lack the physiognomic characteristics of rain forest and so are generally referred to as savanna. Nevertheless, the boundary between savanna and high forest is quite commonly distinct, being sharpened every year by grass fires in the savanna that fail to penetrate islands and peninsulas of forest but sweep through dry grasses between the gnarled, fire-resistant trees typical of savanna woodland. Patches of high forest sheltering villages or following the winding courses of rivers extend far outside the main rain forest belts. Elsewhere, savanna intrudes into humid country, possibly because the soils happen to be dense and clayey with sub-surface water hardly available to trees in the dry season though capable of supporting a dense growth of tall flammable grasses.

There is a good deal of disagreement about the relative importance of the different factors involved in the distribution of savanna and its variation in character from place to place. The overriding importance of climate is indisputable, the rain forest giving way to savanna where the winter dry season becomes marked. Burning has certainly been important more than locally. Burn marks covering large areas appear on air photographs, and fires show up on pictures taken at night from satellites. But the soil and drainage patterns related to the landforms also play a part. Well-dissected, undulating country, usually well-drained and with mature soils, will support forest, whereas level areas nearby, planed by erosion or on the surface of alluvial sediments with impeded drainage and soils subject to alternate water-logging and moisture deficiency, support only grassland.

Savanna plants supply few commodities in demand for export to industrial countries, with the exception of shea-butter, a vegetable oil, and gum arabic from a species of acacia. However, they are valuable to local communities as sources of wild fruits, medicines, dyes, timber, and, above all, firewood. The leaves of certain trees are used in soups; wildfowl and game are abundant in remote areas; honey can be extracted from the nests of wild bees. Domestic animals graze and browse at large. The climate allows both grain and root crops to be grown, and crops such as cotton and groundnuts for local use and for sale are produced extensively. At the same time, sleeping sickness, river blindness, poor soils, or a combination of these and other factors have restricted settlement and population growth in most savanna areas.

2.1.3 Steppe and desert

Approaching the margins of the desert, as the mean annual rainfall diminishes to less than 400 mm (16 in), the proportion of thorny species in the woodland increases, grasses are shorter than in the more humid savanna, and plants are more specialized in their adaptation to drought conditions. Such vegetation typifies the Sahel zone (Fig. 2.2). As the rainfall dimin-

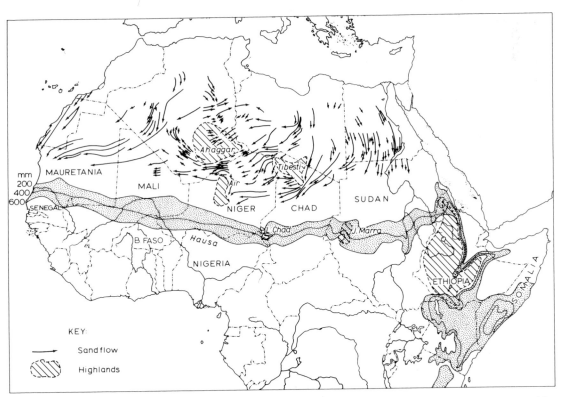

Fig. 2.2 (a). *Various isohyets have been used as limits of the Sahel. The shaded area here is between the mean annual rainfall values of 200 and 600 mm. The Saharan sandflow pattern is adapted from M. Mainguet and L. Canon, 'Vents et paléovents du Sahara, tentative d'approche paléoclimatique,' Revue de Géogr. Phys. et Géol. Dyn. 18: 241–50. (From A. T. Grove, 1978, 'Geographical introduction to the Sahel', Geogr. J. 144: 407–15.)*

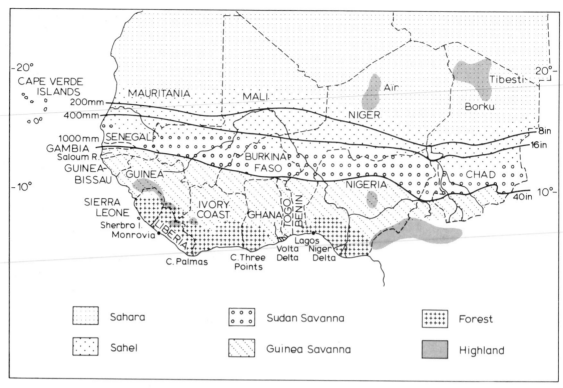

Fig. 2.2 (b). *The biomes of west Africa, where the remarkably regular latitudinal arrangement of the vegetation belts corresponds with that of the isohyets.*

ishes still further, the gaps between plants increase, and eventually vegetation is confined mainly to the margins of storm-water channels and the borders of temporary lakes where trees such as date palms, tamarisk, and certain acacias can obtain water from soil at depth.

In southern Africa the savanna merges southwards into wooded steppe, and thorn scrub in the Karoo, and finally into the sclerophylous bush of the Cape of Good Hope, which is largely made up of evergreen shrubs with some low trees and bulbous plants. Various exotic grasses have been introduced from other continents, and trees able to survive the harsh conditions, like poplar and Australian wattle, have transformed the scene.

2.1.4 High montane vegetation

Vegetation persists to very high altitudes on mountains near the equator, and zones of vegetation can be distinguished at increasing ele-

vation which correspond to some slight degree with those found at progressively higher latitudes (Fig. 2.3). Above the savanna woodland of the plateaux are forests of great white-trunked trees and bamboo thickets. Giant heather, groundsel, lobelia, and other strangely magnified forms make their appearance at about 3000 m (10 000 ft), and higher still these give way to the grasses, herbs, sedges, and bracken of moorland country. The flora becomes more specialized towards the snow-line and is comparable to that found at high altitudes in the Alps.

Montane climates at the equator are peculiar in that seasonal fluctuations are far less marked than in extratropical areas with similar mean annual temperatures. At the top of Kilimanjaro, for example, the mean shade temperature of every month is comparable with that of the cooler parts of the British Isles in January, but the sun is high in the sky and there are long hours of sunshine as well of cloud and mist, so that the conditions for plant growth are rather peculiar.

The vegetation of the summits of the Saharan mountain massifs includes many species which are more typical of the Mediterranean — shrubs, small trees, and aromatic herbs. It is believed that during the last glacial period, with lower temperatures and evaporation and possibly enhanced precipitation, Mediterranean vegetation was able to colonize areas well south of its present limits. Then, as more arid conditions returned and grasses and trees typical of the Sahel moved in from the south, the Mediterranean plants found refuge in the mountains.

2.1.5 North Africa's vegetation

With its high relief and steep decline in precipitation from the coast towards the interior, the vegetation pattern of the Maghreb in northwest Africa is very varied. Left to nature the wetter areas would be clad in mixed forests, including species of oak. However, the Maghreb has been settled by agricultural and pastoral peoples for thousands of years and, though less degraded than the Middle East, its vegetation has suffered considerably. The

blame is sometimes attached to Roman exploitation and more often to nomad Arabs, but it is very difficult to present conclusive evidence of the culpability of either.

The destruction wrought in the last hundred

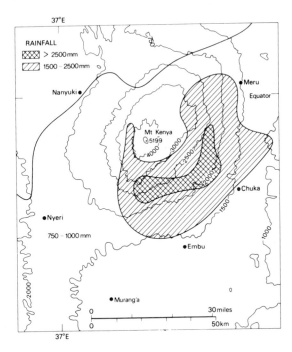

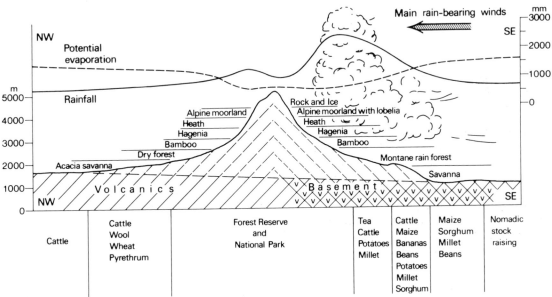

Fig. 2.3. *Altitudinal zoning of the vegetation on Mt Kenya. Rainfall is highest on the south-eastern slopes where mountain forest has been cleared to grow crops such as tea and potatoes. The north-western slopes are drier.*

45

years is more readily authenticated. With a tenfold increase in population and the displacement of a high proportion of the indigenous people towards the interior, the vegetation of the intermontane plateaux and the desert borderlands has been severely mauled. In places like Bou Sa'ada, where the mean annual rainfall is about 150 mm (6 in), the plant cover is much inferior to that of semi-arid regions in some other parts of the world with a similar rainfall but where pressure on the land has been less intense. The French administration was active in promoting afforestation of the mountainous country, but great tracts of plantations and of the surviving natural woodland were burned or cut down during the long years of the liberation war, 1954–62, and have yet to recover.

2.2 Soils

African soils are broadly similar to those developed under similar climates in other parts of Gondwanaland, in places like Brazil, peninsular India and Australia. There are no wide tracts of highly productive soils like the chernozems of the wheatlands of the Ukraine and North America, nor are there such extensive, irrigable alluvial lowlands as the Indo-Gangetic plain of northern India and Pakistan. Nevertheless, the irrigated alluvial soils in the lower Nile Valley are highly productive, and no doubt the clay plains in the Niger and Chad basins and some of the flat-floored valleys of Tanzania hold possibilities for the future.

In the humid regions, the illusion of fertility given to early travellers by the luxuriance of the forests has long since been dispelled and the fragility of the soils is recognized. Once the natural vegetation has been cleared, the organic material in the soils is rapidly burned up by the high temperatures and intense bacterial activity. No longer do falling leaves and twigs, and rain washing the foliage, replenish the soil's nutrient supplies. The impact of raindrops helps to break down the soil's structure, crop yields diminish, and erosion accelerates. The sequence has been followed in many areas and is not easy to halt.

The full potentialities of the land have still to be realized. Yields in Europe were low until a couple of centuries ago and soils tended to deteriorate, to reach low equilibrium levels under cultivation. Improved agricultural techniques involved an integration of crop cultivation and livestock rearing, with animal dung being applied to the fields, and root crops being used to feed the animals in the winter. As a result, cultivation began to improve fertility and production from well-farmed land exceeded that from virgin soil. In the course of the last few decades yields per hectare in Europe and North America have doubled and yields per man employed in agriculture have increased several times. Mechanized implements have allowed heavy soils to be readily cultivated, new varieties of crops have been introduced which can take full advantage of artificial fertilizers, pests and diseases are controlled. Improved breeds of livestock, fed on sown pastures and on high-nutrient feedstuffs, have increased yields of milk, meat, and wool enormously.

Agriculture with high inputs of these kinds is mainly confined in Africa to areas where white settlers have had the necessary capital resources and Africans have learned from them. More productive farming methods appropriate to the different climates and soil conditions are still being worked out. It is known that substantial increases in yields can be obtained by controlling diseases, planting high-yielding varieties, and using fertilizers intelligently. Yields per hectare of cocoa and rubber can be increased five or ten times, and methods are available for multiplying yields of food crops by three to six times. But such methods are too costly in terms of both money and energy inputs for most African farmers and their wives. The Green Revolution has yet to take place.

In each and every climatic region of the continent there are fertile soils and soils that are inherently poor; their quality depends on the parent material from which they are derived and the history of the way in which the land has been managed. The pattern of the soils is complicated because it is effectively compounded of the climatic, geological, and relief patterns superimposed one upon another. Soil maps on a scale of 1 : 250 000 or larger have been made of extensive areas in several countries for the use of agricultural advisory and planning services. Smaller-scale soil maps of the country as a whole are as liable to mislead as to convey any useful information.

2.2.1 Arid zone soils

The desert soils are shallow, have poorly developed profiles, and lack organic matter. Desert plains in the northern Sahara and parts of the Kalahari are commonly underlain by calcrete and silcrete; bare sand and surface pebbly layers called *reg* are characteristic of the driest areas of the Sahara and the Namib desert; upland soils are usually thin and stony. In depressions, water seeping through the regolith evaporates and leaves behind salty or calcareous deposits either in the soil profile or forming surface crusts. So long as salinity and alkalinity are not too great, most desert soils with a sufficient depth of friable material contain fair amounts of nutrients and are capable of yielding crops if water is supplied to them.

In the intertropical semi-arid lands with 250 to 600 mm (10 to 24 in) of rain annually, brown soils and ferruginous tropical soils are widespread. Occasionally they are alkaline but the heavy rains concentrated into a few months of the rainy season have washed out the bases and as a result of this leaching the soils are commonly found to be slightly acid. Duricrusts, mainly ferricretes, outcrop widely on low watersheds, and the soils, because they are so shallow, are not of much value for agriculture. More useful are the brown sands that occupy much of the Sahel–Sudan zone, derived from ancient dune formations. They are sometimes deficient in phosphorus and nitrogen and respond to dressings of the appropriate artificial fertilizers to yield good crops of groundnuts, sorghum, and millet. Over wide areas these soils are deep enough to allow tractor cultivation but, if they are overcropped or overgrazed, they are susceptible to water and wind erosion.

Alluvial plains on the floors of depressions in the semi-arid parts of the continent, flooded by local rains or by large rivers rising at a distance, are widely floored with dark-brown or black, deeply cracking, non-kaolinitic clays. They are sometimes called Black Cotton soils, though cotton is rarely grown on them, or margalitic from the Latin *marga*, meaning 'marl', because they are heavy and calcareous, or simply Tropical Black Earths. They consist mainly of the clay mineral smectite, which expands and contracts strongly with wetting and drying, and in consequence they are churned up to a considerable

depth and lack well developed horizons. The term 'vertisol' is commonly used for this class of soils. They occupy wide areas in the White Nile basin of the southern Sudan Republic and the southern parts of the Chad basin and it seems quite likely that they developed under shallow lakes and on floodplains, especially between 10 000 and 5000 years ago when the climate was more humid.

2.2.2 Soils of sub-humid and humid regions

In the sub-humid savanna lands, with rainfall totals of 750 to 1250 mm (30 to 50 in annually), upland soils are usually red and ferruginous with lateritic ironstone developed locally. An association of gently rolling plains with inselbergs rising sharply from them is widespread, and savanna woodland covering a more or less dissected lateritic ironstone crust is very characteristic of west Africa north of the high forest zone and of the central African plateaux surrounding the Zaire basin.

Soils of the humid regions are deeper than elsewhere on account of the intense weathering and because high forest has protected the regolith from erosion. Red or yellow coloration extends several metres, even tens of metres, below the surface and yet the top horizon, rich in organic matter, is seldom more than a few centimetres thick. Forest litter, leaves, branches, and even tree trunks break down rapidly under the attack of fungi, termites, bacteria, and other large and small organisms. These acid soils are commonly called latosols from the word 'laterite', which is commonly applied to thoroughly leached tropical soils. The term 'ferrallitic' is also used, referring to the presence of alumina as well as iron oxides. Such soils are best used for tree crops such as oil-palms and rubber; under annual cultivation they are liable to deteriorate rapidly.

The influence of original parent material is important. Amongst the best soils are those which are still youthful and retain quantities of soluble minerals useful to plants. Deep loamy soils formed under high forest, chocolate-brown at higher altitudes, red at lower levels, derived from volcanic rocks of Pliocene and later ages are richer than most other soils in Africa. They occupy much of the Kenyan and Ethiopian highlands. Red gritty earth at the foot of rocky outcrops is also well liked by cultivators; it remains moist long into the dry season on account of seepage from the hills behind. It is well drained and easy to till, but liable to be eroded by gullies cutting back into the valley-floor terraces and into the hill masses.

There are other good soils, but great tracts of the continent, above all on the upland plains where weathering has continued for millions of years, have soils that are thin, lack plant nutrients or essential minerals, or at present are for some other reason of little value for agricultural purposes.

The soils of north-west Africa include those typical of the Mediterranean region and of the northern Sahara. Commonly they include an illuvial horizon rich in carbonates, and in the heavier rainfall areas near the coast are often reddish in colour. Because of the high relief in parts of the Atlas region, soil conditions vary greatly over quite short distances, rates of erosion are high, and reservoirs silt up rapidly.

2.2.3 Plants as soil indicators

The vegetation is often a useful guide to soil potential. Shifting cultivators judge when the land is fit for cropping by the nature and density of the plant cover, and soil surveyors are always on the lookout for plant indicators. Over much of West Africa *Borassus* palms are found to be growing on moist alluvial land. *Borassus* is a curious tree, with one or two large bulges near the top of its slender grey trunk. It produces yellow nuts the size of tennis balls that are relished by goats and are ground up to produce a kind of flour in times of famine; the timber is stringy but useful for rough building because of its resistance to the attacks of termites. Small, thorny trees with grey-green trunks, *Acacia seyal*, often characterize heavy black earths derived from basic lavas or clayey limestones in the savanna zone. Coconut palms thrive on freely drained sandy soils at the coast; oil-palms flourish on well-drained red loams, ferrallitic soils derived from sandy sedimentary rocks; cocoa grows most satisfactorily on deep clayey loams underlain by crystalline rocks rich in bases, from which forest has been lately cleared.

2.2.4 Soils and topography

The arrangement of the soil and vegetation types in many parts of the continent when mapped at 1 : 50 000 (i.e. about one inch to a mile, a smaller scale than most air photographs and a similar scale to pictures commonly made from Landsat and SPOT satellite images) conforms to some degree with the relief and drainage pattern. A certain sequence of soil types and related vegetation associations is found to be repeated time and time again across country. Such a sequence is called a toposequence or sometimes a catena, the sequence of soils across a section of a river valley being likened to the links in a suspended chain (Fig. 2.4).

On dissected upland plains, material is constantly being washed away from the soils of facets near the crests of interfluves, dissolved in soil water or carried away in particulate form in water running over the surface. These eluvial soils on slope crests are usually reddish, more acid, and less clayey than the other soils in the toposequence. On the hillslopes are colluvial soils, consisting in part of material derived from upslope and in the process of being moved by degrees to the slope foot. At the border of the valley floor, slope material accumulates giving deep profiles. Successively younger soils are encountered towards the stream, derived from alluvial deposits of various ages and from recently deposited alluvium. In many cases the vegetation distribution displays some relationship to the soil sequence and farmers are seen to have adapted their cropping patterns and the shapes of their holdings to the topographical arrangement of the soils and their suitability for different uses.

On depositional plains of low relief, other kinds of soil and vegetation patterns appear, with sandy soils on old dunes or marking former stream channels, and clayey soils in depressions that were flooded in more humid periods of the past. Such soils are best mapped from air photographs which depict the complicated arrangements very clearly, whereas the surveyor on the ground may have great difficulty in appreciating the overall pattern associated with a local relief of only a few metres. Maps of such areas are particularly important when preparations are being made to irrigate them, because the layout of irrigation channels, plots, and access roads should conform with the soil pattern if the large investments involved are to be adequately repaid.

Small-scale soil maps conceal a multitude of

important soil differences that are important to the individual cultivator. Their usefulness is therefore limited. They are little more than attempts to find some order in a mass of scattered surveys and field observations made by individual soil scientists and surveyors with different backgrounds and using different classificatory systems and terminologies.

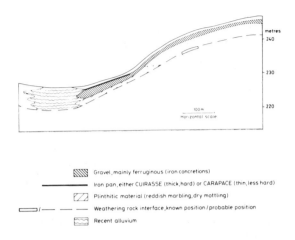

Fig. 2.4 (a). *Soil catena in the forest zone of south-west Nigeria. Developed between upland erosion surface and alluviated valley floor, the catena is of a relatively simple kind with a gravelly layer in the slope soils, iron pan near the surface at the slope foot, and recent alluvium on the valley floor.*

Gravel, mainly ferruginous (iron concretions)

Iron pan, either CUIRASSE (thick, hard) or CARAPACE (thin, less hard)

Plinthitic material (reddish marbling, dry mottling)

Weathering rock interface, known position / probable position

Recent alluvium

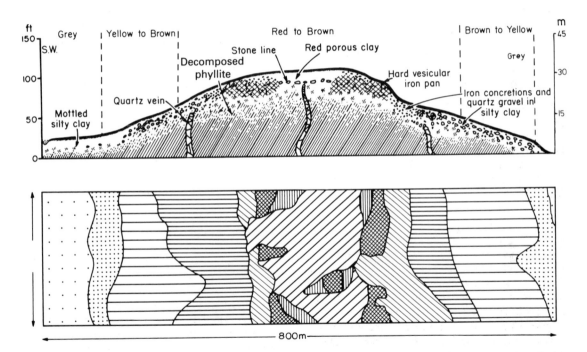

Fig. 2.4 (b). *A more complicated catenal arrangement of soils in southern Ghana. This cross-section shows the distribution of soils overlying phyllites in the rain forest zone. Red clay soils on the erosion surface remnant are underlain by a stone line. Such lines, which commonly appear in soil sections in tropical Africa, are the outcrops of layers of stones more or less parallel to the surface and some metres below it. Some represent old land surfaces, others probably mark the depth to which termite activity penetrates. Ironstone outcrops at the breaks of slope bound the erosion-surface remnant; fragments of quartz and concretionary debris appear in the slope soils. Alluvial terraces on valley slopes and bottoms, resulting from Pleistocene climatic changes, introduce complexities to the lower parts of the catenas. The soil map below the section shows the distribution pattern of the different kinds of soils and simplifies what is a very complicated arrangement. (From H. Brammer, 1962, 'Soils', in J. B. Wills, ed.,* Agriculture and Land Use in Ghana, *OUP.)*

49

2.3 Fauna

2.3.1 Mammals

Africa's mammalian fauna is remarkably rich, consisting of thirty-eight families (not counting bats). Fossil remains indicate that many of the animals now mainly confined to the savannas of the centre and east were much more widely distributed some thousands of years ago, roaming the foothills of the Atlas mountains and the basin of the Vaal river. Ancient rock engravings of hippopotamus, giraffe, and other large beasts have been found in remote desert regions from which they have long since disappeared. Greater aridity over the last five thousand years drove many species out of the Sahara and, in more recent times, the demands of the Roman amphitheatres disposed of most of the lion, elephant, and other large animals that had managed to survive in north Africa.

In west Africa and Ethiopia, large mammals have been all but eliminated by native hunters armed with bows, spears, or muzzle-loaders and by the encroachments of cultivators, so that game is now restricted to remote swampy or mountainous regions. Within living memory elephant have disappeared from parts of northern Nigeria and ostrich from the Algerian Sahara. In eastern and southern Africa great numbers of antelope and other animals have been slaughtered for sport and also in attempts to eliminate carriers of disease harmful to cattle. Fencing of great tracts of grazing land in the Kalahari has interrupted migration routes, cutting off the game animals at times of drought from the last remaining sources of surface water. Many Africans who travel abroad or live in towns have their first sight of lion, rhinoceros, and such creatures on television or in the cages of zoos. Nevertheless, great numbers of wild animals remain, including, for instance, about a million elephant. Efforts have been made to protect the elephant in recent years by banning the trade in ivory in order to deter poachers. However, problems have been arising in Zimbabwe, for instance. By 1992 it was estimated that the number of elephant there had risen to over 70,000, too many to be supported on the area available to them. They were already encroaching on agricultural land and when the drought of 1992 came, several hundreds had to be shot because they were starving. Tusks were in store worth $12 mn, but because of the ban they could not be sold to offset the costs of conservation.

The wild animals of Africa are of very great value because they remind us of a richer natural order of the past. They also provide ecologists with the opportunity to study the complex interactions of vertebrate faunas such

Zebra grazing on the floor of Ngorongoro Crater in Tanzania: the crater rim is in the background.

as once must have existed more widely throughout the world. Such a resource should not be allowed to disappear.

National parks have been demarcated where hunting is forbidden and nearly everywhere, according to the law, licences are required to kill the larger animals. But regulations alone cannot prevent poachers killing rhinoceroses when the horn can be sold for large sums in the East because it is supposed to enhance virility. Crocodiles are becoming rare in well-populated areas, partly because their skins are used to make expensive handbags. Snakes are real dangers to people living in the bush. Baboons, monkeys, and elephants damage farmers' crops and, to a person living on a 1500-calorie carbohydrate diet an antelope, no matter how graceful, is going to mean only one thing—meat.

Parks and reserves have to be guarded and controlled and this is costly. Furthermore, government and local people in many countries are not easily persuaded that they can afford the land needed to ensure the preservation of wildlife. Especially at times of drought, famine, and armed conflict, wildlife protection breaks down and wild animals as well as people suffer.

It has been argued that on marginal and poor land the potential meat production of indigenous fauna is higher than that of domestic animals. The reason for this has been give by E. B. Worthington. He writes:

The wild flora usually comprises herb layer, shrub layer and trees, and in the wild state this is utilized by a dozen or more species of animals from the pig tribe rooting underground to giraffes feeding on the tree tops, with a range of grazers and browsers in between. Also the animals are immune to trypanosomiasis and several other indigenous diseases which are dreaded by cattlemen. In order to eliminate tsetse and to tame such land for the purposes of cattle and sheep, it is necessary to eliminate or depress the upper storeys of vegetation and concentrate upon the pasture, inevitably introducing at the same time the dangers of accelerated soil erosion.

One may hope that 'game-cropping' may be shown to be economic and practicable. But hunting and trapping wild animals can be expensive. Then the carcasses have to be transported rapidly to processing plants where many are found to be diseased and unfit for

Rhinoceros in Ngorongoro.

human consumption. It will be a little surprising if careful hunting turns out to be more productive than careful herding.

The strongest argument for wildlife conservation in practice is the foreign currency to be won from tourists armed with cameras. Nearly every African country is now paying a good deal of attention to its game reserves, and the tourism associated with them is big business, especially in Kenya. Everywhere it is also being recognized that the local people must benefit from conservation if it is to be successful in the long term and the wildlife is to survive.

2.3.2 Birds

The rain forests, savannas, lowlands, and highlands each have their own assemblages of bird species (see Moreau's *Bird Faunas of Africa and the Islands,* 1966). The number of species in Africa is high as compared with temperate latitudes but not remarkably high for the tropics. The rain forest, in comparison with that of Amazonia and south-east Asia, is quite poor in both bird and plant species. An explanation is probably to be found in terms of the comparative simplicity of Africa's topography, with few refuge areas available in millennia of greater climatic aridity, and consequently fewer isolated habitats conducive to speciation.

One of the greatest puzzles to be solved is the origin of the seasonal migrations of birds from

Europe and central Asia across the Sahara, arriving in the Sudan zone at the beginning of the dry season (see Moreau, *The Palaearctic-Africa Bird Migration Systems*, 1972). Some birds carry on south down the coast as far as Cape Province in South Africa. In March and April the migrants consume a great deal of food and put on fat to provide fuel for the long return journey to breeding grounds in the north. In recent years many species have been much depleted because of the harsher conditions associated with drought on the south side of the Sahara. One wonders how the migratory movements were affected in the longer term by the extension of the European ice-caps and the simultaneous expansion of the Sahara and then by its subsequent contraction.

2.3.3 Fish

2.3.3.1 Freshwater fish   Like Moreau's volume, *The Inland Waters of Tropical Africa* by L. C. Beadle is the product of a lifetime's work in the field in Africa and in study in England. The distribution patterns of the freshwater fish reflect the past history of the drainage patterns (p. 26). A mid-Tertiary fish fauna that seems to have been common to most of the continent was presented with a great variety of new habitats as a result of the dislocation of drainage systems resulting from rift faulting.

The fish of the Zaire basin and of Lakes Tanganyika and Malawi differ from those of the great rivers of the Sudan zone. The number of species of fish in the Nile, Chad, Niger, and Senegal is quite small and the assemblages in the different basins resemble one another quite closely. These characteristics reflect the drying up of the Sudan zone 20 000 to 12 000 years ago, followed by interconnections between the rivers in subsequent wet phases until widespread desiccation took place about 5000 years ago. Members of the nilotic or soudanian fauna common to all the basins are the Nile perch, *Lates niloticus*, and also *Tilapia galilaea* and *Citharinus citharus*. Nile perch were introduced to Lake Victoria as recently as the 1960s. They have eliminated more than a half of the 200 endemic cichlid species that had evolved there in the late Pleistocene, but they provide larger fish and bigger catches than formerly.

The fish of Lake Tanganyika and the molluscs

there have some features more characteristic of marine than freshwater species and it was thought at the end of the last century that they must be descended from the fauna of an ancient sea. Such ideas are now discounted and it seems more likely that the peculiarities of these particular creatures are the outcome of adaptation over a long period of time to special salinity and other environmental conditions in the lake. Lake Tanganyika is 1470 m (4800 ft) deep; at depths of more than 200 m (700 ft) below the surface the water is stagnant, deprived of oxygen, and practically uninhabited. Much the same is true of Lake Malawi, which is 760 m (2500 ft) deep. In Lake Malawi there are 245 species of fish, even more than in Lake Tanganyika with 214 species. The main ecological zones in the two lakes are similar in character but the two faunas are rather different, probably because it is a considerable time since the two lakes were last connected.

South of the Zambezi, the number of freshwater species of fish is greatly reduced. Representatives of a few of the tropical families tolerant of low temperatures have managed to survive in the Cape region but all those in the extreme south-west are endemics. In the headwaters of the Cape streams, representatives of an ancient freshwater fauna persist which are related to families and genera in north Africa and absent from tropical Africa. It is possible that the connection was through parts of Gondwanaland that have now drifted away (Fig. 1.2). Some tropical fish are found near the Mediterranean coast, in the Nile delta, and in pools in the southern foothills of the Algerian Atlas mountains; north of the Atlas, the freshwater fish are almost exclusively of Mediterranean origin.

2.3.3.2 Marine fish   African sea fisheries are dominated by pelagic species, fish living near the surface such as herring, tuna, and sardine. Demersal fish, the kind that spend much of their time on or near the sea-bed, are generally lacking because the continental shelf is so narrow in most places. An exception is off South Africa, where Cape hake and stockfish are abundant. The west coasts are especially productive in the zones of cold upwelling water bringing nutrients to the surface in the sea areas off the Sahara and the Namib desert.

3

PESTS AND DISEASES

No one seems to be very much concerned about preserving the smaller creatures in Africa; few of them are in danger of extinction, though much of the scientific attention they attract seems to be directed towards their destruction. There are risks that if some of the smaller, harmless creatures are inadvertently exterminated along with the harmful ones the resulting imbalance could be costly to man in the long run. Some of the smaller creatures are evidently beneficial, bees for instance. Wild honey, scooped from nests in hollow trees or collected from basketwork hives lodged in the branches, sweetens many otherwise dull rural diets.

Many small creatures are harmful because they damage crops and carry disease. Some are a greater menace between the tropics than in higher latitudes because climate, notably the lack of frosts, allows them to live and breed easily. Others present problems because standards of hygiene, water supply, and sanitation are low.

Monkeys and other primates are of medical interest because they are the hosts of some parasites that affect man. Monkeys were the hosts of the yellow fever virus and it has been suggested that green monkeys in Burundi may have been the source of the acquired immune deficiency syndrome virus causing AIDS. By the 1980s AIDs was widespread in central Africa, possibly having been spread initially because cost considerations caused disposable syringes to be used repeatedly, without sterilization, thereby transmitting the disease from one patient to another. Social conditions in cities, migrant labour, and social breakdown have accelerated the diffusion of the disease. Because AIDS destroys the body's natural resistance to disease, cases often appear in the

form of endemic African diseases such as leprosy and malaria. Application of control measures is very difficult and long-term effects on health, population, and society itself must inevitably be very drastic.

From all the continent's creatures and organisms a few have been selected for more detailed consideration here because they are particularly interesting ecologically and are known to play an important part in human affairs.

3.1 Locusts

Locusts are amongst the traditional plagues of Africa. They are species of large grasshoppers, normally living either in small groups or singly in a solitary state. Occasionally they congregate into swarms, probably in the first place when their food supplies are restricted to small areas by drought. Then, when conditions improve, the swarms multiply and break out to occupy much wider areas. A grown locust needs to eat its own weight of food every day, so a large swarm, weighing tens of thousands of tonnes, will eat all the green leaves and crops over several square kilometres, the food supplies of tens of thousands of people.

Locusts did great damage in Africa in the 1930s. During the Second World War, to prevent food shortages, especially in the Red Sea region, an International Locust Organization was set up. This was maintained in the post-war period. When a locust outbreak occurred, experts were flown out from headquarters in London and teams of local people were organized to deal with the locusts before severe damage had been done. Treatment mainly involved spraying pesticides onto infested areas from aircraft. By the time independence came to most African countries, the locust threat had receded, control measures were relaxed, and the organization was run down. Suddenly, in 1985, when the rains returned to many parts of Africa that had been suffering from drought for many years, swarms of locusts of several kinds reappeared and the United Nations Food and Agriculture Organization (FAO) took over responsibility for dealing with them.

The Desert Locust has continued to cause trouble from time to time ever since the Second World War. Its breeding places are widespread at the desert margins in a wide belt stretching from Morocco to Pakistan (Fig. 3.1). Desert Locusts hatching from eggs laid after winter and spring rains in the northern Sahara are carried south with the wind, roosting by night and flying by day. At the southern fringe of the desert, during the summer rains, they breed again and may be carried further south in the early dry season in the wake of the intertropical convergence zone, to arrive in east Africa about October.

Outbreaks north of the equator in 1985 involved not only the Desert Locust but also unprecedentedly large numbers of grasshoppers and the Migratory Locust. The Migratory Locust had emerged from the Inland Niger Basin in 1928 and over the next decade had advanced into the Sudan, Kenya, Tanzania, and south-west Africa, affecting many areas for two consecutive years. In 1985 it erupted into Sudan and Ethiopia. South of the equator in the same year, swarms of Brown Locusts which had hatched in South Africa invaded Botswana. The Red Locust was also a menace. It has two main outbreak areas, one in the grassy plains around Lake Rukwa in south-west Tanzania, the other in Zaire between Lakes Mweru and Tanganyika. Red Locust swarms are known to have afflicted much of south-central Africa in 1847–54, 1892–1910, and 1933–44. After the last of these, experts based at a centre in Mbala (for-

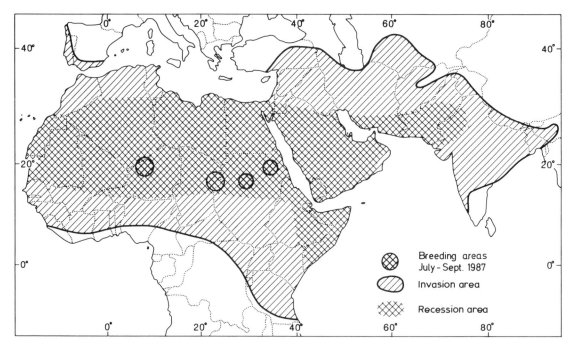

Fig. 3.1. *Desert Locusts are usually confined to the arid recession area, but if water and vegetation conditions are suitable they have been known to invade heavily settled cultivated regions far outside the deserts. Control of the insects in their breeding grounds has been made difficult in the 1980s by armed conflicts and also by the banning of the use of certain insecticides, such as dieldrin, because of their environmental side-effects. Towards the end of 1987 swarms from Chad, Niger, and Sudan moved across the Sahara into Algeria and Morocco.*

merly Abercorn), Zambia, kept the situation under observation and in 1954 directed effective counter-measures when an outbreak threatened by organizing the spreading of poison dust to kill the young locusts, the hoppers, before they got their wings. The outbreak in 1985 was less successfully contained and by 1986 was reported to be affecting Tanzania, Malawi, Zambia, and eastern Zaire.

3.2 Termites

Often miscalled white ants, termites are in fact neither white nor ants but a primitive type of creature related to cockroaches. Like wasps, bees, and ants, they invariably live social lives; they cannot exist in the solitary state as locusts can, but only in the group. More than 400 species are known in Africa, some living entirely underground, some in wood, others in mounds protruding above the ground. They are probably the most numerous macroscopic creatures in Africa, with a biomass of about 100 kg per ha (100 lb per acre) in *Brachystegia* woodland and ten times as much in some rain forest habitats.

Termites play an important part in the ecosystems of both forest and savanna. Forest species commonly build their nests in trees, while termites in open woodland are more commonly subterranean or dwell in mounds. Several species, some living in damp forests and others in humid savanna with soils rich in ferruginous laterite, build mushroom-shaped dwellings. According to Lee and Wood in *Termites and Soils* (1971), the architectural forms are very constant within species and identification of a species is often more readily done by examining the nest than the termites themselves. The mounds represent an adjustment to varying materials, behaviour, and climate. Deep red-earth soils are often characterized by skyscrapers 7 or 8 m high; grey clayey soils, for instance at the north end of Lake Turkana, by vertical pipes of similar height. Flat cones like miniature volcanoes are distributed over wide stretches of semi-arid country; their galleries go down 15 m (50 ft) or more to moist layers and they may include subterranean foodstores and have galleries and covered runways radiating over 30 m (100 ft). Each mound is commonly surrounded by a bare patch so that a field of termitaria appears on an air photograph as a dense rash of white dots. In swampy or clayey grasslands subject to flooding, trees may be confined to termitaria and their ruins rising a metre or so above the general level of the ground and providing relatively well-drained sites: such is the case in the part of Uganda west of Lake Victoria and in Barotseland in Zambia. West of Accra on the coastal plains of south-east Ghana the vegetation shows a striped pattern where fires driven by south-south-west winds have been held up by termite heaps so that strips of shrubby woodland stretch downwind from each mound with grassy lanes, burned annually, running between the bushy strips.

Termites consume dead plant and animal remains and thus perform some of the functions of earthworms in higher latitudes. Leaves and stems and roots of plants are not allowed to decompose gradually; they are comminuted by

A termite skyscraper provides a useful perch for a hawk at the northern end of Lake Turkana.

55

Swampy grass plains in south-west Uganda, where termite mounds provide relatively well-drained sites on which shrubs and trees can grow.

termites to a state in which further more complete decomposition is rapid. This helps to explain the small amount of raw humus in tropical African soils and the rapid turnover of plant remains. Furthermore, by bringing up finer plant material from a depth, the termites provide a gravel-free layer on what might otherwise have been very stony ground.

Quite commonly, road sections in rolling country in Africa exhibit a stone line at a depth of a metre or two, with loamy material above and weathered rock beneath. It is possible that the stony layer is an old 'desert pavement' formed in a past arid period, the loamy layer resting on it having been brought to the surface by termites. The termite mounds or termitaria and the bare areas surrounding them are eroded more rapidly than better-covered soils. It could be argued that much of the lowering of the land surface takes place not only as a result of solution, creep, and wash but also as a result of termite activity.

To the householder, termites are a menace threatening to eat not only paper or cloth but also the wooden framework of his dwelling. To the modern farmer they are pests that eat his fences and buildings, damage his pastures and crops, and construct underground cavities that trap his mechanical equipment. To the historian they are destroyers of documents that might have thrown more light on the African past.

3.3 The mosquito, malaria, and other mosquito-borne diseases

The common form of malaria in Africa is caused by a parasite, *Plasmodium falciparum*, which is transmitted by various species of mosquitoes of which the most prevalent is *Anopheles gambia*. The parasite colonizes the liver and infects blood cells and is one of the commonest causes of death amongst infants, probably killing a million or more every year. Children who survive acquire a measure of resistance to the disease and may only get a fever if it recurs. Many west Africans carry the mutant gene for sickle-cell anaemia, a disease of the blood which can provide a measure of protection against malaria. On the principle of the survival of the fittest for local conditions, this abnormality has increased in malarious parts of Africa, in some of which it reaches a frequency of 30 or 40 per cent; however, the anaemia is itself the cause of many deaths when inherited without a normal gene.

Attacks of malaria greatly reduce physical and mental energy and the general state of health; farmers are liable to be laid low at the beginning of the rainy season just when they need all their strength for preparing the land and planting crops. Some forms of malaria can be fatal to expatriate Europeans who have never acquired resistance to the disease, but they are usually able to protect themselves by proofing their houses against mosquitoes and by regularly taking protective drugs of one kind or another in the form of small pills.

Of the several species of mosquito capable of transmitting malarial parasites of one kind or another, some are more attracted to human blood than others. Malaria eradication in Africa is unusually difficult because *Anopheles gambia* feeds on animal as well as human blood, so that the mosquitoes can survive even if they are temporarily prevented from feeding on man. As mosquitoes usually, though not invariably, breed in standing water they are most numerous near swamps and rivers, and risks of infection are hence greatest in riverside towns and during the rainy season.

Malaria can be controlled in several ways. The larvae can be killed by draining swamps and spraying pools; insecticides can be sprayed on the walls of dwellings; male mosquitoes can be sterilized by radiation so that matings are infertile and mosquito numbers decline; drugs can be used to suppress the activity of malarial parasites in the blood. The disease was eliminated on Mauritius, and successful schemes on the Copperbelt in Zambia showed that malaria can be almost entirely dislodged from towns. But it is now realized that control must be really effective or the anti-malarial projects may do more harm than good. The people in a treated area can lose their resistance to the disease and then, if mosquitoes should reinfest the area, infection may be fatal instead of merely producing a mild fever. Furthermore, Africans who lose their resistance may return to their villages or move to an area where the disease remains endemic; if they become reinfected they may die, and if they live they carry the infection back to the towns they left. Europeans depending on a particular pill may move to a place where the malarial parasite is resistant to that particular drug, and rapid recourse to an effective alternative becomes essential. With air transport, people in places which have been free of the disease may fall ill several weeks after their return from tropical Africa and may even transmit the disease to others.

Mosquitoes also transmit dengue fever and the virus disease called yellow fever. Essentially, yellow fever is a disease of monkeys, but it can be transmitted from them to man by several species of forest mosquitoes. Once it becomes established in an urban area, the mosquito *Aedes aegyptica* acts as a very efficient carrier from one person to another. The disease is commonly fatal, but a vaccine has been known for several decades, and travellers to and from Africa are required to be inoculated against it. Millions of Africans have also received prophylactic treatment. Small parasitic worms called filariae are also transmitted by mosquitoes and can cause great distress to people infected by them; there is now an effective treatment for this disease.

It is thus important to stress the manifold dangers of the mosquito as a disease vector, for many people these days, believing that they are protected by anti-malarial pills, fail to take simple precautions to prevent themselves being bitten.

3.4 The tsetse-fly, trypanosomiasis, and sleeping sickness

The tsetse is a large, bustling brown fly, with greyish stripes or spots on the thorax, and wings that overlap when at rest. It is the main though not the only vector of trypanosomiasis. If a tsetse bites a man or animal suffering from the disease, it swallows blood containing parasites called trypanosomes. These develop and multiply within the fly, and if the tsetse should subsequently feed on another man or animal they are injected into the bloodstream and the disease has been transmitted. The victim usually falls ill within a few days, but in the case of man several days or several months may elapse before death occurs. There are drugs for treating the disease in man, where it is usually known as sleeping sickness, and preventive inoculation is now partly effective in man and animals.

About 10 million square kilometres within 14° of the equator are infested with tsetse-flies of various species (Fig. 5.1). Grassy highlands rising above about 1200 m (4000 ft) are too cold for successful breeding of the fly, as also is open country with an intense and lengthy dry season. Such open terrain is broadly of two kinds; semi-arid country such as occurs in the Horn of Africa (Somalia) with less than 500 mm (20 in) of rain annually and, secondly, heavily settled regions in the savanna zone, around Kano in northern Nigeria for instance, where population densities exceed 100 per km² (260 per mile). Under such conditions, trees under which the fly can breed have been cleared for cultivation or wood fuel, and game animals on which flies normally depend for their food have been wiped out. Typical tsetse-ridden country is sparsely settled savanna woodland with 750 to 1500 mm (30 to 60 in) of rain annually, and with poor soils.

In the past the ravages of sleeping sickness have influenced the distribution of population over much of the continent. An outbreak in Zaire, then the Belgian Congo, towards the end of the nineteenth century, spread to the Busoga area of Uganda, near Lake Victoria and between 1902 and 1905 killed 30 000 people; the area remains sparsely settled. Over the next two or three decades the disease spread north through Cameroon into Nigeria and Ghana. Over 30 per cent of the populations in many villages were infected and people evacuated the river valleys and moved on to the safer but often less fertile interfluves. Hundreds of thousands were treated by mobile teams and eventually, towards the end of the 1930s, the epidemic died out.

Surveys are now carried out regularly to discover victims of sleeping sickness so they can be treated in the early stages before infection can be transmitted to other people living nearby. Villages have been shifted to new sites

free of tsetse-fly, and woodland where the fly might breed near villages has been cleared. But scattered foci of infection remain and recent estimates suggest that about 20 000 new cases occur every year. Sleeping sickness still has the potential to become a major threat to health in Africa.

Attention is now directed mainly towards preventing trypanosomiasis amongst cattle. The disease in animals, nagana, has denied vast areas of the continent to cattle and horses and indeed to most other domestic animals except poultry. This may help to explain the late occupation of south-east Africa by pastoralists and why ox-drawn ploughs have not replaced hoe cultivation. Many pastoralist peoples long ago devised systems of transhumance, seasonal movements by which they pasture their cattle on the highlands or in the drier areas during the rains and then move to the lowland savannas during the dry season, when the fly usually keeps to cool, moist woodland bordering streams and pools. In the past many animals died of nagana on their way to market, trekking from the interior grazing lands to the towns of the Guinea coastlands. Transport of animals by lorry through fly-infested areas has much reduced losses.

More positive control measures have been taken in recent years by dealing with the trypanosomes' hosts and the fly's food supplies and breeding places. In parts of Uganda and Zimbabwe, large numbers of game animals have been hunted out, especially antelope. Recent studies of food preferences of the tsetse have shown that hartebeest, impala, zebra, and certain other species can be spared because tsetse rarely feed on them. Attention is now concentrated on eliminating buffalo, reedbuck, duiker, warthog, and bushpig, which the fly seems to find more appetizing.

In Nigeria, wide areas of grassland were made safe for cattle by clearing clumps of infested woodland. Spraying insecticide from the air carries the risk of upsetting the natural balance, in particular killing the ants that feed on the pupae of the fly. Drugs are available for inoculating cattle, though problems of resistance are arising. There are however some promising developments. In particular, traps containing insecticide have been devised which are impregnated with chemicals that attract the tsetse to their deaths.

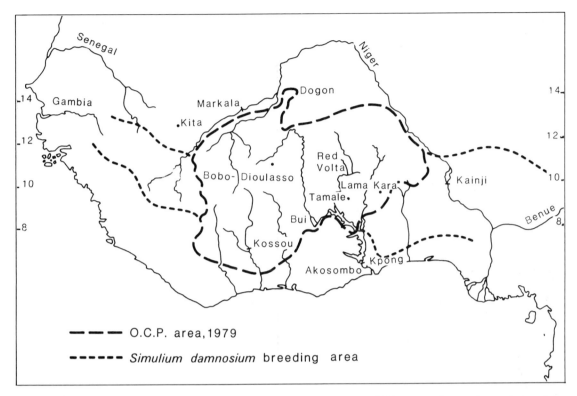

Fig. 3.2. *The breeding areas of the fly* Simulium damnosum, *which transmits onchocerciasis, river blindness, stretch across west Africa from the Gambia to the Benue river basin. A costly UN World Health Organization Onchocerciasis Control Programme (OCP) was originally confined to the central part of this zone, but reinfestation from adjoining areas has required it to be extended. (From J. F. Walsh, 1985, 'Onchocerciasis: river blindness', in A. T. Grove, ed.,* The Niger and its Neighbours, *Balkema.)*

3.5 Parasitic worms

There are a number of kinds of worms that live in the blood and tissues and intestines, the most common being the hookworm. This affliction can be treated fairly easily, but unless local sanitary arrangements are improved or the patients start wearing shoes they are likely to be reinfected from the microscopic eggs of the worm in excreta.

Infection by guinea-worm is very common in parts of west Africa, causing ulceration of the legs and thereby incapacitating people for weeks at a time. It can be avoided if surface water is thoroughly boiled and filtered before drinking, or if reliance is placed on clean water from wells. In both cases the keys to better health are education in hygiene and sanitation,

with quite small improvements in household equipment.

3.6 Onchocerciasis or river blindness

This parasitic disease afflicts about 30 million people, mainly in tropical Africa. It is caused by a filarial worm, *Onchocerca volvulus*, transmitted by a small bloodsucking black fly called *Simulium damnosum*. The worms breed in the human host, producing large numbers of microfilaria only a fraction of a millimetre in length. These cannot develop further unless they are taken up by a *Simulium* fly biting the host. The fly is unable to breed unless it can feed on blood from a warm-blooded creature. Furthermore, the larvae of the *Simulium* need to

59

be in fast-flowing water where they can filter out organic particles. So the *Simulium* lays its eggs on rocks or plants in turbulent water and the flies tend to congregate in the vicinity of natural or artificial falls and rapids; it is near such places that the chances of being bitten and acquiring the filaria are greatest.

The suffering caused by the microfilaria is very great. Those filaria dying just under the skin cause severe itching; however, the main harm is done by worms damaging the eye. This usually happens when a person is heavily infested, and mainly afflicts people 20 years of age or more. Many of them go blind. Onchocerciasis is extremely widespread in the well-watered savannas of west Africa, where rapids are common features of the rivers flowing over crystalline rocks. In some villages near the tributaries of the Volta River, 10 per cent of the population are blind, and 20 per cent of those over 30 years of age. It seems likely that the people had spread out into the river valleys with the peaceful conditions under colonial rule. In recent decades people have been moving away from the rivers on account of the disease and cultivable land is becoming scarce on the watersheds.

Control of the disease might be brought about by treating the sufferers with drugs at an early stage to rid them of the filaria, but this involves regular attendance at a properly staffed medical centre and making sure that patients are not reinfected. Preventing people from settling in fly-infested areas to ensure they do not come into contact with the fly is somewhat easier to arrange, by shifting settlements away from breeding rapids and providing them with alternative sources of water. The World Health Organization, in its largest and most expensive operation, has been attempting since the early 1960s to eliminate the fly from rivers in west Africa by killing the *Simulium* larvae with insecticide (Fig. 3.2). Since 1975 the Onchocerciasis Control Programme has been using helicopters to spray as much as 18 000 km of river per week in the rainy season and about half that length in the dry season. Over much of the region involved, which occupies over three-quarters of a million square kilometres, transmission of the disease appears to have virtually ceased, but two serious problems have been arising. *Simulium* flies can be carried into the treated area by the wind from as much as

150 km away, and so the treated area has had to be successively extended; eventually, if it is to succeed, it will have to include over twice the area currently being treated. Unfortunately the *Simulium* larvae have been acquiring resistance to the pesticides being used and new, more expensive, kinds have had to be introduced. The battle is a costly and lengthy one and the end is not in sight, for the filaria can remain for 10 or 20 years in the individual person, producing new microfilaria which could form the origin of a renewed outbreak.

3.7 Schistosomiasis or bilharzia

Schistosome worms afflict millions of people in Africa who for one reason or another walk or work in streams and lakes. The worm lives in the bladder and intestines of man, feeding on the blood and laying eggs that are passed out into fresh water in the course of excretion. Larvae hatch out of the eggs; if it happens that *Bulinus* or *Biomphalaria* snails are present, the

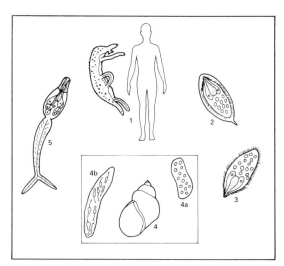

Fig. 3.3. *The life cycle of* Schistosoma haematobium. *Approximate lengths are given in brackets. (1) Paired adult worms (15 mm long) live in man. (2) Egg (0.15 mm long). (3) Miracidium larval stage. (4) Shell of freshwater snail* (Bulinus), *the intermediate host for the organism. (4a,b) Mother sporocyst and daughter sporocyst. (5) Cercaria (0.35 mm). (From D. S. Brown and C. A. Wright, 1985, 'Schistosomiasis: bilharzia', in A. T. Grove, ed.,* The Niger and its Neighbours, *Balkema.)*

larvae penetrate the snails, multiply within them, and large numbers of a different stage of larvae are released which can penetrate the skin of people who enter the water. The larvae develop into schistosome worms, which eventually reach the liver, bladder, and intestines and multiply (Fig. 3.3).

Blood in the urine is the most apparent symptom of schistosomiasis. So common is this condition that many people do not take it seriously, though the infection has a generally debilitating effect on health. It is most prevalent amongst young people, and its prevalence has been increasing with the spread of irrigation and the construction of dams holding back artificial lakes. In many regions more than half the population is affected and, in rural areas, it is only where the weather is too cold because of the altitude or where the ecology of rivers and lakes is otherwise unfavourable for the snail vectors that the disease is absent. Control has not yet been very successful. It is possible, though difficult, to get rid of the snails by using a molluscicide or clearing the plants on which they live. There are drugs capable of ridding people of the disease, but they are likely to become reinfected unless they avoid contact with water containing the larvae. Probably the most effective programmes are those involving a combination of methods including an educational component to persuade people to keep out of water—though it is unlikely that fishermen, irrigation farmers, and small boys will take any notice. Probably an answer will only be found when an effective vaccine is devised, but this may lie several years in the future.

3.8 Rinderpest

This is the old cattle plague, a virus disease that afflicted Europe at intervals until the middle of the nineteenth century, when it was virtually eliminated there by concerted action between governments to ensure the effectiveness of quarantine regulations controlling movements of livestock across frontiers and the slaughter of infected beasts. Such action cannot be expected in Africa at present.

In Africa south of the Sahara, rinderpest does not seem to have been known until a century ago (*nagana*, the disease transmitted by tsetse, is indigenous). It may have been brought into Somaliland from India at the time of the Italian invasion of Ethiopia. The same year it reached Masailand and Uganda; never had cattle been known to die in such numbers. In 1892 it entered the country north of Lake Malawi and by 1896 was reported from both sides of the Zambezi and shortly afterwards from the Transvaal, Orange Free State, and Angola. Next year it reached the southern tip of the continent. West Africa did not escape; thousands of pastoralists lost their entire herds in the 1890s and were forced to take up sedentary agriculture for at least a few years. Eventually the epidemic subsided in much the same way as an influenza epidemic.

The indirect effects were long-lasting. Many pastoral groups lost their dominating positions amongst the surrounding sedentary farming people. Some of the effects were less evident. When rinderpest wiped out the antelope in the Rhodesias it was noticed that the tsetse had disappeared from wide areas, the tsetse-flies having been deprived of their main source of food. Stock-rearing became possible in areas that had been closed to domestic animals. This was the first indication to the early white settlers that eliminating game might be a practicable method of controlling trypanosomiasis.

Since the end of the last century rinderpest has broken out in various parts of the continent from time to time and control of the disease has been one of the main preoccupations of veterinary departments. Inoculation is very effective and co-ordinated campaigns in regional groups of countries have been successful. However, breakdowns in government authority have increased the risks of epidemics. Much depends on effective international co-operation in controlling this and other diseases; such co-operation was easier in the colonial era when it was necessary for only a few metropolitan governments to work together. Now about 50 independent states must co-operate for such purposes and the pan-African institutions involved have not always operated at maximum efficiency.

4

ETHNICITY

One of the characteristic features of Africa, which has an important bearing on economic and political affairs, is the variety of races, languages, and religions, not only on the continent as a whole but also in individual countries. This diversity is a rich cultural heritage. At the same time it presents severe problems to governments attempting to establish their legitimacy and to procure national unity within state boundaries deriving from colonial creations. It is also a source of conflict, both actual and potential.

4.1 Race

Individual racial groups have recognizable characteristics and can be typified but, like geographical regions, they are very difficult if not impossible to define precisely. In many cases, terms used to denote racial groups, such as 'Bantu' or 'Nilotic', are in fact the names of groups of languages. Racial and linguistic boundaries, where they can be defined, seldom correspond exactly, and a different nomenclature should ideally be used for each.

In Africa, Negroes constitute the largest racial group; they occupy most of the continent south of the Sahara. A few thousand years ago they may have been the dominant race in the Ethiopian and Saharan regions as well, both of which have since been invaded by paler-skinned people from the north and east. Bushmen and Pygmies, who preceded the Negroes in much of Africa, are often regarded as the aboriginal inhabitants. The Negroes have interbred with them, with pale-skinned Caucasoid or Armenoid peoples moving down from the north, and with people of Indonesian origin

who came across the Indian Ocean into Madagascar over a thousand years ago (Fig. 4.1).

Bushmen or, as they are often called now, San people, numbering only a few thousand, survive in the remoter arid lands of southern Africa. They have thin lips and hair tightly spiralled to form tufts. Their language, Khoisan, is characterized by a large number of clicking sounds. It was probably the early ancestors of the San who were responsible for the rock paintings widely scattered over the southern and central parts of the continent.

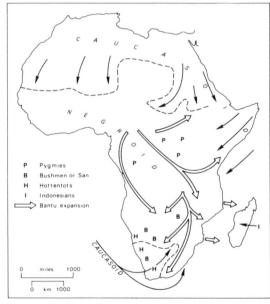

P	Pygmies
B	Bushmen or San
H	Hottentots
I	Indonesians
⟹	Bantu expansion

Fig. 4.1. *The main races in Africa. Arrows indicate in a very general way the main movements of people of different racial groups over the last two thousand years.*

Now the San are confined to the Kalahari and its borders, where they took refuge from invading Negroes and Europeans. Those who continue in their old ways of life live in small bands, hunting all manner of animals and collecting food from wild plants.

Some of the San interbred with cattle-owning people from the north, the Hottentots or Khoi-Khoi who roamed most of south-west Africa south of the Cunene river. Most of the Khoi-Khoi were eventually absorbed into people of mixed origin, the Cape Coloureds of Cape Province.

Pygmies, the other aboriginal group, are confined mainly to the equatorial forests of the Zaire basin. Hunters, trappers, and collectors, they are dark-skinned, shy people with an average height of only about 142 cm (4 ft 8 in). They seem to live on good terms with their Negro lords, receiving grain and bananas from them in exchange for meat.

The Negroes can be roughly divided into two great groups of approximately equal size, a south-eastern group mainly speaking Bantu languages and a north-western group speaking a variety of languages which have been classed as Nigritic, Sudanic, and West African. In addition there are a relatively small number of people in the Chad basin who speak certain central African languages.

It is generally believed that the Bantu-speakers originated from two streams of people who moved outwards from the Chad/Cameroon region a few thousand years ago, possibly about the time of increasing desiccation around 3000 BC. One set of migrants moving east along the Sudan zone learned how to grow cereals, to raise cattle, and to make iron. By 1000 BC they had reached the Rift Valley and over the next millennium moved south into the Zambezi region. The second stream of migrants took the Bantu language south from the Cameroons into the Zaire basin, moving along the coast and rivers; they were root-crop cultivators who continued to rely on stone tools. The two Bantu streams rejoined in south-central Africa about 1500 years ago.

Pale-skinned people, Caucasoids or Armenoids, have entered Africa from time to time over thousands of years. Amongst the earliest arrivals were the Berber-speaking peoples of north Africa who intermingled with Negroes living in the Sahara and on its southern fringes. About 10 million people, mainly living in Morocco, still speak Berber languages.

Scarcely distinguishable from the Berbers physically are Arabs who invaded Egypt and the rest of north Africa in the seventh century AD, bringing with them the Muslim religion. Over the last five hundred years they have infiltrated the Sahel and Sudan zones and have also settled on the seaboard of east Africa. Originally traders or nomadic pastoralists, many of them have settled down to become sedentary cultivators; they continue to speak Arabic and remain Muslims. Numbering about 150 millions, they constitute about a quarter of the total population of Africa; one cannot be precise because of miscegenation. Interbreeding of the different peoples has given rise to all gradations from typical Negro to typical Caucasoid, and, especially in the Nile valley, people with mixed physical characteristics have acquired the language and culture of later Arab invaders.

The latest Caucasoid arrivals in Africa, the Europeans, number little more than 6 millions, of whom the majority live in the Republic of South Africa. More than half of them, mostly speaking Afrikaans, are descended from Dutch and German settlers at the Cape in the seventeenth and eighteenth centuries, and the remainder are largely descended from British immigrants who have arrived over the last 180 years. The next largest coherent European group is made up of about 100 000 Whites in Zimbabwe, with similar numbers in Algeria and Morocco and lesser concentrations in Kenya, Egypt, Tunisia, Zaire, Nigeria, Ivory Coast, and Senegal. Their numbers have been changing rapidly as a result of political shifts. In the Maghreb there were nearly 2 million Europeans in the mid-1950s, about 8 per cent of the total population. Four-fifths of them lived in the towns but they occupied two-fifths of the cultivated land in Algeria and a fifth of that in Tunisia. Between 1956 and 1962, during the Algerian war of independence, over half the white colonists in north Africa left for France, abandoning nearly all the land they had farmed. There was a similar sudden exodus of Belgians from the Belgian Congo when it was suddenly granted independence in the early 1960s, and most of the half million Portuguese in Angola and Mozambique returned to their home-country or moved to Brazil when those countries became independent in the 1970s.

Asian people, mainly from India, arrived in large numbers on the east coast in the latter half of the nineteenth century to provide labour for railway construction and plantations. Many of them returned home and most of the Asians now living in east Africa are the descendants of people who came over to start businesses. They do not form a homogeneous group; there are both Hindus and Muslims and amongst both there are differences of religious belief. Of the total of about a million Asians, the majority live in the Province of Natal in South Africa, especially in Durban. In Natal and in the east African countries, Kenya, Uganda, Tanzania and Mozambique, Asians outnumber Europeans.

The Europeans and Asians are divided amongst themselves and are still separated from the majority of the Africans by language and culture as well as by colour. In the towns, where most of the Europeans and Asians are concentrated, the different races have until recently lived in their own separate quarters, each group retaining its own peculiar ways of life and scarcely ever intermarrying. Naturally there are and were exceptions. In Angola and Mozambique, Portuguese and Africans have interbred for centuries, and in the Republic of South Africa over 2 million Cape Coloureds, living mainly in and near Cape Town, are the outcome of White, Negro, Khoi Khoi and Indonesian interbreeding over the last three hundred years. The Republic of South Africa had laws against miscegenation (interbreeding of the races, especially Whites and non-Whites) for several decades, but they were repealed in 1986.

4.1.1 Racial tension

Racial tension arises where one section of a community assumes that it is superior to the others and seeks privileges not accorded to the rest. As Philip Mason wrote in *An Essay on Racial Tension*: 'When the sections involved correspond with racial groups, then the tension is displayed to the world and becomes identified in the minds of the contestants with racial differences.'

There are no sound scientific grounds for believing that differences between races allow them to be placed in an order of precedence, some being superior and others inferior. Clearly there are physical differences, and tests could perhaps be devised to discover the relative physical efficiency of different racial groups so long as the confusing effect of variations in diet and care of children could be eliminated. But to compare the mental capacities of racial groups is a much more difficult task; tests are likely to indicate a person's cultural environment rather than his inherent intelligence, whatever may be implied by this term. That the San and Pygmy are incapable of reaching as high a level of performance as other African peoples would be extremely difficult to prove or disprove for, although their ability in most intellectual spheres would seem to the outsider to be limited, their skills in certain specialized fields is undoubted. Again, there is no conclusive evidence as to the relative ability of brown, black, and white people. Black people can certainly compete very successfully with white people in sport, sculpture, music, and scholarship. The fact that black Africans are in general less advanced technically and economically than white ones does not imply that they are incapable of reaching the same level. They have had a different history, they have their own cultures and traditions, and they are making their own contributions to the sum total of human knowledge and awareness.

Racial tension is the expression of antagonism based not so much on the inherent antipathy of one race towards another as on one group's fear of another, stimulated by economic or cultural differences. In Africa, the early white settlers were separated from the black Africans by a wide cultural gulf which can be attributed to the fact that until the sixteenth century most of Africa had been isolated from the rest of the world. It had not shared in the accumulation of knowledge and wealth that began in the riverine areas of Egypt, Iraq, and India and which, from a European viewpoint, is seen as having culminated in the spread of Roman civilization from the Mediterranean basin to north-west Europe. The art of writing and all that it involves in historical continuity was largely unknown in Africa south of the Sahara. It escaped the culturally unifying influences of medieval Christendom and Islam. There could be no African Renaissance. To the eighteenth-century European, the African was a savage; the white man was master, the black man a slave. It is not very surprising that differences in race should have been automatically associated with all manner of economic and political privileges and restrictions, class reinforcing colour in the differentiation of indigenous and European. This class/colour stratification has persisted anachronistically into the latter part of the twentieth century and continues to dominate human affairs in the southernmost part of the continent.

4.2 Culture

4.2.1 Language

It has been estimated that more than 800 languages are spoken in Africa, some spoken by only a few hundred people, some by several millions. Attempts have been made to trace their genealogy (their origins and inter-

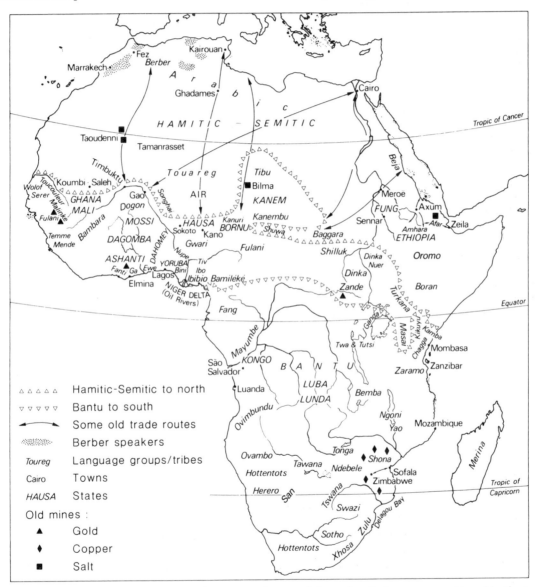

Fig. 4.2. *States, tribes, and languages. The names of some of the main ethnic groups mentioned in the text are shown. Between the Bantu-speaking peoples of southern Africa and people speaking Semitic and Hamitic languages a latitudinal belt stretching across the continent is the home of groups speaking a great diversity of tongues. The states named existed in pre-colonial times; only a few of the old trade routes are shown.*

relationships), but with only limited success so far. The Bantu languages which are spoken by most of the peoples of the south and east appear to be derived from one ancestral language, and from studies of the present distribution of languages, their nature, and structures it has been concluded, as mentioned earlier, that ancestral Bantu was spoken in the Chad/Cameroon region (Fig. 4.2).

In a country like Nigeria, where thirty languages are in common use, the multiplicity of tongues causes difficulties in education and commerce and hinders the spread of ideas. It is also a great obstacle in the way of creating a national feeling amongst all the people of this large and varied country. In many countries no one African language is dominant and so the language of the former imperial power has been adopted to transact official business. In such countries English, as in Ghana, or French, as in Senegal, is now being spoken at home, especially in families where mother and father are educated and happen to come from different tribes (Fig. 4.3).

In the Sudan Republic, Arabic was adopted as the official language, thereby depriving the

people in the south of the country of the opportunity to involve themselves fully in national affairs. Hausa is widely used in northern Nigeria and locally in other parts of west Africa and even in the Sudan Republic, where there are a large number of west African immigrants. In the Belgian Congo, both French and Flemish were official languages as they were in Belgium; Flemish has now been dropped in Zaire. Both French and English are official languages in the Cameroon Republic. Swahili was adopted as the language of government in Tanzania, but it has been found to be a handicap in higher education and it would not be surprising if English were to be adopted either instead of or alongside Swahili. English and French are likely to emerge as the main common languages in Africa. Already some of the minor languages are spoken by only a few old people; such a loss entails the disappearance of an irreplaceable element of the world's culture; it is as serious and significant as the wiping out of a biological species.

4.2.2 Society

Typically African societies are based on kinship, the network of relationships woven by descent and marriage. Descent is reckoned in various ways: patrilineally, that is from father to son, over most parts of the continent, matrilineally especially amongst the southern Bantu in the zone between Angola and Mozambique.

The unit of social organization is the family, not just a man, his wife, and their children, but the extended family embracing three or four generations and including cousins. The lineage, the group tracing its descent back through three or four more generations, retains its cohesion. People belonging to the same clan with a common ancestor, say, ten generations back, recognize certain ties and, especially if they occupy the same territory, will act in concert in certain circumstances. The individual and his family traditionally have a right to the use of land, a usufructuary right, as members of such a territorially based society.

In most African societies, lineages and clans are exogamous; that is, sexual relations between members of the same lineage are regarded as incestuous and marriages take place only with people outside the lineage. This

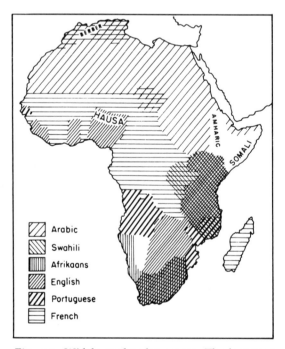

Fig. 4.3. *Widely spoken languages. The language map is extremely complicated, but some languages, most of them introduced, are now widely spoken.*

In the Tongo area of northern Ghana in the early 1960s people were still living much as their ancestors had done, in traditional round mud huts with conical roofs in the shade of baobab trees.

leads to the development in time of a web of interconnecting strands between families through a wide area.

The transference of bridewealth from the husband's family to that of the bride signals the completion of a marriage. The bridewealth is not simply a payment for property; it is a measure of esteem and amongst other advantages it has the effect of stabilizing marriage, since it may be reclaimable if the couple separate. Polygamy, according to which a man may have more than one wife at a time, is traditional in most African societies. It does not mean there are more women than men; women marry early and often marry again later, while men marry late and may then have more than one wife at a time.

Cutting 'horizontally' across the 'vertical' lineage and clan structures are age-grade organizations, craft guilds, and other associations. Several hamlets and villages or lineages and clans may recognize certain individuals as having a particular religious status or function, perhaps as oracles or rain-makers. The people inter-linked in these ways—with similar traditions, sharing a common ancestry, speaking the same language, and perhaps occupying a particular tract of country—constitute a tribe.

The word 'tribe', like the word 'native' is considered objectionable in some quarters these days, but it seems a better word than 'nation', which has been suggested as an alternative. A tribe does not necessarily occupy and claim a well-defined piece of country; it may have been scattered by war or divided in two by a nineteenth-century frontier; on the other hand it may grade almost imperceptibly into another neighbouring tribe. Some tribes have chiefs and paramount chiefs, others are acephalous, having no important rulers. Language is the best guide to tribal identity, but languages have dialects and some people speak more than one language fluently.

In spite of the difficulty in defining what is meant by the word 'tribe', tribalism remains of great importance in Africa at the present day. Membership of the tribe and tribal education impose upon boys and girls the standards of behaviour which will be expected from them in adult life. The kinship structure within the tribal context provides links between rich and poor, and between townsman and country-dweller. Associated restraints and responsibilities continue to be felt even in countries where a majority of the children attend school and a large proportion of the population is now urban. This kinship and lineage system is the aspect of African society that most clearly distinguishes it from Western society, in which kinship ties rarely stretch far outside the small-unit family. Increasing mobility and commercialization of life are straining traditional African social linkages and this entails increased stress for the individuals involved.

4.2.3 Religion

Details of religious observance vary from one tribe to another. In most of them some form of ancestor worship is practised and the existence of a supreme being is recognized, together with that of a number of other spirits believed to have some control over natural phenomena. Various practitioners act as intermediaries between the spirits and the individual or group, and in some cases these priests came to be regarded as chiefs or kings. Religion forms an integral part of the life of the individual person and the community, but traditional religion is particular to the clan or large social group.

Christianity and Islam brought into Africa ideas about God that were in some ways new. They are monotheistic religions; that is, they teach the existence of one God, and both stem from the Jewish religion. Christianity had been widely adopted in Egypt and north-west Africa at the time when the Roman Empire in the west was collapsing. The influence of the Christian Church in Africa crumbled when the Arabs brought Islam to north Africa in the seventh century AD. Christianity survived only amongst the Copts in Egypt, the Nubians living alongside the Nile to the south of Egypt, and in the Axumite kingdom of northern Ethiopia. All of them looked towards the Patriarch in Alexandria as spiritual leader.

Arab traders and missionaries brought the teachings of Muhammad as they are enshrined in the Koran to the trading centres of the Saharan region and to the coastal settlements along the shores of the Red Sea and Indian Ocean. Islam was at least partly responsible for the emergence of large political states in late medieval times in the western parts of the Sahel and Sudan zones.

From the sixteenth century, Christian missionaries were active, first the Catholics in west and east Africa and later Catholic and Protestant missionaries from various European countries. Until the colonial period, these new universal religions made little impression on Africa south of the Sahara. Christianity was confined to certain coastal stations and the impress of Islam was restricted outside north Africa and the lower Nile valley to the larger towns at the southern end of the trade routes across the desert. The mass of the people, country-dwellers, remained pagans, mainly animists.

The most important factor promoting the dissemination of the new religions, both Islam and Christianity, has been the improvement of communications since the end of the nineteenth century, which allowed ideas as well as people and goods to travel more easily. Tribes and tribalism were never static, but the rate of change has greatly accelerated over the last hundred years. People have been moving from the country into the towns and traders have been travelling through the country districts. Under the stresses of a new money economy the old cults have been breaking down. The individual person is no longer confined to his tribal homeland. He goes to school, he reads newspapers and listens to the radio, he works in the mines and in offices and shops. His boss is no longer a tribal elder but someone, possibly from another tribe, who has authority because of his education, experience, or wealth. Some old beliefs and ceremonies may be retained but, in the new settings of time and space, Islam and Christianity have provided supernatural ideas codified in holy books that have become widely accepted.

Now, a large proportion of the population north of latitude 10°N is Muslim and increasing numbers of Muslim converts are being made towards the west African coast, particularly in south-west Nigeria, and also down the east coast into Tanzania and Mozambique. It is not possible to give the numbers or proportions of people who now belong to either Islam or Christianity, because there are many intermediate stages between being a pagan and being a monotheist (a believer in one God); and the new religions in Africa are being influenced as much by African beliefs as they have influenced Africans.

5

TRADITIONAL WAYS OF LIFE

Until the penetration of Africa by European commerce and capitalism in the nineteenth century, most Africans were involved directly in winning a livelihood from the resources around their homes. However, their societies were not static, either economically or technically. Nor was everyone producing simply for his own or his family's use and consumption. Amongst many tribes, slavery was a feature of the social structure. So, even at that time, some people were working to the advantage of others who could command their services and were in positions of authority because of their religious, hereditary, or commercial status. Many people were producing a surplus for sale to purchase foodstuffs, salt, metalware, or ornaments, and certain towns had long existed that were dependent on long-distance trading.

5.1 Hunting and collecting

Today, especially in more remote areas of the continent, groups of people can be found still living in the Stone Age. The San and the Pygmies, numbering only a few tens of thousands, have already been mentioned. They present to African governments the kinds of problems that are facing countries in other parts of the world, like Australia with its Aborigines. The question is whether such 'backward' people are to be encouraged to persist in their traditional ways of life or not. Unless special attention is paid to them they may perish miserably like the Ik, the mountain people who live amongst the rocky hills where the Sudan, Kenya, and Uganda adjoin. Deprived of their hunting areas, and faced with starvation, they have ceased to function as an organic community and each person is concerned only with his

own survival. If such people are to retain their own cultures and flourish, then extensive tracts of land have to be set aside for them, almost as if they were animals needing nature reserves. If they are allocated such land, can they then be permitted to keep it if valuable minerals are discovered? Should they receive medical care and, if so, should they be provided with other social services, even though they make little or no contribution to the state? If they are deliberately to be 'brought into the modern world', how can they best be educated and enabled to compete effectively with people who are better prepared to cope with life at the end of the twentieth century? These are questions to which there are no easy answers.

5.2 Pastoralism

Some of the same problems arise in the case of nomadic pastoralists, especially those in the more remote areas who have been accustomed to move freely through the semi-arid lands at the desert margins. Before the beginning of this century there was plenty of room for them to nomadize in search of grazing and water for their animals. Now their grazing lands are crossed by international frontiers and encroached upon by cultivators, while the numbers of pastoralists and their animals have multiplied.

The majority of pastoralists are not nomadic but are involved in transhumance, moving regularly between dry-season and wet-season grazing grounds. Increasing numbers are settled in one spot in the dry season, near a source of water, either a well or riverine swamp. Others have a base where crops are cultivated by the women and older people while the herds are away in the rains, when

Pastoralists encamped on the outskirts of Timbuktu.

there is surface water and abundant, nutritious grazing at the desert margins. All these gradations may exist in a single pastoralist tribe, and families are commonly split into two sections, one wide-ranging and the other more restricted in its movements or even settled down to farming. Where this is the case, adjustment to adversity and to modernization can more readily occur.

In the Saharan region, pastoralists were the dominant social groups. Being mobile, with their camels and meagre equipment, they were able to engage in the caravan trade or to extract protection money from traders, and they were powerful enough to enslave people to cultivate food crops for them in the oases. In the wetter regions of the Sudan zone to the south, on the other hand, political power was in the hands of town-based chiefs to whom the pastoralists paid tribute. With the coming of colonial rule and the decline in trans-Saharan trade, the

A Boran encampment in south-west Ethiopia.

Fulani cattle being grazed on the sub-humid coastal grasslands of south-east Ghana.

dominance of the pastoralists at the desert margins was undermined. Everywhere taxation became more rigorous but, at the same time, the cattle owners began to benefit from veterinary services and from wells and boreholes and their flocks and herds increased. With the end of colonial rule they found themselves unrepresented in government and at a disadvantage in dealing with the sedentary people. In southern Algeria, for instance, government forced Touareg children to attend boarding schools and as a result their whole culture began to disintegrate.

To buy such goods as they need, especially cloth and grain, pastoralists sell milk and clarified butterfat and silvan (woodland) produce in local markets. They rarely eat meat, just occasionally goat or mutton, scarcely ever beef. Amongst some groups blood is taken from a vein in the necks of live cattle, especially by herdsmen, and mixed with the milk as a convenience food. Milk is the essential item of diet and lactation depends on the cows having calves. The family herds have often been compared to a bank balance, the interest being milk and calves, and the deposit account being drawn upon when unusual demands are made on the family finances. Such demands are greatest when marriage by one of the male

members is in view. The young men who perform the hard and tedious work of tending the animals are anxious to see their flocks and herds grow in size so that they may have wives and rear children who will enable them to lead the more leisured existence of their fathers. To cover major expenses and pay taxes, cattle are sold to itinerant traders for consumption in nearby or distant towns. Mainly male animals are sold, the females being kept to maintain the milk supply and to keep up herd numbers.

The area of land available to livestock has increased as game animals have been eliminated and as tsetse flies have been confined to less extensive areas where woodland has not been cleared (Fig. 5.1). Boreholes have been put down to provide water in areas where its absence had prevented grazing. Inoculation and vaccination have reduced stock losses from disease, especially rinderpest. Livestock numbers have increased alongside pastoralist populations, probably increasing fivefold since the beginning of the century; the figures available are far from reliable, usually being based on taxation or inoculation counts, and varying from time to time on account of droughts and epidemics.

A stage has now been reached where it is clear that nearly everywhere in Africa rangelands are supporting more stock than they can sustain indefinitely. In the 1950s and early 1960s in west Africa, with rainfall more abundant than it had been for some decades, cattle rapidly increased in number and the pastoralists extended their ranges further into the desert. When, eventually, drought years returned in the 1970s and 1980s, pastoralists suffered more from famine than other people. Grazing was eaten out. Many families lost their herds and had to seek refuge in famine relief camps where food aid was distributed to them; the people of the semi-arid lowlands of Ethiopia and Somalia as well as the zone south of the Sahara were particularly affected. The disaster attracted the attention of the whole world to the problems of life in such marginal environments.

Government and international agencies are anxious to reduce the density of stocking and at the same time to increase the supply of meat for the towns. If herd owners could be persuaded to dispose of a greater proportion of their stock each year, both problems might be solved. But an individual livestock owner is anxious to maintain his herd numbers so as to ensure there is enough milk to feed his family and to improve the chances that some of his stock will survive in case of losses from disease or drought. Improvements in transport and growing urban populations have increased the demand for livestock products, but nomadic and semi-nomadic pastoralists on semi-arid rangelands cannot be expected to meet it.

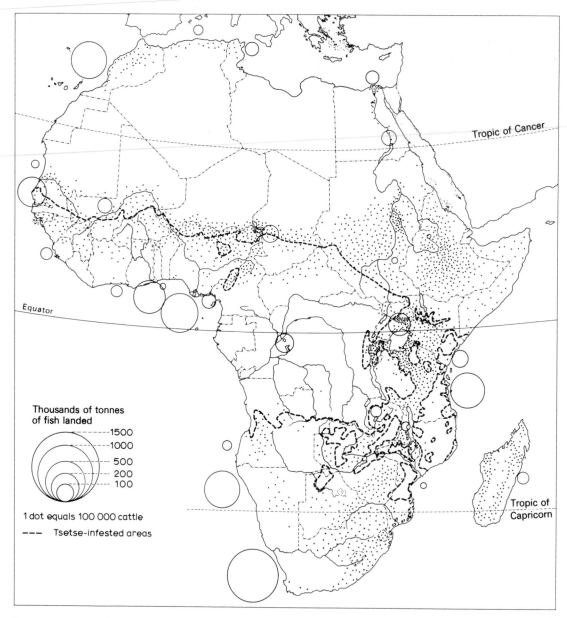

Fig. 5.1. *Cattle and fisheries about 1987. In addition to the fish landed at African seaports, large tonnages are caught by fishing boats from Japan and Europe. In spite of droughts, numbers of cattle increased markedly between 1974 and 1987, according to UN statistics, especially in Sudan, Mali, Tanzania, Kenya, and Madagascar.*

Oxen ploughing in Ethiopia.

Ploughs are usually primitive.

5.3 Cultivation

Although the plough was used by the Egyptians in the days of the Pharaohs and was certainly in use elsewhere north of the desert 3000 years ago, it appeared south of the Sahara only in Ethiopia until the colonial period. Cultivation over much, possibly most, of the continent is still done with the hoe, not a small-bladed implement of the kind used by gardeners in Europe but a much larger tool, usually with a short handle. Except in some Muslim countries, where many of the women are confined to the house, the hoe is wielded as often by the womenfolk as by the men, for preparing the ground for planting and sometimes to help with weeding. The division of labour between the sexes varies a good deal according to tribe and time of year.

The crops first grown in Africa were mainly wheat and barley north of the Sahara and in Ethiopia, date palms in desert oases, sorghum and millet in the savanna lands, yams and oil-palms in the high forests, with locally domesticated rice in west Africa between the Inland Niger Delta and Sierra Leone (Fig. 5.2). The range of crops widened from time to time, as it did in Europe. Coco-yams, sugar-cane, and probably plantains and bananas, mangoes, citrus, and breadfruit were introduced from south-east Asia, perhaps via Madagascar, between one and two thousand years ago. The Portuguese brought a whole range of South American crops to Africa from newly discovered Brazil in the years around AD 1500, and these spread quite rapidly into the interior

from several points around the coast. Prominent amongst the new arrivals were maize, now the staple foodstuff for most of the Bantu peoples, and cassava (manioc), now the chief foodcrop in the wetter, western parts of the continent. In addition there were groundnuts (perhaps better known as monkey nuts or peanuts), beans, sweet potatoes, and papaya (or pawpaw). They allowed cropping to be diversified, they improved nutritional standards, modified farming methods, and may

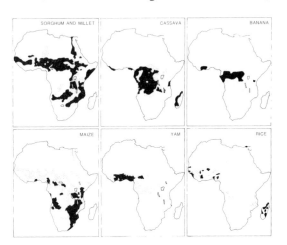

Fig. 5.2. *Distribution of some important crops. Staples or co-staples are shown by black shading; crops of economic importance are shown by dotted shading. Cassava is now grown widely in semi-arid lands as a famine reserve crop. In recent decades, rice, of which there are many new varieties, has become a staple food in West Africa for 65 million people.*

well have caused populations to increase, first in the coastlands to which the new crops were initially introduced and then further inland.

The assemblage of crops that can be grown varies from one climatic zone to another. Within each climatic zone the implements used, the field and farm patterns, and the customs of holding land vary from one tribe or ethnic unit to another and according to the stage they have reached in the process of modernization. Within a single tribal area, the intensity of farming varies with the pressure on the land, which is a function of the population density, the inherent productivity of the land, and the inputs it receives in the form of water and fertilizers.

In detail, land use varies with soil conditions, slope angle and 'nearness to the sound of the human voice'. Very often, land close to dwelling-places is well manured and cropped every year. Land at a greater distance, to which it takes a long time to walk or cycle, may be cleared and cultivated for only a year or two and then rested to recover its fertility. Beyond lies the forest or woodland, more or less degraded but usually a significant source of wild produce. The same family commonly employs intensive methods in one area and extensive methods in another, varying them according to local drainage and soil conditions. Some of the produce they consume themselves, the rest they sell in local markets or, these days, at produce buying stations.

Four main agrarian regions can be distinguished on an ecological basis; those of the rain forest, the savanna, the desertlands, and the winter rainfall zone.

5.3.1 Forest cultivators

Relatively few African farmers have the chance to clear high forest for cultivation, for much of the remaining high forest persists only in very sparsely settled country.

While the Mbuti Pygmy hunters and gatherers in the Ituri forest of north-eastern Zaire form an integral part of the ecological picture, as Colin Turnbull describes them, adapting to the forest and living in sympathy with it, neighbouring Bira cultivators regard it as a hostile world, cutting it down to plant their crops and moving every few years as the soils become exhausted. Such methods of land use can support only a sparse population because so much land is needed if there is to be time for the forest to grow up and restore fertility.

The Zande who live on the north-eastern borders of the forest, in a remote part of the continent where the Sudan Republic adjoins Zaire and the Central African Republic, are shifting cultivators. They are made up of some 50 small tribes, assimilated by a conquering group nearly 200 years ago and now speaking, in the main, a single language. Primarily hunters and collectors when they were first described by European explorers more than a century ago, they now cultivate a wide range of crops and have acquired new ones from their neighbours in quite recent years.

A section of the Zande has been described by de Schlippe in *Shifting Cultivation in Africa* (1956). He emphasizes that an orderly arrangement can be discerned in what at first seems to be a chaotic distribution of farm plots and bush around the settlements. Homesteads are usually built on the valley slopes, particularly on the fertile soils at the edge of gallery forest, that is, the forest bordering streams. The grassy upland plains, underlain by lateritic ironstone at a shallow depth, are mainly left unused except for hunting and occasional cultivation, and are burned every year. Around the living-huts, crops are planted here and there: tobacco in the shelter of the eaves, bananas on old refuse heaps, pumpkins and sweet potatoes on rich soil swept from the courtyards and including ash and other household waste. The main farms are established in forest clearings where eleusine millet and groundnuts are planted in the first year, followed by maize and gourds in the second, with cassava interplanted for harvesting in the third year, when the plot is allowed to revert to woodland. The gardenland near the houses is planted up with oil-palms, mangoes, and bananas. As the years go by they cover an increasing area, expanding down the slope toward plots of dry-season maize alongside a stream-bed. But every year the main food farms have to be established further away from the homesteads and eventually, after a decade or two, the decision is made to move to another site. Usually there are other reasons for moving; poor harvests, misfortunes, quarrels may influence the decision as much as soil exhaustion and the distance to be travelled to the cereal farms.

The Ibo, who live between 80 and 240 km (50 and 150 mls) from the coast of south-east Nigeria, contrast strongly with the Zande (Fig. 5.3). They are more densely settled than almost

any other people in Africa outside the Nile valley in Egypt. Although archaeological finds in the centre of Iboland, at Igbo, suggest that many centuries ago they were integrated into a

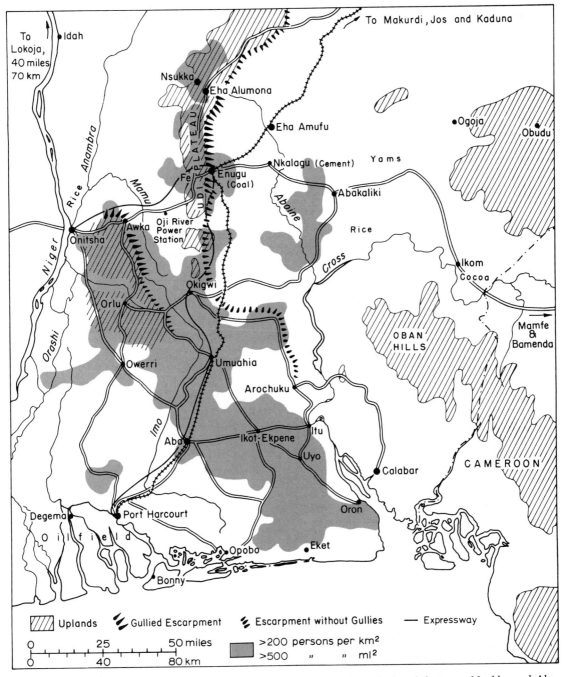

Fig. 5.3. *The heavily settled area of south-east Nigeria, with Ibos in the north between Nsukka and Aba, Ibibio around Ikot-Ekpene, and other peoples in the south.*

west African trading network, they have no important chiefs at the present day. Many of them are Christians and have attended schools started by Christian missions. Traditionally they are village-dwellers, living in rectangular huts thatched with straw or palm-fronds and surrounded by fences or mud walls. In general such compounds are spaced a few tens of metres apart and are surrounded by gardens where root crops and vegetables are grown in the shade of oil-palms and other useful trees. In the old days these wooded villages were surrounded by an earthern wall and a belt of forest. Several of them have populations of 10 000 or more but they are still villages, not towns. In the south the wooded compound land stretches from one village to the next almost without a break, just with less heavily settled oil-palm woodland in between. In the drier north, on the Udi Plateau, the villages are large islands of trees surrounded by open grassland providing rough grazing for a few dwarf cattle and thatching grass for the houses. Most of the food is grown in the oil-palm gardenland which is fertilized by leaf-fall and household wastes, including the dung of goats and sheep kept in the compounds. Wine is obtained from raffia palms growing by the streams. Cassava is grown in the grasslands around the forest villages. Fertility of the grassland plots is maintained by planting them up with shrubs, notably *Acioa barteri*, the leaves of which help to build up soil nutrient levels.

The many people in these northern Ibo villages could scarcely survive today on the product of their own land. The steep slopes are deeply incised by gullies, and yields of all the crops are quite low. Most of the young people have been emigrating to towns all over Nigeria, sending money back to their relations, sometimes sending their children back to be educated and building houses in their home villages with a view to retiring there in later life. Even for some of their foodstuffs the villagers depend on less congested districts and imports from overseas.

5.3.2. Savanna cultivators

In the savanna lands a similar kind of spatial variability and internally generated change can be found to that in the forest zone. Some savanna peoples live in much the same way as

they did half a century ago, when they were described by agriculturalists like Trapnell, Clothier, and Allan in Northern Rhodesia.

On the northern plateau in what is now Zambia, cultivation of the *citimine* (ash-planting) type is still practised by the Bemba. It involves felling trees over a much larger area than is to be planted, perhaps 30 to 60 hectares for every hectare to be cultivated. Branches are lopped off the trees, taking care to preserve the leaves, and laid in stacks or flattened piles for burning on the patches to be cropped. Crops are then planted in the ash-covered soil. Such methods allow sorghum, millet, maize, cassava, and numerous lesser crops to be grown for a year or two before soil exhaustion and weeds force the cultivators to move on. Shifting cultivation of this kind can support a population of up to 6 persons per km^2 (15 per square mile). With greater densities the equilibrium is liable to be upset, for the fallow period has to be reduced, fertility declines, larger areas have to be cultivated each year, and so the resting period is still more abbreviated.

Now the old way of life is fading, mainly because the young men have been attracted away to work in the Copperbelt or in the mines in the Republic of South Africa. No one is left to do the hard work of cutting down the trees. The Bemba have been leaving their small clusters of huts and concentrating in townships along the Great North Road linking southern and east Africa. Cassava, sweet potatoes, and other crops not needing too much labour are now grown by the women on more permanent plots nearby. Millet, no longer the staple, is mainly used for making beer. There is more irrigated farming than formerly, and crops are grown and processed for sale to hungry travellers on the road.

The Hausaland region of northern Nigeria in the Sudan zone of West Africa has a long history of sustained, permanent cultivation (Fig. 5.4). The country around the ancient cities of Kano, Katsina, and Zaria is heavily settled, with population densities commonly exceeding 80 persons per km^2 (200 per square mile). Wild game has been almost eliminated and woodland where tsetse can breed is confined to limited areas, so trypanosomiasis is not a serious menace. Fertility is maintained by applying animal manure to the fields. Goats, sheep, and cattle go out daily to graze on the uncultivated land at the village outskirts and on patches of poor land nearer the centre. At night they are kraaled near the houses or within compounds, and their dung, together with other wastes, is carried out to the fields by donkeys. The plant nutrients from a large area left uncultivated are thereby concentrated on the cultivated fields. After the grain harvest, herds of cattle belonging to transhumant pastoralists pass through the heavily settled agricultural districts, on the way from wet-season grazing lands to riverside pastures. The cultivators welcome them and may be ready to build huts, dig wells, or pay a considerable sum of money to persuade them to spend a few days or weeks in the neighbourhood, the stock feeding on crop residues and in recompense leaving dung to enrich the fields. The cultivators and the pastoralists are said to be symbiotically related, in that they depend on each other for their livelihoods.

Farmers rely to some extent on the waste

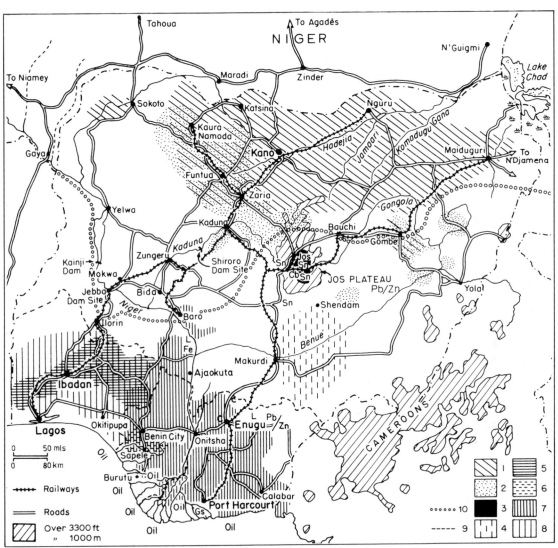

Fig. 5.4 (a). *Nigeria: main crops and minerals. 1—groundnuts, 2—cotton, 3—tin, 4—benniseed, 5—cocoa, 6—rubber, 7—palm-oil, 8—palm kernels, 9—regional frontiers before the civil war of 1966–70, 10—southern limits of predominantly Muslim areas; Muslims are also in a majority around Ibadan. Gs—natural gas, C—coal, Cb—columbite, Fe—iron, L—limestone, Pb/Zn—lead–zinc, Sn—tin.*

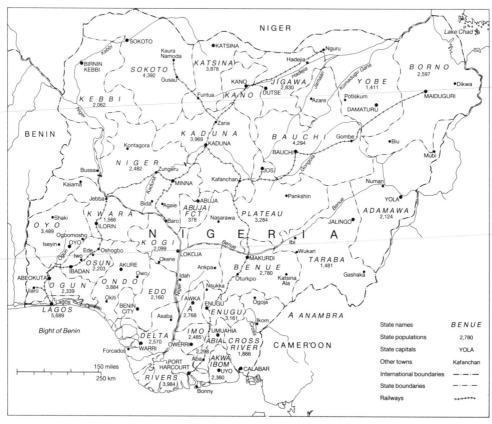

Fig. 5.4 (b). *Nigeria: the States: since 1991 Nigeria has been redivided into 31 States each with a population, according to a 1991 census, of between 1.4 and 6 millions (except for Abuja Federal Capital Territory which had fewer people than the rest).*

products of nearby towns to enrich their fields. They bring into the town donkey-loads of wood lopped from trees left growing on the cropland and return with panniers full of manure to put on their fields. The slaughter-houses, pit latrines, and other sources of waste in big towns like Kano thereby enable the small fields of the surrounding country to remain under cultivation year after year. Rural areas and towns like these depend on each other, but such old-established towns are rare in Africa. Many of the village people in Hausaland are craftworkers; as well as farming, they make mats, pottery, and other articles. Craftsmen near the larger towns used to sell their cloth and leather articles to merchants in the towns, who traded them over long distances, even across the desert. Now such craft products have difficulty in competing with factory-made tex-

Shallots being grown on beds in the linear depressions between sandbars fronting the Volta delta, south-east Ghana.

tiles and imported plastics, and so more and more people from the countryside are finding work in the towns, and the built-up areas are expanding into farmland.

Irrigation has been a traditional feature of certain sub-humid to semi-arid lands. In Hausaland, sugar-cane, wheat, and vegetables have long been cultivated in the dry season, especially on fadamaland, seasonal swampland, in the vicinity of large towns, using *shadufs* to lift water from shallow wells. On the coastal sandbar of the Volta delta, in the coastal dry zone that extends from eastern Ghana to Togo and Benin, two or three crops a year of shallots, small onions, are grown (Fig. 5.5). In linear depressions between the low sand ridges making up the sandbar, raised beds are made with much expenditure of labour, by bringing in sand. Heavy dressings of manure are applied; bat dung, masses of small fish, and cattle dung

A channel leading water from the middle, well-watered southern slopes of Kilimanjaro to the lower slopes where it is needed to irrigate bananas and coffee.

Women puddling the soil preparatory to planting rice on the plains at the foot of Kilimanjaro near Moshi in Tanzania.

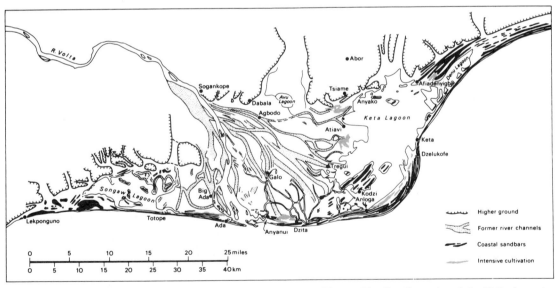

Fig. 5.5. *The Volta delta in the coastal dry zone of south-east Ghana. The distributaries of the Volta have in the past formed a delta which probably extended further south than it does now. Coastal processes have built up coastal sandbars with lagoons behind them, especially on the east side of the delta. The linear depressions between the sandbars are intensively cultivated, making use of fresh water at a depth of a few metres. The lagoons, when they are well supplied by local streams from the north, are used for fishing; the lagoons dry up when rains are poor and salt is collected from the lagoon floors.*

79

are brought by canoe across the lagoon separating the bar from the mainland. The seed is brought from a particular locality in Togo. Water is applied in the drier parts of the year. The shallots are sold mainly in Accra. In east Africa, channels lead water from springs in the Elgeyo escarpment, on the western side of the rift valley in Kenya, to irrigated fields at its foot. On the south side of Kilimanjaro in northern Tanzania, the Chagga people lead water from the well-watered middle slopes to the drier and warmer lower slopes to allow the production of bananas and coffee. Other systems of channel irrigation exist on the northernmost highlands of Malawi.

5.3.3 Oasis cultivators

In areas with a mean annual rainfall of less than 250 mm (10 in) within the tropics, and less than 150 mm (6 in) in north Africa, crops are largely dependent on flooding or artificial watering, and so cultivation in these semi-arid lands and deserts is confined to relatively small areas with favourable soils and water supplies.

The volumes of water required for irrigating crops is very large when compared with those needed by livestock or human beings. While a cow or a man can manage with about 20 litres (4 gallons) of water per day, a hectare of millet (enough to support several people for a year) demands about 2500 litres (220 gallons per acre) every hour of the day for about three months. Such large volumes of water, which must be free from damaging salts, can be obtained cheaply only in restricted areas. The Nile valley is quite exceptional, with its sources near the equator and on the Ethiopian highlands providing the northern Sudan and Egypt with 80 km³ (20 cubic miles) of water every year, enough to flood about 40 000 km² to a depth of 2 m and support about 40 million people. Large volumes of water are also brought into arid lands with less than about 250 mm (10 in) of rain per year by the Senegal, Niger, Chari–Logone, and the Awash river of Ethiopia. The annual discharges of such seasonal rivers are highly variable and their control is as yet imperfect. While modern, large-scale irrigation requires storage dams, pumps, and canals, traditional irrigation involves planting crops on floodplains and channel slopes where they can use moisture left in the soil by the floodwaters.

Quite sophisticated methods of irrigation are employed in the oases of the Algerian Sahara (Fig. 6.4). The oasis dwellers have long depended on the date palm, a tree that can withstand great heat, high rates of evaporation, and soil water containing a moderately high content of common salt in solution. The fruit grown for local consumption is hard and floury, very different from the fat, sticky dessert varieties exported to Europe. As a hectare of date palms requires about 10 million litres of water annually for 50 trees (about a million gallons per acre) reliance cannot be placed solely on water hauled up from wells; the roots of the trees must be able to draw on sub-surface water at a shallow depth, so the oasis sites are localized depressions and the channels of river systems formed in wetter periods of the past.

It has been estimated that two and a half million date palms grow in the Sahara south of

An Algerian oasis with date palms in a hollow where their roots can reach groundwater.

An Algerian oasis abandoned because groundwater has been lowered by excessive abstraction of water lower down the wadi.

the tropic of Cancer. Only about one-third of these bears dates, for summer rains towards the south prevent the proper maturing of the fruit. Oases in the recesses of the Tibesti and Ahaggar mountains are watered from springs breaking out of the sandstones or by percolating water brought to the surface by rock bars across the sandy floors of deeply incised wadis. After you have been walking in the heat of the day over a barren, rocky plateau, it is delightful to drop down into a shady oasis and hear the trickling water and laughing children. Millet, sown in August or September after the date harvest and ripening three or four months later, is grown beneath the trees on plots made up of squares with sides a few metres long built up into ridges to control the flow of the precious water. There are tobacco and onions as well, small tomatoes for drying and use in soups, and henna used by the women as a cosmetic, to

stain their teeth red. Peas, beans, and melons are locally important; occasionally figs and vines manage to survive in the shade of the palms.

While date palms rely chiefly on sub-surface water, annual crops are irrigated from surface channels. Spring water is only occasionally available and, when it is, a reservoir is needed to store the water overnight for use in the daytime. In a few Saharan oases such as Adrar, underground sources have been tapped by deep wells and the water is led to the oasis depression by a tunnel or *qanat* marked at the surface by a line of ventilation holes. Usually reliance is placed on wells, which used to be three or four metres deep, though some are much deeper, each one capable of watering, say, 400 m² (one-tenth of an acre). On each plot every square metre must receive its due and all through the day the squeaking of the balancing

81

Sowing millet in Goubonne, Tibesti.

Date palms in Goubonne, an oasis in Tibesti.

Water from a spring being used to water plots in Tibesti.

arms of the *shadufs* sounds through the oasis. A donkey or camel can be used to haul a large leather bucket by a rope passing over a pulley, and then ten times the area can be irrigated from one well, but additional labour is required to control the flow of the water and the beast has to be provided with fodder.

Oasis cultivators must remain at work all the year round to produce their meagre harvests. Many of them were until recently serfs or slaves, settled in the oases by Arab, Tibu, or Touareg masters, who depended largely on livestock but found it useful, generations ago, to have slaves working for them. Now the slaves have become share-croppers or tenants but are little better off than they were before.

Many have moved away to work on the oil-fields or in the towns near the coast and the pastoralists must assist with the cultivation. In some oases money from oil has been invested in pumps intended to reduce labour requirements and increase the irrigated area, but pumping in one area can lower the water table and cause neighbouring shallow wells to dry out, so that little may be gained from such developments.

5.4 Fishing

Fish constitute only a minor part of their diet for many Africans but it is an important source of protein, needed especially by people in the forest zone. The fisher-folk themselves consume large amounts of their catch; the women usually preserve the surplus by drying, smoking, or salting it for sale. Fresh fish will not keep long enough to be sold more than about 10 km (6 mls) from where it has been caught; preserved fish is traded over hundreds of kilometres.

African sea fisheries have not been fully exploited by traditional methods, partly because the best fishing grounds lie off sparsely settled desert coasts (Fig. 5.1). Cool upwelling waters, partly responsible for the aridity inland, are rich in nutritive salts, and the plankton they support provide the food supply for great quantities of sardine, pilchard, tuna, hake, and a variety of other fish. The cool seas off the coast of south-west Africa and Angola and between Morocco and Senegal have attracted much attention from fishing fleets with factory ships in attendance, from Spain, eastern Europe and Japan. Some of the fish is sold in the coastal ports, but much of it is exported to countries outside Africa in the form of oil and fish-meal.

Crates of sardinella at a fish-processing factory in Senegal about 160 km south of Dakar. The fish are either frozen or converted into fish-meal. The United Nations Development Programme has been lending assistance to fisheries in Morocco, Senegal, and Ghana. The coastal states have extended their exclusive economic zones (EEZ) 200 miles from the shore, and while the local share of the catch has risen that of vessels from foreign countries has fallen.

The fisheries of the warmer coastal waters are fished by a number of coastal tribes. Amongst the most active are the Ewe who live on either side of the Ghana–Togo border, the same people who grow shallots. They put out to sea in large dug-out canoes and employ long seine nets hauled in from the shore. The nets are costly and the large indigenous companies operating them display a good deal of enterprise and organizational ability. New techniques and equipment such as nylon nets and outboard motors have been adopted as they have proved to be profitable—and so far as the availability of foreign exchange has allowed. Distribution of the fresh fish has been a weakness and attempts have been made, not always successful, at a centralized system of freezing and marketing.

Inland fisheries are very varied in character. The most productive are shallow lakes like Lake George and Lake Naivasha in eastern equatorial Africa, which may yield annually 20 tonnes of fish per km² (50 tons per square mile) of surface area. Lake George gains nutrients from hippopotamus which graze around the lake at night and defecate in the lake where they keep cool in the daytime.

The waters of deeper lakes are not so rich as the shallow ones; below a certain depth the water is cool and stagnant and incapable of supporting many fish. Lake Kivu is particularly noteworthy in this respect. As a result of its violent history in recent geological times,

A fishing boat on a sand ridge with the sea behind, near Keta in south-east Ghana. In the background a team of fishermen is hauling in a seine net.

involving its formation by a volcanic eruption blocking off a headwater of the Nile and diverting it into Lake Tanganyika, it contains few species of fish and the water more than 70 m (230 ft) below the surface is so saturated with sulphuretted hydrogen and methane as to make fish life at depth impossible.

Amongst the most productive inland fisheries are the great swamps—not those that are stagnant, for the decaying vegetation deprives the water and thus the fish of oxygen, but those with a throughflow like the Malagarasi swamps in Tanzania, Lake Bangweulu in Zambia, and Lake Chad. They yield millions of fish annually but they also fluctuate in size, so that shore facilities are not always readily available. The Malagarasi swamps are remarkably clear and have a sparse plankton population. The abundance of fishlife there is due to the presence of two species of small fish which feed on water lilies and other plant material and pass out a partly digested mass which forms the main food of other species of fish, especially *Tilapia*.

About one and a half million tons of freshwater fish are caught annually in Africa, about half in rivers and on floodplains. According to a diagram in Welcomme, *Fisheries Ecology of Floodplain Rivers*, (1979), p. 210, the potential annual fish catch from a river in a year can be calculated very roughly by dividing the area of the drainage basin in km^2 by a factor of about 50, where floodplain development is normal, or by 10 where the floodplain is extensive. Year-to-year variation in yields is considerable, depending on the size of the seasonal flood; droughts result in reductions in catch size and in the number of larger fish species caught over the next year or more. From floodplains, catches are roughly of the order of about 50 kg per hectare so the food value obtained is not very different from that derived from an equal area of unirrigated cropland. In some rivers, the Ouémé in Benin for instance, hedges are planted on the edge of the river channel at low water which act as refuge traps or fish parks when the floodplain drains in the following dry season; catches from such traps may exceed 3 tonnes per hectare. If fishing is excessive, fisheries will fall below their optimum productivity and it is wise to leave some reaches and floodplain lakes unexploited so that stocks can recover rapidly after droughts or overfishing.

Some tribes are more skilled at fishing than

Fish trap in a stream flowing towards Lake Rukwa in south-west Tanzania.

others, being more specialized and employing a greater variety of methods. Usually the men fish and maintain the boats and gear; the women treat the catch by drying and smoking it and market the produce; small boys play an important role, paddling canoes, baiting lines, and lifting traps.

On the upper Niger the Bozo are specialist fishermen who migrate up and down the river according to the season and in particular according to the movements of shoals of small fish called *Alestes*. At the end of the dry season, the shoals move upstream from Lake Debo in the Inland Niger Delta towards Koulikoro, the Bozo setting traps for them successively further up the river channel (Fig. 5.6). In September, as the flood comes down from the Guinean highlands and the river spreads over its floodplain, the Bozo move downstream with the Black Flood through the Inland Delta and as much as a thousand kilometres into the Niger Republic. In the dry season they return to the Inland Delta, where they build reed fences, supported by wooden poles, that guide the fish into basketwork traps as the waters drain from the floodplain. The Bozo buy millet with the cash they get for their dried fish. Mopti has always been an important market for them, the dried fish being traded by lorry down to the Ivory Coast and Ghana; in return kola nuts from the southern forests come north.

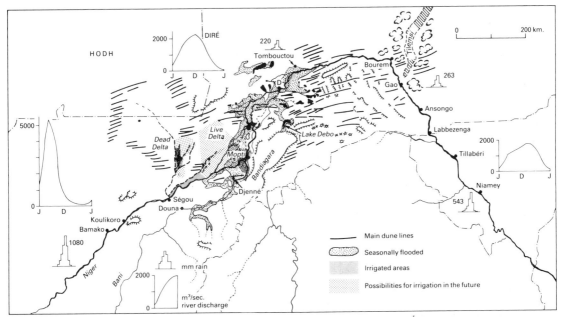

Fig. 5.6. *The Inland Niger Delta where the Niger and Bani rivers which rise in the highlands of Guinea come together at Mopti. Between the ancient trading centres of Jenne and Timbuktu their seasonal floods spread over grassy plains and fill shallow lake basins. Fishermen move up and down the river according to the season; pastoralists graze their cattle on the riverine plains late in the dry season and then move to rainy-season grazing lands at the desert margins; cultivators grow rice on the floodlands; a barrage at Sansanding raises the water to a level at which it can flow along canals following old distributaries in the Dead Delta of the Niger.*

Lake Debo in the Inland Niger Delta, seen from the Space Shuttle on 3 December 1985.

Some groups of Hausa farm in the rains and fish in the dry season, whole families of 20 or 30 persons moving hundreds of kilometres upstream from Nigeria and Niger into Mali towards the end of each year. The Songhai of the Niger bend in Mali are primarily rice farmers; they plant riverside fields in June for harvesting in October and fish in the following dry season, preserving some of their catch until the next rainy season when they can exchange it with Fulani pastoralists for milk and butter.

Floodplains and seasonal swamps in semi-arid country are grazed by cattle in the latter part of the dry season. Cattle and fishing are complementary, for the cattle convert the grass into readily dissolved organic and mineral nutrients which enrich floodwaters to the benefit of the fish. Lakes, rivers, and their floodplains thus support complex ecological and social systems, systems that can be seriously disrupted by river development schemes unless care is taken to understand them and act accordingly.

85

6

AFRICA BEFORE THE COLONIAL PERIOD

Interest in African history was greatly stimulated by the upsurge of nationalism and the emergence of self-governing African states about 1960. New institutes and area study centres sponsored research into the subject, both within and outside Africa. More recently, television documentaries and books such as *Roots* have made the subject much more widely known.

Most of Africa south of the Sahara has no written history before the sixteenth century; writing was introduced with Islam and Christianity. Before the coming of these universal religions, written contracts and codes of law were unknown. Tribal histories were preserved in folklore, and lists of great chiefs were handed down by word of mouth. The memory of events persisted but was so symbolized and distorted by oral transmission that fact and fiction are difficult to disentangle. Consequently much reliance has to be placed on archaeological remains: artifacts, tools, pottery, and buildings, often in fragmentary form and requiring imagination as well as skill in their interpretation.

North of the Sahara, especially in Egypt, the situation is very different. Pictorial records, hieroglyphics on monuments and clay tablets, household and state accounts, laws, and obituaries provide a political and social history over a period of 5000 years unequalled elsewhere in the world, except possibly in China.

6.1 Prehistory

The position of Africa in prehistory is similar to that of Egypt in ancient history. The very early prehistoric record is fuller in Africa south of the Sahara than anywhere else. The discoveries of *Australopithecus*, a manlike creature that lived in the early Pleistocene, by Raymond Dart in South Africa and the sequence of finds by members of the Leakey family and others in the East African Rift Valley over the last half century provide a collection of hominoid remains that is unrivalled elsewhere. Associated with the remains are the tools used by early man and the bones of the animals on which he preyed. The earliest implements are of crude workmanship, not always easily distinguishable from natural objects. Later tools vary from one region to another according to the materials used and, presumably, the purpose for which they were intended. Dating is always a problem, especially for the times before about 50 000 years ago; after that time radio-carbon (C14) methods begin to be useful.

It is possible that modern people, *Homo sapiens sapiens*, first appeared in Africa a hundred thousand years ago, spread to the Middle East, and eventually eliminated or interbred with their Neanderthal predecessors. The story has yet to be worked out.

Greater aridity in the northern tropics between about 20 000 and 12 000 years ago must have greatly impeded movements of people and the interchange of knowledge between the people of the Mediterranean lands and those south of the Sahara; some of the racial and cultural differences between the peoples north and south of the desert may have developed at this time. Then came the early Holocene pluvial period when the Sahara was much less of an obstacle than it is now, with people hunting and grazing their cattle in areas that are now extremely arid, but discrepancies in technology either side of the Sahara seem to have persisted through this wet period. Livestock were reared in the Sahel at an early stage but crop cultivation was delayed until about 3000 years ago. By that time, copper was being mined in various places on the southern edge of the desert and copper ornaments and implements were in use, though not bronze so far as we know. In the vicinity of the copper mines, and probably dating from the same period more than 2000 years ago, there are rock paintings and engravings of chariots drawn by horses. They could have been Carthaginian or conceivably Egyptian. No one knows what use was made of the chariots but their presence would suggest that the Sahara was a much less barren place than it is today.

6.2 Ancient history

The emergence of Egypt as a unified state about 5000 years ago coincided with the period when current aridity was becoming established in northern tropical Africa. The desiccation of the Sahara dates from this time. The discharge of the Nile was diminishing, its flood levels falling as the monsoon rains in Ethiopia became less intense and its low-water levels being reduced as supplies from the White Nile dwindled when the rift valley lakes of southern Ethiopia ceased to overflow to Lake Turkana, and Lake Turkana no longer spilled north-west to the Pibor and White Nile. As droughts increased in severity, fringing forests alongside the Nile in Egypt were cleared or died; wild fauna disappeared from the valley and the borderlands became more desertic as the climate deteriorated.

The population of the Nile valley in Egypt increased, the landscape becoming a product of man's handiwork as much as nature's. Settlements grew up on levees bordering the main river channels and crops were grown on the adjacent soils as the floodwaters retreated every autumn. Gradually the irrigation system was refined, banks being constructed to control the flooding and channels dug through the natural levees to ensure the proper watering and cropping of greater areas of the floodplain. Cropping was extended into the spring and early summer by digging shallow wells to reach groundwater in the alluvium, the water being lifted by *shadufs*. The irrigation system extended along the distributaries in the delta, and by degrees greater areas of marshes and ponds formerly used for fishing and hunting were drained for cultivation.

Everyone is familiar with the pyramids. Built over 4000 years ago, they are the most prominent and spectacular of the architectural and engineering structures of the ancient Egyptians. The Nile valley and delta during the Pharaonic age can be pictured as a busy, integrated, and productive fragment of the continent: a land with numerous towns and cities and a population of perhaps 3 or 4 millions. Ships carrying timber and other commodities imported from Asia, as well as local produce, sailed up the Nile before the northerly winter winds to dock in riverside harbours excavated in the floodplain. Wharfs were backed by storehouses and overlooked by temples and palaces on a gigantic scale. These are amongst the structures that are being excavated by archaeologists to supplement knowledge of the country gained already from the monuments to the dead standing on the higher ground overlooking the alluvial plain.

The end of the Pharaohs came with the conquest of Egypt by the Assyrians in the seventh century BC, bringing with them knowledge of iron-working. Technical innovations continued with the introduction from Persia of the *saqiya*, a great wheel capable of lifting water through a height of several metres. Driven by animal power, it allowed more land to be cultivated before the annual flood arrived, and led to a general increase in productivity. The coming of Alexander and the 300-year rule of Ptolemy (one of Alexander's generals) and his successors over Egypt revivified administration and urban life. The drainage and irrigation of the Faiyoum, a large oasis depression west of the Nile upstream of the delta, was extended, the supply of water from the Nile being improved and more effectively controlled by the construction of a great canal, the Bahr el Yusuf. The capital of the country was transferred to Alexandria, a new city on the Mediterranean shore of the delta. This Ptolemaic period saw the full development of the northern part of the delta and a shift northwards in the demographic centre of gravity of Egypt.

An appreciation of the great antiquity of Egyptian civilization and the scale of its endeavours and accomplishments enables one to understand why so much attention has been paid to the possibility of Egyptian influences

Ghardaia, the home of a Muslim sect in northern Algeria, the members of which are renowned as traders throughout the country.

having radiated through Africa in early times, well before Bantu expansion. The Egyptians were in touch with the Nubians of the Nile valley south of Aswan in what is now the Sudan Republic. Meroe, about 160 km (100 mls) downstream of Khartoum, was a flourishing city 3000 years ago. Enormous slag heaps nearby indicate the considerable scale of an iron industry where now there is scarcely any wood for making charcoal. Meroe had trading links with the Red Sea and the Gulf of Aden and also with Axum, the chief centre of an empire that had been established in northern Ethiopia about 400 BC by immigrants from the Yemen region of Arabia. It is possible that knowledge of iron-working was transmitted to Africa south of the Sahara from both Meroe in the north-east and Carthage in the north-west.

North Africa west of the Nile delta was occupied as much as 6000 years ago by pastoralist peoples who occupied not only the Maghreb but also much of what is now the western Sahara. When Phoenicians from what is now Lebanon founded Carthage about 800 BC, on a site now occupied by a suburb of Tunis, and also a number of other trading centres further west to the Straits of Gibraltar and beyond down the Atlantic coast, they found there a people speaking a language called Tamazight, related to languages spoken in the Nile valley. Later on, Greek traders and colonists regarded these aboriginal inhabitants of north-west Africa as barbarians and called them Berbers, a name that has continued to be applied to them. Though primarily pastoralists, they were also cultivators, growing tree crops and cereals on terraces that can still be distinguished on air photographs of the uplands in the interior.

Carthage was overwhelmed by Rome in 147 BC; Cleopatra's Egypt was conquered in 32 BC. For the next five centuries north Africa, including Egypt, formed a part of either the western, Roman or the eastern, Byzantine empire.

Whereas the Carthaginians had confined their activities to the coast, the Romans extended their rule far inland, especially in what is now Tunisia. Called Ifriqiya, it was eventually to give its name to the whole of the continent, not merely to the eastern part of the Maghreb. Vast areas of semi-arid steppe in west-central Tunisia and along the coast of the Gulf of Gabes were planted with olive trees; the oil from them was refined locally and together with corn was exported in large quantities to Rome. In northern Tunisia and Algeria, much of the land was under the plough and thousands of square kilometres were laid out in rectangular fields. This system, called centuriation, was designed to facilitate administration and taxation. The pattern survives into the present landscape, showing on air photographs as an east–west and north–south grid marking the roads and ditches of Roman times (not very different from the regular field boundaries of the present-day North American high plains). In the drier areas of Libya and the eastern Maghreb, dams were built across wadis to trap sediments and provide deep, moist soils on which crops were grown. Camels began to be widely used in the Sahara about the second century AD and the Romans constructed forts and other defensive works in the remote interior to protect settlers from raiding nomads. The sites of the forts have been used by later settled peoples; their remains are the *qasrs* often remarked by travellers through the region at the present day.

Many of the townspeople of Roman Egypt and north Africa were converted to Christianity: St Augustine of Hippo was one of them, Simon Stylites another. Byzantine rule in the West was undermined by the Vandals who settled in Tunisia, but the end of a period of several centuries of European rule in north Africa came suddenly and dramatically with the Arab invasions in the middle of the seventh century AD. Inspired by the teachings of Muhammad, who had died in AD 632, the Arabs rapidly conquered Egypt and swept on into the Maghreb. The Berbers, as they have always done, resisted the new invaders and succeeded in retaining their ancient tribal structures by retiring to the mountains. Christianity in northern Africa had been weakened by theological disputes and by confusion in the Byzantine empire, and within a century the majority of the population had adopted Islam and the Arabic language and customs. In the Maghreb, Christianity was entirely eliminated. It persisted in Nubia and in Egypt, where Coptic Christians formed a sizeable proportion of the population, as much as a fifth, until the middle of this century. But Mediterranean Africa and in time the desert lands to the south became overwhelmingly Arabic in language and Islamic in culture, a part of the Middle East as much as a part of Africa, and this state of affairs has persisted to the present day.

Greeks and Romans seem to have penetrated south to the swamp grasslands of the Sudd, but the Nile valley did not provide an easy route to the south and there is little information in classical writings about intertropical Africa. The first close contacts of Africa south of the Sahara with the civilizations of the Mediterranean basin and Mesopotamia were made by sea. Greeks and Arabs sailed down the Red Sea to east African ports quite regularly and a pilot book of about AD 120, the *Periplus of the Erythraean Sea*, written in Alexandria, gives some details of the coast as far south as the Mozambique channel and also indicates that ships from India were visiting the western shores of the Indian Ocean. Discoveries of Chinese porcelain of the twelfth century at various points along the east African coast and on the offshore islands of Tanzania show that trade with the Orient was on a considerable scale for several centuries before the coming of the Portuguese.

Other sailors along these sea routes included Indonesians. They introduced to Africa yams, breadfruit, and bananas, which were adopted by the Bantu-speaking peoples. The Indonesians went on to settle in Madagascar, which had remained uninhabited until this time. By the end of the first millennium AD they were firmly settled:

a mixture of Indonesian and African (although at that stage the Indonesian element was probably still dominant) and speaking an essentially Indonesian language with the addition of some African vocabulary. With their rectangular wooden huts, on stilts in the wetter zones, and their slash-and-burn rice cultivation, supplemented by the cultivation of the other Indonesian crops which they brought with them and by fishing on the coasts and in the rivers, their way of life was close to that of their Indonesian forebears. But they had acquired new techniques in Africa notably in relation to domestic animals, and they had brought with them the forerunners of the great herds of hump-backed zebu cattle which are now an essential feature of the Malagasy landscape. (Mervyn Brown in *Madagascar Rediscovered*, 1978.)

Bantu expansion into south-central Africa was aided by their adoption of Indonesian food crops. By about AD 1000 Bantu were established between the Zambezi and the Limpopo, trading gold and copper down to the coast. They built the great stone walls, towers, and gateways at Zimbabwe from which the country takes its name. Within the ruins have been found Chinese porcelain, beads from India, and other goods of foreign origin almost certainly imported through the ancient port of Sofala some 400 km (250 mls) away to the east (see Fig. 4.2).

6.3 Medieval times

6.3.1 The western Sudan zone

The early history of the medieval Sudan zone is relatively well-known because camel caravans linked the region to the Mediterranean and accounts of the states on the southern margins of the desert were brought back by Arab travellers. The medieval states depended on their control of north–south trade in gold and slaves from the forests, salt from the Sahara, and European metal manufactures from the Mediterranean (Fig. 4.2). The earliest state was Ghana, the name adopted by the Gold Coast in 1957 on gaining independence from Britain. Old Ghana, with its capital at Koumbi Saleh

about 320 km (200 mls) north of Bamako near the Senegal–Niger watershed, controlled the trans-Saharan trade in Guinea gold. The Negroes gave their gold in exchange for salt excavated by slave labour from ancient lake beds in the Sahara and the gold paid for European goods brought south by desert Arabs and Berbers from Morocco. Many of the northern traders who came to settle in Koumbi Saleh were Muslims. They attracted many converts to their religion amongst the leading members of the community and their influence increased. About AD 1040 a warlike Muslim sect, the Almoravids, gained many adherents amongst the nomadic peoples of the region. One group moved north and quite rapidly conquered Morocco and Spain; the remainder took control of Ghana. According to legend, the people who fled to the south-east from the original Ghana at this time were the ancestors of the Akan people of the modern state of Ghana.

A federal union formed in 1960 by the former French colonies Senegal and Soudan adopted the name Mali, which had belonged to a Mandingo kingdom, a successor to ancient Ghana. Flourishing in the thirteenth century, its capital lay on the upper Niger far to the south of Koumbi, probably at Niani in the Republic of Guinea. Like Ghana it traded in Saharan salt and Wangara gold. When Mali's ruler, Mansa Musa, made a pilgrimage to Mecca in the early fourteenth century he displayed so much wealth in Cairo and elsewhere en route that his fame spread to Europe and he is to be seen depicted on several maps of the period. At his death the Mali empire extended across the southern Sahara and western Sudan zone from the Atlantic coast to the Aïr mountains. Like all the great states that have evolved in this region, it was a loose confederation consisting of several towns and tribes, paying tribute to the paramount chief or king when he was powerful, and going their own way in times of stress.

After Musa's death, the Songhai people of Gao, which is located on the Niger where it turns south-east, broke away from Mali, and troubled times followed. Nevertheless, the writings of Ibn Battuta, who was travelling in the region in the 1350s, indicate that commerce remained active. Ibn Battuta described Gao as the largest, richest, and most beautiful city in the Sudan. In the fifteenth century, under Muhammad Askia, its influence extended over much of the western Sudan and came to include the Hausa states on the Niger–Chad watershed. These states had been established in the eleventh century, possibly by Berber immigrants from the north. Further east, extending either side of Lake Chad, was Kanem, another state of similar antiquity.

In 1586, Songhai was attacked by an army from Morocco whose rulers wished to gain control of trans-Saharan trade and the source of Guinea gold to the south. The Moorish army suffered heavy losses in the desert crossing, and though it managed to defeat the armies of Songhai its efforts brought no benefits to Morocco. The Moors were unable to gain control of either the gold mines of the south or the elusive people who worked them. In the turmoil that followed the invasion, trade routes shifted eastwards to Kano and Katsina. The Moors settled down in Timbuktu, married local women, and in time lost contact with the Sharif of Morocco, but Moorish influence is discernible to this day in the pottery, dress, and diet of the people of the middle Niger.

The modern states of the western Sudan zone are far from being directly derived from their medieval predecessors but they all have a great deal in common as a result of their former commercial and political connections. Islam has impressed a certain cultural uniformity on the zone; the languages of the old imperial peoples are spoken more widely than most African tongues, and tribalism is less divisive than in many other parts of the continent.

6.3.2 North and east Africa

A second incursion of Arabs into north Africa in the eleventh century is regarded by some writers as having been more momentous than the first invasion, four centuries earlier. It involved large numbers of nomadic pastoralists, and some have argued that they were responsible for a deterioration of the 'habitat values' of Mediterranean Africa, attributing the impoverishment of the plant cover until the present day to the voraciousness of the nomads' goats. Both invasions have been invoked to explain the southward movement of Berbers and the formation of new states in the western Sudan. Such arguments are not easily disproved but neither is the evidence to support them very strong.

Both the Maghreb and Egypt in medieval times, and also the Sudan zone, experienced periods of prosperity and decay according to climatic and political conditions. Low flood-levels resulting from the failure of the rains in the source regions of the Nile have been causes of famine throughout Egypt's long history. In the eleventh century the Nile floods were so reduced for several years in succession that the Egyptians sent an embassy to the Ethiopians requesting them to desist from diverting the flow of the river. Political problems, as now, resulted from discordances within the Islamic world and deterioration in relations with the countries to the north-east.

In the Maghreb, as in Egypt, Byzantine technology and knowledge deriving from the earlier civilizations of Greece and Rome were fused with those of Persia, within Islam. Both Kairouan in the east and Fez in the west of the Maghreb, established as capitals by the Arabs, became centres of philosophical, theological, and legal learning. Their trade links extended east to Mesopotamia and south into the Sahara (Fig. 4.2). New irrigation works were undertaken; new crops were introduced from the east; industries grew up, based on local products such as wool, linen, sugar, lead, and iron; architecture, music, and literature flourished. Scholarly writers such as Ibn Khaldun and Ibn Battuta came into prominence, and it is from their works that we derive our knowledge of the western Islamic world at this time.

Civilization in north Africa in the medieval period compared favourably with that of the merchant states in Italy; indeed the roots of the European Renaissance can be traced by way of Spain and Sicily to Tunisia, through which much of the Greek and Roman learning of Alexandria was transmitted to western Europe.

The eleventh and twelfth centuries were turbulent periods for the Maghreb. Norman pirates raided the coastal towns, then came the nomadic invasions from Egypt, and many sedentary communities inland disappeared about this time. With the reconquest of Iberia from the Moors by Christian Portugal and Spain, thousands of Arab and Jewish refugees moved over the Mediterranean into the Maghreb from Andalusia and, later on, several coastal cities were occupied by Portugal in the west and by Spain in the east. In the early fifteenth century Ottoman Turks came to dominate the eastern and southern Mediterranean, thereby gaining control of trade routes from Europe to the Orient. They took possession of Byzantium (now Istanbul) in 1453 and in the following century occupied Egypt and established three military domains in the south-west Mediterranean, based on Algiers in the west, Tunis in the centre, and Tripoli in the east. It was the Turks who dislodged the Spaniards from the Maghreb; the Moroccans themselves expelled the Portuguese from their country.

By the end of the fifteenth century, the Americas had been discovered and, more important to the Mediterranean countries, the Portuguese had found a sea route to the East Indies. From this time onwards until the nineteenth century, the Islamic countries of north Africa declined; their cities decayed, their populations diminished and, with the rest of Africa, they failed to benefit from the cultural and technical developments that spread from Italy to the Low Countries and Britain and sowed the seeds of the Industrial Revolution.

6.4 Expansion of Europe into Africa

6.4.1 Portuguese exploration

The Portuguese were anxious to reach the source of Guinea gold and to find a sea route to the Orient. In the course of the fifteenth century they systematically explored the west coast of Africa and about 1470 at last discovered a land where gold was mined. They built the castle of São Jorge da Mina, now Elmina on the coast of Ghana, to be the headquarters of a royal governor and to try to ensure that none but Portuguese merchants should trade in that area. Their captains continued to explore further south and in 1498 Vasco da Gama rounded the Cape of Good Hope and reached Calicut on the Indian Malabar coast, thereby opening a new era in the history of Africa and the world.

Within ten years the Portuguese had conquered the Arabs in the east coast ports and they continued to dominate the trade of the Arabian Sea until the end of the sixteenth century. The settlements they established along the west and east coast of Africa were at first little more than stopping-places for watering and repairing ships on the way to the Indies. The Portuguese were relatively few in number and mortality amongst them was high, but they succeeded in making several notable journeys into the interior of Africa, journeys that were not to be repeated by other Europeans until the nineteenth century. An official Portuguese embassy reached Mali in 1534; Edward Lopez travelled in the Kingdom of the Congo, south of the lower course of the river, for four years in perfect safety. Pires was well received by the Oba of Benin, a kingdom west of the Niger delta; da Silveira reached the court of Monomotapa more than 320 km (200 mls) up the Zambezi. Copper, gold, and ivory from Zimbabwe may have helped to purchase spices from India. Conditions in Africa at this time are not to be compared too unfavourably with those in Europe at about the same time.

6.4.2 The slave trade

At first the Portuguese and the other Europeans who followed them down the west coast wanted gold, ivory, and pepper; in return they supplied mirrors, knives, cloth, and later firearms, bar iron, and rum. African demand for these goods outstripped what they could pay for them in gold and ivory; in exchange for the European manufactures they offered slaves. In 1530 the first slaves for sale in America were carried across the Atlantic to work on the new sugar plantations in Brazil and in the West Indies—the first, it has been estimated, of some 10 million. In the sixteenth century, when the trade was almost entirely in Portuguese hands, about a quarter of a million were exported. The demand spread to Spanish America, the Caribbean, and North America, all the European maritime countries competing for the profits. The number of slaves carried each year mounted until in the eighteenth century about 60 000 were being shipped annually. At that time Britain was the principal maritime power. Half the slaves were carried in British ships—over 2 million between 1701 and 1810—bringing great profits to West Indian plantation owners and to the merchants of Liverpool and Bristol, and providing a great stimulus to British manufacturing and industrial growth.

The slaves were procured from the hinterland by African traders who were careful to prevent the Europeans from penetrating far inland. The Europeans stayed on the coast, living in forts built along the rocky shores of the Gold Coast, in hulks tied up in the creeks of the Niger delta and in large towns like Luanda in Angola. The great number of men, women, and children exported at this time, approaching half a million in some decades, must have been a considerable drain on the tribes living in the interior. Their populations generally were much smaller than now; one might make a guess of twenty millions living between Senegal and Angola.

Nearly everywhere, it seems, social life was disrupted by the trade. Coastal peoples, armed with European firearms, raided far into the interior. In west Africa, old states like Oyo and Benin took advantage of the new commercial opportunities; small states emerged at the coast and grew strong and wealthy; larger states like Dahomey and Ashanti grew powerful towards the end of the seventeenth century, supporting standing armies and attempting to dominate both coast and interior. For the peoples of western Africa, the period between 1550 and 1850 must have seen years of turmoil, with armed bands and mercenary troops as constant threats to settled life. Even in south-central Africa, the Luba, the Lunda, and the Bemba on the Zambezi–Congo watershed, becoming involved in the trade in ivory, gold, and slaves, expanded as plundering, military powers. African works of art discovered in recent decades, mostly undated but clearly of considerable antiquity, such as the Ife bronzes and the brass figurines from Igbo in Nigeria, point to earlier streams of cultural development that were dammed back or diverted at this time, an African dark age that reached its nadir little more than a century ago.

To plantation owners and merchants, slavery became an economic necessity; if it were to be abolished they would be ruined, or so they thought. If one country were to prohibit the trade, others would persist in it to profit at the expense of the first. Nevertheless, slavery in England was recognized as illegal in 1772 and about 15 000 slaves there were set free as a result. Some of them, with 1200 Negroes from Nova Scotia who had fought on the British side in the American War of Independence, were shipped to Freetown. They settled there to a European way of life under the influence of Christian missionaries and formed the nucleus of the British colony of Sierra Leone. In 1820 free negroes from the USA were settled by the American Colonization Society at Monrovia,

later to become the capital of Liberia. The black colonists belonged to tribes from other parts of Africa or to no tribe at all; they were as much American as African. Nearly all of them stayed at the coast and their descendants continue to form groups quite separate culturally from the indigenous people inland, who now outnumber them in Freetown and Monrovia.

6.4.3 The settlement of South Africa

A Dutch supply station, founded at the Cape in 1652 to provide corn and cattle for ships en route to the Indies, developed into a civilized, compact community. It attracted Dutch and German Protestants and French Huguenots, all of whom arrived in the latter half of the seventeenth century. The settled area expanded, with wheat and vines being grown on farms up to about 100 km (60 mls) from Cape Town, with Malay, west African, and also local slave labour (Fig. 6.1).

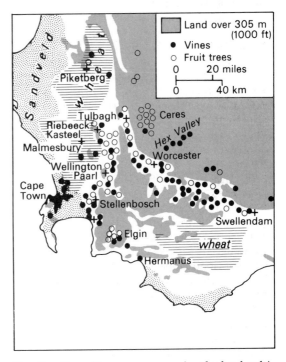

Fig. 6.1. *Cape Town now occupies the land cultivated by the first Dutch settlers at the Cape. In the decades around 1700, arable farming spread to the areas now covered with vines and fruit trees while graziers moved northwards and eastwards between the mountain ranges to more distant areas.*

As the settlers increased in number, they spread north-east into the drier country more remote from Cape Town and took to rearing cattle and sheep. The climate was more favourable to pastoral than arable farming and it was easier to walk the animals to Cape Town than to carry corn over long stretches of difficult country. Farms were large, often covering several square kilometres and, as they were inherited according to Roman–Dutch law by the eldest son, younger sons constantly pushed north and later east, cutting out new holdings for themselves from country which seems to have been sparsely inhabited. The birth-rate was high and the frontier of settlement advanced rapidly into the interior.

In the course of the eighteenth century a distinct, new nation emerged in South Africa. It was a nation of farmers, isolated on their great, lonely farms from the civilized life of Cape Town by distance and steep mountain ranges. They spoke Afrikaans, a language with a simpler pronunciation and grammar than the Dutch from which it was derived and including in its vocabulary many African and eastern words. They were Calvinists, clinging to the harsh orthodoxy of the seventeenth century and finding in the Old Testament justification for the master and slave relationship between themselves and their Hottentot servants. These rough country farmers formed the nucleus of the new nation, the Afrikaner or Boer (farmer) element in the Union and Republic of South Africa, a country with a strong colour-consciousness, with the white man master of the black.

The main conflicts now so apparent in South African society began to develop early in the nineteenth century. While the Dutch settlers advanced steadily inland and then east along the valleys and plains south of the Nieuwveld range, Bantu tribes were occupying the east side of the continent. Both were immigrants to a land which appears to have been only sparsely inhabited by nomadic Hottentots and Bushmen. Boer and Bantu met in the vicinity of the Great Fish river which reaches the sea between Port Elizabeth and East London and there were several clashes between them before 1800 (Fig. 6.2).

During the Napoleonic wars the Cape came under the control of the British government, anxious to maintain control of the sea route to

India. About 1820 several hundreds of British immigrants arrived, and many of them were settled in the eastern districts to populate the frontier area against the Bantu. Each colonist was allocated 40 hectares (100 acres) of land to encourage him to farm intensively. This was too small an area to be rewarding and before long most of the settlers had sold their land or had rented it to Bantu tenants and had moved into the coastal towns. A large Bantu-speaking Xhosa population built up east of the river in what became native reserves and are now the Ciskei and Transkei. The British continued to be predominantly town-dwellers and were always far exceeded in numbers by the Boers in rural areas.

Friction arose between the Boers and the British in the Cape. The British colonial authorities attempted to enforce laws that were foreign to the Dutch settlers; they refused to annex African territory to satisfy the farmers' demands for more land and in 1834 they forbade the Boers to keep slaves. To escape British interference, Boer farmers began to trek northwards, west of the Bantu territories and across the Orange River. On the high veld they found good pasture land and, taking their possessions on ox-wagons, they gradually occupied the plateau as far north as the Limpopo, and set up their own republics of the Orange Free State and Transvaal. Other Boers moved east through the passes in the Drakensberg, and coming down towards the wetter lands of Natal they encountered the Zulu and came into conflict with them.

The Zulu had been a minor clan of the Nguni tribe, occupying a territory between the Portuguese at Delagoa Bay to the north and the Xhosa to the south. About 1800, under a succession of charismatic chiefs, they developed into a powerful military state. The first of the great chiefs, Dingiswayo, diverted the loyalty of the age-sets of the Nguni lineages and clans to himself by assigning successive generations of the same lineage and compound to different regiments. He very successfully adapted to warfare a traditional hunting technique, the crescentic deployment that develops into a pincer movement. His successor, Shaka, introduced a new weapon, the assegai, a short stabbing spear. This combination of centralized authority and greater military efficiency enabled the Nguni within a few years to domi-

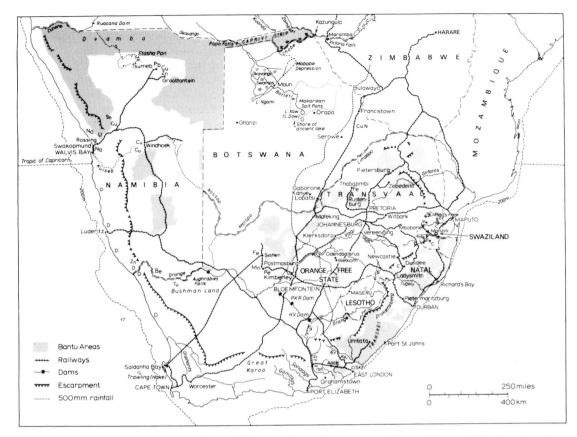

Fig. 6.2. *Southern Africa. About the end of the eighteenth century, white settlers and Bantu came into contact near the Gt Fish river. In the 1830s a group of Afrikaans farmers left the Cape Colony, which had come into British hands in 1806, and moved into the interior, settling in the areas that were to become the Orange Free State and Transvaal. The economic importance of South Africa at the present day is based on its mineral resources. Amongst the first to be discovered were the diamonds of Kimberley and the gold of the Witwatersrand. Later a whole range of valuable minerals was found to be available: Be—beryl, C—coal, Cu—copper, D—diamonds, Fe—iron, Mn—manganese, N—nickel, Na—salt, Pb—lead, Sn—tin, Tu—tungsten, Ur—uranium, Zn—zinc.*

nate surrounding peoples. In the first half of the nineteenth century, a complicated 'domino effect' resulted in a centrifugal expansion of Nguni groups. The people they conquered and effectively fused together into new tribes adopted patterns of organization comparable in some respects to those of the Zulu. Amongst the descendants of these new political entities are the Swazi, the Ndebele (Matabele) of western Zimbabwe and the Ngwato of Botswana.

British settlers had established themselves in the Durban area in the early decades of the nineteenth century. Impelled by the threats of Zulu power and Boer penetration, the British government intervened in 1843 to establish the colony of Natal. The Province of Natal has remained to this day the most British part of the country. Bantu groups that had been broken by the Zulu swarmed into southern Natal and, lacking chiefs and tribal organization, were settled like refugees in locations, later to become native reserves.

The Boer Trekkers who occupied the high plains numbered only about 10 000. They took what land they wanted. The Africans in the area at the time were few in number because in the decades before the arrival of the Trekkers, they had been involved in inter-tribal warfare associated with the Zulu expansion that had depopulated wide areas. In any case, they were

95

primarily pastoralist people with tribal areas large enough to allow a considerable degree of nomadism. After the Trek, the land most suitable for farming and grazing was rapidly taken up by the white settlers and only a relatively small area was set aside for the Bantu.

Along the coast of Natal a number of sugar plantations were established by British settlers before 1850. They needed a big supply of labour. There were many natives in the reserves nearby, but they had no desire to work for the white man and so the planters were allowed to import indentured labour from India. Of the several thousands of Indians shipped across, some returned at the end of their contracts, but most elected to settle in the country and sent home for their families. Indians continued to arrive until 1913, when further immigration of Asians was stopped by law. Since then they have increased in number faster than the Whites but remain concentrated in coastal Natal.

6.4.4 Nineteenth-century penetration

At the beginning of the nineteenth century, little was known in Europe about the African interior, and far less than about South America. Much of the map of the continent remained a blank. The rivers, except for the Senegal and Gambia, had been unhelpful in giving access to the interior, but tracing their courses provided the pretext for several of the most important exploratory journeys. Scotsmen were especially prominent amongst the early explorers.

6.4.4.1 *The Nile valley* James Bruce, a Scottish laird who travelled through Ethiopia and the Sudan about 1770 with the source of the Blue Nile as his main objective, was amongst the earliest scientific explorers. He found the Abyssinian highlands divided between a number of independent feudal lords warring amongst themselves. In spite of the fact that immigrants from the Yemen had brought the art of writing to northern Ethiopia hundreds of years before the time of Christ, and the kings of Axum had been converted to Christianity by Byzantine priests as early as AD 300, the country was little more advanced than other parts of Africa. For nearly a thousand years Ethiopia had been isolated from the world, not only by its formidable mountain rim and desert bord-

ers, but also by the hostility of the Muslims and pagans surrounding it on all sides. Wars against Somalis and Arabs attacking with Turkish support in the sixteenth century had been successfully concluded, after much destruction, with the help of 400 musketeers sent by the King of Portugal. Then there was conflict between the Amhara and settled Oromo people in the Bale mountains to the south which weakened both of them and Oromo pastoralists (often called Galla) were able to occupy wide areas. Ethiopia fell into the depressed state in which Bruce found it: backward, disunited, and with rulers whose cruelty was extraordinarily revolting. The utter disregard for life and the sadistic caprices of chiefs are amongst the features of African life at the time that strike the readers of explorers' journals most forcibly, and this is particularly true of the accounts of Christian Abyssinia.

Ethiopia remained in a fragmented state until the middle of the nineteenth century, when the regional chiefs were conquered in turn by the Emperor Theodore. He died in 1868 after failing to repel a British expeditionary force led by Napier, but his new empire recovered from the attack in time to defeat the armies of Egypt pushing south from the Sudan. Later, by destroying an Italian army at Adowa, the Abyssinians preserved their independence of European rule for another forty years.

In 1798 Napoleon, the dynamic ruler of revolutionary France, burst into Egypt. For three hundred years the country had been ruled by a decadent oligarchy, the Mamluks and, under their rule, Egypt had fallen into a state of social degradation and industrial inertia, bypassed commercially, a backwater. The population of Cairo, the capital, was still a quarter of a million; a mere 8000 people found shelter in the ruins of Alexandria. French scholars swarmed over the pyramids and other ancient monuments and for some years afterwards there was a vogue for ancient Egyptian styles in French furniture and fashion. But Napoleon's army and his experts were stranded by Nelson's victory over the French fleet off Alexandria and had to find their way home as best they could.

Following the French invasion, Egypt acquired a new ruler, Mohamet Ali, who swept away the Mamluks. He and his successors as Viceroys, though still subject in theory to the Sultan in Constantinople, responded to the intrusion of revolutionary Europe by attempting to bring Egypt into the modern world by following the lead of the newly industrialized countries. The system of land tenure was transformed, peasants being granted ownership of their land and the larger properties being offered to individuals capable of developing them commercially. Alexandria, linked by canal to the Nile, was made the capital, roads were built, machinery and technicians imported from Europe, and the pace of industrialization was forced. By 1830 about 40 000 people were employed in factories producing textiles, sugar, paper, glass, and chemicals. Hundreds of students were sent to Europe and many more attended schools of medicine, engineering, chemistry, accountancy, and languages. Egypt by the middle of the nineteenth century was far ahead of any other African country and of many in Europe.

The Sudan came into existence as a political unit as a result of Mohamet Ali's need for gold, his expeditions up the Nile in search of it, and his subsequent ambitions for imperial expansion when the gold turned out to be a delusion. The first places to be occupied upstream of the first cataract at Aswan were settlements along the Nile in Nubia which had remained Christian until the fourteenth century. South of the desert and west of the Nile, Negro cultivators had been forced to retire to the Nuba mountains and the Jebel Marra by Arab pastoralists moving south from Egypt over the centuries (Figs. 4.2 and 6.3). East of the river, where the Arabs were less numerous, the pagan sultanate of Fung had arisen in the sixteenth century with its capital at Sennar on the Blue Nile. According to Bruce its population in 1700 had been a quarter of a million and it had trade links with Abyssinia, the Red Sea, and the state of Darfur that had arisen in the west. Southwards lay the Sudd and the pastoralist peoples, Shilluk, Dinka, and Nuer, and beyond them, in the savannalands and forest country over towards the Zaire watershed, were Negro cultivators including the Zande. By degrees these lands were brought into the Egyptian empire, in a state with Khartoum as its capital, at the confluence of the Blue and White Niles (Fig. 6.3).

The Fung and Darfur dynasties were swept away by the Egyptian conquest. Arab slave traders began to operate in the south, profiting from the protection afforded by some of the Egyptian administrators. The problems of the present-day Sudan Republic, which have involved in effect a state of war between north and south for most of the time since the country became independent in 1956, stem from this Egyptian colonial episode.

6.4.4.2 *East Africa* The Sultan of Muscat at the entrance to the Persian Gulf, whose ancestors had driven the Portuguese out of the east African ports about 1740, was recognized by Britain in 1822 as overlord of the east African coastlands. The Sultan had captured Mombasa and transferred his capital from Arabia to the island of Zanzibar. Some 30 km (20 mls) from the continental shore and with a good harbour, Zanzibar was in an excellent position for trading along the coast (Fig. 11.1). Cloves were introduced from the East Indies and soon became an important export, but for long their value was exceeded by that of slaves and ivory from the mainland.

The Arabs on the east coast, unlike the Europeans in the west, did not depend on African middlemen for their supplies of slaves, but sent caravans far inland themselves and by the middle of the century had established small settlements in places like Tabora in the centre of the Tanganyika plateau and Ujiji on the east side of Lake Tanganyika. The slaves brought to the coast were sold in the market at Zanzibar and exported to Turkey, Arabia, Persia, and India. The treaty of 1822, recognizing the Sultan, had been aimed at limiting the trade, particularly with India, and British naval patrols attempted to stop the traffic. Yet, in the middle of the century, about 15 000 slaves were still passing through the Zanzibar market every year, and as many were perishing on the way to the coast. Explorers like Speke and Livingstone, who followed the slaves' routes on their journeys in the interior, brought back to Europe horrifying accounts of the suffering and destruction they encountered and suggested that the raiding and enslaving went far towards explaining the emptiness of the lands they had traversed. Public opinion in Britain was aroused, and by 1873 naval and diplomatic pressure had eliminated the slave trade along the coast, though in the interior it was rooted out only at the end of the century, when Euro-

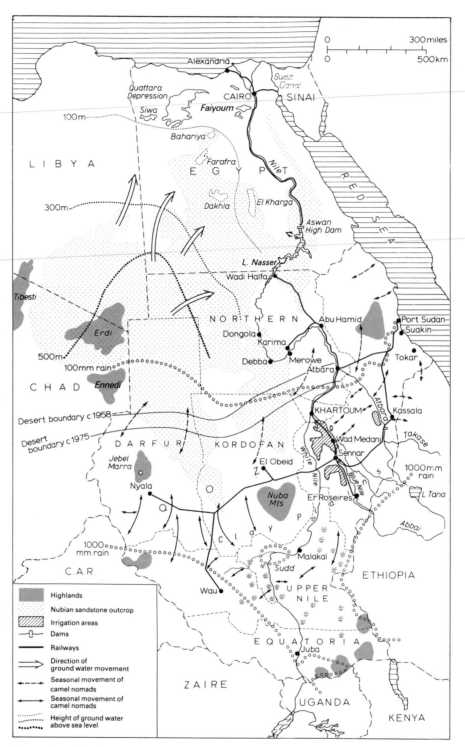

Fig. 6.3. *The Nile valley in Egypt and the Sudan. The Sudan came into existence as a result of Turco-Egyptian imperial expansion up the Nile valley in the nineteenth century. Evidence of the shift in the edge of the desert between 1958 and 1976 is not entirely convincing.*

A church built at Galula, a remote area in south-west Tanzania, early in this century by German Catholic missionaries.

pean administrations were properly established.

The early missionaries entered the country as explorers. Rebmann brought back news of a snow-capped mountain, Kilimanjaro; Krapf was the first European to see Mt Kenya. But Livingstone's travels in southern Africa were unrivalled; they were so extensive and revealing that he must be regarded as the greatest of all European explorers of Africa. By the last quarter of the century, missionary influence was being felt in many parts of east Africa. In Zanzibar, a cathedral church was built on the site of the slave market; French Catholic and English Protestant missionaries were received at the court of the Kabaka of Buganda, and German mission stations were established in the neighbourhood of Lake Tanganyika. Besides making converts and bringing back information about the interior, the Christian missions compiled dictionaries of the native

The interior of the church.

99

languages, introduced all manner of trade goods and, above all, brought schools and new ideas. Little though they may have wished it, their activity necessarily had political implications, and in many cases the flag of his country followed the missionary inland.

6.4.4.3 West Africa Tracing the course of the Niger to the sea was the initial stimulus for much of the exploration of west Africa. Mungo Park, travelling there under the auspices of the African Association, which had been founded in 1788 to promote the discovery of the interior parts of Africa, was able to show that Leo Africanus had been wrong in describing a great river at Timbuktu as flowing west (Figs. 1.24 and 5.6). The Niger flowed to the east, but where did it reach the sea? At the beginning of the nineteenth century it was still not realized that the Oil Rivers, where Europeans had been trading in slaves for centuries, were in fact a network of creeks forming the delta of the Niger. Park had drowned at the Bussa rapids (which are now submerged beneath the water held back by the dam at Kainji in western Nigeria) and when Oudney, Denham, and Clapperton were sent to the western Sudan zone by the British government in 1823, tracing the course of the Niger was still a pretext for their journey, though there was a greater anxiety in some quarters to secure treaties with the rulers of the interior both to put a stop to the slave trade and to stimulate legitimate commerce.

Clapperton's party followed an old caravan route across the Sahara from Tripoli to Borno (or Bornu) on the west side of Lake Chad. While Denham explored the country around the lake, Clapperton travelled west to Sokoto, which he reached safely in spite of the fact that the Shehu of Borno was at war with the Sultan of Sokoto (Figs. 4.2 and 5.4). The Sultan was the leader of a group of Fulani Muslim revivalists who had revolted in 1804 against the Hausa rulers of the ancient states which make up the western parts of present-day northern Nigeria. They had succeeded in taking over the reins of government and had pressed south and east, continuing to threaten Borno for several decades.

The country between the Hausa–Fulani states and Borno (where the majority of the people are Kanuri, not Hausa) and on their southern borders was devastated by slave-raiding, but the explorers brought back to Europe a vivid picture of active commercial life still managing to flourish in the western Sudan zone. 'Kano', Clapperton wrote,

may contain some 30 000 to 40 000 resident inhabitants of which more than one half are slaves. This number is exclusive of strangers who come here in crowds during the dry months from all parts of Africa, from the Mediterranean and the Mountains of the Moon, and from Sennar and Ashanti.

The market was well regulated, with fair prices and produce from the local country and afar displayed for sale. One large section was for slaves; 'slavery is here so common', writes Clapperton inconsequentially, 'that they always appear much happier than their masters'. The explorers were unable to secure the Sultan of Sokoto's signature to a treaty ending the trade and it continued until the end of the century. I recall meeting old people in Katsina in 1952 who had been slaves. The very detailed descriptions of the country between the Niger bend and Lake Chad in Barth's journals of his travels in the 1850s show that the heavily settled rural areas differed little in appearance from the present day, away from the main roads. The more remote pagan areas were always liable to be devastated by raiding horsemen and the villagers driven off into slavery.

Several states between Hausaland and the Atlantic coast, in the early nineteenth century, were under the rule of Fulani Muslim revivalists. In the Inland Delta region of the Niger, for instance, Fulani under Hamad Bari defeated the Bambara king of Segu, captured the ancient trading centre of Jenne, and occupied Timbuktu (Fig. 5.6). People were encouraged to come together into large villages for greater ease of political control. Long-distance migratory pastoralism was regulated, and rules were laid down about grazing on the delta. Towards the end of the century, three of the states were united under El Hadj Omar. When he died his successor was unable to resist growing French pressure from their old-established bases on the lower Senegal.

On the west coast, the slave trade was still vigorously alive in the 1840s and the number of slaves being carried overseas was increasing rather than diminishing, even though the trade had been made illegal for most north-west European countries for many years. A British naval patrol based on Freetown operated in west African waters specifically for the purpose of searching ships for slaves. More than 130 000 were found and released between 1825 and 1865, many in Freetown, but nearly 2 million are believed to have been exported in the same period, mainly to Brazil and Cuba. It was clear that more positive measures were needed.

In the 1830s, after the Lander brothers had at last shown that the Niger reached the sea at the Oil Rivers, two expeditions were sent up the Niger to trade, establish mission stations, and plant a model farm near the confluence of the Niger and Benue. The paddle-steamers used were more manœuvrable than sailing vessels,

but the enterprise failed, mainly because of many deaths from malaria. Some years later, however, when news arrived that Barth had reached the upper Benue, and an expedition under Baikie steamed far up the river to try to meet him, quinine was used and no one died. From that time forward the Niger could be used as a route to the interior; safe, except for the hostility of local people anxious to prevent trade in the interior falling into the hands of Europeans.

Legitimate trade along the west coast steadily expanded and by 1840 the palm-oil trade alone was worth a million pounds a year to British merchants. The French at that time were interested mainly in the Senegal area and as late as 1870 would have been willing to

The high country behind Alger and the northernmost ranges of the Atlas.

exchange French rights along the seaboard from Ivory Coast to the Cameroons for the Gambia. While other countries lost interest in west Africa, Britain's influence grew. British missionaries were active in Freetown, on the Gold Coast, and in Yorubaland, and their schools were largely responsible for spreading European ways of thought and political aspirations. On the Gold Coast, agreements made with chiefs of the coastal states led to intermittent conflict with the Ashanti further inland. Lagos was annexed in 1861 to stop slave-trading there. By 1870, Britain was too deeply involved in west African affairs to relinquish her interests, but she failed to take the opportunity to secure a monopoly along the coast, a momentous failure —or restraint—which has resulted in the present political and economic fragmentation of west Africa.

6.4.4.4 Central Africa

By 1870 the Great Lakes of east Africa had been reached by Europeans, the White Nile was known to emerge from Lake Victoria, and Livingstone had traced the southern headwaters of the Congo/Zaire. The falls on the lower river still prevented any expedition penetrating far upstream and all the centre of the basin remained unknown to European geographers until Stanley reached the Lualaba from the east coast and sailed down the Congo to Stanley Pool and found his way to the mouth of the river (Fig. 7.3).

The reports brought back by Stanley were of special interest to Leopold II, King of the Belgians, who was in the process of organizing expeditions to explore central Africa from a base in Zanzibar. Stanley met the King and agreed to lead an expedition to build a road from Stanley Pool to the sea and open up the Congo basin. Within five years, treaties had been made with hundreds of native chiefs, five steamers were sailing on the river above the falls, and the Congo Free State had begun to take shape.

6.4.4.5 North-west Africa

The three Turkish vilayets in the Maghreb, known as the Barbary States, had long been notorious for their privateers, who attacked shipping and enslaved their captives. Diplomatic pressure was ineffective in securing safe passage for ships, and in 1830 the French used this situation as a pretext for landing troops in Algeria.

The French government was not anxious to

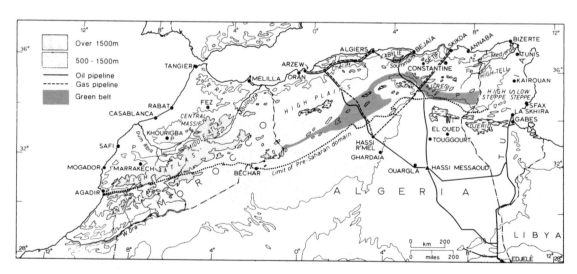

Fig. 6.4. *The Maghreb, the Atlas region on the north-west side of the Sahara, was colonized by the French between 1835 and 1962. The Green Belt is a zone being planted with trees, mainly by the Algerian army, in an effort to prevent the desert encroaching northwards. Fe—iron, P—phosphates. Pipelines lead oil from the Edjelé and Hassi Messaoud region and natural gas from Hassi R'Mel to the coast of Algeria and Tunisia.*

encourage European settlement, but settlers arrived none the less from Spain, Italy, and Malta, as well as from France. For their own safety they established themselves not on isolated farms but in villages and towns scattered over the coastal plains of Oran, Algiers, Philippeville (now Skikda) and Bone (Annaba), around Setif, and in the Cheliff valley (Fig. 6.4). After a time the French government found itself in a position where it had to support the newcomers against the indigenous Muslims. Taking advantage of their privileged position before the law, the settlers acquired more and more land. The frontier of European settlement advanced south, beyond the Tell mountains and on to the interior steppes, the native Algerian population being forced to accommodate itself to the intruders by retiring to the Kabylie, Aures, and other highland retreats. Before long the settlers, *colons*, acquired Algerian nationalist sentiments and in France, Algeria became officially Algérie française. Whenever the home country found itself in difficulties, as in the revolutions of 1848 and 1871, the *colons* seized the opportunity to exert their influence locally, and even rejected particular individuals sent as governors from France. However, they were too near the seat of government in France and too aware of the strength of the Muslim majority to break away in the style of the Boers in South Africa. After a thousand years of middle-eastern predominance, the Maghreb thus came to experience ever closer and more burdensome relations with southern Europe until independence came in the early 1960s.

THE COLONIAL ERA AND THE COMING OF INDEPENDENCE

7.1 The partition of Africa

Most African states as we see them on the map at the present day first took shape at the end of the nineteenth century, when the continent was rapidly carved up by European powers and shared amongst them. Why this imperialist scramble took place is still not altogether clear; even some of the statesmen involved at the time looked upon it as rather absurd. No general theory fully explains the partition. British governments were more concerned with events elsewhere, in India, Canada, and Australia, where British investments were far greater and prospects for the future were very much more attractive. At first, governments had no intention of procuring territory and becoming encumbered with the costs of administering unhealthy and relatively unproductive lands. However, a number of pressure groups, including manufacturers and missionaries, were pressing for intervention and as time went on local European consular and military interference in native affairs increased.

A good deal seems to stem from events in Egypt. Mohammet Ali and his successors had attempted to force development there in the same way that it was to be attempted in parts of tropical Africa more than a century later. Egyptian development had faltered and failed to take off into sustained growth. Inflation and mismanagement at home prevented Egyptian manufacturers from selling abroad. At the same time, pressure from European countries, notably Great Britain, forced the Viceroy in Alexandria to comply with agreements made with his Turkish Sultan in Constantinople which permitted foreign traders to sell anywhere within the Ottoman dominions. Egyptian factories, thereby deprived of tariff protection against foreign competition, were unable to produce at a profit and few survived.

The attempt to leap from a subsistence to a complex economy failed. Egypt acquired an export-oriented economy based not on manufactures but on cotton. Cotton had been grown in Egypt since early Christian times but had been of little commercial value until, in 1816, a French technician called Jumel happened to notice, growing in a garden in Cairo, a cotton plant with extraordinarily long fibres. Other plants were bred from its seed, their seeds were multiplied and distributed to farmers, and the production of long-staple cotton grew from 20 tonnes of lint in 1820 to 1000 tonnes in 1835. The crop did not interfere with wheat and barley because it was planted in March and April after they had been harvested. It grew through the summer and needed watering before the arrival of the flood in July. So work began in the delta to store the water from the flood and deliver it to the cottonfields in the early summer. This was done by building earthern banks across the Nile distributaries each year as the flood was falling and leading the water accumulating behind the banks along canals to the fields.

By 1861 cotton was providing over a third of Egypt's export earnings. When supplies of cotton to the world market from the Southern States were interrupted by the American Civil War, Egypt profited greatly. It was able to contribute £18 million, about a third of the total cost, towards the construction of the Suez Canal. But the Civil War came to an end, the price of cotton fell sharply, and the Viceroy of the time, the Khedive Ishmael, soon found himself paying interest rates of 12 to 26.5 per cent on loans for railways and other projects that had been started when there was plenty of money available.

Too much had been started in too short a time with insufficient internal savings, and too much reliance had been placed on foreign businessmen and bankers. The British government bought a majority of the shares in the Canal from the Egyptian government in 1874. In spite of this, the external debt became unsupportable and in 1878 an Anglo-French Commission inquiring into the financial situation by degrees took control of the Egyptian treasury. The Khedive was deposed and when in 1882 'proto-nationalists' mounted a violent demonstration in Alexandria against European interference, a British warship opened fire while the French warships sailed away. It was an incident rather than a premeditated action, but the British government found itself in a situation where it could see no alternative but to occupy Egypt.

At the same time that the Egyptian government was collapsing and its administration was being rendered ineffective, a revolt in the Sudan gathered strength and swept away Egyptian rule. The *jihad* was inspired by an Islamic revivalist leader, el-Mahdi, who established his seat of government in Omdurman, across the White Nile from Khartoum (Fig. 6.3). El-Mahdi soon died and his successors were the Khalifs whose regime persisted for about 15 years, until 1898 when the Sudan was reconquered by combined British and Egyptian forces. Henceforth, throughout the first half of the twentieth century, both Sudan and Egypt were effectively subject to Britain.

In many respects, events in Africa were side-issues of internal politics and rivalry between the 'Great Powers' in Europe. The early 1880s saw the end of a period of Anglo-French collaboration in overseas affairs. The French were pursuing an increasingly aggressive policy abroad in an attempt to distract attention from troubles at home and, after the British occupation of Egypt in 1882, they felt they were in a position to apply pressure in Africa with relative impunity. British influence in the critical coastal zones had been growing stronger over the years; in the early 1880s French and German activity also increased in these areas and

friction between them grew. When Leopold's ambitions in the Congo conflicted with those of France, Britain, and Portugal, a pretext was provided for Bismarck, Chancellor of Germany, to call a conference of the powers involved. At the Berlin Conference of 1884–85 it was agreed that new annexations on the African coast were not to be recognized as valid unless they were accompanied by effective occupation. The Conference marks the beginning of a colonial era that was to last into the second half of the twentieth century (Fig. 7.1 (a)).

In west Africa the French advanced rapidly east from Senegal, engulfing the remains of El Hadj Omar's empire and pushing on to Lake Chad. Their advance barred the way to British expansion into the interior and prepared the foundations for modern Muslim states such as the new Mali. Behind the Guinea coast Britain had already gained the most productive territories; the French merely prevented them from spreading laterally, by expanding into the interior from their coastal bases at Conakry, Abidjan, and Porto Novo. Upstream of Bathurst, which had long been in British hands, the Gambia was confined to a narrow strip on either side of the river which was consequently no longer able to serve its natural hinterland. Sierra Leone blocked direct access to the sea from the interior of French Guinea. The British penetrating inland from Accra and the Germans from Lomé agreed on a frontier between Gold Coast and Togoland that split both the Ewe and Dagomba peoples (Fig. 4.2). British trading companies on the lower Niger and Benue united to resist competition from other countries and managed to secure sole trading rights in the region from the Sultan of Sokoto. The British government, mainly to prevent the French taking over the lower Niger and raising a tariff barrier, declared a Protectorate over the region and handed it over to be ruled by the Royal Niger Company.

In west-central Africa, Britain, Germany, and France sought access to Lake Chad, which was one of the few definite features appearing on maps of the interior and which was thought to have greater potentialities than in fact it possessed. From a short coastal strip in the Cameroons, where Britain had long been influential, Germany rapidly acquired a large triangle stretching inland to the lake, and French expeditions pushing north from the forests of the

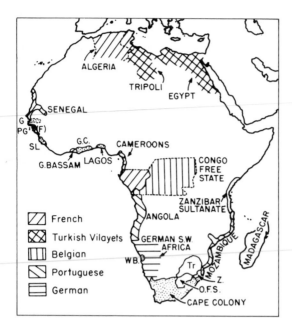

Fig. 7.1 (a). *Africa after the Berlin Conference.* B—Basutoland, E—Eritrea, G—Gambia, GC—Gold Coast, K—Kamerun, L—Liberia, N—Nyasaland, NR—Northern Rhodesia, OFS—Orange Free State, PG—Portuguese Guinea, RM—Rio Muni, SL—Sierra Leone, SM—Spanish Morocco, SR—Southern Rhodesia, Sw—Swaziland, T—Tunisia, Tr—Transvaal, U—Uganda, WB—Walvis Bay, Z—Zululand.

Fig. 7.1 (b). *Africa at the outbreak of the First World War (key as for Fig. 7.1 (a)).*

Congo at Brazzaville linked up with their compatriots advancing across the desert from Senegal and Algeria. In the Congo Free State, exploration and occupation went on simultaneously, with the Belgians keeping Mahdists from the Sudan out of the Uelé basin in the north-east and forestalling the British in the south by acquiring Katanga, now called Shaba, an area which is outstandingly rich in economic minerals.

South Africa shared in the revolution (Fig. 6.2). Diamonds were found near Hopetown, south of Kimberley, in 1867. Prices of agricultural produce in the neighbourhood soared as Africans came out of their reserves to earn money in the mines. Exports trebled in value, capital was attracted from abroad, and a railway was soon built from Cape Town to Kimberley. Rhodes, Beit, and Barnato gained control of the mines by buying out small opera-

tors, and when gold was discovered in the Transvaal in 1886 the financiers of Kimberley were able to supply or attract the capital required for its exploitation. Gold-seekers from Britain flocking into the Boer republics soon outnumbered the early settlers, and tension between the two peoples—which eventually led to the Anglo-Boer War—gradually increased. By the end of the century the Rand was producing a quarter of the world's gold supply, and the Boers and the British were at war.

The Germans established themselves in south-west Africa. In 1886, before they could link up with the Boers in the Transvaal, Rhodes, who was by then the Prime Minister of Cape Colony, annexed Bechuanaland. He thereby succeeded in securing a British routeway to the north along the tracks that had been followed a few decades earlier by the missionaries Moffat and Livingstone. The chief of the Matabele was persuaded to grant mining concessions to Rhodes and by 1890, when the British South Africa Company assumed responsibility for administering the lands north of the Limpopo, British influence extended north to the headwaters of the Congo and the far northern end of Lake Nyasa (Malawi).

The French had gained an early foothold in Madagascar and in spite of a British presence occupied the whole of the island in 1883. French activities on the mainland of east Africa were limited to Djibouti in Somaliland. Britain and Germany, both operating from Zanzibar, were the main competitors, and, in contrast to the situation in west Africa, government interest was greater than that of the merchants. German claims to the land south of Lake Victoria were recognized by Britain in 1886, partly to gain support over Egypt, and a few years later the Imperial British East Africa Company took over the administration of the territory stretching from the lake north and east to the indeterminate borders of Sudan and Ethiopia.

The Italians arrived late on the scene. Britain and Germany warned them off the Sultan of Zanzibar's southern possessions and they proceeded to occupy the desert coasts of Eritrea and Somaliland. A resounding defeat at Adowa in 1896 halted their advance on to the Abyssinian highlands, and it was not resumed until 1935 when Ethiopia, though a member of the League of Nations, was conquered by Fascist Italy.

7.2 The beginning of the colonial era

By 1900, the continent had been partitioned, only Morocco, Libya, Ethiopia, and Liberia remaining independent (Fig. 7.1 (b)). The new colonial governments of the European powers were beginning to delimit frontiers, assess the economic resources of their new possessions and organize the administration of the African peoples they had come to rule. They stamped out the slave trade and after some initial disputes brought peace to a continent that was sorely in need of a period of tranquillity.

The nineteenth century had been a time of wars and uncertainty associated with the impact of Europe. Many pastoral peoples had lately suffered from rinderpest; various epidemics such as sleeping sickness, measles, and smallpox had caused much loss of life; black military states had terrorized their neighbours; at the end of the century, severe droughts afflicted many areas. When there were rebellions in German East Africa they were crushed with marked severity. In the Congo, Leopold's administration gained notoriety for its harsh treatment of native labour. But for most Africans conditions probably improved under the new order; people began to move down onto the plains from mountain refuges and to travel around more freely.

There was little thought at this time of systematic economic development of the new colonies. Goverments had far less control over world capital than they have today, and the bankers and financiers were unwilling to invest in countries that seemed to be so poor and unprofitable, except for South Africa. Local colonial governments were chronically short of cash and relied on revenues derived from import duties and head taxes. On the west coast, where people had long been trading with Europe, exports of groundnuts from Senegal and palm-oil from the forests further south steadily increased. Cocoa was introduced to the Gold Coast from Fernando Po in 1879 and within a few decades the local people had planted tens of millions of trees, and exports of cocoa exceeded those of gold in value. But the continental interior remained scarcely touched until communications improved, allowing bulky produce to be exported economically.

7.3 Railway construction

The railways were planned with various political and economic ends in view. Their importance lies not simply in the effects they had on transport costs but also on the fact that they explain the location of most of the present urban centres in Africa. The fastest growing towns were those chosen to be the ports, coastal or riverine, at the termini of the railways. They were the obvious centres for trade and commerce and in many cases they were chosen to be colonial capitals and remain the capitals of the independent states of today.

Many of the earliest railways were built from coastal ports to new mining centres inland, notably in southern Africa (Fig. 7.2). Even in these cases, political advantage was involved as well as economic interests. The first lines to the Rand goldfields were from Durban and Port Elizabeth, both in British territories (Fig. 6.2). The Boer republic of the Transvaal therefore gave financial backing to a line reaching the sea at Lourenço Marques (now Maputo) in Portuguese East Africa. It refused to allow the line from Cape Town to Kimberley to be extended north through the Transvaal, and eventually the railway to Rhodesia was laid across the fringe of Bechuanaland, reaching Bulawayo in 1902. Over the next few years it was extended to Wankie, with the prospect of traffic from the coalfields, to Broken Hill (now Kabwe in Zambia) where lead and zinc had been discovered, and finally to the enormously rich deposits of copper extending from Northern Rhodesia across the frontier of the Belgian Congo into Katanga (Fig. 9.2).

In the Congo, the railways were designed originally to supplement the navigable reaches of the river with its main tributaries (Fig. 7.3). First the essential link was constructed from the seaport of Matadi to Leopoldville (now Kinshasa) above the falls, a difficult task for which

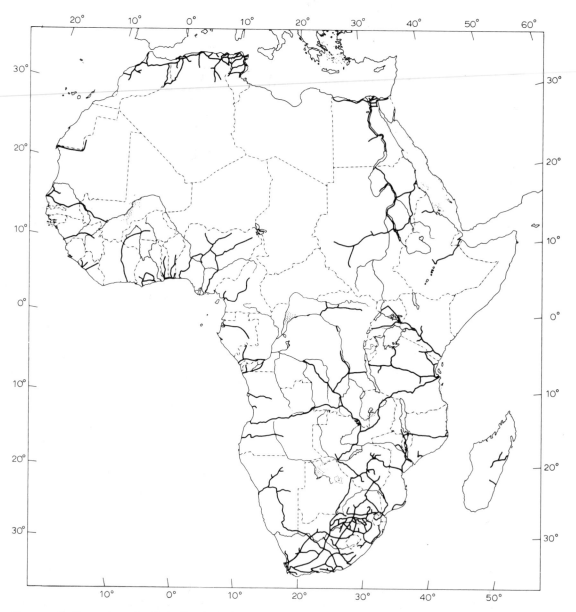

Fig. 7.2. *Railways in 1987. Only South Africa and Tunisia can be said to have railway networks.*

forced labour was employed. Thereafter additional track was added so as to reduce the number of switches needed from rail to river and back to rail, especially between Katanga (now Shaba) and Kinshasa.

In Nigeria, reliance on river transport diminished at an early stage. At first, Baro on the Niger was visualized as the outlet for the north of the country but within a few years, before the First World War, Kano was connected by rail right through to the coast at Lagos by a line crossing the river at Jebba and with the line to

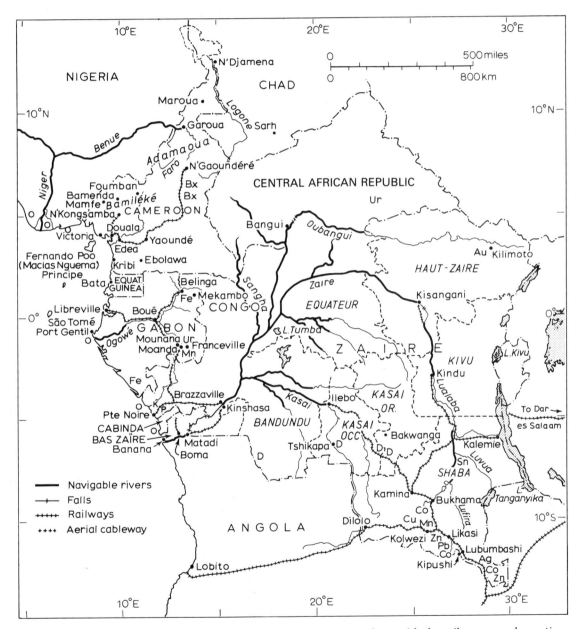

Fig. 7.3. *West equatorial Africa. River transport remains important here with the railways supplementing it, especially where rapids prevent use of the waterways. The line from the mining areas of Shaba to the coast at Lobito is not in use, because of conflict in Angola and poor relations between Angola and Zaire.*

St Louis, the early French settlement near the mouth of the Senegal river.

Baro relegated to a spur running down to the Niger (Figs. 5.4 (a) and (b)). Traffic on the Niger and Benue rivers remained moderately heavy but most of the groundnuts from the Kano area and tin from the Jos Plateau took the direct rail route to Lagos. In Gold Coast, a railway built primarily to serve the goldfields at Tarkwa was extended to Kumasi and provided carriage to the coast for Ashanti cocoa (Fig. 11.2).

An early line from St Louis to Dakar greatly stimulated groundnut production in Senegal and proved to be a profitable enterprise (Fig. 10.7 (a)), but other French lines directed from ports on the coast towards the Inland Niger Delta were planned in the first place for rather vague strategic purposes and have always lost money.

In east Africa, Germany and Britain were both anxious to establish rail links between the coast and Lake Victoria. The British line from Mombasa to Kisumu was the first to reach the lake (Fig. 11.1). As much of its total length of 1422 km (884 mls) ran across country unproductive at the time, there appeared to be little prospect of it paying and it was partly to alleviate the financial burden that white settlement on the Kenya highlands was encouraged a few years later. Meanwhile, the German line inland from Tanga towards Lake Victoria was left uncompleted to serve the fertile highlands of Meru and Kilimanjaro while efforts were

concentrated on a line further south from Dar es Salaam following the old slave route to Tabora and on to Kigoma on Lake Tanganyika.

The new railways and the steamers on the main lakes and rivers reduced the costs of transport in the interior to a fraction of those for head-loading or rolling barrels, which in many cases were the only alternatives. Long-distance trading in bulky goods suddenly became profitable and agricultural production for export in the interior was greatly stimulated. Furthermore, telegraph lines alongside the railways allowed administrative instructions and business orders to be transmitted rapidly from the coast instead of being carried by runners. The ports served by the railways had to be extended to cope with the new bulky traffic generated, while others with restricted hinterlands fell into disuse. Large numbers of Africans who had never before worked for wages were employed by the railway contractors as labourers and learned to use and need cloth, matches, and metal goods. At the same time, locally produced iron work, pottery, and textiles were unable to compete with imported manufactured goods from Europe, thereby removing from many African artisans their sources of income and making them entirely dependent on the produce of their farms and thus more at risk from climatic hazards than they had previously been.

Tanga from the air.

Kabara, the port for Timbuktu on the Niger in Mali, with a river steamer made in East Germany in the background and slabs of Saharan salt in the foreground. There was a socialist government in power at the time (1969), and amongst the cargo was Cuban sugar and Czechoslovakian beer.

7.4 The First World War and its aftermath

By 1914 France had established a protectorate over Morocco, and Italy had created a colony, Libya, out of Tripolitania and Cyrenaica. The desert boundaries to the south of both countries were vague and remain a source of conflict to this day (Fig. 7.1 (b)).

South of the Sahara, most of the colonies had been pacified and organized into new administrative units which sometimes, but not always, conformed with tribal and other traditional areas. Tribes and villages found their boundaries had suddenly become more rigid than hitherto. In some colonies, notably the Rhodesias, Tanganyika, and Kenya, Africans found that land they had hitherto regarded as available for cultivation and grazing had been occupied and fenced by European settlers. Taxation gradually became more effective and to earn cash to pay their taxes people had little option but to work on European farms or in the mines, or to grow crops for sale. European codes of law, including land law, were applied in the towns, while native law and custom continued to apply in the rural areas. Roads were built to link the main settlements to the railways and navigable rivers; traditional markets that happened to be well placed grew in importance; quite new market towns developed.

For six years during and after the First World War progress was limited. German colonies in the west were occupied by French and British troops after relatively little fighting, but the

Woman selling salt and rice in the traditional fashion in a Timbuktu market.

campaign in Tanganyika dragged on for years, involving only small forces, but causing much general destruction and heavy loss of life, particularly amongst native porters, in country which had yet to recover from earlier upheavals. Veterinary work was neglected and once again rinderpest spread through much of east Africa.

After the war the German colonies were administered by individual allied powers as League of Nations Mandates; Togoland and Kamerun were both subdivided between Britain and France; in east Africa, Tanganyika became a British Mandate, while Ruanda-Urundi was ruled by Belgium. South-west Africa became effectively part of South Africa.

7.5 The inter-war years

The 1920s saw a general improvement in conditions. Prices for agricultural products were rela-

tively high, and some territories such as the Gold Coast embarked on ambitious development projects. Commodity prices slumped with the general contraction of world trade between 1930 and 1936; government revenues shrank and, since a large proportion was required to maintain administrative services and pay the interest on loans for railway construction, programmes for expansion were curtailed. Roads, water supplies and schools were needed everywhere; the factories of Europe needed orders for equipment, but economic development practically ceased.

In some fields, steady, unspectacular progress continued. European District Officers, touring their districts on horseback and in boats, supervised native courts and treasuries, made maps and organized the building of bridges and market places. Technical officers, though pitifully few in number, began to make an impression on the control of disease amongst people and livestock. Missionaries built churches and helped to collect support for them by building schools and hospitals as well. Education was largely in the hands of the Christian missions. Educated Africans in small numbers were reaching universities in Europe and the USA and joining the professions, especially the law. As the possibility of acquiring wealth and power equal to that of the Europeans became more apparent, so did the political fermentation begin which was to culminate in the post-Second World War struggles for independence.

In each colony much depended on the size of the white-settler element and the policies followed by the administering power.

Algeria was regarded by the French as being a part of France. Non-Europeans were treated as French subjects, but as French citizens only if they chose to live by the French civil code of law in preference to Muslim law and custom. In general, French rule was repressive not only in Algeria but also in the neighbouring protectorates, where the Muslims were nominally the subjects of the Bey of Tunis or the Sultan of Morocco. In these two countries traditional society was subjected to lesser pressures than in Algeria, but French control was strict. Spain's authority extended over the Rio de Oro in the western Sahara and also over the northern portion of Morocco, though it always had difficulty in exerting its will over the freedom-loving Berbers of the Rif highlands.

The relaxation of British control over Egypt at the end of the First World War was one of the first instances of a liberal response by an imperial power to nationalist agitation. By the Anglo-Egyptian Treaty of 1936 the country's independence was acknowledged, but as the prospect of war loomed again Britain's continued concern for the Suez Canal route to India caused her to reimpose her effective authority over the Egyptian government for several more years.

In the Union of South Africa nearly everything achieved in agriculture, mining, transport, and industry was the result of European skill, capital, and organization combined with non-European labour. Africans were prohibited from owning land except in the reserves, which formed only 13 per cent of the country. Laws restricted their movements and prevented them from performing a large num-

ber of skilled jobs, and while class distinction throughout the world was weakening, South African life became increasingly based on colour distinction. Nevertheless the Whites could claim that standards of living amongst Bantu in the Union were higher than anywhere else in Africa and could point to immigration from surrounding countries as an indicator of worse living conditions outside South Africa.

In Southern Rhodesia (now Zimbabwe), the trend of events after it became a colony governed by the white minority in 1923 was similar to that in South Africa. Separate European and native areas were delimited, the former close to the railway from Bulawayo to Salisbury (now Harare), on the best land and with reliable rainfall. Africans in towns were required to carry passes and were discriminated against in industry, but policies were generally more liberal than in the Transvaal.

Nearly 44 000 km² (17 000 mls²) of land in the Kenya Highlands were reserved for European ownership. Whereas in Southern Rhodesia there could be no question but that the Whites intended to remain in control, Kenya was recognized by British governments as being primarily African territory, where the interests of Africans must eventually be paramount.

British policy in Africa was not based on any general theory of colonialism, and the pattern of government varied widely according to local circumstances. In territories with few white settlers, much reliance was placed on traditional native rulers in both the administration of justice and local government affairs. The same was true to a lesser degree in other territories, because it was the only way in which small numbers of Europeans could rule large numbers of Africans cheaply. Whereas the French did away with the higher traditional offices and operated through local chiefs, the British often retained the full traditional hierarchy and confirmed the native rulers in their powers. On the other hand the British have been criticized as having been less willing than some other Europeans to accept educated Africans on an equal footing socially.

While each British territory had a good deal of responsibility for the policies. it adopted, policy in French territories was directed from Paris. Each French colony was represented in both houses of the French parliament and was regarded as an integral part of the French

Union. Within each colony government was strongly centralized and authoritarian. More attention was paid to the towns by French administrations than to rural areas; the reverse seems to have been the case in British territories. The underlying French philosophy was to regard the colony as actually or potentially a part of the motherland; the African was to be turned into a black Frenchman. The results were to be apparent in the political scene after independence, with many African leaders in francophone countries, especially Senegal and the Ivory Coast, being strongly influenced by their experience in French public life.

The Belgians were able to concentrate on governing their one great colony, a hundred times the size of the mother country, and they ruled it in a businesslike way, in effect from Brussels. Educated Africans were given special privileges, but there were very few of them because little attempt was made to develop higher education. The emphasis was placed on technical training. Native institutions were carefully studied and, where possible, supported. Little attempt was made to educate the people politically; such luxuries, it was argued, could come later when the economic base had been prepared and the people were ready for it. Standards of living in Katanga and the large towns elsewhere came to be higher than in most other parts of tropical Africa, thanks to the copper, gold, and diamond mines. But African leaders remained inexperienced; they were known only to their own tribal groups and lacked national support when the time came for independence to be granted.

Portuguese policy was somewhat similar to that followed by France, but more extreme. There was a desire to produce a small native elite owing allegiance to Portugal as the source of civilization. Mozambique and Angola were looked upon as provinces of Portugal, closely linked to the mother country, and any growth of national feeling was deliberately prevented by allowing political rights and privileges to neither Portuguese nor Africans.

7.6 The coming of independence

7.6.1 The Second World War and its sequel

Colonial rule seemed well established in Africa in 1939 (Fig. 7.4 (a)). Only the Union of South Africa and Egypt were independent states; Southern Rhodesia had dominion status, which gave it a good deal of local autonomy under the British Crown. Liberia, though politically independent, relied heavily on the great rubber plantations of the Firestone Rubber Company, and its voice was unheard in international affairs. The Ethiopian Empire was being modernized by its Italian conquerors, who saw themselves as successors of the Romans. In many of the tropical dependencies limited numbers of Africans were gaining experience in legislative assemblies, but as these were dominated by European officials or settlers and had little real authority, the African members were often looked upon by their compatriots as tools of the white man.

As the European nations rearmed, prices of tropical produce rose uncertainly, but before new development projects could gain momentum the war supervened. France and Belgium were occupied by Germany and in consequence their possessions in Africa enjoyed somewhat greater responsibility for their own affairs than hitherto. Italian armies were defeated in Ethiopia and Libya, and German armies in Algeria, Tunisia, and Libya were eventually squeezed out of Africa between Americans advancing from the west and British from the east.

While shortage of shipping space and the blockade of continental Europe reduced the demand for African agricultural produce, mines yielding tin, copper, and other metals vital in wartime rapidly increased production. Manufacturing in the Union of South Africa and in Egypt expanded enormously and the value of Southern Rhodesian manufactures multiplied five times in the 1940s. Many airfields were built to serve supply routes to the Middle East from across the Atlantic. In general, however, economies stagnated for lack of skilled technicians and equipment, and progress remained slow for several years after the end of the war for the same reasons.

Political development accelerated during and after the war. Africans who joined the allied forces were promised better conditions after the war. They fought in Ethiopia against the Italians and helped to defeat them, and saw service in India, where the movement towards independence was far advanced. In west Africa the circulation of nationalist newspapers

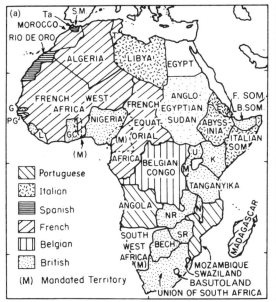

Fig. 7.4 (a). *Africa at the outbreak of the Second World War. B—Benin, Bu—Burundi, CAR—Central African Republic, D—Djibouti, EG—Equatorial Guinea, GB—Guinea Bissau, Gh—Ghana, IC—Ivory Coast, K—Kenya, Le—Lesotho, M—Malawi, R—Rwanda, S—Senegal, Ta—Tangier, BF—Burkina Faso, Zim—Zimbabwe. For other abbreviations see p106.*

Fig. 7.4 (b) *Africa in 1993 (key as for Fig. 7.4 (a)). CV—Cape Verde Is, CI—Comoro Is, Re—Réunion, STP—Sao Tome and Principe.*

increased and demands for independence swelled in volume. To most Europeans it still seemed that several decades of economic and political growth lay ahead before Africans could be in a position to govern their own countries, and many of the African intelligentsia seem to have thought likewise.

In 1948 riots in Gold Coast instigated by ex-servicemen and the nationalist party received much popular support. They were followed by a British government commission of inquiry that recommended far-reaching constitutional changes, giving much greater responsibility to Africans. At the same time African affairs began to attract attention in the United Nations, where a number of Asian states which had recently thrown off European rule were itching to fight imperialism wherever it persisted. In 1952, after Britain had removed its troops from the Suez Canal zone, Egyptian army officers overthrew King Farouk, the suc-

cessor of the Khedives, and established a revolutionary government. It was a precedent that was to be followed in many Muslim states and later in newly independent African countries. However, the event that can be identified as effectively marking the end of the colonial period was the 'Suez Affair' of 1956.

Colonel Nasser, who had become head of the Egyptian military government, recognized the urgency of increasing production to feed Egypt's growing population and decided that a scheme to build a great new dam at Aswan was the answer. He entered into negotiations with the United States of America and other western countries to obtain funds and equipment. However, various difficulties arose over Egypt's intention to purchase arms from Communist Czechoslovakia, and America withdrew its offers of assistance. Nasser responded by nationalizing the Suez Canal, which was still owned by shareholders including the British and French governments. Income from the Canal had been rising rapidly as a result of the increasing volumes of oil from the (Persian/Arab) Gulf being shipped to Europe, and it seemed to Nasser that this was his best hope of obtaining the funds he needed for building the dam. Egypt had been nominally at war with Israel since 1947 and now the three countries, Britain, France, and Israel, conspired to co-operate in seizing control of the Canal. The Israelis successfully advanced across Sinai while British and French troops landed in the Canal Zone by sea and air. However, pressure from both the USSR and the USA forced them to withdraw ignominiously and Nasser was left holding the Canal. The Russians agreed to assist in the construction of the dam and it was successfully completed in the mid-1960s.

The former Italian colonies, Libya and Ethiopia, had acquired independence by the early 1950s. Somalia emerged in 1960 with the union of the former Italian and British Somalilands. Sudan, which had been at least in name an Anglo-Egyptian condominium, became independent, as did the French Protectorates of Morocco and Tunisia. The British and French governments accepted that no profit or prestige was to be gained from resisting nationalist movements once they had gained momentum with popular backing. Gold Coast and Nigeria saw the road to freedom stretching broadly ahead and the reins of government were handed over in an agreed manner. The main difficulties arose in colonies where there was a large and vocal white-settler element.

7.6.2 White settlers and strife

In south-central Africa, in spite of misgivings by the people and governments of the countries concerned, the Rhodesias and Nyasaland were brought together in a federal state (Fig. 9.2). There were hopes that the complementary qualities of its components would produce a strong economic unit, with Nyasaland's abundant manpower, Northern Rhodesia's mineral resources, and Southern Rhodesia's skilled and experienced Whites coming together to the advantage of all of them. But the hopes were never realized. Within ten years, by the end of 1963, Nyasaland and Northern Rhodesia had asserted their independence of white domination and become independent Malawi and Zambia.

In east Africa, white settlers were farming very small areas in Uganda and Tanganyika, and government was firmly in the hands of the British Colonial Office. In Kenya, on the other hand, much of the most productive land was in the hands of commercial companies and a few thousand settlers from Britain and South Africa, while Kikuyu tribal lands nearby were becoming increasingly overpopulated. What is more, new settlers had arrived in the years following the Second World War and the voice of the Europeans was heard more loudly in government than that of the Africans. Anti-White emotion erupted in 1952 in the form of the Mau-Mau rebellion, which was suppressed only after some years of military action and civil unrest, and on the clear understanding that majority rule for the Africans was not to be long delayed.

The situation in Algeria was much more serious. Its ties with France, like its geographical position, were much closer. A million Whites were living in the country, constituting about a tenth of the population. Of the Muslim majority, some had much to lose from a diminution of French influence, and the aim of nationalists had been equality of Europeans and Muslims rather than independence. When large-scale violence at length broke out in 1954, the struggle was long and virulent, involving large numbers of French troops and the supply of arms to the Muslims from their newly independent neighbours to east and west. The prize at stake was increased by the discovery in 1956 of oil in the Algerian Sahara.

War in Indo-China and then in Algeria, following the experience of the Second World War, was holding France back economically and emotionally. Eventually, in 1958, there was a change in the regime with the return to power of Charles de Gaulle. The African colonies were given the opportunity to decide whether to remain within the French Union, with the prospect of receiving economic assistance, or of becoming fully independent. Only Guinea chose the latter course and for the next twenty years attempted, rather unsuccessfully, to develop as a non-aligned, socialist state. Algeria won its independence in 1962, but the fierceness of European reaction within the country and the equally violent response of the Muslims were such as to force the settlers to abandon their farms and the city-dwellers as well to decide that life in France, Spain, or Italy offered more to them than would independent Algeria. Within a year or two the European population of Algeria dropped from over a million to less than 80 000, that of Morocco from

450 000 to half that number, and of Tunisia from a quarter of a million to 125 000. It seems likely that as many Europeans emigrated from Africa in the early 1960s as had ever gone there to settle.

The Congo (Zaire) demanded independence and, all unprepared, was granted it by Belgium with a delay of only a few weeks, to fall into a state of anarchy from which it has yet to recover. A state of civil war which had existed in the Sudan Republic between the Arab north and the black south since independence in 1956 was interrupted in the 1970s but has since been resumed. The Mali Federation comprising the former French colonies of Senegal and French Soudan separated into its component parts a few months after its formation, the name Mali being retained by the Soudan. A Central African Federation intended to include the former colonies of French Equatorial Africa—Oubangui-Chari, Chad, French Congo, and Gabon—never came to birth, though Oubangui-Chari assumed the name Central African Republic. Uganda and Kenya patched up their internal divisions, at least temporarily, and followed Tanganyika into independence. In Nigeria, the largest of all the African states in terms of population, tribal differences allied with political rivalry led first to the division of the Western Region into two parts and then to the overthrow of the Federal government in 1966 and the murder of some of its ministers, the substitution of a military government, Ibo pogroms in the north, and civil war between Ibo Biafra and the rest of the country.

By the end of 1963, the only African countries of any size remaining under European rule were those bordering South Africa, by this time a Republic outside the Commonwealth. Marxist freedom fighters forced the Portuguese to grant independence to their colonies, Mozambique, Angola, and Guinea in 1975; most of the settlers, numbering in all about half a million, returned to Portugal. Resistance to the revolutionary governments in Angola and Mozambique by guerrilla forces was supported by the South African government and persisted into the late 1980s. The Whites in Southern Rhodesia responded to pressure from Britain for greater African representation in government by unilaterally declaring independence (UDI) in 1965. Sanctions imposed by countries other than South Africa were not very effective and

the illegal Rhodesian regime persisted for 15 years until it was eventually brought down by black guerrillas. Renamed Zimbabwe, the country gained its independence under a government elected by both Blacks and Whites.

A century after the Berlin Conference, all of the African countries were under the rule of African governments, with only two exceptions—South Africa and its dependency Namibia (Fig. 7.4 (b)). The government in Pretoria was determined that Whites should retain control of South Africa, in spite of the fact that they numbered only about one-sixth of the total population. It attempted to arrange this by a geographical contrivance, establishing several semi-autonomous states within the Republic, homelands to which all the Blacks should belong as citizens, leaving the rest of the country as the homeland of the White establishment. However, neither the majority of the Blacks nor the rest of the world were prepared to accept this as a viable solution. The states bordering South Africa, the so-called frontline states, clubbed together in an organization called SADCC (Southern African Development and Co-ordination Conference) with the aim of liberating South Africa from its white masters.

By 1990 it was becoming apparent that Communism was a spent force and USSR intervention in African affairs ceased. Some complicated problems which had persisted for many years began to unravel. The Communist government in Addis Ababa was dislodged and the civil war in Ethiopia, which had lasted for nearly 20 years, came to an end. Cuban troops left Angola, and the way was opened for Namibian independence. In South Africa, the White government released Nelson Mandela, leader of the African National Congress (ANC),

A Kenya–Tanzania border post. The frontiers between African countries are sometimes not at all well marked on the ground.

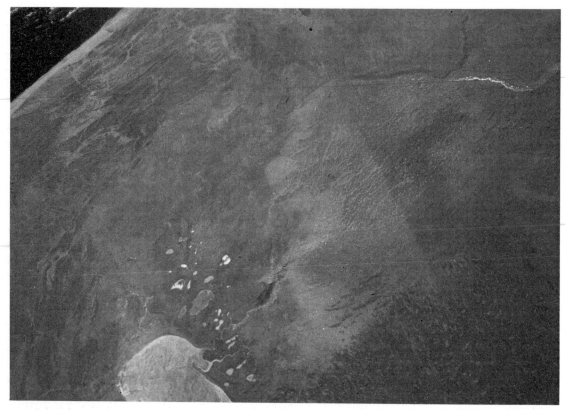

Looking west towards the Atlantic from the Space Shuttle. The more heavily grazed country around the Etosha Pan in northern Namibia (lower left) is clearly distinguishable from the less heavily grazed Angolan landscape on the right.

from prison and negotiations began that must inevitably lead to a transfer of power. This was a signal for old tribal enemies to surface, especially in the black townships on the Rand, with the Zulu Inkatha movement on the one side and the largely Xhosa ANC (African National Congress) on the other.

Tension and violence were not confined to the southern part of the continent; strife and disorder afflicted several African countries north and south of the equator and for most Africans life became more difficult in the last quarter of the century than it had been.

Africa had been partitioned by politicians in European countries motivated by desires of various kinds, prominent amongst them being the promotion of national prestige, commercial advantage, and settler security. The independent states of Africa are derived from the colonial territories which consequently took shape towards the end of the nineteenth century. They vary in size and resources; most are composed of several ethnic groups; their institutions, deriving from Europe, are grafted on African rootstocks. It is not surprising that their progress has been uneven and uncertain.

7.7 Development

The term 'development' has come into general use in relation to Africa and other less prosperous parts of the world especially since the Second World War. The countries concerned have been called successively the underdeveloped, developing, and less-developed countries (LDCs). Essentially development means change for the better, involving economic growth but also social betterment. It carries with it ideas of planning, the putting to good use of latent resources, and the elaboration of the socio-economic system.

Change of this kind is not necessarily a continuous process nor has it been entirely confined to the last half century. Social and economic development were not entirely lacking in Africa before Europeans reached the lands south of the Sahara, and it might even be argued that it was as apparent in the colonial period as it has been since. Now, in the 1980s, Africa is not only poorer than most other parts of the world, but in many if not most African countries conditions are deteriorating rather than improving. In this sense, development has ceased.

Economic development in Africa in colonial times and since independence has involved money coming into widespread use, improvements in transport, communications, and water supplies, less disease, longer life expectancy, and the spread of education. It has also involved the production of agricultural and mineral commodities for sale overseas. Funds received from the sale of these commodities allow the purchase of manufactured goods, notably textiles, petroleum products, and latterly foodstuffs from abroad, and investment in buildings, roads, and factories. Local trading, involving the sale of foodstuffs and craftware, has always been important and it continues to be. However, trading between African countries has never been very important because they all tend to produce the same kinds of things. The exception is the southern part of the continent, where the industries of the Republic of South Africa have supplied the needs of neighbouring countries for manufactured goods, while those countries have supplied labour for the mines in the Republic.

A newly constructed railway in Malawi, 1977.

7.7.1 The growth of commodity exports

The agricultural commodities produced in Africa for export consist largely of crops which grow best in low latitudes. Amongst the most important are coffee, cocoa, tea, and palm-oil, all obtained from perennial bushes or trees that grow in the rain forest and montane forest regions, and groundnuts well suited to the sandy soils of the savanna lands. All of these crops are grown by African smallholders alongside their foodcrops, though a proportion is grown on large estates. Sisal and sugar-cane, bulky crops which require a good deal of factory processing before export, have been grown almost entirely on estates. Rubber trees mainly grow in large plantations, but some trees have been planted by farmers and the latex sent to local factories for processing. Cotton is grown on large irrigated schemes and also by small-scale upland farmers; ginning to separate the seeds from the lint can be carried out either by small machines or in large factories, as can compression of the lint into bales. Tobacco is another crop, grown both on large estates and by smallholders, which can be cured and otherwise processed on either a small or a large scale.

The requirements for the production of such agricultural commodities are primarily environmental, in that they require appropriate climate and soil conditions. In addition they call for sufficiently knowledgeable and numerous cultivators, plus adequate transport and marketing arrangements. The areas producing cash crops are widely dispersed over the continent, but a relatively small number of regions, each covering a few thousands of square kilometres, are responsible for the bulk of the production.

Mineral-producing areas have a different kind of distribution pattern from the commercial agricultural areas (Fig. 9.1). By far the most important mines, certainly until 1960, were those of the Transvaal in South Africa and the Copperbelt extending from Zambia into the Shaba region of Zaire. In addition there were goldfields in south-west Ghana, tinfields on the Jos Plateau and coalmines in the Enugu area of Nigeria. All of these had been promising enough to stimulate the construction or extension of railways from the coast early in the century. After the Second World War, increasing attention was given to mining iron ore and bauxite, both of which are bulky in relation to their value. Mining for these ores had to be fairly close to the coast to reduce rail haulage to a minimum, and preferably close to Europe to keep down shipping costs; it was concentrated in Mauritania, Liberia, and Guinea. Phosphate deposits were also located near the coast, mainly from Senegal to Morocco and also in Togo, Tunisia, and Egypt. After 1957, oilfields and natural gas were discovered in regions of Mesozoic and later sedimentary rocks extending along the northern side of the Sahara from Egypt into Libya and Algeria, and down the west coast from the Niger delta, through Cameroon, Gabon, and Congo to Cabinda, that small portion of Angola north of the Zaire estuary. In the 1970s minerals and oil won fairly readily from the sedimentary rocks along the northern and western margins of the continent came to equal in value those extracted, often at greater cost, from the ancient hard rocks of the south and south-centre of the continent.

The main areas producing agricultural and mineral commodities in demand overseas offered opportunities for wage employment and attracted migrants from surrounding less well-endowed regions. By the middle of the twentieth century relatively few Africans remained in traditional subsistence economies, untouched by the demands of international markets. Most of them had become dependent on the state of world trade and on the requirements of the industrial countries. The mining industry was almost entirely in the hands of companies based in Europe, America or, in the case of southern Africa, in Johannesburg. Cultivators producing crops for export were very much at the mercy of large, European-based commercial companies involved in importing manufactured goods and exporting agricultural commodities. They made their purchases through local agents, many of whom were Indians in east Africa, Lebanese in west Africa. Transport and marketing costs were always high because of the wide spacing of roads and railways and so returns to the agricultural producer were low and uncertain. White-settler farmers with their ability to borrow from banks, hire labour, and invest in labour-saving machinery were able to run large farms and make a good living, but the opportunities for African smallholders to save and invest in equipment were limited. Many of

The machine escaping from the wooden box in the foreground was intended to assist in the extraction of coal from a mine to be opened in south-west Tanzania. It was damaged when the lorry carrying it on the last lap of its journey from Shanghai ran out of control on a steep, winding road.

those who were enterprising saw much better chances of improving their lot in the towns than in their villages, especially with independence, when Africans came to power and gained access to the resources of government.

7.7.2 *The development decades*

During and after the Second World War, both British and French governments recognized the need to do more than keep law and order and provide facilities for trading with their African colonies. They set aside considerable sums of money for colonial development and welfare. These were expended in a variety of ways on health, education, road construction, and soil conservation schemes; all was on a modest scale, and little attempt was made at first to procure integrated development within each colony. The colonial economy was still seen as complementary to that of the metropole.

At the same time, colonial governments in British territories instituted Marketing Boards in an effort to improve the quality of produce and to even out prices by underpaying the producers and accumulating monetary surpluses in times of high prices, with a view to subsidizing producer prices when world demand should slacken. With the post-war recovery of the industrialized countries and rapidly increasing demand in the 1950s, prices for most commodities rose, and Marketing Boards accumulated surpluses that were banked in London—to the benefit of the British economy. As price levels continued to rise in the 1950s these funds were seen by colonial governments as being available for general development purposes, not necessarily for the benefit of producers in rural areas.

At about the same time, in the 1950s, the Communist bloc and the western countries began to compete for support in the United Nations and elsewhere by providing aid in the form of loans and grants to African countries. As a result, African governments came to have increasingly strong control over the money available in their countries for development and other purposes. With the coming of independence to most African states in the years around 1960, Africans replaced European admistrators and technical officers in government, rapidly in some countries such as Zaire, more slowly in some of the former French colonies.

The General Assembly of the United Nations designated the 1960s the organization's First Development Decade. Governments were encouraged to produce comprehensive development plans to ensure economic growth. They were advised to aim at growth rates of at least 5 per cent annually, with the aim of reducing the gap between the under-developed and the industrial countries and in the hope that some of them, at least, would 'take off' into sustained growth in the way that Rostow's model of economic growth had indicated they should. For Africa as a whole the target of 5 per cent growth was reached in the 1960s and the early 1970s. Overall, the shares in national output of mining, manufacturing, construction, administration, and defence all increased. Agriculture remained the dominant sector of the economy, but its share of national output diminished from over 40 per cent in 1960 to little more than 30 per cent in 1975. These could be taken to be signs of progress, but there was no take-off. It began to be realized that increases in 'production', especially if production figures included expenditure on defence and administration,

were not necessarily very beneficial, except to soldiers and civil servants.

Economic growth in some African countries slackened as early as the 1960s, notably in Ghana, where the economy had always depended heavily on cocoa, whose price on the world market fell at a time when government expenditure was becoming increasingly lavish. Growth in the Sahelian states was also very limited. This was a serious matter because rates of population growth in the Sahel were increasing so fast as to equal or even exceed rates of economic expansion; some people were becoming wealthy but most were staying poor. Rural dwellers were moving out of agriculture into the towns. Agricultural methods showed few signs of improvement and food production was scarcely keeping up with population. In the course of the 1970s, imports into Africa from overseas increased in relation to both exports and total production, and a growing proportion of these imports consisted of food.

7.8 Crisis conditions

The oil price rises in 1973 and again in 1978 differentiated the African countries in a striking way. Oil exporters, notably Libya, Algeria, Nigeria, and Gabon, benefited enormously from their increased oil revenues, and these four countries together came to account for over a third of developing Africa's total output. Large sums of money came into the hands of their governments. The situation in Nigeria was particularly important because of the scale of the opportunities for development that seemed to be made possible in this, the most populous country in Africa. Government expenditure in the cities attracted people from the rural areas and from surrounding countries. The internal demand for palm-oil and groundnut oil exceeded home-produced supplies and, from being an exporter of these commodities, Nigeria became a net importer. Public works of all kinds were constructed, notably roads and irrigation projects. Manufacturing expanded. Some people became very wealthy; dependence on imported food and consumer goods in the towns rapidly increased; but for most people in the rural areas conditions scarcely improved at all.

Most African countries have no oil or gas-fields and, after 1973, they suddenly found their import bills vastly increased. They had become dependent on road transport; petrol and diesel oil were essential for everyday life as well as for transport and industry. Nearly every country was running into debt because the price of imported manufactured goods was increasing faster than that of the commodities being exported (Fig. 13.8). The general increase in energy costs had caused a slowdown in the economic growth of the industrial countries and they were not requiring as much copper, manganese, and iron ore as before, so both the prices and the volume of exports fell. Even nature seemed to have a grudge against the African continent, especially against the poorest, semi-arid countries along the southern side of the Sahara. The rains were deficient year after year from 1970 to 1973, and from 1980 to 1984 there were severe droughts in southern Africa as well as in the lands along the south side of the Sahara.

The situation was relieved for a time in the later 1970s by increased rainfall and by loans being made available by Western banks, governments, and international agencies. Money was being accumulated by oil-rich countries, especially Saudi Arabia and other Gulf states and was being deposited in Western banks. The banks were prepared to make loans to developing countries, loans that were often guaranteed by Western governments; the loans enabled African countries without oil to continue to pay their way, at least for the time being. However, the loans had to be repaid, and interest had to be paid on the outstanding amounts owed. This was difficult enough for many countries because of their reduced incomes from the exports on which they had normally depended. Their difficulties were accentuated in the early 1980s, when American government financial policy, involving the borrowing of large sums of money from overseas at high rates of interest, boosted the exchange rate of the American dollar. As repayment of the loans and the rates of interest payable by the African countries were frequently linked to the dollar and to interest rates prevailing in the

USA, many African countries found that servicing their debts, that is paying interest on them and repaying the capital sums, was becoming unsupportable. Their currencies lost value and imported goods became very scarce. Many professional people and skilled technicians emigrated to the oil-exporting countries. Services provided by government agencies, such as hospitals, education, post and tele-communications, justice, and civil security deteriorated.

More money was flowing out of Africa in the 1980s than was moving into it. Many countries were effectively bankrupt. The situation was ameliorated to some extent by a sudden fall in oil prices after 1984 and some improvement in climatic conditions about the same time. The fact remains that between 1975 and 1985 many African countries, in terms of national output, ceased to develop, and in terms of output per head of population they declined economically. Not only did the gap between the rich industrial countries and the poor African countries increase but the poor became poorer. With the fall in oil prices in the mid-1980s, even the oil-producing countries suffered. Many people in Nigeria went hungry, for food production had fallen far behind home demand and now there was little money to spare for importing food from overseas.

Since the mid-1980s the realization has come to many governments in Africa, and elsewhere, that politicians and civil servants are not necessarily the people most capable of operating productive commercial enterprises. The collapse of centrally controlled economies in Communist countries and the relative success of market economies in liberal democracies has made this very evident. The problems of building up new economic structures from scratch to replace the old ones are enormous. Fortunately, in most African countries there are many individuals and groups who have continued to operate independently as farmers, fishermen, artisans and traders in spite of past government policies.

POPULATION, MIGRATION, AND URBANIZATION

8.1 Numbers of people and population growth

The number of people in Africa in 1993 exceeds 600 million, about one-ninth of the world's population. The figure is approximate, for reliable counts have yet to be made in most countries. A full census is costly, and succeeds only if enough enumerators are trained and efficiently organized, and if the people being counted are able and willing to give the information required. Numbers in the Republic of South Africa, Egypt, Zimbabwe, Kenya, and Ghana are known with a fair degree of accuracy, and for most other territories the estimates given, for instance, in the *United Nations Demographic Yearbook* are probably within about 15 per cent of the truth.

Uncertainty about the population of two of the most populous countries, Ethiopia and Nigeria, is particularly great, and their actual populations may differ by several million from the figures given in the statistical table at the end of this book. Ethiopia has never had a census. In Nigeria the situation is confused because of political interventions. In the 1960s the seats in the Nigerian Federal House of Assembly and a proportion of the revenue were allocated to the regions comprising the federation on the basis of their population. Censuses made in 1962 and 1963 are suspected to have been highly inaccurate, as a result of each region attempting to push up its numbers to get 'a bigger slice of the cake'. Most people thought that the national figure that emerged, 55 million, was too high. A more recent figure from a 1974 census put Nigeria's population at 84 million and the U.N. Demographic Yearbook gives the 1989 population as 109 million. How-

ever, in March 1992 the provisional results of an official census in November 1991 gave the total population as only 88.5 million. Even this is very much greater than the numbers in any other country in Africa.

Governments everywhere are coming to realize that census data are essential for sound economic and social planning, so increasing efforts are being made to obtain more detailed and reliable statistics. Probably the most valuable figures to planners are rates of population increase. They are only now becoming available for many countries, for the first counts of any reliability were made after 1948, and later figures to compare with them are relatively scarce. An alternative means of assessing rates of change, by comparing birth-rates and death-rates, can seldom be used because records, if they are kept at all, are incomplete. However, information of one kind or another is accumulating; taxation figures provide a guide to changing numbers in the first half of the century and sample surveys can reveal current trends.

It is known that Egypt's population, which is believed to have been about 5 million at the beginning of the nineteenth century, began to increase markedly about 1870, doubling in the second half of the century doubling again in the first half of this one, and doubling again by 1980 (Fig. 8.1). South of the Sahara there was not much sign of population increasing at all rapidly until eighty years later than in Egypt, about 1940; since then numbers have doubled about every 25 years (Fig. 8.2). It would seem likely that Africa's population as a whole in the 1990s is increasing at a rate of about 3 per cent annually, which involves a doubling every 25 years (Fig. 8.3). In Ivory Coast, Kenya and

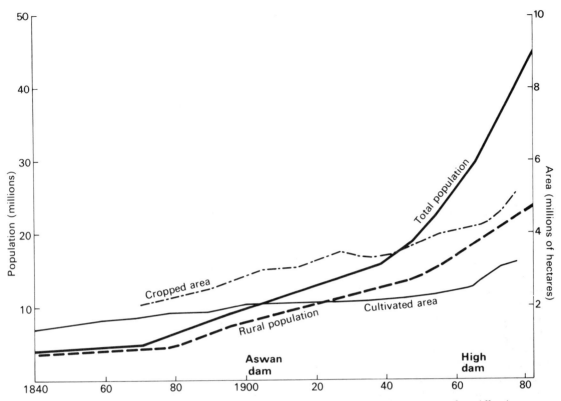

Fig. 8.1. *The population of Egypt began to grow markedly after 1870 and has increased rapidly since 1940. By 1988 it was about 50 millions. The cultivable area has grown more slowly but the spread of year-round irrigation and the use of fertilizers has allowed more than one crop per year to be taken from the land. This explains why the cropped area has grown more rapidly than the cultivated area.*

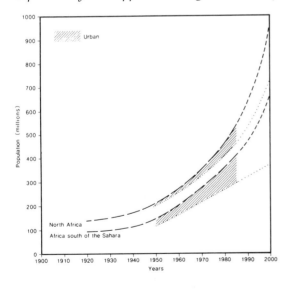

Fig. 8.2. *Population increase in Africa, 1920–85. The values until 1950 are taken from Hailey's* An African Survey, *OUP 1957. Those for later years from the US Bureau of the Census, 'World Population 1983—recent demographic estimates for the countries and regions of the world', Washington 1983, and the 'World Bank Development Report', OUP 1985. Urban populations—the numbers living in settlements of more than 20 000 people, are uncertain. The extrapolation to AD 2000 for the total population south of the Sahara is taken from the World Bank report.*

Swaziland, rates of growth exceeded 4 per cent in 1989. Only in the island states, Mauritius, Réunion, Sao Tome and Principe and the Seychelles was population growth less than 2 per cent. In African mainland countries, rates of increase were everywhere more than 2 per cent, except for West Sahara where the people, normally nomadic in any case, have been involved in fighting for several years. No continent has ever had such a high growth rate; in European countries, annual rates of increase have seldom approached 2 per cent.

Why is this population explosion occurring in Africa? Birth-rates have increased somewhat; certainly they are now very high, above 45 per 1000 per year in all but a few countries, with each woman bearing on average about six children in her lifetime and as many as eight in some countries. However, the increase in population growth rates is mainly to be attri-

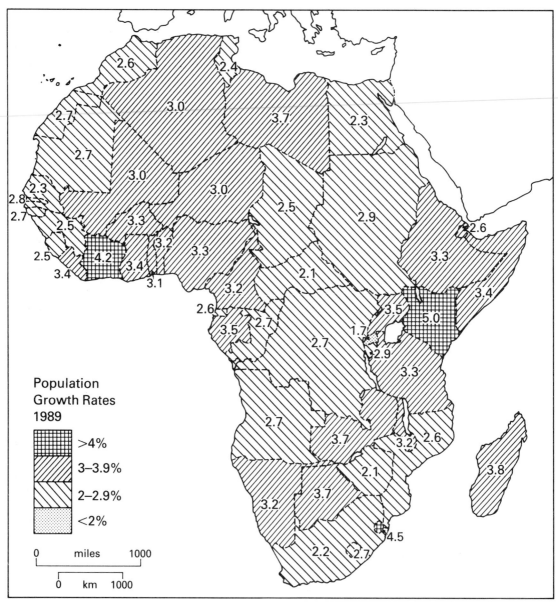

Fig. 8.3. *Population growth rates in African countries in 1989 according to the Demographic Yearbook, 1991. In none of the mainland countries were annual rates of increase less than 2 per cent (except in West Sahara, which is a very special case); overall growth rates were about 3 per cent.*

buted not so much to increased fertility as to fewer children dying in infancy. About 20 per cent of children in tropical Africa still die before they reach the age of five, but the percentage has been diminishing. Medical services have not improved to such a degree as to provide an explanation for more infants surviving. Presumably they do so as a result of better living conditions: cleaner water supplies, fewer local famines, less destructive epidemics. When they expected many of their children to die parents saw no need to limit the size of their families, and most are still unprepared to do so.

Now, Africa has the fastest-growing population of all the continents. Birth-rates are high even in the towns and amongst women who have attended school. In Europe and most other industrialized parts of the world, with higher standards of living and much lower mortality amongst infants, rates of increase are relatively low, even negative in several states, because parents are deliberately limiting the number of children in the family. In very few African countries does the use of modern methods of contraception exceed 10 per cent. Most Africans are still ready to accept children as they come, and it is impossible to foresee if and when they will adopt the restrictive attitude of Europeans.

Greater numbers provide additional supplies of labour and a growing market and it has been argued that both of these are prerequisites of economic growth. But unless the labour can be employed productively, rapid population growth aggravates existing problems of housing, food supply, land shortage, and poverty. Under the existing conditions there is a high dependency ratio, with children under 15 constituting half the population. The cost of education is correspondingly high and constitutes one of the major components of government expenditure.

8.2 Distribution of population

8.2.1 Regions of sparse settlement

Extensive areas of the continent remain sparsely settled, with fewer than 4 persons per km² (10 per square mile; see Fig. 8.4). They include the deserts of the north and south-west, swampy plains in south-east Angola, Zambia, and central Zaire, and the tsetse-

ridden plains of the Zaire watershed. In such country, people live either in small groups exploiting the resources of wide tracts extensively, or in larger groups spread at wider intervals, farming intensively. Belonging to the first group are the pygmies in eastern Zaire and the Kalahari bushmen (San), both of whom are collectors and hunters. In the second group are the oasis-dwellers of the Sahara. In such difficult environments, though people are not usually dependent entirely on their own surroundings, their ways of life are so finely adapted to their habitats that they find it extremely difficult to change. Thus, unless they abandon their homelands for more favoured areas, they have little opportunity for sharing in any overall improvements in national standards of living. They continue to retain their old customs and occupations; they are anachronisms—interesting specimens for the anthropologist, traveller and tourist, but a source of some embarrassment to their progressive compatriots in the towns.

Most sparsely settled regions, if they lack mineral resources, remain poor and empty, though there are exceptions. Semi-arid western Cape Province has long been the source of one of South Africa's main exports, wool, and in recent years boreholes have allowed much of the Kalahari in Botswana to become available for herding cattle. Tractor ploughing of the plains east of the Blue Nile in the Gedaref region of the Sudan, first sponsored by government and later financed by private companies, has allowed half a million hectares (over a million acres) to be brought under cultivation and cropped with grain and cotton. But agriculture is usually problematic where labour is in short supply for clearing bush, building roads, and digging for water; and the high costs of developing such land deter large-scale investment. So the empty lands of Africa are often liabilities rather than assets to the countries possessing them, increasing the costs of transport between more productive regions and often absorbing capital that could be invested more profitably elsewhere.

8.2.2 Regions of dense settlement

The heavily settled regions have an economic importance out of all proportion to their extent. This is particularly true of (1) the southern Transvaal industrial and mining region and (2) the Nile valley and delta in Egypt, but it also applies to four essentially agricultural regions between the tropics (3 and 4) with population densities of between 40 and 400 per km² (100–1000 per square mile). Together, these six relatively small areas contain roughly half of Africa's population on about 2 per cent of its land area.

8.2.2.1 The southern Transvaal The greatest concentration of industry in southern Africa lies on the interior plateau of Africa (Fig. 8.5).

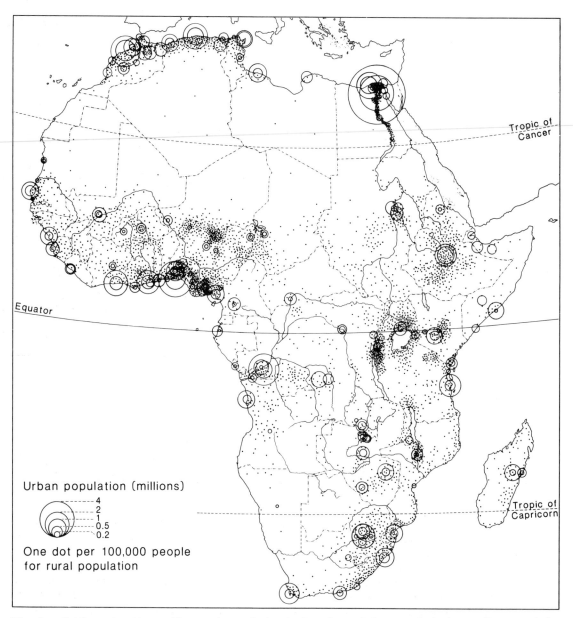

Fig. 8.4. *Settlement patterns. The rural population is densely settled over relatively small areas of the continent with wide areas still sparsely populated. Clusters of large towns and cities are concentrated in the Nile delta, the Maghreb, southern Nigeria, and the southern Transvaal. Concentric circles give some idea of the growth of the larger cities between the mid-1970s and the mid-1980s.*

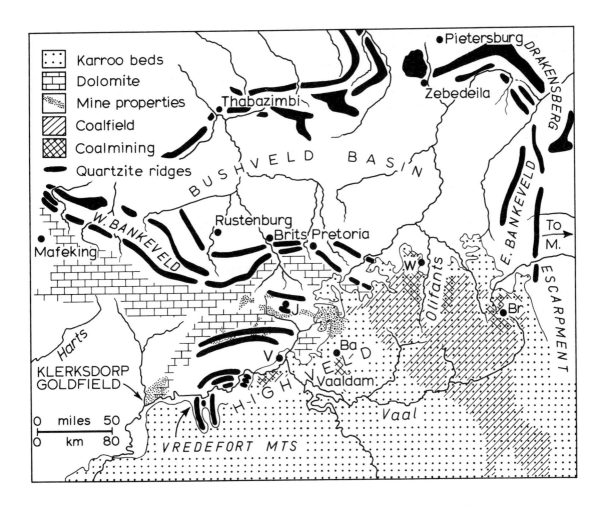

Fig. 8.5. *The industrial heartland of southern Africa, centred on Johannesburg (J), Pretoria, and Vereeniging (V), includes the Vaal river, the Bankeveld and the Bushveld basin. The gold-bearing rocks of the Rand and Klerksdorp goldfields, belonging to the Witwatersrand system, consist of varied, hard sedimentary rocks folded into a large syncline of which the northern limb forms the ridges of the Rand running east–west under Johannesburg. Overlying them are the dolomites and igneous rocks of the Bushveld complex which are mineralized, especially in the vicinity of quartzites. Karoo beds which once overlay the whole region have been stripped away from the north and the drainage system superimposed upon the older rocks, allowing the rivers to breach the quartzite ridges as at Pretoria and Thabazimbi, thereby providing routeways and dam sites. The Karoo beds remaining in the south-east include coal measures which are now extensively mined to generate power locally and for export from Richards Bay to Japan and elsewhere. M–Maputo, W–Witbank, Br–Breyton, Ba–Balfour.*

Far from the coast or any navigable river, within 80 km (50 mls) of Johannesburg, on the watershed between the Vaal and the Limpopo and far from the coast or any navigable river, it is the only industrial complex in Africa comparable in scale with the conurbations of Europe and North America. Its location and development were determined in the first place by the existence of the Witwatersrand goldfield, secondly by the proximity of coal and other minerals, and thirdly by the availability of good supplies of labour and capital and a large market created by the gold-mining industry.

The southern Transvaal industrial complex, with a population of about 7 million, is much greater than any other centre of industry on the continent. It contributes possibly as much as a quarter of Africa's total manufacturing industrial output and provides a livelihood not only for the people dwelling on the Rand and in its vicinity, but also for the families of workers whose permanent homes are hundreds of kilometres away in Mozambique, Malawi, Botswana, and northern Namibia.

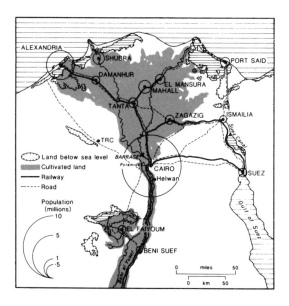

Fig. 8.6. *The Nile delta. Industry and population have been concentrating in Greater Cairo, in the towns of the delta and alongside the Suez Canal. TRC—Tenth of Ramadan City—is the prototype of a network of industrial towns intended to provide for Egypt's growing population.*

8.2.2.2 *The Nile valley in Egypt*   Below the High Dam at Aswan, the Nile enters a long, narrow, trough-shaped valley with steep scarps overlooking the flat, irrigated silts of the old floodplain. Several barrages have been built within the last hundred years to raise the level of the river and allow its waters to be led along irrigation canals. The main canal, the Bahr el Yusef, leaves the Nile below Asyut and delivers water to the fertile basin of the Faiyoum (Fig. 8.6). Below Cairo the river divides into two main branches that traverse the delta. These days, very little Nile water entering Egypt reaches the Mediterranean; over a tenth of it evaporates from the surface of Lake Nasser; nearly all of the rest is used for irrigating about 2 million hectares (5 million acres) and also for industrial puposes. Industrial activity and the main urban centres in Egypt are concentrated in the west of the delta between Cairo and Alexandria, and alongside the Suez Canal. About 37 million people are concentrated in the quadrilateral in between the two, with an additional 17 million on the essentially agricultural land of Upper Egypt.

Of the populous regions south of the Sahara, two (3 *a* and *b*) are in Nigeria and adjacent parts of West Africa; others (4 *a* and *b*) occupy parts of the rift valley region of east Africa.

8.2.2.3 (a) *The Guinea coast*   The largest of all these concentrations of population borders the Gulf of Guinea, including the Ibo, Ibibio, and Yoruba peoples of Nigeria, southern Benin (formerly Dahomey), Togo, and Ghana (Fig. 11.2). The eastern part within the high forest belt receives more than 1400 mm (56 in) of rain annually, the western part in the coastal dry zone less than 1000 mm (40 in). Some 75 million people living there depend on root crops, plantains (large bananas), rice, and maize for food; their external trade is based on exports of cocoa and kola, phosphates, and oil (Figs 5.4 (a) and 9.1). Rubber, timber, and palm-oil products were once important items in southern Nigeria's overseas trade, but with the growth of mineral oil exports and the expansion of urban populations, especially that of Lagos, the palm-oil, rubber, and timber are mostly consumed locally.

8.2.2.3 (b) Hausaland Northern Nigeria is very different from the Guinea coast. The annual rainfall of 500–1200 mm (20–48 in) comes in only 4 months of the year, and the majority of the people, who number about 30 million, are engaged in growing sorghum, millet, and beans for themselves, and cotton and groundnuts for local processing and mainly for local use. Kano is the main urban centre.

8.2.2.4 (a) The Lake Victoria region On either side of the equator, within about 320 km (200 mls) of Lake Victoria, about 40 million people live around the lake and on the highlands to east and west (Figs. 8.7. and 11.1). The rain comes in two seasons and in the well-settled areas exceeds 1000 mm (40 in), allowing the production of all manner of tropical tree, root, and grain crops.

Southern Uganda is naturally fitted to be one

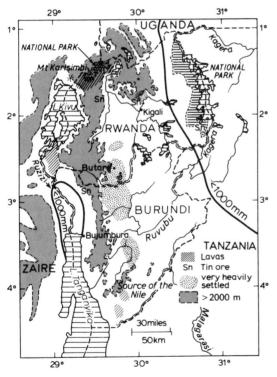

Fig. 8.7. *Rwanda and Burundi, with a total population of more than 10 millions, are the two most heavily settled countries in Africa. They have quite a high rainfall and fertile soils but they are situated over 1000 km from the sea and have no rail connection with the coast.*

of the most productive agricultural regions in Africa, producing in peaceful times big crops of coffee and cotton for export as well as plantains and maize for local consumption.

The volcanic highlands of Rwanda and Burundi to the south-west are amongst the most congested rural areas in the continent (Fig. 8.7). The people live in groups of huts scattered through a mosaic of small banana and coffee plantations, interspersed with fields of beans, sweet potatoes, and sorghum. No railways link these countries to the coast, which at its nearest is 1200 km (750 mls) away to the east. In each country about 6 million people are living off 26 000 km² (10 000 mls²), a situation in striking contrast to that in neighbouring parts of Tanzania and Zaire where mean densities are less than a tenth as great.

Sukumaland and Nyanza on the south and east sides of Lake Victoria are populous upland plains with numerous livestock as well as much cultivation. The Sukuma, numbering about 2 millions, occupy a region of about 50 000 km² (19 000 mls²) which has been reduced to a cultivation steppe where the only trees surviving are either useless for firewood or bear edible fruits. Pressure on the land is also high in Nyanza, and efforts are being made there to increase productivity by draining and irrigating swampland.

The highlands on either side of the eastern rift between Nairobi and Kitale, largely underlain by volcanic lavas, plus the southern lower slopes of Mt Kenya and Mt Kilimanjaro have a high population density overall, though it is somewhat unevenly distributed. The hills and plateaus rising above the 1500 m (5000 ft) contour and occupying in all about 170 000 km² (65 000 mls²), support about 8 million people belonging to several different tribes, of which the largest is the Kikuyu. Nairobi is by far the largest urban centre in the entire region.

8.2.2.4 (b) Ethiopia Central Ethiopia is also widely underlain by volcanic lavas, and because of its altitude is well watered in most years. About 25 million people, mostly living on the highlands west of the rift valley, extending from Tigrai in the north to Sidamo in the south, are almost entirely agricultural (Fig. 8.8). In the north, cereals are the main crops. Ensete, the false banana, is a staple in the south. This plant, growing 3 to 8 m (10 to 25 ft) high, is

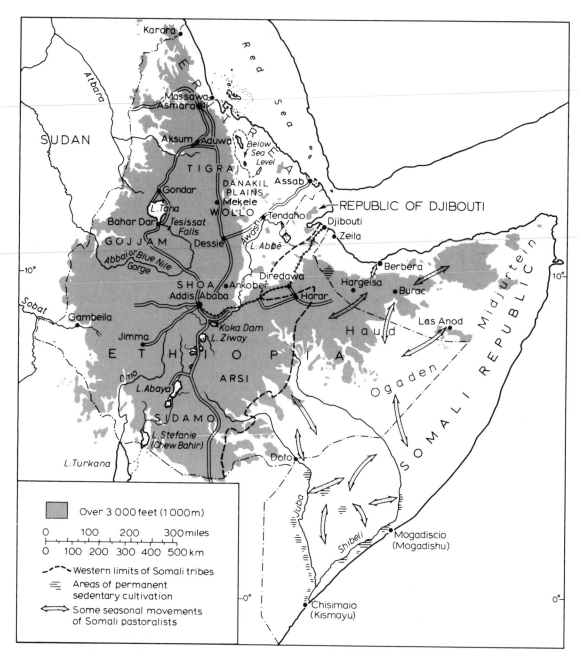

Fig. 8.8. *Ethiopia occupies most of the Horn of Africa. Fighting in Ethiopia between central government forces on the one hand and Eritrean and Tigrean guerrillas on the other disrupted life in the north of the country from 1961 to 1991. In the 1980s, a Marxist government in Addis Ababa forced people to move from the troubled, heavily settled north to the relatively sparsely settled south-west of the country. Eventually, in 1991 the central government forces were defeated and Eritrea became virtually independent. A government set up in Addis Ababa was dominated by Tigreans and Oromo (Galla). The people who had been forced to move to the south-west were allowed to return to their homes. Conflicts between the various political parties and clans in Somalia in the early 1990s brought the country to a state of complete collapse and destitution. Many Somali sought refuge in northeast Kenya and many died of starvation.*

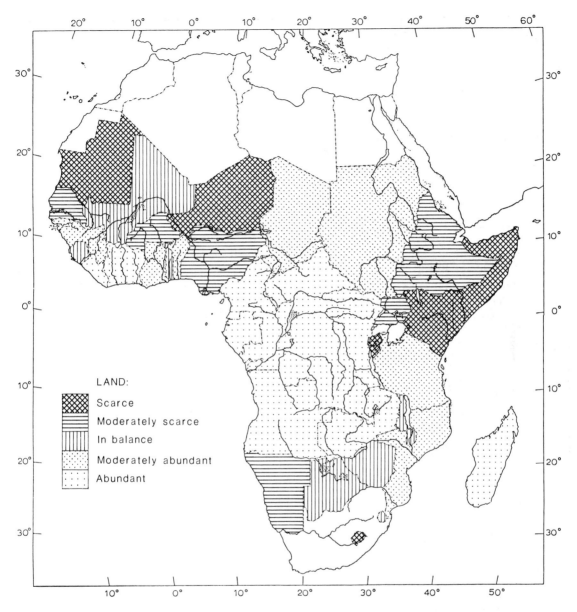

Fig. 8.9. *Abundance and scarcity of land for agriculture in African countries. This attempt to indicate the relationship between population and agricultural land resources was made in a report, 'The state of food and agriculture', by the UN Food and Agriculture Organization (1985). There are few instances where movements of population between states offer a means of obtaining a balance, for political obstacles are strong. Even within states, tribal and linguistic differences, community cohesion, and existing claims to land restrict the possibilities for redistribution of the population. Resettlement programmes have been attempted, notably in Ethiopia, but voluntary migration between rural areas by individuals and their families probably far exceeds in sum total the results of deliberate government intervention.*

usually planted around the houses on plots well manured with dung and ashes. The pseudo-stem formed by the sheaths of the leaves is the edible part, yielding a starch of high nutritional value which can be used for making bread or a kind of porridge. Population and cattle densities are high in the ensete-growing areas.

8.2.2.5 Other populous regions Additional concentrations of population occur at the northern and southern ends of Lake Malawi and along the coasts of the Maghreb and east Africa. Urbanization in Morocco is far advanced, whereas the vast majority of the population in the Lake Malawi/Nyasa region remains rural.

The probable reason why these populous areas were well-settled originally is that they have adequate rainfall and cultivable soils and are capable of supporting large agricultural populations. Most of them were relatively well provided with communications in the colonial period and became exporters of cash crops. Except for their major urban centres they remain to a large degree self-supporting in foodstuffs (Fig. 8.9).

There are other smaller well-populated areas which are more remote and less well-suited to cash crop production for other reasons. People may have concentrated in them in the past for defensive or other political reasons. Some were formerly 'native reserves', created by the governments of white-settler colonies, as in South Africa, Rhodesia and Kenya.

Instances occur of sparsely peopled areas within or alongside congested districts which have remained unattractive to settlers because of tsetse infestation or the prevalence of river blindness. Some empty areas are forest or game reserves, or lack water, or are liable to seasonal flooding. From the congested areas with limited economic opportunities people move to the mines, the commercial agricultural areas, and the towns to obtain paid employment.

8.3 Migration

Groups of people have migrated across Africa since early times; mention has already been made of the southward expansion of the Bantu-speaking peoples and the advance of the Arabs west and south from the isthmus of Suez. From the Maghreb and the western part of the Sudan zone, Muslims as individuals or in groups have made the pilgrimage to Mecca for several centuries (Fig. 8.10). In the early nineteenth century, warring Zulu groups fought their way west into the interior of southern Africa and northwards to the Great Lakes, attracting adherents from other tribes and eventually settling down in various locations as far north as Zambia, Malawi, and Tanzania. The last hundred years have seen migratory movements of a different kind, involving millions of individuals seeking employment in cities, in mining, and in commercial agriculture. A sad feature of the 1970s and 1980s has been the large numbers of refugees escaping from famine, oppression, and conflict in their home areas (see p. 207).

8.3.1 Migrant labour

Early in the colonial period, people in Africa

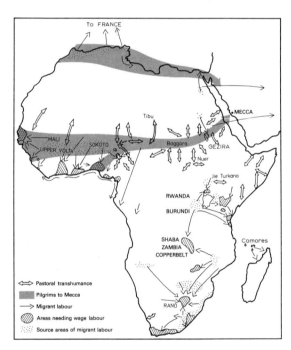

Fig. 8.10. *Migratory movements. Pastoralists shift their grazing grounds seasonally. Labourers move to the mining and export crop regions and back to their homes. Muslims make the pilgrimage to Mecca, usually by air these days. Not shown here are the movements of refugees and those from rural to urban areas, which are now more important than all the other migratory movements on the continent.*

found they needed money. They wanted to purchase the manufactured goods appearing in markets, and they had to pay taxes to their new rulers. Money could be earned by selling commodities like palm-oil and rubber, cotton, and groundnuts to European traders and by working on European farms and plantations or in newly opened mines. They found they could travel around safely, outside their own tribal territories. A redistribution of the population began in response to the new opportunities and pressures.

Before the end of the nineteenth century, people from the interior of the Sudan zone were moving seasonally to work in the groundnut-growing areas of Senegal, some of them becoming sharecroppers. In succeeding decades, the cocoa plantations established by the local people in southern Ghana (Fig. 11.2) attracted immigrants from the north of the country and from Upper Volta (now Burkina Faso); many of them settled down as tenants and eventually became incorporated in local societies. Thousands of Hutu from Ruanda who found work on the coffee plantations of southern Uganda, became farmers themselves and were eventually accepted as Baganda. Kikuyu moved from congested reserves to become labourers and squatters on European farms. Such movements were largely from rural areas with dominantly subsistence economies into other rural areas offering wage labour in money economies.

The results of rural–rural migration varied. From some districts, such as Sokoto in northern Nigeria, the number of migrants was very large; figures as great as a quarter of a million a year have been given. But the majority were away from their homes, working in the cocoa-growing areas, for only a few months during the dry season, when farmwork in the semi-arid zone ceases, and so the effects were less drastic than in some other cases.

In the last quarter of the nineteenth century men were being attracted from all parts of southern Africa to the diamond and gold mines in South Africa. In Malawi, until 1974, about one-third of all the able-bodied males were working abroad at any one time, mainly in Rhodesia (Zimbabwe) and South Africa. Individuals stayed away from home for a year or more at a time, and, in the absence of the young men, society was disrupted. Women found

themselves taking on more and more responsibilities and performing arduous tasks which were formerly undertaken by men; agricultural production suffered. In countries such as Mozambique, Swaziland, and Lesotho the national economy and government revenue became more and more dependent on the earnings of the men abroad.

The basic reason why Africans have moved from their tribal areas into employment as wage labourers is the growth of mining, industrial, and agricultural enterprises in places remote from centres of African population. This is particularly true of the area rich in minerals stretching from Shaba through Zambia and Zimbabwe to the Rand, where white capital, technical skills, and organization stimulated economic development of all kinds. This engendered a very great demand for labour. To meet it, Africans were lured from their homes by the need for money to purchase manufactured goods. In many cases colonial governments ensured that labour would be forthcoming and at the same time increased state revenues by imposing head taxes which could only be paid if people went to work for wages. In southern Africa, transport was provided by recruiting agencies. Underlying the whole situation has been the relative poverty and lack of opportunity, and sometimes shortage of land, in the migrants' homelands.

Whereas in Europe, and indeed in most countries, people have been moving into towns from rural areas for well over a century, and have settled in them permanently, the majority of Africans until recent years continued moving periodically to and from their villages. In part, this 'circular migration' has been their own desire, for the environment of the town was alien to them; they wished to retain ties with their families; they had a secure base with a right to land in their home villages and many wished to return home as soon as they had sufficient cash to achieve the objects for which they originally emigrated. In some ways this was advantageous for the mining companies employing labour and for the governments of the countries receiving migrants. Both could avoid the responsibility for establishing communities of immigrants and the costs of providing housing and education, and of looking after the welfare of the members of workers' families too young or too old to work. Those costs fell on the labour source areas. In the past, labourers were provided with bachelor accommodation only (and very basic it usually was) and there was no opportunity for them to bring their families. The migrant looked back to the village as his real home, where his relatives lived, where he had his land or his rights to land, where he was secure and could eventually retire and lay his bones.

Since the middle of the century, increasing numbers of Africans have been settling and raising their families in the towns. A new generation has grown up, with slackened tribal ties and with the town its natural environment. Government offices and industry have required skilled and semi-skilled workers, which temporary migratory labour could not provide. A permanent work force, made up of people in regular employment and with relatively high salaries, has created demands for all kinds of services. These are provided by other people who are described as being in the informal sector; they commonly form the majority of the

A maker and repairer of shoes at work under a shelter on the edge of the bus station in Moshi, Tanzania.

urban labour force. In this way a class system is emerging in the towns, cutting across the older tribal groupings.

In recent years some of the migratory movements have gone into reverse. Not only were the French forced out of Algeria in 1962 and Portuguese out of Mozambique and Angola in 1975, but Asians were ejected from Uganda by Idi Amin's government in the 1970s. In 1969 the Ghana government, in order to preserve jobs for local people, forced many foreigners, mainly from Upper Volta and Nigeria, to leave the country. Ghanaians were in turn the main sufferers in 1982, when the Nigerian government decided to enforce the rule that all foreign workers must have work permits. The Malawian government, after many migrants had died in an air disaster in 1974, restricted the number of Malawian workers in South Africa; only 12 000 were employed there in 1976 as compared with 100 000 two years before. The South African government in pursuing its apartheid policies forced whole communities of Bantu families to leave urban areas where they had settled, to be resettled in Black Homelands which some of them had never seen. Many highly trained technicians and academics from African countries that are experiencing economic and political difficulties have been finding jobs in international organizations or have emigrated to oil-producing countries, those from Egypt and the Sudan, especially, going to the countries of the Arabian peninsula.

8.4 Urbanization

Until the end of the nineteenth century about 95 per cent of Africans were cultivators, herdsmen, and fisher-folk, living in small settlements, in groups of huts clustered on rocky hills scattered through the forest and savanna, or along the coast and river banks.

In the towns strung along the Nile and in the Maghreb, mosques and markets were prominent features of the central areas; artisans' workshops and cubical mud houses lined narrow, shaded streets. Such towns could trace their histories back through hundreds, even thousands, of years. But many of them were in decay, for urban life in north Africa had suffered a recession between the fifteenth and early nineteenth centuries. Algiers in 1830, at the time of the French occupation, had no more than 30 000 inhabitants. As the influence of Europe increased and trade flourished once more, so city life burgeoned. Large ports became administrative centres; new towns were created; villages in the interior became flourishing market places.

The French established new commercial and administrative centres alongside the old towns, the medinas in Tunisia; in Morocco the policy was to build at a distance and form twin cities; in Algeria the medinas were in many cases taken over by the French, who erected new buildings and modernized the central areas. As time went on, indigenous people were attracted to the towns in growing numbers, so that shanty towns, bidonvilles, began springing up in close proximity to skyscrapers. Soon the European town-dwellers were outnumbered by the Muslims. Now, in north Africa, more than half the people live in towns of over 5000 inhabitants and about one-third in cities of over 100 000.

South of the Sahara, ancient trading settlements like Timbuktu and Gao, Katsina and Kano, lay at the termini of caravan routes across the desert. Arab ports such as Lamu and Malindi were dotted along the east coast from the Red Sea to Mozambique. In the interior, Kampala, Addis Ababa, and Kumasi in the nineteenth century were capitals of martial states, war camps that attracted large numbers of chiefs and their retainers and slaves. These were exceptional. In the Zaire basin and the lands to the south there seem to have been few towns of any size, other than those established by European administrators, traders, and settlers. Only in Yorubaland in south-west Nigeria was any larger proportion of the population not rural (Fig. 8.11).

The core area of south-west Nigeria is Oyo State, with its capital at Ibadan. It contains most of those large towns that characterize Yorubaland, tracing their origin back a thousand years to Ile-Ife. The daughter settlements, laid out on the same plan, reproduced its social and political institutions. From the centre, where there stood the walled palace of the Oba priest-king and a market alongside, wide roads radiated out to neighbouring towns. The traditional unit of settlement was the compound,

Cairo: the largest city in Africa, with a population estimated to be about 10 millions.

consisting of a number of rooms grouped round a central square courtyard, the whole compound covering 2000 m² (half an acre) or more. Such compounds lined rectangular networks of streets between the main roads and the whole town was surrounded by a wall or a ditch (Fig. 8.12).

Early in the nineteenth century the Yoruba towns were attacked from the north by Fulani rulers of the Hausa states and the towns were also at war with each other. Ibadan, just within the forest belt, became an important centre for military operations and when peace came retained its dominant position both politically and economically. At the end of the century it was linked to Lagos and to the north by the railway and became successively a provincial headquarters, a regional capital, and the site of the first University in Nigeria. It has a population of about 2 million and is reputed to be the largest essentially native African city south of the Sahara.

In colonial times much power was left in the hands of the traditional rulers, the Obas, and administrative headquarters were set up at the outskirts of the main towns where they lived. A growing class of educated Nigerians was attracted from the crowded old settlements to the new quarters with their stores and offices and new-style, single-family houses. Consequently, many of the larger towns now have two distinct parts, an older one rather broken-down and congested with the big compounds split up into a large number of separate parts, and a newer quarter with modern buildings, good water supplies, and a car-owning population.

Towns such as Ogbomosho, Ife, Ilesha, Ede, Ikrun, Ikire, Iwo and Oshogbo, all with populations well in excess of 100 000, have little in the way of manufacturing industry. Considerable numbers of people are still engaged in such crafts as weaving and dyeing and leatherwork, and many of the women as well as men are traders on a large or small scale. Specialization of labour is increasing, but many of the townspeople still own land nearby and gain at least a part of their living from farming. In some ways these Yoruba towns resemble medieval European cities. In Oshogbo, Iwo, and Ilobu, amongst others, many of the males are primarily agriculturalists. Many live for part of the year in farming villages several kilometres from the town where their families are established

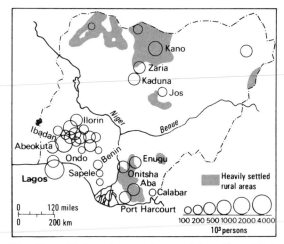

Fig. 8.11. *Main urban centres and heavily settled rural areas in Nigeria in the mid-1980s. The large towns are concentrated in Yorubaland in the south-west of the country. The towns named are the main industrial centres.*

and to which they feel tied. They hire strangers, mainly Hausa from the north to help them with the farmwork and derive a cash income from the sale of cocoa.

In the colonial period, many of the pre-existing towns in Africa were adopted as administrative and commercial centres and were linked together and to the coast by railways and roads. Old towns bypassed by the new means of communication declined. The fastest-growing towns were those chosen to be the ports, coastal or riverine, at the termini of the railways. They were the obvious centres for trade and commerce. In many cases they were chosen to be colonial capitals and are now the capitals of the independent states.

Some large towns seem to have started by chance. The site of Nairobi was first selected as a suitable location for railway workshops on the new line being built from Mombasa to Lake Victoria at the very end of the last century. Other urban centres are mining towns which have become communications nodes and have subsequently developed in other directions. Johannesburg, springing up where gold was developed on the Rand, is now a great commercial and industrial city. On a much smaller scale, Enugu, established in connection with the newly discovered coal seams in the Udi

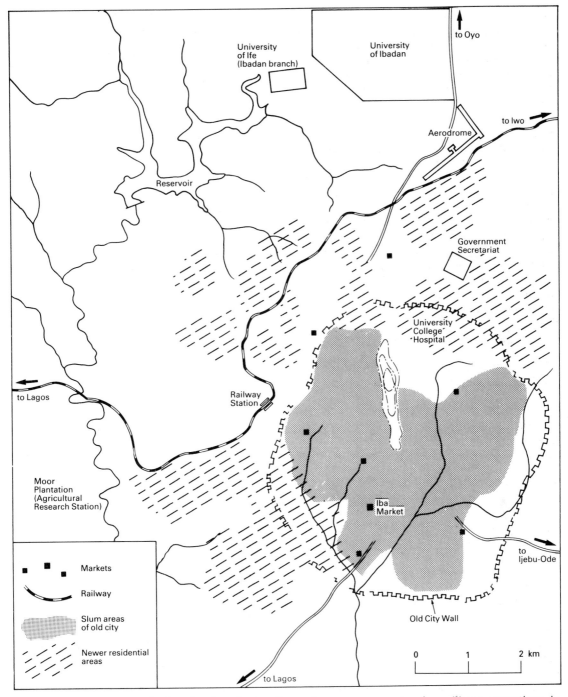

Fig. 8.12. *Yoruba city. Ibadan, in the nineteenth century, was a centre for military operations in Yorubaland. The walls protecting the compounds, where 100 000 people lived, formed a circle centred on the palace of the ruler, the Oba, and the Iba market. When it was joined by rail to Lagos and the north, with the station built outside the walls to the west and the colonial government residential area to the north, housing and commercial activity spilled outside the old city. The compounds were subdivided and many of the old dwellings deteriorated into slums.*

139

A street scene in the central part of Nairobi.

escarpment and linked by rail in about 1917 to the new creek port of Port Harcourt, became the capital of Eastern Nigeria. Now Enugu has been far surpassed by Port Harcourt, which is the most important centre of the Nigerian petroleum industry, and the old slave port of Bonny has become an important oil tanker terminal.

It is quite possible that new towns will develop in the future, for instance near new mineral discoveries or as a result of government planning. The Copperbelt towns of Zambia are only about 60 years old (Fig. 9.5). Tema in Ghana was a little fishing village until the 1950s, when a great artificial harbour was constructed to serve the Volta dam and Accra, the country's capital. In Nigeria, work is far advanced on building a new capital at Abuja in a sparsely settled region near the centre of the country, because Lagos has become one of the most congested cities in the world. In Tanzania too the seat of government is in the course of being shifted from Dar es Salaam on the coast to a more central location, at Dodoma on the dry plateau 480 km (300 mls) inland.

Future urban growth is likely to take place mainly in cities that are already important and were already in existence at the beginning of the century. Minor ports are declining as container vessels come into general use and the harbour installations and overland links of major ports improve. Government spending on public works and the employment offered in government offices attracts ever more people to the main administrative centres, above all to the national capitals. The big towns, with their good water supplies, schools, hospitals, shops, cinemas, and bright lights attract swelling numbers of young and old, rich and poor. The rate of increase of population in the biggest cities is higher than that in the rural areas; figures suggest that they are doubling in size every ten to twenty years (Fig. 8.13).

Most African towns differ from European ones in their spatial arrangement. In large European towns the central areas are the main business districts. Further from the centre there is commonly a ring of decaying property possibly being taken over for offices or being reconditioned. Then comes the sprawling resi-

Central Dar es Salaam looks run-down in comparison with Nairobi.

The sea front at Dar es Salaam remains attractive.

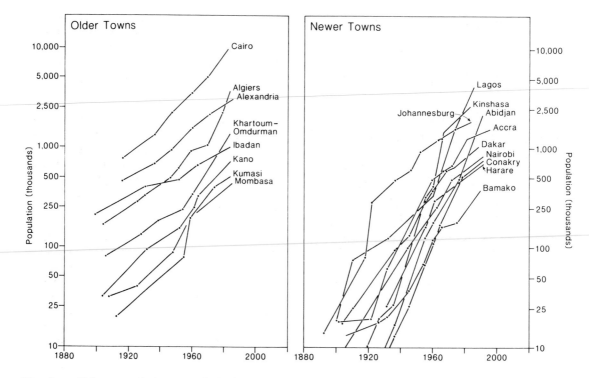

Fig. 8.13. *Urban population growth. Values are uncertain because of inaccurate counts and because the city limits vary from time to time.*

dential housing of this century, new factories, and out-of-town shopping facilities. This ring structure is less apparent in Africa; there the towns are remarkable mainly for distinct quarters or sectors. In southern Africa and until recently in east Africa, Europeans, Asians, and Africans lived in separate parts of the town, either because of legal restraints on mixing or because only Europeans and relatively few others could afford the high-class houses, and the Africans had to be satisfied with the third-class residential districts.

In west Africa, government offices and houses for European civil servants were commonly built two or three kilometres away from the 'native' townships for reasons of health and security; the commercial area lay near the docks or railway station and one or more 'stranger settlements' sprang up, each dominated by a particular ethnic group. The old government areas retain their character, with roads laid out in a rectangular grid and shaded by avenues of flowering trees. In the business districts, rising

land values are causing multi-storey buildings to be erected.

The Yoruba towns remain peopled overwhelmingly by Yoruba people and are organically parts of the surrounding countryside. The newer towns, especially the capital cities, usually have a very mixed population with representatives of several different tribes. People from the nearby areas and the largest tribes in the country predominate. Each large ethnic group tends to be in the majority in one or other part of the city and there its language is the one most commonly used, alongside English in the case of Accra, French in Abidjan, Swahili in Dar es Salaam, and Portuguese in Maputo.

Costs of house construction are high, much higher than all but a few can afford, and many of the immigrants live in shanty towns, where houses are constructed of mud, scrap metal, and packaging materials, possibly with some basic facilities such as standpipes and latrines being provided by local authorities. It is to such

Queueing for water from a standpipe in a self-built settlement a few miles outside Durban, South Africa.

settlements that immigrants first come, often to live with relations while they seek work and their own accommodation. The successful move into better housing and newcomers take over the abandoned premises. Such unplanned settlements develop their own institutions, sometimes harking back to a particular rural area from which the majority of the people come. The spontaneous settlements are now seen by governments as deserving assistance rather than being condemned as illegal and insanitary, for the state has not the funds to provide the facilities needed and it can best operate through the informal institutions that are emerging. In this sense, indirect rule has come to the urban areas of independent African countries.

Over one-third of the people in South Africa are urban dwellers. Under apartheid, the white government attempted to control the number of immigrants by forcing people to carry identification papers and obtain permits to live in the towns. But many people evaded the law in order to be with their families and to get jobs, and they were often abetted by their white employers. This policy has now been abandoned and Blacks are in the majority in every urban centre in South Africa.

In Zambia, where the economy has long been highly dependent on copper mining and the industries associated with it, about half the

population now lives in towns. In Zaire, the urban population multiplied five times between 1945 and 1960 and has been further swollen by people seeking security from the disturbances and lawlessness that have afflicted various parts of the country since independence. There are still some countries like Tanzania and Sudan, where 80 per cent of the people are rural; but the proportion of the population in Africa living in towns of over 20 000 exceeded 15 per cent in 1975 and had increased to over 25 per cent in 1987. If present trends continue it will exceed 50 per cent in the early years of the next century.

Even in the less urbanized countries the importance of the towns is very great. Their inhabitants have a higher income than the country people; they are more conscious politically and set the fashions in thought and behaviour for the youth of the country. They provide a rapidly expanding market for agricultural produce. At the same time they present immense problems. In most towns the influx of people combined with the natural increase exceeds the opportunities for paid employment. The kinship system of social security functions less effectively than in the villages, leading to destitution and the neglect of children. Jobless youths turn to crime in the absence of other means of getting a living.

In order to gain the support of the urban dwellers and allow people to survive on low wages, governments have been inclined to attempt to keep food prices down by importing foodstuffs from abroad and putting them on the market at subsidized low prices. One way of doing this has been by supporting an artificially high rate of exchange for the local currency. This can have the effect of discouraging local farmers from producing for the market and so it further increases dependence on imports. This is one feature of what has been argued to be a bias, not necessarily always intended in the policies of government in many African countries, in favour of the towns and harmful to the rural areas.

There are signs that urban dwellers are looking back to the rural areas from which they came and seeing them in a new light. Salaried people living in the towns have been amongst the entrepreneurs in agricultural development. In Ghana, where foreign exchange has been so scarce that imported foodstuffs have not been available and local currency so lacking in value that country people have been unwilling to take their produce to market, townspeople have been growing their food in their home villages or begging it from their rural cousins. In Nigeria, cereals for local consumption have become more rewarding to farmers than export crops. It is possible that the balance between the country and the town is swinging back in favour of the country-dwellers.

Migrants on the move.

9

MINERAL EXTRACTION AND OIL PRODUCTION

Salt, gold, and copper were mined in many parts of the continent long before Europeans arrived on the scene. Guinea gold was the main lure attracting Europeans to the lands south of the Sahara; the word 'Guinea' is probably derived from Jenne, an ancient trading city of the Niger through which gold from mines to the south passed on its way to Timbuktu and caravans crossing the Sahara. The Portuguese found native peoples winning gold from shallow mines in Ashanti and also in Zimbabwe. When the British arrived in Nigeria, tin was being extracted from alluvial deposits on the Jos Plateau by the local Birom. Slabs of salt, dug from desert depressions, were traded long distances by camel caravans. In most parts of Africa, locally occurring iron ore was smelted in mud furnaces, using charcoal, until bar iron from Europe became available.

9.1 The mining industry in High Africa

9.1.1 South Africa

Most of the economic minerals first exploited were situated far inland and it was not until the latter part of the nineteenth century that Europeans became involved in large-scale mining activities. Their attention was drawn to the interior of the Cape in 1875, when diamonds were discovered in the vicinity of Kimberley. It soon became apparent that the source was a cylindrical pipe of rock, called kimberlite, an igneous intrusion containing carbon crystallized as diamonds. Miners digging deeper and deeper into the pipe at Kimberley soon found that they needed expensive drilling, lifting, and pumping gear. Those able to procure funds for the equipment were able to buy out the smaller operators until a few individuals dominated the workings.

About ten years later, gold was discovered 400 km (250 mls) north-east of Kimberley on the Witwatersrand in the southern Transvaal. Production was first centred at Johannesburg and later extended east and west along the gold-bearing reefs. The gold occurs in a very finely divided state, as a powder in bands of quartz–pebble conglomerates called bankets, which are believed to have accumulated in the very distant past as shoreline pebble deposits. In the central districts of the Rand, near Johannesburg, the reefs lie quite close to the surface, but in most places they are at great depths, some mine shafts going down over 3 km (2 mls) where temperatures exceed 43 °C (109 °F) and rock bursts are liable to occur under the intense pressure from the overlying rock. The workings at the western and eastern ends of the Rand are endangered by flooding from large volumes of water contained in cavernous dolomites overlying the Witwatersrand system of rocks; pumping is essential, shafts passing down through the water-bearing beds have to be lined with concrete, and subsidence is liable to occur as the result of collapse into caverns beneath the workings.

Extracting great volumes of rock under these conditions calls for exploitation by large concerns. Expensive equipment and large, skilled staffs are needed to prospect for new reefs, to sink shafts over 7 m (25 ft) in diameter, to pump out water at rates of millions of litres per day, to ventilate the deep workings and finally to extract the gold from the tough ore-bearing rock. To deal with such problems large companies evolved on the Rand, companies that were organized originally by the Kimberley diamond-mining magnates, and financed by them and by thousands of private and institutional investors in South Africa, Britain, and North America.

In recent years the most productive mines have been those about 65 km (40 mls) west of Johannesburg. Great reserves of gold remain but much of it is too deep for profitable working, at least with present techniques and prices, and in the future only a limited number of mines are likely to remain open on the Witwatersrand itself.

The increase in the value of gold relative to the world's currencies that took place during the economic depression of the 1930s initiated a comprehensive series of geological surveys in

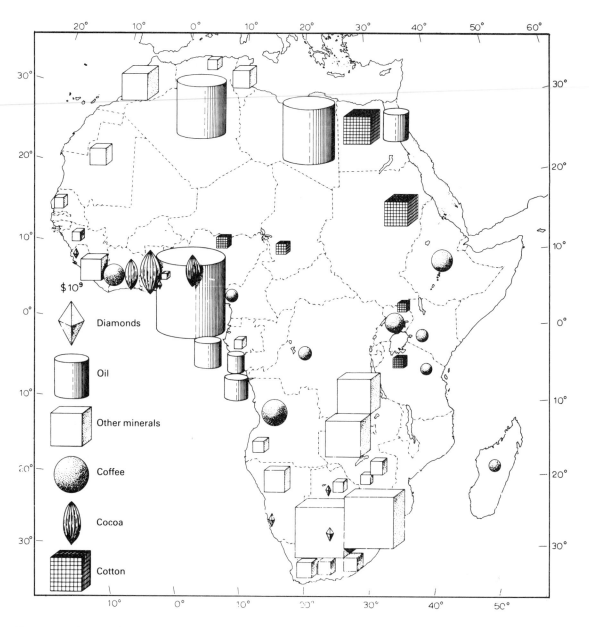

Fig. 9.1. *Values of the most important commodities produced in African countries in* (a) *the mid-1970s*

South Africa. They revealed gold-bearing conglomerates and quartzites lying concealed beneath thousands of metres of Karoo beds and other sedimentary rocks in the northern Orange Free State. Since 1950 a number of new mines have been brought into operation in this area, about 200 km (120 mls) south-west of Johannesburg, the most important being at Klerksdorp, Odendaalsrus, and Welkom. The ores are remarkably high-yielding, and as a result of opening these mines and others on the eastern Transvaal high veld, and the introduction of more efficient mining methods, production of gold in South Africa increased from 370 tonnes in 1953, to 700 tonnes in the 1960s, and over 1000 tonnes in 1970. It has since declined to about 700 tonnes, but is still worth something like $10 billion annually and constitutes

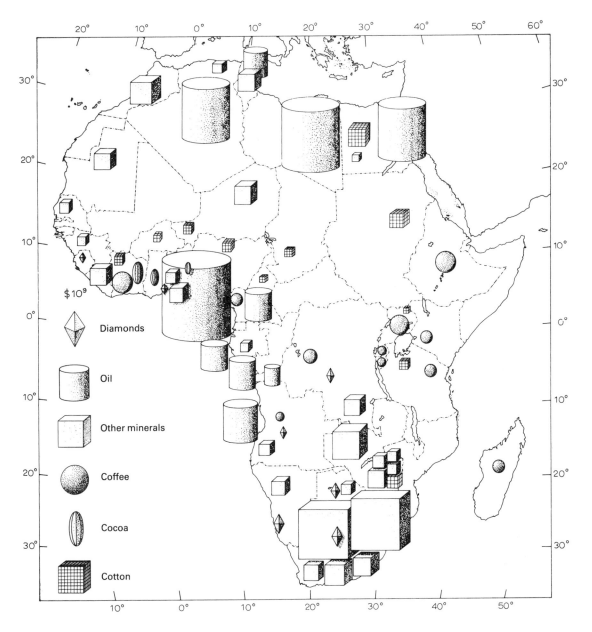

$10⁹

Diamonds

Oil

Other minerals

Coffee

Cocoa

Cotton

(b) the mid-1980s (in both cases in 1975 $US).

Work in progress on a mining shaft in the Moab area which by 1997 is expected to produce 13 tonnes of gold a year.

about half of world production. The demand for gold bullion is lower now than it used to be. Instead of being used to make coins or to underpin the value of a country's money, most of the gold produced is used these days for making jewelry. The goldfields already being worked in South Africa ensure that gold can be mined well into the twenty-first century.

The Witwatersrand goldfields continue to depend on migrant labour from beyond South Africa's frontiers. The workers are drawn mainly from Lesotho and Mozambique. In the newer gold-mining towns in the Orange Free State Bantu workers have their wives and families living with them. Welkom is a good example of a new-style mining town, with broad roads, residential suburbs radiating from the centre, and green wedges of open space between. On the east side a trading estate has attracted over a hundred assorted industrial plants.

For each ounce (30 grams) of gold produced, about 3 or 4 tonnes of rock have to be dug out, hauled to the surface, crushed and sorted. It is worth extracting other economic minerals from the crushed rock, even if they occur in small quantities, because the extra cost is relatively small. Uranium, which has been the most important of these other minerals in the ore, is recovered from those parts of the gold reef

where concentrations of the ore are highest. Sales in the 1980s increased to over 5000 tonnes, worth about $500 million. However, demand rapidly diminished in the early 1990s when the USA and CIS (the Commonwealth of Independent States; the former USSR) agreed to dismantle nuclear warheads, and stocks of weapons-grade uranium came onto the market which could be processed for use in power-stations.

The headwaters of the Limpopo river cut through the quartzite ridges of the Witwatersrand near Johannesburg and the Bankeveld east and west of Pretoria to flow northwards across a remarkably level plain (Fig. 8.5). Called the Bushveld basin, this plain coincides with the surface of an enormous mass of granitic and norite rocks around the rim of which, at the base of the igneous complex, are a number strongly mineralized zones. One of the most important economically includes the iron ore of Thabazimbi. In addition copper, antimony, platinum, asbestos, tin, and chrome ores are being worked. Half a million tonnes of phosphate concentrate are produced annually 240 km (150 mls) east of Pietersburg, not far from the Kruger National Park. Diamond mining is important near Pretoria; the largest diamond in the world, the Cullinan diamond, weighing over 0.5 kg (about 1.5 lb) was found in the Premier Mine there.

South-east of the Bankeveld, the high plains are underlain by horizontally disposed beds of sandstone, shale, and coal measures belonging to the Karoo system. Thick seams of coal, constituting the southern hemisphere's largest coalfield, are extensively worked near Witbank, Balfour, and Vereeniging. Westwards from Johannesburg, dolomites underlying the rocks of the Karoo system outcrop over an extensive area. These dolomites are some of the most productive water-bearing rocks in southern Africa, boreholes less than 30 m deep commonly yielding more than 450 000 litres (100 000 gallons) per day. The dolomite areas are also important economically because they are locally overlain by diamond-bearing gravels.

The richness of this assemblage of valuable metallic ores, diamonds, coal, and underground water, all within an area of a few thousand square kilometres, is scarcely to be rivalled anywhere else on earth, and it goes a

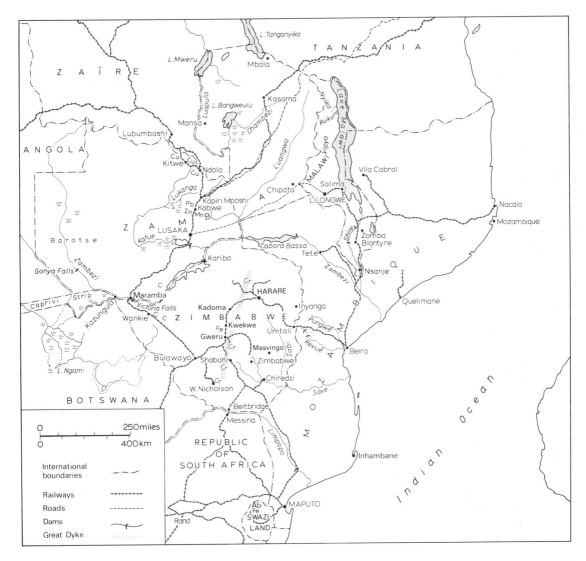

Fig. 9.2. *Zimbabwe, Zambia, Malawi, and Mozambique. A number of economic minerals are associated with the Great Dyke which cuts across Zimbabwe from north-north-east to south-south-west. Ab— asbestos, C—coal, Cr—chromite, Cu—copper, Fe—iron, M—manganese, Pb—lead, Zn—zinc.*

long way towards explaining why South Africa is such a prosperous country in comparison with other Afro-Asian states.

9.1.2 Zimbabwe

Mineralized zones extend northwards from the Transvaal into Zimbabwe, Zambia, and Zaire (Fig. 9.2). In Zimbabwe the metallic ores are associated with igneous intrusions which invaded volcanic and sedimentary rocks a thousand million years ago. The magma devoured great masses of the sedimentaries and altered others by heat and pressure. The molten rocks cooled down and solidified and by degrees were eroded away to reveal granite bosses surrounded by metamorphic aureoles. Gold, asbestos, and chrome are found in the altered rocks, especially in the vicinity of the Great Dyke. This elongated mass of intrusive

149

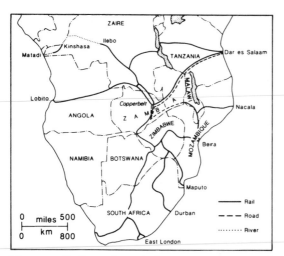

Fig. 9.3. *Rail, road, and river routes to coastal ports from the Copperbelt. From Zambia, the most convenient outlets are by rail via Beira or Maputo and for Shaba in Zaire the line via Lobito. Conflicts in Mozambique and Angola have interrupted these routes. Alternatives via East London and Dar es Salaam involve increased costs and reduced returns to producers.*

rocks, the most conspicuous feature of the geological map of Zimbabwe, runs north-north-east to south-south-west across the centre of the country from near Harare, the capital, to West Nicholson. It consists of four separate igneous complexes, flaring out towards the surface and aligned along a gigantic fault. The mining in this belt is on a considerable scale, but Zimbabwe's mineral wealth does not compare with that of the southern Transvaal.

In the western part of Zimbabwe and extending south-west into Botswana, and north-east into Zambia, the rocks of the Karoo system include extensive coal measures. Coal has been mined at Wankie (Hwange) for several decades and pits have also been opened in Botswana and in the Gwembe valley of Zambia. From Wankie, coking coal is brought by rail 500 km (300 mls) to an iron and steel plant at Que Que, about half-way between Harare and Bulawayo, where vast reserves of high-grade iron ore and limestone are available.

The railway from Cape Town to Kimberley runs north-north-east along the eastern side of Botswana, passing quite close to coal mines at Molepolole and copper and nickel mines at Selibe-Pikwe. At Bulawayo one line goes on to Harare; the other runs straight to Wankie,

crosses the Zambezi at the Victoria Falls, serves a declining lead and zinc mining area at Kabwe (formerly Broken Hill) and eventually reaches the Copperbelt extending from Zambia into Zaire (Fig. 9.3).

9.1.3 Zambia

The copper-bearing strata are vertically disposed, pre-Cambrian sedimentary rocks of the Katanga sequence resting on Basement Complex. It is thought that the ores were precipitated in a nearshore marine environment several hundreds of millions of years ago. The copper, which occurs as sulphides in layers about 50 m (170 ft) thick, is accessible at intervals along a belt some 320 km (200 mls) long and 50 km (30 mls) wide which extends from south-east to north-west across the Zambia–Zaire border (Fig. 9.4).

At first, in the 1920s, the copper was reached by shafts. After 1950 these were replaced by open pits from which enormous shovels extract the ore. The copper is concentrated by flotation techniques, smelted using electricity, and refined electrolytically before being exported. The ores are amongst the richest in the world, with a metal content exceeding 0.7 per cent, and the scale of production is very large. Production in terms of metallic copper increased from 370 000 tonnes in 1953 to 835 000 tonnes in 1970. It declined to 700 000 tonnes in the early 1980s, worth approximately $1 billion annually.

The mines in Zambia employ several hun-

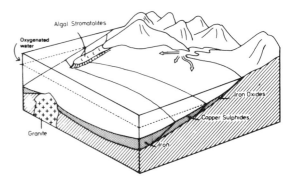

Fig. 9.4. *The origin of Copperbelt ores. It is believed that the metallic ores were precipitated in a nearshore environment beneath the level of oxygenated water.*

dred Europeans and about 40 000 Africans. Most of the African workers are Zambians who have worked there for the mining companies over ten years and have their families with them. Ownership of the mines is in the hands of a small number of large companies, registered in Zambia but subsidiaries of large international conglomerates, transnational companies (tncs) with important South African interests.

The population of the Zambian Copperbelt, which exceeds one and half million, is concentrated in seven towns spaced roughly 50 km (30 mls) apart, the largest being Ndola and Kitwe (Fig. 9.5). Each of the seven towns is situated close to an ore deposit and is separated from the other towns by sparsely settled woodland which is quite rapidly disappearing as it is cleared to provide fuel for the townspeople. Industries in the area are closely associated with the copper mining and involve smelting and refining but little in the way of metalworking. The mines remain dependent on South Africa for supplies of explosives and electrical and earth-moving equipment; consumer goods are largely imported from Zimbabwe and the Republic. A petroleum refinery at Ndola is capable of processing three quarters of a million tonnes of oil annually; this is pumped along a pipeline from Dar es Salaam.

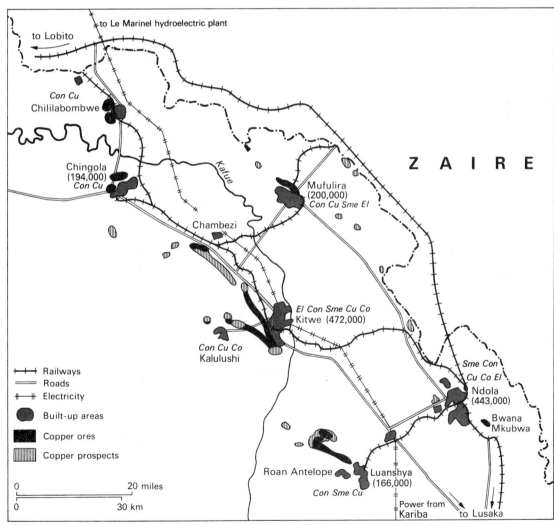

Fig. 9.5. *The Zambian Copperbelt. Co—cobalt, Cu—copper, Con—concentrator, El—electrolytic refinery, Sm—smelter. Figures in brackets are populations.*

9.1.4 Zaire

In Shaba, mining is on an even greater scale than in Zambia, about half a million tons of metallic copper being produced annually and in addition a number of other valuable metals. At Kipushi, in the south, copper-zinc sulphide ores are mined underground. The concentrated ores are railed 25 km (15 mls) to Lubumbashi for smelting and conversion to blister copper (Fig. 7.3). In the central area, copper and cobalt oxides are quarried from open pits and the concentrates are refined at Likasi, where there are also foundries, metal-working, and electrical plants. The most important mining area is in the north-west, where Kolwezi is the focus for processing ores, including some 15 000 tonnes of cobalt (about half the world's output), a metal widely used in steel alloys. Other mines produce concentrates containing about 150 000 tonnes of manganese and 100 000 tonnes of zinc annually, plus cadmium, silver, and germanium sulphide ores, and practically all the world's supplies of radium. Treatment of the sulphide ores at Likasi and elsewhere yields as a by-product sulphuric acid, which is used for treating the copper ore and for many industrial purposes. The Shaba industrial complex is probably more important than any other in Africa apart from the Witwatersrand. However, it has suffered in recent years from political confusion in Zaire and the spread of AIDS amongst the working population.

9.1.5 Mining elsewhere in High Africa

In addition to these mining operations, mention should be made of tin, also produced in Shaba, and diamonds at Tshikapa in Kasai (to the north-west of Shaba). Outside South Africa, Zimbabwe, Zambia, and Zaire there are other important mineral workings. Diamonds are mined at Orapa, Jwaneng and Letihakane in Botswana and are also extracted from alluvial sediments in north-east Angola and from an unbroken 160 kilometre stretch of raised beach material along Namibia's coastline between the Orange and Kuiseb rivers. A short distance inland from Walvis Bay, an opencast mine at Rossing is one of the world's major sources or uranium, production there being comparable to that of South Africa. Copper is mined near Windhoek, the capital of Namibia, and nearly a million tonnes of copper, zinc, and lead concentrates are produced annually at Tsumeb in the far north of the country. In Mozambique, coal suitable for coking is mined at Tete on the Zambezi, where abundant iron ore is near by. Gold, copper, manganese, asbestos, and titanium are amongst a number of minerals known to be present in the area but scarcely worked at present. In contrast, minerals of much economic importance are on the whole lacking in East Africa and Madagascar.

9.2 Mining and the petroleum industry in Low Africa

North-west of a line from the mouth of the Congo/Zaire to Ethiopia, the only minerals regarded as being of any importance until about 1960 were gold in Ghana, tin in Nigeria, diamonds in Ghana and Sierra Leone, rock phosphate in Morocco, iron ore in Algeria, and iron ore and bauxite in 'the western triangle' of west Africa (Fig. 9.6). Mineralization in the crystalline rocks was less intense than in southern Africa and a large proportion of the minerals extracted came from alluvial deposits where heavy minerals had been naturally concentrated by water sorting, that is by fluvial action in the past. A beginning had been made in the exploitation of bauxite, iron ore, and phosphate deposits situated not too far inland from the coast and, as the size of ocean carriers increased, these bulky minerals seemed to have considerable possibilities for the future.

9.2.1 Oil

The scene was transformed in the mid-1950s when, after several years of geophysical and geological prospecting by major companies, oil was discovered in large quantities in two main areas in the northern Sahara and also in southeast Nigeria. This was at a time when the sea route from the Arab/Persian Gulf to Europe via the Suez Canal had been interrupted by the conflict between Egypt and Israel, and tankers had been diverted round the Cape. Now there was the possibility of shipping oil to Europe and the east coast of America from Libya, Algeria, and Nigeria, and in the future it might be possible to export natural gas in liquefied form.

The oilfields were rapidly developed. Pipelines up to 300 km (180 mls) long carried oil

Fig. 9.6. *The western triangle of west Africa. Minerals constitute the most important exports of these countries. Bx—bauxite, D—diamonds, Fe—iron. Diamond mining is now largely in the hands of individual operators. The iron and bauxite mining is by large overseas companies.*

from the Libyan fields to tanker terminals on the Gulf of Syrte (Fig. 9.7). In Algeria pipelines up to 1000 km (600 mls) long carried oil from Edjelé, far south near the Libyan border, to La Skhira on the Gulf of Gabes in Tunisia, and oil from Hassi Messaoud and gas from Hassi R'mel to three terminals on the Algerian coast: Arzew near Oran, Algiers, and Skikda (Fig. 6.4). Oil in Nigeria was first located in the eastern Niger

delta and was subsequently discovered off the western part of the delta as well, terminals being constructed at Bonny, Warri, and also offshore (Fig. 9.8).

Oil exports from Africa began about 1961 and production increased through the 1960s. The export began of liquefied natural gas from Algeria to Canvey Island in the United Kingdom, but this soon came to a halt when abundant natural gas was discovered in the North Sea. However, oil production had already reached high levels when the price rises of 1973/4 and 1978/9 took effect. Quite suddenly Libya, which in 1954 had been one of the poorest countries in the world, found itself in 1974 one of the richest, with income per head in excess of $5000. Algeria's socialist government invested much of the new wealth from oil in industrial plants in the vicinity of the pipeline terminals on the Mediterranean. Nigerian oil revenues, with the world price at about $30 per barrel (about $200 per tonne), reached as much as $20 billion annually in the early 1980s, though this sum had to meet the demands of

nearly 100 million people in 19 States (Fig. 9.9). Other discoveries of petroleum were made in Egypt, Tunisia and in coastal Cameroon, Gabon, Congo and Cabinda (a small Angolan enclave north of the Congo/Zaire estuary).

The search for oil and then the drilling and construction of pipelines had provided employment for local people, mainly as labourers, transport drivers, and contractors; the majority of the skilled engineers were European and American. With the initial construction complete, most of the Europeans departed and the demand for local labour diminished. Before long, African governments in the producer countries took control of the oil industry

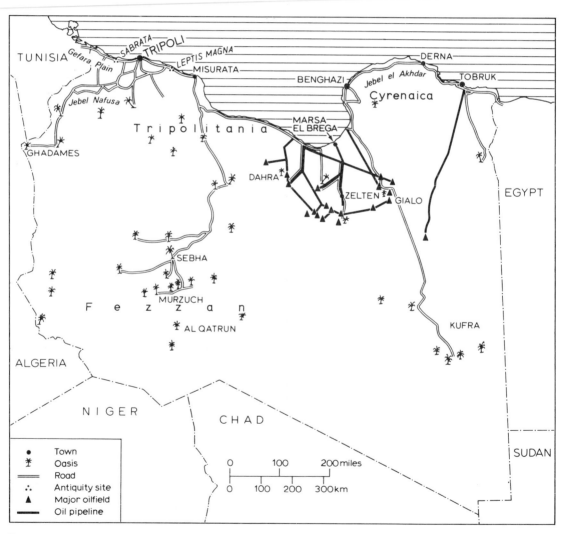

Fig. 9.7. *The oilfields and pipelines of Libya.*

by establishing national companies. These bought the oil from the companies extracting it and received a large part of the profits from its sale on the world market. They now had enormous sums at their disposal for development purposes and to meet current government expenditure.

The value of oil production in Low Africa far exceeded that of any other mineral or in fact of any other commodity produced in the region. Phosphate mining in Egypt and the Maghreb, Sahara, Senegal, and Togo had greatly expanded and was worth over $1 billion at the high prices being offered around 1974. Morocco was responsible for most of the phosphate produc-

tion, exporting about 10 million tonnes annually in the early 1970s; since then demand has slackened, and prices fell in the 1980s.

The total value of African production with oil at its peak price around 1980 was about $40 billion annually, of which a large part was at the disposal of nine African governments—Nigeria, Libya, Egypt, and Algeria being the main recipients.

By 1980, South Africa's income from minerals was greatly exceeded by that of the oil producers, and much of the returns from mining in that country had to be spent on the equipment, electricity, water supplies and labour required to extract the ores and refine the metals before

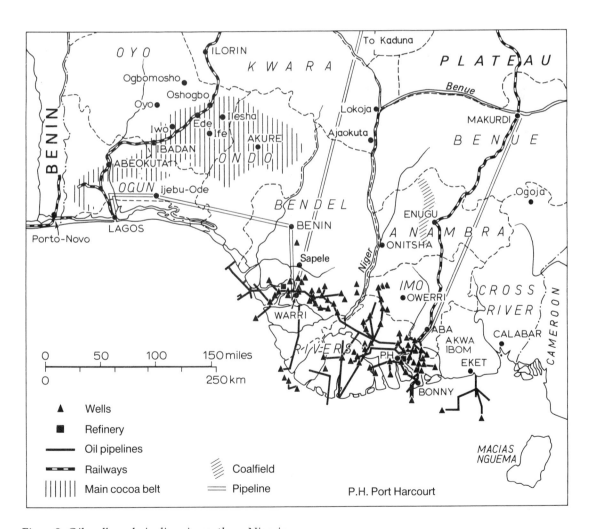

Fig. 9.8. *Oil wells and pipelines in southern Nigeria.*

they could be sold on world markets. A considerable proportion of the profits from the sale of the minerals was available to the mining companies and their shareholders to reinvest in South Africa or elsewhere and was not, in general, available to the South African government directly. Its revenue depended on taxation of the mining company profits and the earnings of people employed in the mineral and associated industries. In the oil-producing countries, on the other hand, governments were presented with the profits made by the national oil companies as well as with taxes paid on their profits (so far as they were declared) by the foreign companies extracting the oil. Governments' use of the funds provided by the oil was not always to the long-term advantage of the countries concerned; some were spent on arms, some on expensive but not very successful development projects, and quite large sums found their way back into private bank accounts in Europe and America.

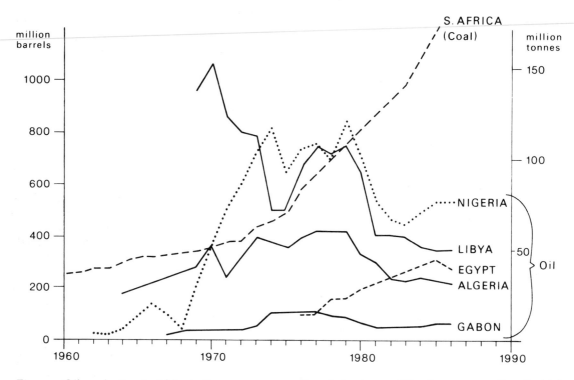

Fig. 9.9. *Oil production in Africa in the 1970s was running at about 300 million tonnes annually, of which Libya contributed half. In the early 1980s production fell to about 200 million tonnes but by 1991 had recovered to 360 million tonnes. Well over half was coming from north African countries and most of the rest from Nigeria. Meanwhile, South African production of coal (which has an energy content per tonne somewhat less than that of oil) increased from 50 million to 170 million tonnes annually.*

10

WATER RESOURCE DEVELOPMENT

Rivers and lakes in Africa have been controlled for two purposes: firstly, to generate electricity for mining and industry, and secondly, to supply water for irrigation projects. Some projects are multi-purpose, involving storage for both power generation and irrigation. On some rivers, notably the Nile and the Orange river, attempts have been made to integrate a number of different projects in schemes intended to make the most efficient use of the water resources of entire basins. Problems can arise with such schemes, because nearly all the largest African rivers run through several countries, each of which wants to maximize its share of possible benefits (Fig. 10.1).

The great seasonal fluctuations in discharge typical of African rivers require the construction of large reservoirs to even out the flow. The lakes created displace people living upstream of dams, while those living downstream may find the change in river regime disadvantageous. Floods may no longer reach land where formerly crops depended on moisture left in the soil when the water subsided. Dams interfere with fish migrations. Silt settles out in artificial lakes and clear water below dams picks up sediment from channel floors, causing downcutting and bank erosion. In the clearer water, plant growth and biological productivity may increase; on the other hand bottom water released from a storage reservoir is likely to be cool, lacking in oxygen, and harmful to fishlife. Changes in flow regime can thus have all manner of environmental consequences, some of which have been aggravated in recent years by droughts of a severity not previously experienced this century.

The economics of large water control schemes depend heavily on the terms under which finance is procured. Such control schemes are very expensive and in some cases

the benefits do not seem to outweigh the costs. Nevertheless, funds are still being made available for more such schemes, partly no doubt because the countries providing the funds also supply the machinery and expertise required to put them into effect. Furthermore, governments like dams as Pharaohs liked pyramids: they are highly visible and very permanent reminders of their builders.

10.1 Hydroelectric schemes

The energy of a river is the product of its discharge and the height through which it falls. Water power is thus most abundantly available where rainfall and runoff are high, the altitudinal range is great, and sites exist that allow the energy available to be harnessed relatively cheaply. In Africa, hydroelectric potential is greatest at locations where large rivers with extensive catchments in the humid regions of the continent descend from interior plateaus to lower levels, and valley gorges allow the construction of dams to store water, even out seasonal fluctuations in discharge, and provide high falls for the water. Such sites are widely distributed around southern and equatorial Africa.

The demand for hydroelectricity has been greatest where power has been needed for mining and industry, and alternative energy sources have been lacking. Amongst the earliest hydroelectric stations in Nigeria were those on the Jos Plateau, built where streams toppling over the western and south-western escarpments provided power for alluvial tin-workings. Other early schemes were undertaken on the Lufira and Lualaba headwaters of the Zaire river to supply power for the mines in Katanga (Fig. 7.3). These schemes were on a modest scale as compared with more recent

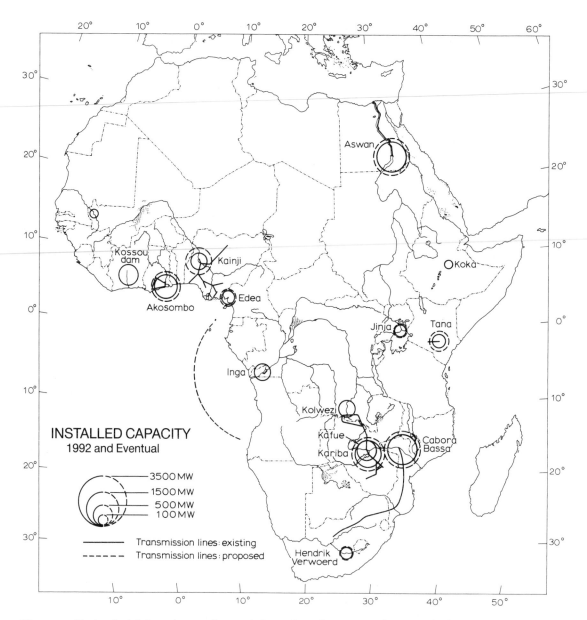

Fig. 10.1. *Hydroelectricity schemes. Some of the major schemes are shown with their transmission lines. The very great potential of the lower Zaire at Inga as compared with the present installation's capacity is apparent.*

ones on the great rivers of Africa, several of which have already received mention.

10.1.1 The Zambezi

In the 1950s, when Northern and Southern Rhodesia were in the Central African Federation, both countries contributed towards the construction of a dam on the Zambezi at Kariba

(Fig. 9.2). It cost £100 million at the time, equivalent to more than £1000 million today. The deep lake behind the dam, with a volume larger than that of any other man-made lake in the world, was intended to supply both countries with power for mining and industry. The power station, with a capacity of about 700 MW, was located on the south side of the river, so when the Federation broke up in 1963, Southern Rhodesia found itself in control of the power supply and eventually bought out Zambia's share. Kariba is now a significant sporting attraction on the tourist circuit from Harare to Victoria Falls and the Chobe and Wankie game reserves. Its generating capacity has been increased and it supplies about half of Zimbabwe's electricity needs.

Since the early 1970s, Zambia has been supplied with electricity from a 108 MW plant at Victoria Falls, and from a powerhouse on the north side of Kariba with a capacity of 600 MW. A new power station with a capacity of 900 MW at the Kafue Gorge was so severely damaged by fire in March 1989 that it was out of action for over a year. Then in May 1992, the flow of the Kafue river fell so low that power output was cut by a third and instead of exporting $18 million worth of electricity to Zimbabwe annually, Zambia had to import from Zaire. Most of the power generated is used by the copper mining industry; the people depend on wood and charcoal for 90% of their needs. In the future, electricity will probably be generated in the Batoka Gorge downstream of the Victoria Falls.

Downstream of Kariba, below Tete in Mozambique, the Cabora Bassa dam, with a capacity of 680 MW, was completed in 1976. Financial assistance came from Portugal and from South Africa. Initial filling of the reservoir in the early months of 1975 severely reduced the flow of the river downstream of the dam; then it was found that the level in the reservoir was rising too fast and an emergency release of water gave a massive unseasonal flood, seriously disrupting ecological conditions. The retention of silt by the dam is likely to have affected the delta of the Zambezi and possibly the adjacent Mozambique coast. Guerrillas destroyed transmission lines to South Africa in the mid-1980s and consequently neither Mozambique nor South Africa has yet derived much benefit from Cabora Bassa.

From the mid-1940s until 1980 the mean discharge of the Zambezi at Victoria Falls was 40 per cent higher than it had been in the preceding score of years, probably because of higher rainfall over western Zambia and eastern Angola (Fig. 1.22). The energy available was therefore greater than seemed to be the case when the present hydro schemes were being planned. However, droughts in the early 1980s greatly reduced the discharge. It is evident that projects of this kind must have some built-in flexibility if they are to adapt to the climatic fluctuations typical of Africa, fluctuations which persist over several years and involve decadal variations of mean discharge between 50 per cent more and 50 per cent less than the centennial means.

10.1.2 The Akosombo dam on the Volta River, Ghana

The Akosombo dam was built across the Volta in the early 1960s where the river transects the Akwapim range in a gorge about 80 km (50 mls) inland of the coast of south-east Ghana. The intention was that the project should provide a basis for the industrialization of the region. After early difficulties in obtaining funding, agreement was eventually reached between the newly independent Ghana government and the Kaiser Corporation of California.

In association with a number of other companies, the Corporation agreed to build the dam in conjuction with an aluminium plant at Tema which would use a large part of the power produced. At first, bauxite from Guiana and Jamaica would be converted into alumina in the south-eastern USA and shipped over to Ghana for conversion into aluminium to be exported to the USA and north-west Europe. It was visualized that at some time in the future Ghanaian bauxite would be used as the raw material in an integrated plant, but no firm promises were made on this score.

A large rockfill dam and a power station were built rapidly and economically at Akosombo, paid for jointly by the aluminium company and the Ghana government. Over the years 1964-68 the Volta Lake filled with water, to become the most extensive artificial lake in the world with an area of 9600 km² (3725 mls²). Though the flooded area had been fairly sparsely settled, about 85 000 people were forced to move from their homes. The provision made for their resettlement and compensation was not altogether satisfactory. Some of them were provided with small, simple houses, but they were unsuitable for an extended family and settlements were not always sited in places where the displaced people wanted to live. The lake has cut off the eastern side of the country from

Looking downstream across the Akosombo dam under construction in 1963.

The Akosombo dam in 1987 with power plants in the foreground and the main mass of the dam behind.

the rest, greatly reducing its accessibility. It is suspected that coast erosion east of the Volta mouth may be a consequence of sediment being trapped in the Volta Lake that would otherwise have been supplied by the river. On the other hand, the lake fisheries have been a great benefit, attracting over 10 000 fishermen and their families from further downstream and yielding over 30 000 tonnes of fish annually in the 1960s, though smaller quantities later (Fig. 10.2). As usually happens, some people have gained from the project while others have lost.

Most of Akosombo's electricity went to the aluminium plant at Tema, its American owners benefiting financially from being able to purchase electricity from one of the cheapest sources in the world and for the first years of the scheme's operation not being required to pay taxes. A number of small factories were established in the Tema area and transmission lines were constructed to carry electricity to many urban centres not only in southern Ghana but also in Togo and Benin. For domestic consumers the electricity was not cheap

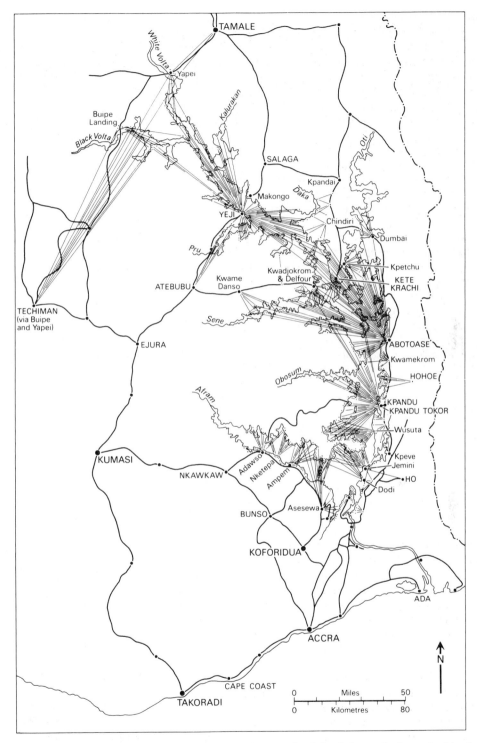

Fig. 10.2. *Settlements and markets around the Volta lake. Much of the fish caught is smoked in the small settlements on the shores of the inlets on the west side of the lake, and then carried to large markets that have grown up near the road on the east side for transport to Accra.*

161

because the expense of constructing transmission lines was heavy in relation to the demand for electricity.

The capacity of the Volta Lake was large enough to even out the variations in the discharge of the river from season to season. A much smaller dam constructed downstream of Akosombo on the Kpong rapids in the late 1970s increased the reliability of power supplies. But in the years around 1980 a succession of dry years reduced Volta discharge and lake level until eventually a drought in 1983 was so severe that flow through the turbines could not be maintained, power supplies were interrupted and the aluminium plant had to cease production. (The level of the Kossou lake and power production from the Bandama River in the Ivory Coast were reduced at the same time.)

Closure of the plant was probably felt more by Ghana than by the aluminium company because, as a result of economic recession, there was an oversupply of aluminium on world markets. However, production was resumed in 1985, on a somewhat smaller scale than before and with the aluminium company paying rather more for its electricity. More of the metal was made available for local factories making domestic equipment. By the late 1980s studies were in progress to discover how water from behind the Kpong dam could best be used for irrigating the Volta floodplain and low terraces downstream in the coastal dry zone of south-east Ghana.

10.1.3 The Niger

Power is developed from the upper Niger at a plant on the Sotuba rapids, not far downstream of Bamako, capital of Mali. Most of the development works have been on the lower river, notably the Kainji dam in Nigeria, planned before Nigerian oil became available. Completed in 1968, the dam holds back a lake which floods the Bussa rapids where Mungo Park met his death. The lake displaced 50 000 people, who were resettled in specially built villages. As in the case of Volta resettlement, many people found the housing and the siting of the villages unsatisfactory, but on the whole there were not too many complaints.

Lake Kainji has quite a limited storage capacity, but the flow of the lower Niger is fairly well distributed through the year, the Black

Flood from the headwaters arriving in the early months of the years to supplement supplies derived from local rains in succeeding months. Nevertheless, power supplies were curtailed from time to time in the early 1970s and 1980s partly as a result of droughts and low river discharges.

Other dams are at Jebba, not far downstream of Kainji, and in the Shiroro Gorge of the Kaduna river which enters the Niger downstream of Jebba. Evening out river discharge through the year has improved navigation on the lower Niger somewhat and has also allowed more irrigation alongside the mainstream. The electricity produced from the dams on the lower Niger is transmitted to Kano and is also distributed by a grid linked to the oil- and coal-powered generating stations in the southeast of the country.

10.1.4 The Tana

The headwaters of the Tana river, which flows from the slopes of Mount Kenya to the Indian Ocean, have been harnessed to generate electricity for Nairobi and nearby industrial areas at Thika and elsewhere (Figs 10.3 and 11.1). Water storage by the Seven-Forks Hydroelectric complex has reduced the height of seasonal floods in the lower river, thereby threatening the survival of floodplain forests which seem to have depended on occasional extreme floods for regeneration.

10.1.5 Other hydroelectricity schemes

Other important schemes have harnessed the energy of rivers in the humid regions of equatorial Africa (Fig. 10.1). In west Africa, the Kossou dam on the lower Bandama river in Ivory Coast (520 MW), and a dam at Edea near the mouth of the Sanaga river, 50 km (30 mls) south-east of Douala (275 MW), are entirely devoted to the production of electricity. The same is true of the Inga power station on the Zaire river downstream of Kinshasa, which serves the Shaba mining region 1860 km (1160 mls) away. Inga's potential capacity is enormous, some 30 000 MW, and it is well able to supply all Zaire's electricity needs for many years to come. However, Shaba's needs for electricity would probably have been provided by a power station nearer at hand with lower transmission costs had there not been a political need to ensure that Shaba should be dependent on a power station near the capital Kinshasa and thus less likely to attempt to make itself independent of central government.

10.2 Irrigation schemes

Several large irrigation schemes have been developed in Africa since 1975, especially in the Sudan–Sahel zone. The aim was to provide a reliable source of food and income in a region liable to suffer from drought and famine. In Nigeria, there was the added incentive to invest in large schemes in the semi-arid north in order to spread the benefits of oil revenues around the country. The Gezira scheme in the Sudan Republic was looked upon as a model to be followed (Figs 10.8 and 10.9); less regard was paid to a large west African scheme in the

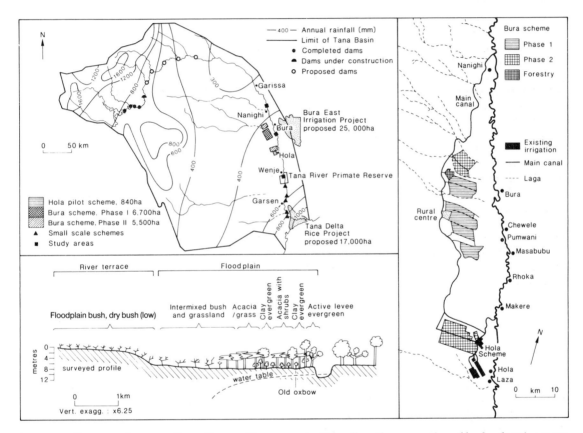

Fig. 10.3. *Dams on the upper Tana, Kenya. These were built to allow the generation of hydroelectric power for Nairobi and other towns in Kenya and have evened out the flow of the river downstream. After experience had been gained on the Hola pilot scheme, it was hoped that a larger area would be irrigated in the Bura area. Settlers arrived from various parts of Kenya and the scheme was put into operation. However, yields have been disappointing because of soil conditions. A weir intended to lift the level of the water to irrigate land on the east side of the river as well as the west has not been built. The pumps used to lift water from the river into the west bank main canal have presented many problems and the whole scheme may be abandoned. The floodplain forest, which is of considerable ecological interest, is being modified by the reduced incidence of flooding and as a result of wood-cutting for firewood and house-building by the immigrants. If the dams proposed for the upper Tana are built or the weir is constructed, interruption of sediment discharge is likely to affect erosion of the lower Tana channel banks and floodplain more drastically. (From F.M.R. Hughes, 'The Tana river floodplain forest, Kenya: ecology and the impact of development', University of Cambridge PhD dissertation, 1984.)*

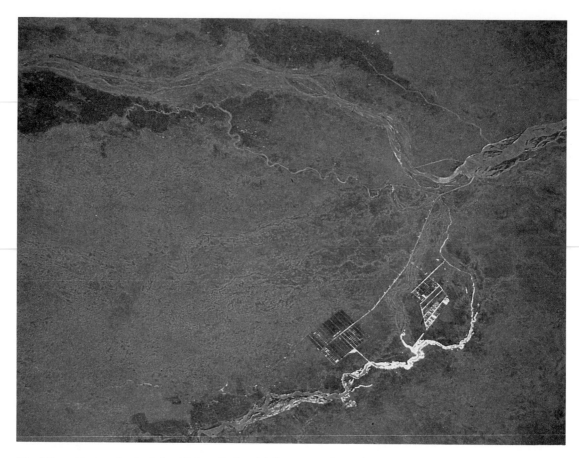

The Niono Project in the Inland Niger Delta, Mali, as seen from the Space Shuttle on 3 December 1985. The Niger, its flow diminished by drought, is flowing from left to right at the bottom of the picture. Water is being led from the river towards irrigated fields on either side of the river and north towards the top of the picture.

Inland Niger Delta which had been in operation for many years but had never been a success (Fig. 5.6). Furthermore, insufficient importance was attached to the great variablity of river flow in the western Sudan–Sahel where the rainfall is even more variable than in the headwaters of the Nile (Fig. 1.22).

10.2.1 The Inland Niger Delta

Attempts to irrigate the country lying to the north of Ségou, a 'dead' part of the Inland Niger Delta in Mali (Fig. 5.6) were begun under the French colonial administration in 1919. In 1946 a barrage was complete at Sansanding to raise the level of the river and divert it along river distributory channels that had long ago ceased to function naturally. Villages and roads were built and Africans given plots of land, with the aim of growing cotton to supply the French textile industry as the Gezira supplied Lancashire. It was hoped to put a million hectares (2.5 million acres) under cultivation, and very large sums of money were spent, but by the time independence came to Mali, only about 40 000 ha were were being cropped successfully. The soils are not as fertile as those between the Blue and the White Nile, the Niger carries less plant nutrients as silt and in solution, and the variability of the rainfall in the headwaters together with the lack of a storage reservoir mean that water supplies are uncertain. Not surprisingly, colonists have never been attracted to work on the scheme.

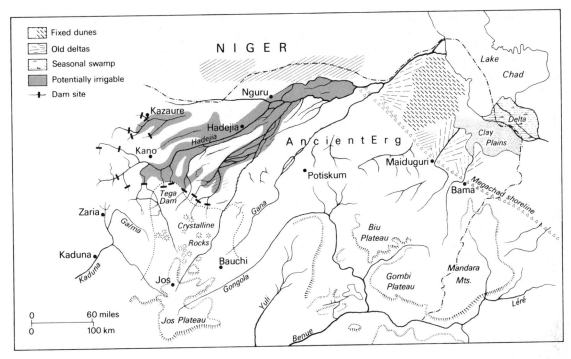

Fig. 10.4. *North-eastern Nigeria. Dams have been constructed in the headwaters of rivers draining towards Lake Chad for irrigating the plains downstream. East of Nguru, farmers are using small petrol engines to pump water from wells to grow wheat.*

10.2.2 The Kano river scheme

The Kano river project, started in 1971, covers 18 000 ha (46 000 acres) in northern Nigeria (Fig. 10.4), including a part of the closely settled zone near Kano city. It is a large-scale, technically complex, capital-intensive project, intended to be the first of several such schemes which were to cover 60 000 ha (146 000 acres). The aim was to increase food supplies, especially wheat for the growing urban population.

Many of those who formerly farmed the land are now involved in the scheme but many people who were displaced by the Tega dam, which covers 176 km² (68 mls²), and by roads, canals, and a government farm, do not feel they were adequately compensated. Problems have arisen from the fact that the best time for planting wheat as a dry-season, 'winter' crop overlaps the time for harvesting guinea corn grown as a wet-season crop. Substituting maize for guinea corn may help to resolve this

conflict. Some of the poorer farmers have difficulties in meeting the costs of inputs provided by the scheme—water, seed, fertilizers, and tractor cultivation—and are being bought out by people with capital or who have been able to obtain loans. Properly trained extension staff are scarce.

10.2.3 The Bakolori scheme

In north-west Nigeria, the Bakolori irrigation scheme is also a product of the 1970s, built at a time when it was felt politically necessary to spend oil revenues in the north of the country and at the same time reduce the risks from drought and desertification. Farmers in the Sokoto valley were dependent on the annual flood, which was always unpredictable (Fig. 10.5). It was argued that a storage dam, built on the crystalline rocks of the upper river, would help to increase the reliability of water supplies. Irrigation of some 12 000 ha (30 000

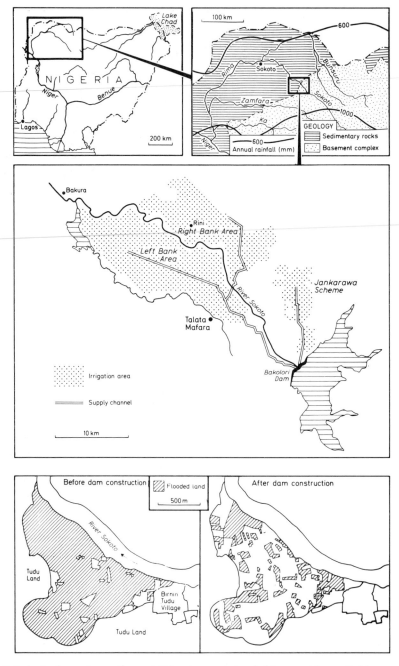

Fig. 10.5. *The Bakolori scheme in north-west Nigeria was intended to provide a reliable source of water for irrigating the alluvial plain bordering the Sokoto river. The results have not been commensurate with the heavy cost of the project. Owing to the droughts of the 1970s and 1980s less water has been available than was expected. Farmers living downstream, near Birnin Tudu for instance, find that the scheme takes so much water that much of the village floodplain on which they formerly depended for growing rice is no longer inundated and so they have to grow alternative crops like sorghum and bullrush millet, which are less rewarding. (From W. M. Adams, 'Downstream impact of river control, Sokoto Valley, Nigeria', University of Cambridge PhD dissertation, 1983.)*

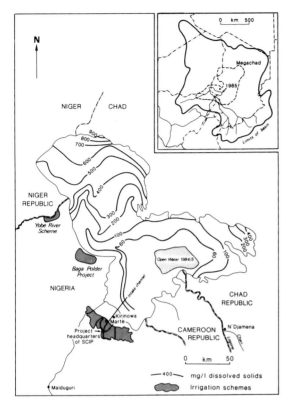

Lake Chad as seen looking north from the Space Shuttle on 15 January 1986. A canal intended to lead water to the Nigerian South Chad Irrigation Project in the bottom left of the picture does not reach the shrunken remnant of the lake—the roughly circular pale patch at the southern end of the lake floor.

Fig. 10.6. *Irrigation near Lake Chad. In the 1960s, when the lake was at a high level, water in the southern part, mainly brought in by the Chari–Logone, had a solute load of only 60 mg/l (i.e. 60 parts per million of dissolved solids). As the water moved north and east, evaporation caused the solute load concentrations to increase. Some calcium and magnesium carbonates were taken up by plants and snails. The proportion of sodium salts increased towards the extreme north and east and these salts were precipitated where seepage water reached the surface and evaporated in shallow basins at a distance from the lake. In the 1970s it was decided to use the fresh water from the southern part of the lake to irrigate a large area of the clay plains of Borno, bringing it by an intake channel to a pumping station which would lift it to a distribution point from which it could be led to the fields. In the early 1980s, when the project was in operation, the lake fell to very low levels (Fig. 1.22) and in mid-1985 its area shrank from about 26 000 km² to less than 3000 km². The intake channel no longer reached the lake and irrigation came to a halt. (From V. A. Kolawole, 'Irrigation and drought in Borno, Nigeria', University of Cambridge PhD dissertation, 1987.)*

acres) was recommended by FAO. The project implemented rather hurriedly in the 1970s was much larger, involving the storage of sufficient water to irrigate 30 000 ha (75 000 acres). The results have so far been unsatisfactory owing to drought and the large size of the project. Cultivators downstream of the irrigated area find flood levels too low during the rains for growing rice and have had to switch to millet; dry-season cultivation has much diminished in area. Farmers who were displaced by the project are dissatisfied with their compensation and the quality of alternative land offered to them; yields on the scheme are lower than had been predicted.

10.2.4 The South Chad Irrigation Project

The most serious failure has involved the South Chad Irrigation Project (SCIP, see Fig. 10.6). It was intended to make use of water led from Lake Chad by an intake canal 30 km (19 mls) long, pumped to a higher level, and distributed by feeder canals over 106 000 ha (260 000 acres). The level of the lake is normally lowest during the rainy season and it was intended to grow rice at this season, using the rains supplemented by irrigation, followed by wheat as a dry-season crop. Since the inception of the scheme in 1974 the lake has scarcely ever been high enough in the rainy season to reach the intake canal. Wheat was grown in some winters in the years around 1980, though yields were lower than had been expected. In 1984 the inflow of water to the lake from the Chari river was so small that the level of Lake Chad never rose high enough to allow water to be pumped from it and neither rice nor wheat could be grown.

The people living in the SCIP area had formerly grown dry-season crops of sorghum, a variety called masakwa, on the land included in the irrigation scheme. Many of them survived the twin disasters of drought and the failure of the irrigation project in the early 1980s by moving onto the lake floor, where they were

able to grow good crops of maize and cowpeas. They were joined by employees from the project, which had been left without water or funds. It remains to be seen how they will all survive when wetter conditions return and the lake floor is flooded, especially if in the meantime the irrigation works have fallen into disrepair.

10.2.5 Senegal river schemes

In spite of the lack of success of these large schemes, large dams have recently been constructed on the Senegal river (Fig. 10.7). The Manantali dam on the Bafing headwater in Mali is intended to regulate the flow of the Senegal river, improve navigation, and produce electric power for Dakar and Mali as well as allowing a

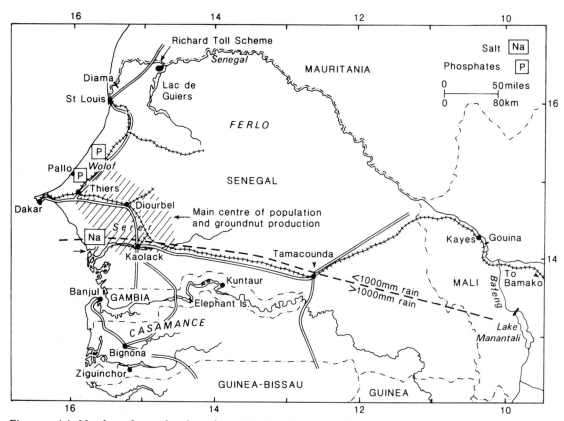

Fig. 10.7 (a). *Northern Senegal and southern Mauritania have suffered severely from droughts in the 1970s and 1980s. A scheme is being completed which is intended to allow irrigation of the plains on either side of the lower Senegal river. The Richard Toll scheme has been in operation for many years, making use of floodwater stored in the Lac de Guier (which is also used as a reservoir for Dakar). A dam on the Bafing river far upstream at Manantali in Mali will generate electricity and store water to reduce the seasonal variation in the flow of the lower Senegal.*

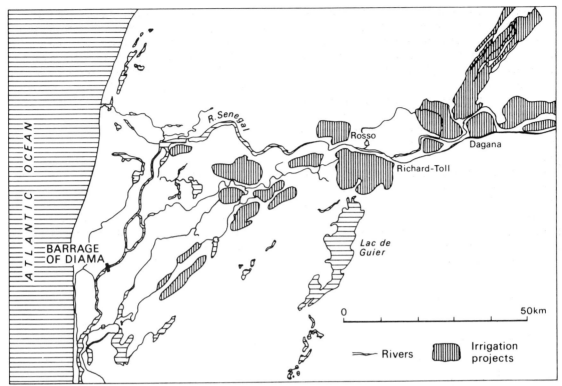

Fig. 10.7 (b). *The barrage at Diama will increase freshwater storage and prevent sea water flooding up the river. Irrigation with water pumped from the river will replace the traditional flood-recession farming. (From Club du Sahel/CILSS, 1979.)*

quarter of a million hectares on the Senegal side of the river to be irrigated. Completion of the power project has been delayed by border

Rice-threshing on an experimental rice plantation near Kaédi in the Senegal valley.

disputes with Mauritania which demands that power should be made available there. A barrage across the lower river at Diama, completed in 1986, is intended to store floodwater and prevent seawater penetrating up the Senegal early in the year when the flow of the river is much reduced. The new structures will make the traditional flood-recession farming more or less impossible, and water for irrigation will have to pumped from the river. The risks of failure are considerable, and the hazards faced by the local people are possibly greater now than before the schemes were initiated.

10.3 Integrated river control projects

On most of the larger African rivers a number of water control projects are now in operation. They have often been planned independently of one another and may even have conflicting effects. In the case of Lake Chad, for instance, in spite of the existence of a Lake Chad Basin Commission, which includes representatives from all the countries around the lake, the South Chad Irrigation Project (SCIP) in Nigeria was designed with little consideration being given to the intentions and activities of the Chad and Cameroon Republics. Both countries are abstracting water from the Logone river to irrigate the plains south of the lake, thereby accentuating the problems of the Nigerian SCIP which, it must be emphasized, are primarily caused by drought reducing the lake to unprecedentedly low levels (Fig. 1.22).

In the development of the Nile waters, greater attention has always been paid to the conflicting interests of the various countries involved. However, as fuller use has been made of the river flow the competition for water has increased, with countries downstream feeling themselves vulnerable to abstraction of water by those upstream.

The Orange river scheme is confined to the Republic of South Africa, except for a large reservoir in Lesotho, and risks of this kind do not exist, so that more rational planning is possible.

10.3.1 Development of the Nile waters

The discharge of the Nile is about eight times that of the Orange river, on average about 86 km³ (21.5 mls³) per year. It leads water from the well-watered east African and Ethiopian highlands across the savannas of the Sudan and the eastern Sahara desert to the Mediterranean. Rational development of Nile water is complicated by the fact that its sources are in five countries far removed from the Sudan and Egypt, where the water is most needed. In the first half of this century, when most of the Nile basin was under British control, plans were made to use the river economically and efficiently by successively constructing a number of storage dams and power stations and keeping wastage to a minimum. The situation changed completely between 1950 and 1960, when all the countries concerned became independent.

At the beginning of this century a dam had been constructed at Aswan on the lowest cataract of the Nile to store water for perennial irrigation in Egypt. Its size was limited at first by the desire not to flood the ancient temple of Philae. Eventually the need for more storage was so great that the temple was rebuilt on a

higher site and the crest of the dam was raised on two occasions, its storage capacity being increased from 1 km³ to 5.7 km³ (1.4 mls³). Other storage reservoirs were built in the Sudan: the Sennar dam on the Blue Nile, to serve the needs of the Gezira, and the Jebel Aulia dam on the White Nile, which was primarily intended to store water for use in Egypt (Fig. 10.8).

The first post-war Nile project to be completed was the Owen Falls dam across the White Nile where it leaves Lake Victoria. This was built primarily to generate electricity for industrial and other uses in eastern Uganda (Fig. 10.1). It was also claimed that the dam would help to regulate the discharge of the White Nile from Lake Victoria, and Egypt was

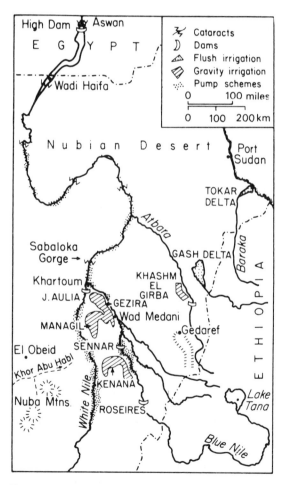

Fig. 10.8. *Irrigation schemes in the Sudan Republic.*

accordingly persuaded to contribute to its cost. The design of the dam was based on the assumption that the discharge from Lake Victoria would continue to be about 21 km³ annually, as it had been on average over the previous half century. However, after 1961 the discharge from the lake doubled, owing to increased rainfall over its catchment, and flow at Jinja remained at an unexpectedly high level for the next 20 years. There was naturally some concern as to the long-term structural adequacy of the spillway, which has had to cope with discharges greater than those for which it was originally designed, and it was evident that much more power could have been developed —had the high discharges persisted.

Until the 1950s, national rights to the Nile waters had been governed by the Nile Waters Agreement which was reached when all the countries concerned were under British suzerainty. According to the Agreement, the Sudan had the right to only 4 km³ (1 cubic mile); the rest was available for use in Egypt. When the High Dam at Aswan was being planned, it became apparent that the lake behind it would flood Wadi Haifa in Sudan. As compensation, Egypt agreed to increase Sudan's share of the water to 18.5 km³ (4.5 mls³). It also provided funds for the resettlement of about 100 000 displaced Nubian people. They were sent·away from their comfortable riverside towns and villages and resettled far to the south-east on a bleak new irrigation scheme supplied with water from the Atbara tributary of the Nile. This scheme at Khashm el Girba has suffered not only from droughts in recent years but also from the capacity of the reservoir having been greatly reduced by sediments brought down from the highlands of Eritrea in northern Ethiopia.

10.3.1.1 The Gezira scheme The Gezira irrigation scheme has been regarded as one of the great achievements of imperial rule in Africa (Fig. 10.9). It was not an intensive scheme; in order to minimize water use and risks of soil salinization, cropping was mainly confined to the winter months when evaporation losses were least. To serve the scheme with water in the first half of the year when most of the Blue Nile's water was needed by Egypt, the Sennar dam was completed in 1925; after the Second World War another dam was built further

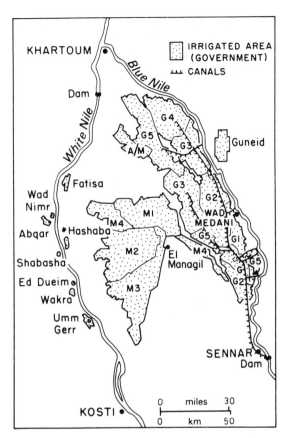

Fig. 10.9. *The Gezira irrigation scheme and Managil extension. (After K. M. Barbour,* The Republic of the Sudan, *1961.)*

upstream at Roseires to generate electricity and allow extension of the irrigated area. The Gezira scheme now provides a livelihood not only for hundreds of thousands of local Sudanese but also for immigrant labourers from the west. The cotton produced provides badly needed foreign exchange and has helped to underpin the Sudanese economy, which is otherwise very insecure.

Criticisms have been made in recent years that the scheme does not allow the tenants to exercise their initiative and that little has been done to improve the amenities of the settlements where the people live. More land is now being devoted to maize and wheat and less to cotton, but production is becoming more intensive than was formerly the case, and water consumption is increasing.

171

10.3.1.2 The Jonglei scheme With Egypt's population growing by over a million every year, and the Sudan making use of all the water it is allowed by treaty, nearly all the flow of the river in the lower Nile valley is being put to use. Attention has therefore been directed towards the possibility of increasing the amount of water available by reducing losses from the Sudd, the swamps of the southern Sudan (Fig. 1.23). Some 10 km^3 (2.5 mls^3) of the White Nile's discharge are lost from this region annually by evaporation of floodwaters and it has long been apparent that such losses could be greatly reduced by leading the White Nile across the swamplands by a canal.

Work began on such a canal in the early 1980s. Careful surveys had been made with a view to limiting its impact on the pastoralist people, the Nuer, Dinka, and Shilluk, who depend on grazing their cattle on the *toiches*, grassland flooded annually by the river. Only about a half of the natural flow of the White Nile was to be canalized and it was planned that a small canal running parallel to the main one should provide water for local irrigation and enable sugar-cane to be grown for processing at factories to be built at Mongalla, Melut, and Renk. It was proposed that a paper factory at Malakal might make use of papyrus from the swamps and marshes that would remain, and that fisheries could be commer-

cialized. An additional 5 km^3 (1.2 mls^3) of water thus saved would be available for use in Egypt and the northern Sudan.

Many ecologists were not satisfied with the precautions being taken to safeguard the environment. Some people were concerned that reduced evaporation from the swamps would diminish the local rainfall; this is unlikely, for the reduction of evaporation from the Sudd would only be a few per cent, and most of the water that falls as rain on the region is brought in from the Indian and Atlantic oceans. The most vehement objections came from the non-Muslim people of the southern Sudan. They were extremely suspicious of a scheme which in their view involved a transfer of benefits from them to the northern Muslim Arabs who form the government in Khartoum. From 1955 to 1972 the southern Sudan had been in a state of turmoil and no work on the Jonglei scheme had been possible. In October 1974, when the scheme was being mooted again, rumours quite without foundation spread amongst the southerners that thousands of Egyptians would be settled on the land reclaimed from the swamps, and serious rioting broke out in Juba. At last, in the early 1980s, a great machine operated by a French company started to dig its way southwards from Malakal. When the canal was over 100 km long and more than half way to Jonglei, civil war broke out again between north and south, and work was suspended. It has been noticed on satellite imagery that the banks of the unfinished canal pond back shallow lakes which form a new element in the complex hydrography of the Sudd plains and may inadvertently benefit game animals and pastoralists.

The Jonglei Canal photographed from the Space Shuttle on 14 January 1986. It extends south, towards the left-hand side of the picture, from the confluence of the Sobat and the White Nile.

10.3.1.3 Risks of conflict over water Some concern has been felt in Egypt and Sudan in recent years over Ethiopia's plans to develop the water resources of the Nile headwaters. There have been rumours that Ethiopia plans to build a reservoir on the Blue Nile and take water to irrigate plains east of the Sudan frontier. It has also been claimed that Ethiopian resettlement schemes on highlands drained by the Blue Nile are yielding heavy loads of sediment that threaten to diminish the capacity of the Roseires dam. Neither of these fears seems to have a substantial basis.

10.3.2 *The Orange river scheme*

Much of South Africa is semi-arid, with no river as big as the Niger, Zaire, and Zambezi. Its main water control project involves making the best use of the waters of the Orange river, which discharges on average 11 km³ (2.7 mls³) annually into the Atlantic (Fig. 10.10).

The main tributary of the Orange is the Vaal river, which flows through the industrial complex of the southern Transvaal, about 65 km (40 mls) south of Johannesburg. The Vaal is already carefully controlled, not so much for irrigation as to supply the industries of the Witwatersrand and Vereeniging. Its flow has been supplemented by water from the eastward-flowing headwaters of the Tugela river, which have been dammed and their waters pumped up 500 m (1600 ft) over the continental divide to supply the Sterkfontein dam in the upper valley of the Vaal.

The Orange river itself is deeply entrenched and offers few opportunities for irrigation. The new project involves diverting a large part of its flow through a tunnel 83 km (51 mls) long and 5 m (17.5 ft) in diameter into the upper reaches of the Great Fish river. From the Great Fish, water will be led by another tunnel and canal system into the valley of the Sundays river. These tunnels, plus various dams and pipelines, will allow about 300 000 hectares (0.75 million acres) to be brought under cultivation. A network of 20 hydroelectric stations is being constructed as part of the project to provide power for industry, especially at demand peaks, and to pump water from the new dams to cities in need of additional supplies. The scheme is an important contribution to the nation's economy, making land available for at least 9000 new farms, and greatly increasing the production of fruit, cotton, wheat, and livestock.

10.4 Small-scale irrigation

In the 1980s there has been a good deal of concern about large river control schemes involving large, expensive dams, expatriate experts, and heavy environmental impacts. Many of the sites most readily developed for big schemes are already being exploited and the costs of new ones mount ever higher. Now, in reaction to this, the virtues of small schemes are being stressed, schemes that can be locally operated with irrigation based on traditional farming practices.

Small schemes, such as those on the floodplains of the seasonal rivers in northern Nigeria, often make use of small petrol- or diesel-driven pumps lifting water from shallow wells and allowing farmers to water 10 times the area they could manage with a *shaduf*. They are attractive because they entail lower costs for initial construction work, fewer staff, and no central marketing organization. They can be operated by local smallholders who can grow the crops most advantageous to themselves, adjusting the cropping pattern in detail to local soil, slope, and water supply conditions, and with their wives doing the marketing of the produce. Smallholdings can be adjusted to changing family age, size, structure, and composition, and farmers can continue to hold their land according to local law and custom. Work on the irrigated plots might be combined with some members of the family looking after livestock or engaging in craftwork, so that lifestyles need not be drastically transformed. Most important, perhaps, is the opportunity such schemes provide for farmers and their wives to exercise their own initiative and judgement, and for enterprising operators to invest in improvements and enlarge their holdings.

Some small schemes have been developed in connection with large dam projects. Thus some of the 36 000 Gwembe Tonga people displaced by Lake Kariba are being encouraged by FAO to take part in simple basin-irrigated cultivation of the drawdown land along the north shore of the lake. The people have long been accustomed to flood-recession farming; the intention is that they should produce rice and vegetables as dry-season crops, supplied with water from the lake by portable low-lift pumps, and also continue to grow rain-fed sorghum. A fall in the level of Lake Kariba of about 20 m in the 1980s has been causing considerable difficulties.

People have long been irrigating on a small scale without government or other outside interference. Shallot farming in the Volta delta has already been mentioned (pp. 79–80). At the outskirts of large towns like Zaria and Nairobi, individuals irrigate vegetables and sugar-cane for the nearby urban markets. Such activities are likely to multiply and deserve

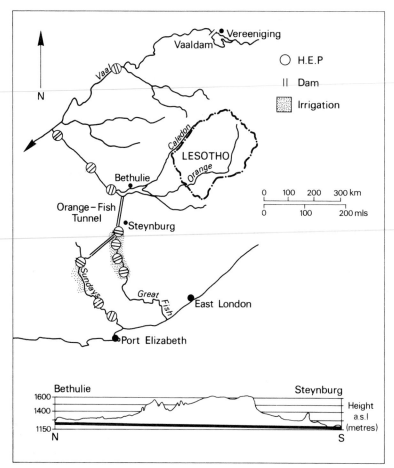

Fig. 10.10. *The Orange-Fish Tunnel, 82.5km long and with a diameter of 5.35m, diverts water from behind the Dam on the Orange River near Bethulie into the Great Fish River near Steynburg in NE Cape Province. The water is used for irrigation and to supplement the water supply of the Sundays River and the Port Elizabeth area.*

stimulus, but possibly not too much interference from aid and development agencies.

There is always a risk of costs, especially of pumps, spare parts, and fuel, outrunning income, especially in remote areas. Training farmers and mechanics requires qualified staff and, especially where schemes are small and scattered, the numbers of such extension staff may have to be high in relation to the area irrigated. Farmers in upstream situations commonly have an unfair advantage over those downstream and conflicts may also arise between cultivators and pastoralists accustomed to using the low ground for dry-season grazing. Irrigated farming is essentially a com-

munity exercise, whereas rain-fed farming is more of an individual family affair. Always in irrigation there are hazards presented by crop pests, salinization, unreliable rainfall, and water-borne diseases such as bilharzia.

It may be concluded that in some settings large-scale water control projects are appropriate, in others small-scale schemes are more likely to succeed; there may even be a mixture of the two. Selection and planning must take into account all the relevant features of the geographical setting, physical, biological and economic. Above all, the social considerations, the needs and desires of the people involved must have priority.

11

INDUSTRIALIZATION IN AFRICA

Industrialization is the spread of techniques of organization and production which enable the environment, especially its energy resources, and the abilities of people to be exploited for the production of a whole range of goods and services. The result is to raise output and consumption per head and thereby improve standards of living. In recent history industrialization has been the means of developing nationally integrated economies capable of self-sustained growth. In consequence, many African countries with economies characterized by the export of unprocessed commodities and the import of consumer and capital goods have adopted development strategies with an emphasis on industrialization.

Starting from a low base-level at the beginning of the Second World War, industrial output in Africa grew remarkably rapidly in the following quarter century, the growth rate approaching 10 per cent annually. Since then the rate of expansion has slackened. The number of Africans who have obtained employment in industry is still relatively small and the proportion of the population employed in manufacturing has scarcely increased over the last thirty years. The continent remains the least industrialized of the world's regions and its share of world manufacturing will still be less than 1 per cent in the year 2000. Its people are in the same position in which they have been for so long, wanting and needing the manufactures that industry can provide, manufactures for which, in the past, they were even willing to sell their fellows as slaves.

The distribution of industrial growth in Africa has been very uneven. It has been concentrated in South Africa, where the influence of Europeans has been longest and greatest, where they have used their skills and money and attracted foreign funds, made use of African labour, and reinvested profits locally. Otherwise, Egypt is of considerable importance, partly because of its position in the Arab world and in relation to the other oil-producing countries of the Middle East. After Egypt come Zimbabwe, Nigeria, Algeria, Morocco, and Zaire, all of them producers of oil or other valuable minerals.

Few African countries, apart from some of those mentioned above, have been in a position to manufacture the vehicles, machinery, electrical equipment, and chemicals which constitute the bulk of present-day capital and consumer goods production in industrial countries. Such an inability has little to do with colonialism, except perhaps in the case of Egypt where a take-off attempted in the nineteenth century was abortive, partly because of the inability of the state to protect its embryonic industries against European competition.

The early stages of industrialization in Africa, as elsewhere, involved processing locally produced commodities for export. These commodities include crops such as cocoa, coffee, tea, cotton, groundnuts, sugar, and palm-oil, and natural products, notably timber and fish. The extraction and processing of gold, copper, phosphates, and other minerals and the development of electrical energy from the continent's water resources may be seen as early stages in the industrialization process, providing the essential inputs for many productive activities. Another stage in laying the foundations for industry has been the manufacture of heavy constructional materials such as cement and concrete blocks to avoid the high transport costs of imported materials. Building and road construction constitute a sizeable proportion of the industrial activity in all African countries and provide an important part of the necessary infrastructure required for further growth. An area of activity of a different kind which is widespread involves the repair and maintenance of vehicles, farm machinery, and electrical and other equipment, though such activity has been restricted in recent years by foreign exchange shortages and consequent difficulties in obtaining spare parts.

The industrial base has been widened by the manufacture of products intended to replace imports of foodstuffs, beer and soft drinks, tobacco, textiles, and metal utensils. Demand for such articles was generated in the 1950s by the boom in commodity prices which raised the incomes of agricultural producers; since then it has been mainly a response to urban expansion. Shoes, plastic products, and similar relatively simple articles are manufactured to supply local demand; radios, bicycles, and tractors are assembled from imported parts.

Many of these and other import-substitution industries have had to be insulated from international market forces to provide protection against overseas competition. The tariffs and quotas consequently imposed have incidentally had the effect of reducing the need to promote efficiency in production and have increased the prices of articles for the consumer. So the incomes generated by import-substitution industries go mostly to urban dwellers, but consumers in both rural and urban areas often have to pay relatively high prices for the home-produced articles, and the choice available is often limited.

Indigenous entrepreneurs have been most active in South Africa and North Africa. Lebanese have played an important role in trade and industry in west Africa; Greeks and Italians have been involved as entrepreneurs in Egypt, the Sudan, and Ethiopia. In east Africa, Asians dominated the clothing, furniture, metalworking, and soap-making industries in Kenya at the time of independence and continue to play an important role in manufacturing. Asians were expelled from Uganda in the 1960s and their entrepreneurial activities were curtailed in Tanzania.

Transnational companies (TNCs) with financial and technical bases overseas have established soap, tyre, and other factories. Their production techniques have been capital-intensive and their output has sometimes undercut that of local entrepreneurs. In some cases individual plants and industries have been established by tncs on the understanding that they will receive protection from government against potential competitors by being given sole manufacturing rights. To maximize time-saving and minimize costs of production and distribution such companies have tended to concentrate operations in capital cities and ports. This does not apply so much to meat-packing and sugar-refining, coffee-cleaning and suchlike operations, where the raw material is bulky in relation to the final product and processing is usually done in the source areas, but even when these plants are included the effect of the activities has generally been to increase regional inequalities of employment opportunity.

In many countries the state has played an important role in promoting industrial growth, the means adopted reflecting the make-up and ideology of the particular government in power at the time and sometimes the personalities involved. In some instances the state's role has mainly involved providing tax and other incentives and ensuring that capital is available for private entrepreneurs through the banking system. In countries with a more socialist orientation, state-supported, parastatal organizations have been set up to establish and operate industries. Even in these cases of direct state involvement, foreign participation has commonly been sought, especially in the early stages of setting up an industry, and tncs may thereby have acquired a dominant position. The situation can scarcely be regarded as satisfactory in view of the hostile attitude of the capitalist world to socialist enterprise and the need for governments to try to ensure the development of balanced and integrated economies.

On the whole, industrial efficiency in Africa has been low for various reasons; costs of capital equipment are high, most of it being imported and taking a long time to acquire; expatriate staff have to be paid high salaries if they are to be attracted away from their home countries; delays are inevitable in procuring spare parts and service engineers when machinery breaks down; management and office procedures are often inefficient because of language difficulties and educational inadequacies. For many manufacturing operations semi-processed inputs have to be purchased from abroad; for instance, the chemicals used as raw materials, not only for plastics factories but even for fertilizer plants, are usually imported. When foreign exchange is scarce such inputs are in short supply, plants run at far below capacity, and unit costs of production rise sharply. Markets are restricted in size because of the small populations and limited purchasing power of most countries. In many, the cost of promoting import-substitution industries has, so far, exceeded the benefits received. Only in the cases of South Africa, Zimbabwe, and Ivory Coast, and of Egypt and other north African countries have manufactured products been able to compete in export markets.

In spite of the emphasis often placed on the production of capital goods (especially in the eastern bloc socialist countries) as being of prime importance in the development process, products like iron and steel and machine tools have scarcely figured amongst import-substitution industries except in South Africa, Zimbabwe, Egypt, and Algeria. Competition from established industries in the developed countries and from producers in the newly industrialized countries in Asia is strong, because of excess world capacity, and in most countries in tropical Africa the market is too small to support such heavy industries. Furthermore the required 'know-how' and skills are unavailable, and both 'backward and forward linkages' are lacking.

By 'backward linkages' are meant the suppliers of the basic equipment and components needed for making machinery, and by 'forward linkages' the likely purchasers of the products for use locally. On the whole, linkages within industries in Africa are of a simple kind, with most operations relying heavily on overseas suppliers or overseas markets. Firms processing raw materials to produce rubber, sugar, and tea are in many cases involved in growing the crops themselves locally and in selling overseas through their own marketing organizations. Companies producing articles made of aluminium and plastics for the African market usually import the raw materials from their plants abroad and set up their factories at the ports of entry. If manufacturers are to be convinced that it is worth their while to build satellite industries locally to supply the inputs or consume the outputs of the plants they have established in Africa they need to be prepared to take a very long-term view, investing in staff training as well as in equipment and being ready to wait a long time for returns. Most firms investing in developing countries are not prepared to do this, especially when shifts in currency values are unpredictable, risks of nationalization exist, and political regimes show signs of being insecure. Stability is an essential requirement.

With declining export prices for commodities since the 1960s, the lack of foreign exchange for purchasing capital goods, and the increasing demand for imported foodstuffs, many developing countries in Africa are turning their attention away from promoting import-substitution industries for development purposes and towards encouraging 'import-substitution agriculture' for survival. In any case, if the momentum of such industrial activity as has been achieved is to be maintained an increase in agriculture production is required.

11.1 Industralization in mineral-rich, 'white settler' countries

11.1.1 South Africa

Industry in South Africa had a relatively early start and benefited from a number of special conditions. The development of the Witwatersrand goldfields a century ago called for engineering skills and equipment on a large scale. As a result, people with technical and financial skills were attracted to Johannesburg from Europe and before long, factories were making wire ropes, explosives, chemicals, and other essentials for the mining industry.

Large numbers of Africans were recruited to work in the mines; government assisted the mining companies by imposing taxes on the black population. By the end of the nineteenth century the number of black mineworkers had reached 100 000 and between the Wars that figure trebled. Since 1960, when foreign black workers constituted two-thirds of the labour force in the mines, the proportion has fallen to less than a third, mainly from Lesotho. Wages paid to the Blacks were always low, constituting altogether about 15 per cent of total gold-mining costs. Even so, the rate of return on capital was not much above 5 per cent and it could be argued that without cheap labour goldmining on the Witwatersrand would never have been economic. In the course of the 1980s labour costs increased to over 30 per cent of the total. Consequently, other costs have had to be reduced in order that the mines shall continue to be profitable. The economies involved include the concentration of activity on high grade ores, which automatically shortens the lives of mines, and improving efficiency underground—without shortening the lives of miners.

Agriculture developed in the southern Transvaal and Orange Free State to provide maize and other foodstuffs for the mining population. At first it involved African sharecroppers working on farms owned by Afrikaners. Later, as farming became more heavily capitalized, the farm-owners exerted the legal claims they had acquired to the land and employed the Africans as labourers. The black farm labourers were paid even less than the mineworkers but were willing to do the work because of legal restrictions that had been placed on African ownership of land outside the reserves.

The market for consumer goods in South Africa was limited in the early stages mainly to foodstuffs, beer, and clothing for the mineworkers; the Europeans' needs were generally supplied by imports from overseas. After 1925, tariffs on consumer goods were applied to stimulate local manufacturing and, in 1928, the state established an iron and steel industry, ISCOR. With the rise in the price of gold in 1932, in contrast to the situation in most of the rest of the world, prosperity increased in South Africa. Then came the Second World War, which cut off imports and resulted in an expansion of manufacturing, so that by 1945 it was the leading sector of the economy. It now provides employment for over 1.3 million people.

South African manufacturing industry is very varied, the main components being foodstuffs, textiles and clothing, chemical products, metalwork, machinery, and assembly of motor vehicles. Though some of the products are much more sophisticated than those manufactured elsewhere in Africa, industrial research and development have been limited and there is still heavy reliance on foreign technology.

Industrial activity is heavily concentrated in the Witwatersrand–Vereeniging conurbation which has a total of about 7 million people. This southern Transvaal industrial complex is greater than all the other centres of industry in the country put together. It contributes about half the Republic's industrial output and provides a livelihood not only for the people dwelling on the Rand and in its vicinity, but also for the families of workers whose permanent homes are hundreds of kilometres away in Mozambique, Malawi, Botswana, and northern Namibia. Of lesser importance are the industrial areas in the Durban–Pinetown–Pietermaritzburg area and around Cape Town. There are factories at a number of lesser centres, notably Port Elizabeth, East London, Kimberley, and Bloemfontein, but the value of production in all four towns put together is much less than a third that of the southern Transvaal. Finally mention must be made of Border Industries; the outcome of apartheid, they were deliberately established on the outskirts of white towns, at the periphery of the Homelands, and enabled almost a million black workers to travel daily to work in White-owned plants.

The concentration of industry in a few urban centres is not unusual in newly industrializing countries. In South Africa industrial location has been influenced by the freight- and traffic-sharing policies of the state-owned railways. Traffic between the coast and the interior has deliberately been spread over several rail routes to make full use of the tracks and the facilities at the different ports. This has allowed all the main ports in the Republic, and Maputo (formerly Lourenço Marques) in Mozambique as well, to function economically. Freight rates were deliberately designed to promote agriculture and industrial development in the interior by charging low prices for the carriage of raw materials and high ones for mining equipment and other finished products. As a result, industries established near their markets were at a great advantage because of their relatively low costs of distribution for finished goods over the local area. The railways remain the chief means of freight transport because of the long distances between the big population clusters and the bulky nature of much of the traffic such as coal and mineral ores. Passenger traffic also remains at a high level because the non-white population is largely dependent on public transport.

11.1.1.1 The southern Transvaal

11.1.1.1 The southern Transvaal The industrial complex of the southern Transvaal is composed of the Rand, which stretches 50 km (30 mls) east and west of Johannesburg, the Witbank coalfield to the east, Vereeniging on the Vaal river to the south, and Pretoria near the margin of the Bankeveld and Bushveld basin to the north (Fig. 8.5). While Pretoria is the capital of the Repubic, Johannesburg is the commercial and industrial metropolis of southern Africa, at the centre of the transport web of the sub-continent with varied industries all around. The first factories were built on confined sites between the ridges and mine dumps in and around the city. Now the central parts of Johannesburg are crowded with skyscrapers and the industrial areas lie out on the Rand to the east where there is more room and industrial estates allow orderly development. Steel production began near Pretoria and a larger plant was later built near Vereeniging. Heavy engineering has concentrated near by, making use of water from the Vaal river dam and coal and coke available in abundance. In 1955 the world's largest oil-from-coal plant was established at Sasolburg; this consumes about 30 million tonnes of coal annually and makes a sizeable contribution towards the country's oil requirements.

11.1.1.2 Durban–Pinetown Second in importance to the southern Transvaal is the industrial area around Durban–Pinetown and Pietermaritzburg. With a population of over a million, Durban is closer to the Rand than any other South African port and is the busiest in Africa, handling about 30 million tonnes annually. Oil refineries and a variety of other plants have been established there. Generating stations using coal mined at Newcastle provide power and there is plenty of water available from the Umlaas and Umgeni rivers. Cane grown on large estates along the coast north of Durban provides between one and two million tonnes of sugar annually, some of it being used in fruit-processing and confectionery industries. Pietermaritzburg, 80 km (50 mls) inland and much smaller than Durban, is the capital of the Province of Natal. It has a big aluminium plant. Wattle tree plantations established near the

railways within a radius of about 100 km (60 mls) and at altitudes of between 600 and 1200 m (2000 to 4000 ft) provide a useful raw material. When the trees reach an age of about ten years the bark is stripped off and sent to factories for the tannin to be extracted; the trunks are sold for pit props. Stock-rearing is also important in the region, and a tannery has been established capable of treating 150 000 hides and 120 000 skins annually. With so much tanned leather available other manufactures have developed, notably the largest shoe factory in the Republic. The big Kwa Zulu population in Natal provides a large market for cheap manufactured goods and a pool of labour; approaching half a million find employment in local industry.

Durban itself remains an attractive city and tourism is one of its main sources of income; thousands of Whites take their winter holidays on the coast nearby, which is pleasantly warm at a time of year when the interior plateau can be cold and windy.

11.1.1.3 The Cape Cape Town is second in importance to Durban as a port and as an industrial centre. The original settlement is now the commercial centre. Railway yards and offices occupy land reclaimed from Table Bay in the course of dock construction. The suburbs of the city cluster on the northern slopes of Table Mountain and stretch for several miles to the south. Much of the export trade consists of agricultural produce from the immediate hinterland, the scene of early Dutch settlement. The economy of the lowlands stretching north and east of Cape Town is based on wheat and wool. Vineyards climb the lower slopes of well-watered rocky hills within a radius of about 100 km (60 mls) of the city. Further inland, in valleys experiencing low winter temperatures, apple orchards occupy valley floors where cool air collects at night, with peach trees on the slopes. Electric generating stations on rivers like the Hex provide power for pumping irrigation water to fields and orchards and also for the electrified section of the railway between Cape Town and Beaufort West. The agricultural produce forms the basis for local industries: brandy and cigarettes, woollen cloth and preserves in the provincial towns, textiles and clothing in Cape Town, mainly intended for the market provided by the south-west Cape.

Fishing in the waters off the west coast and

by trawlers on the Agulhas Bank is highly productive. The fish feed on phytoplankton utilizing mineral salts brought to the surface by the upwelling Antarctic water on coming into contact at the southern tip of the continent with the Agulhas current. The majority of the catch consists of mackerel, pilchards, and anchovy, which are either canned or turned into fish-meal and oil.

11.1.1.4 Border Industries The Border Industries are mainly located in the vicinity of Durban, Pietermaritzburg, East London, and Pretoria. Almost a million black workers live in towns that have been established near by in the Homelands and travel daily to work in white South Africa. So far there has not been much sign that the wages earned in factories are creating significant economic growth in the Homelands themselves, but stores, garages, and small businesses are being operated by Bantu, and as wages increase there may be some spread of prosperity.

South Africa has had the advantage of the impetus provided by the goldmining industry in the first place, other mining activities at a later stage, an entrepreneurial class, and foreign exchange for purchasing capital equipment. A proportion of the total manufactured product is exported, over 10 per cent in 1980. Much of it goes to African countries lying to the north, but exactly how much is uncertain, because official statistics are not necessarily accurate and may be deliberately obscure. Gold continues to constitute about 40 per cent by value of the country's total exports.

An Asian residential area on the southern outskirts of Durban.

The economic growth of South Africa has been restricted for over a quarter of a century by the lack of capital investment from overseas on account of uncertainty about the future of the country and latterly because of internal racial and tribal conflict. Future prospects depend on whether a stable government emerges with multi-racial involvement and inter-tribal peace. If it does, then the future of the country will be brighter than that of any other in Africa. If it does not, then the economy could sink to levels similar to those further north.

11.1.2 Zimbabwe

The main attraction of Rhodesia to early settlers was gold. White farming became a success in the 1920s and 1930s. Secondary industry was stimulated by the Southern Rhodesian government during the Second World War, with the construction of an iron and steel plant at Que-Que and with cotton spinning at Gatooma (Fig. 9.2). These state industries were denationalized when they became commercially viable.

With a large influx of Europeans and white South Africans at the end of the Second World War, the value of gross output rose rapidly. A high proportion of the manufacturing output was exported to Northern Rhodesia (now Zambia) and Nyasaland (now Malawi). At the same time agriculture flourished, Southern Rhodesia's tobacco being much in demand on account of the world-wide shortage of dollars needed for buying American tobacco. Industrial expansion continued into the period when the Rhodesias and Nyasaland together formed the Central African Federation. Large amounts of capital were attracted from abroad and, by 1965, manufacturing output was worth over six times that of mining and three times that of European agriculture in the country. The copper revenues of Northern Rhodesia financed much of the investment, and cheap supplies of labour were forthcoming from Nyasaland. Both countries provided markets for products that were protected by a Federation tariff wall against imports from the rest of the world, including South Africa, and also by the high costs of transport from the coast that had to be carried by imported goods. The end of Federation about 1963 was a setback, but before capital outflows had become serious, the economy was partly closed as a result of sanctions on trade imposed by many countries after the white Rhodesian government made its Unilateral Declaration of Independence (UDI) in 1965.

During UDI, investment was directed towards the luxury end of manufacturing in order to maintain supplies for the Whites. While rural areas suffered from unemployment, manufacturing output increased absolutely and in relation to other sectors of the economy. It now accounts for a quarter of the GDP (Gross Domestic Product). Zimbabwe is now more industrialized than any other African country apart from South Africa and possibly Algeria and Ivory Coast.

Since African majority rule was established in 1980, gold, nickel, copper, and chrome have all continued to be mined and exported on a considerable scale and many other minerals on a smaller scale. The iron and steel plant at Que Que (or Kwe Kwe) has an annual capacity of 1 million tonnes. Textile production and metal-working have increased over the years; although phosphatic fertilizers are made, Zimbabwe is otherwise dependent on imported chemicals. Local manufacture of petrochemicals including nitrogenous fertilizers has been held up by interruptions to oil supplies carried by pipeline from Beira. A plant was opened in 1980 which converts sugar-cane into ethanol which is a petrol substitute. Blended with petrol in a 15:85 mix, it helps to reduce Zimbabwe's reliance on imported fuel.

About half of the investment in Zimbabwean industry is South African and that country has continued to take most of Zimbabwe's exports of minerals, steel and manufactured goods. With the downturn in the South African economy in the early 1990s, manufacturing in Zimbabwe has ceased to grow. Efforts are being made to strengthen economic ties with the SADCC (Southern African Development Co-ordination Conference) countries in order to develop new markets.

11.2 Industrialization in oil-producing countries

11.2.1 Egypt

Egyptian industrialization started in the nineteenth century but was impeded by foreign competition. Much manufacturing and commercial activity fell into foreign hands, though the construction industry remained under Egyptian control. During the Second World War, with imported manufactures unobtainable and Commonwealth troops providing cash and employment, industrial production increased by 50 per cent. However, it still contributed less than 20 per cent of the national output, and when peace came local factories were unable to compete with imports from established manufacturing countries. Wealthy people invested their money abroad if they could and in property in Egypt if they could not, and the sterling and dollar balances that had accumulated during the war rapidly dwindled.

In 1956 foreign concerns were nationalized and, under Nasser, assistance was given to state manufacturing enterprises. Conflict with Israel in 1967 closed the Suez Canal and resulted in the Israeli occupation of Sinai and the destruction of industrial plant in the growing towns of Suez, Port Said, and Ismailia. With increasing American influence in the 1970s, the policy of state socialism was reversed. At the same time the economy benefited from self-sufficiency in oil, from hydroelectric power generated at Aswan, the recovery of Sinai from Israel and the reopening of the Canal in 1975, and American aid.

It had been intended that manufacturing plants should be located in all the different provinces, but in practice the last few decades have seen the development of a major industrial belt along the roads and railway running across the Nile delta between Cairo and Alexandria and a minor one alongside the Suez Canal (Fig. 8.6). In general, development has suffered from lack of skilled people; many such people have been attracted by the high salaries offered by other Arab oil-producing countries in the Middle East.

11.2.2 Algeria

Under French rule, industry was concentrated in Algiers and its immediate neighourhood. Under Algeria's Marxist government the petroleum industry was nationalized, and pipelines distributed the oil and gas to a number of coastal ports (Fig. 6.4). Investment has been concentrated in refineries and plants at these ports which liquefy and utilize natural gas.

Ammonium nitrate and other fertilizers are being manufactured at Arzew, and a huge plant produces plastics at Skikda. An iron and steel complex established by the French at Annaba has been enlarged; cement, paper, and other factories have been built. Industry now accounts for a half of Algeria's national output and farming for only 10 per cent. But farming still involves half the country's population, and industrial growth, though active, is unlikely to be capable of absorbing the rapidly growing number of young people looking for jobs.

11.2.3 Nigeria

At independence Nigeria's industry was mainly based on a limited range of agricultural and natural products. Little encouragement had been given to industry under the colonial regime and there was little local expertise. Vegetable oils were extracted from groundnuts and from oil-palm fruit and kernels, and some went towards manufacturing soap and related products. Textile factories using locally grown cotton were concentrated in Kaduna. Various consumer goods were produced in the Lagos–Apapa area.

After independence, the state gave greater protection and financial incentives to manufacturers and provided infrastructure in the form of water supplies, electricity, and industrial sites. At first reliance was placed on funds from agricultural produce Marketing Boards and loans from overseas. After the civil war of 1966–70 and with the rises in oil prices after 1973, federal government oil revenues were made available in abundance through banks and state investment corporations. Nevertheless, control over funds was and still is concentrated in the hands of a relatively small number of people, many of them active in politics, who are in positions to obtain loans and invest in existing or new enterprises. There continues to be an informal alliance in the promotion of industry between such individuals and foreign-based technical partners and multinational corporations. This goes far to explain the high cost of all development projects in Nigeria, with costs of government contracts in the early 1980s two or three times higher than those in some other developing countries.

Frequent changes in regime and the lack of national solidarity have meant that there has not been a generally accepted development plan for Nigerian industry and changes in direction have been frequent. For instance, a very large electricity generating station, with a capacity of 1350 MW, had been completed at Egbin near Lagos by 1985, but three years later it still stood idle because construction of the pipeline to bring natural gas to it from the delta region had yet to begin, no agreement having been reached as to which firm should undertake the work. Meanwhile enormous quantities of gas, the equivalent of 20 million tonnes of oil, were being flared annually in the delta and offshore oilfields.

The distribution of activities through the country has depended in some instances on regional political pressures. In most cases manufacturing has been attracted to places close to markets and where imported inputs are readily obtainable. The outcome is a great concentration of activity in and around Lagos/Apapa which sustains half the value added and half the employment in large-scale industry. There is a lesser concentration around Kano, which is afforded some protection against competition from factories in Lagos/Apapa by distance inland. Kaduna has also attracted a number of manufacturing plants, including an oil refinery supplied by pipeline from the coast and a small superphosphate factory. Natural gas and other industries based on petroleum are mainly situated near Port Harcourt and the oil terminals of Bonny and Warri. The opportunities for 'downstream activities' based on petroleum products have as yet scarcely been exploited.

Manufacturing industry as a proportion of national output increased from 4 per cent in 1960 to 9 per cent in 1977 and 12 per cent in 1985 but has since fallen back to only 8.5 per cent in 1990. Textiles, beer, soft drinks, cigarettes, soap, and detergents account for about 60 per cent of the value added. Production of paint and roofing materials, flour milling, and vehicle assembly grew quickly in the 1970s but all of them are dependent on imported materials, backward linkages not having developed to any great extent. By 1987, following the collapse of the oil market, only about 30 per cent of manufacturing capacity was being utilized, mainly on account of lack of foreign exchange.

An important new development has been the building, with West German assistance, of a direct reduction steel plant at Aladja in Bendel,

near the coast. This is supplied with energy by a gas turbine station at Ughelli. Ore is shipped in from Liberia and Brazil and converted into steel for use in rolling mills at Oshogbo, Katsina, and Jos. The Aladja plant has a capacity of 1 million tonnes of steel annually but in 1987 was working at only 20 per cent capacity on account of power cuts, rises in the price of gas and electricity, and competition from cheap imported steel. The rolling mills were also working at only 10–15% capacity in the early 1990s.

An even larger iron and steel plant constructed with Russian assistance at Ajaokuta in Kwara State was completed, six years behind schedule, in 1992. It was planned to excavate 5 million tonnes of ore annually at Itakpe 52 km away and concentrate it in a beneficiation plant so as to have an iron content of 55 per cent. The treated ore was to be carried by rail to Ajaokuta for conversion into 1.3 million tonnes of steel. Eventually, steel production at Ajaokuta was visualized as increasing to 5.3 million tonnes annually. This is not likely to be the case for many years because of the huge costs involved and the lack of demand in Nigeria and worldwide.

A large petrochemical plant near Onne, Rivers State, has been more successful, producing over a million tonnes of nitrogenous fertilizers and saving $100 million of foreign exchange annually.

Other basic industries are required if the economy is to survive the inevitable downturn in oil production likely to occur early in the next century, when the country's population is likely to be approaching 200 million. But production and transport costs are high and although oil production was on the increase in the 1990s the Nigerian economy may not be strong enough to support such developments.

Nigeria remains very dependent on imported consumer goods, especially durables. Processing of foodstuffs has made only slow progress in recent years, partly because of the low prices offered to farmers by state commodity-buying agencies but also because of drought. With the fall in the price of oil in the early 1980s, government revenues from oil were halved within two years. In 1983 a fifth of the country's industrial plants had to close down for several weeks and many firms went out of business altogether because of the shortage of foreign exchange and of imported raw materials. The evolution of an integrated industrial base has been impeded by the financial switchback created by the rise and fall of oil revenues, and the future is full of uncertainty.

11.3 Industrialization in countries with economies based on agriculture

11.3.1 Kenya

Industrial development in Kenya during the colonial period was stimulated by the presence of European settlers and an Asian population. The Europeans set up factories to process agricultural crops, mill grain, can butter and meat, and tan leather. They were influential enough to obtain some tariff protection against imported manufactures and ensure free entry of Kenyan-made goods to Tanganyika and Uganda. Asians were active in commerce, vehicle and machinery repair work, and also in small-scale manufacturing of items such as clothing, furniture, and soap. Both of the immigrant communities invested a considerable proportion of their profits locally.

The main centre of manufacturing is Nairobi, with its satellite Thika 42 km (26 mls) to the north-east, where factories produce textiles, clothing, and paint, and assemble radios and vehicles. They are dependent on hydroelectric power from the Tana river, the largest river in Kenya, and oil coming by pipeline from Mombasa. Other smaller centres of industrial activity include Mombasa, Nakuru, Kisumu, and Eldoret (Fig. 11.1). Since independence, Africans have played an increasingly important part in manufacturing, often in collaboration with multinational companies. As a proportion of national output, manufacturing production has not made great strides; it stood at 10 per cent in 1964, and 13 per cent in 1977, but by 1992 it was down to 11 per cent. Nevertheless, a higher proportion of the working population in Kenya were employed in manufacturing than is the case in most other African countries. The main products are beverages, cigarettes, textiles and processed food; the most important manufactures exported are those produced at the Mombasa oil refinery.

11.3.2 Tanzania

Tanzania's white and Asian population was smaller than that of Kenya and it was also more scattered and less effective politically and economically. Although crop processing emerged at an early stage, other industrial activities were on a very limited scale before independence, and many manufactured items were imported from Kenya. In the early 1960s, the Tanzanian government made efforts to ensure that newly established industries should be located in Tanzania as well as in Kenya. Partly as a result of this factories assembling radios, and making cigarettes, shoes, aluminium ware, and tyres were located by multinational companies in Dar es Salaam and Arusha, but Tanzania has not been able to reduce Kenya's lead.

After the Arusha Declaration of 1967 an attempt was made under President Nyerere to create a socialist economy. Government development corporations were established to run nationalized banking, insurance, and industrial enterprises, and a policy of decentralization was adopted to spread benefits around the country. Wage employment and value added in manufacturing trebled between 1964 and 1976. As a proportion of national output, value added by manufacturing increased from 3.5 per cent in 1958 to 9 per cent in 1977, figures which are very comparable to those for Nigeria over the same period.

Some of the large plants established in the late 1960s and 1970s have been very costly failures. A cement plant built 25 km north of Dar es Salaam to obviate the need for importing cement from Mombasa in Kenya was oil-fired, and costs of the product were very high on account of the rise in oil prices and the large sums that had to be paid to foreign personnel for management. A large fertilizer plant at Tanga failed because of the high cost of raw materials, all of which were imported.

It has been argued that the cement plant should have used Tanzanian coal, but the coalfields have yet to be opened up and they are located hundreds of miles away in the southern part of the country (Fig. 11.1). The cement plant, it has also been said, should have been built at Kilwa, where gypsum is available locally, and then the sulphuric acid which would have been produced as a by-product could have been used to treat Tanzanian phos-

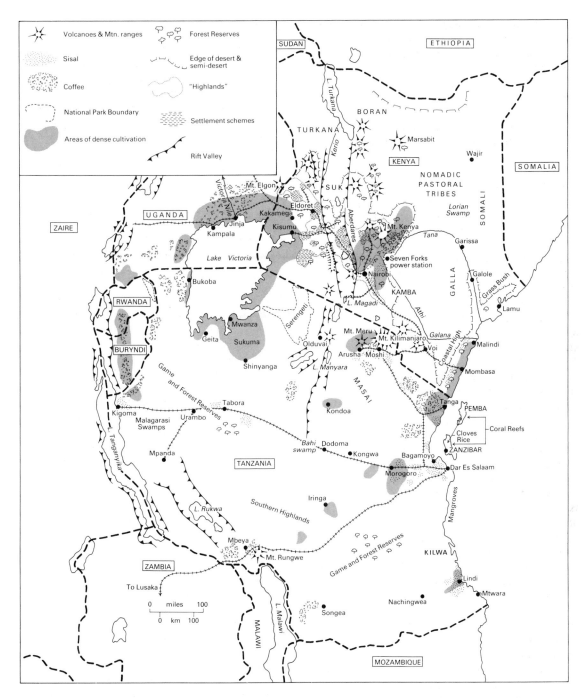

Fig. 11.1. *East Africa. The economically productive areas of East Africa are mainly the highland areas in the vicinity of the rift valleys and great volcanoes, the country around Lake Victoria, and certain stretches of the coast.*

phates from the east side of Lake Manyara to produce superphosphate fertilizer. Near Mbeya, in the south-west of the country, abundant coal and iron provide the potential basis for a steel industry. But building up a heavy industry complex is far beyond Tanzania's own capacities under present circumstances.

Since the droughts of the 1970s, disruption caused by villagization, rises in oil prices, and the war against Amin in Uganda, foreign exchange has been very scarce and the country has fallen deeply into debt. Unlike Kenya, Tanzania has failed to attract tourists in sufficient numbers to provide hard currency. Government and its resources in the 1990s are fully occupied with the problems of feeding the people and ensuring they have the necessities of life. Since 1987, socialist policies have been abandoned, greater encouragement has been given to private enterprise, and business has begun to pick up.

11.3.3 Ghana

Ghana, in the inter-war years, was the most prosperous country in tropical Africa, mainly as a result of its cocoa and other exports. In the early years of independence after 1958, under President Nkrumah, an attempt was made to industrialize. It was supposed that power from Akosombo had a vital part to play in the process (Fig. 11.2). The financial basis for expansion was at first provided by money accumulated in the 1950s by government Produce Marketing Boards selling cocoa for high prices on the world market and paying low prices to producers. Industrial expansion was thus to be at the expense of the rural people.

Large sums of money were invested rather inefficiently and extravagantly between 1961 and 1965 in various industrial and other concerns at a time when the price of cocoa on the world market was falling. At first production of cocoa continued to increase but, not surprisingly in view of the low prices paid to producers, this did not persist and the basis for industrial expansion disappeared. Ghana's exports of cocoa in the mid-1980s were, according to official statistics, about 200 000 tonnes annually, only about one-third those at the peak twenty years earlier, and prices on the world market were depressed. Nevertheless, cocoa exports provided over 50 per cent of the

Tourism can be a useful source of foreign exchange and provides a market for locally produced craftwork.

country's foreign exchange earnings.

After 1963, while Ghana's public sector continued to expand excessively, national output per head was in decline. Ghana had its own Central Bank; its currency was no longer tied to sterling and by the early 1980s it was greatly overvalued. There had been frequent changes of government as a result of military coups. Salaries and wages had greatly diminished in real terms, many public services were scarcely functioning and more than half the country's top-level professionals and skilled workers had emigrated to Nigeria and elsewhere. Industry, which had been massively protected, was in a state of collapse because shortage of foreign exchange prevented it obtaining essential spare parts, raw materials, or components from overseas. There were signs of recovery in the late 1980s, but most industrial plants were still running at little more than 20 per cent of capacity.

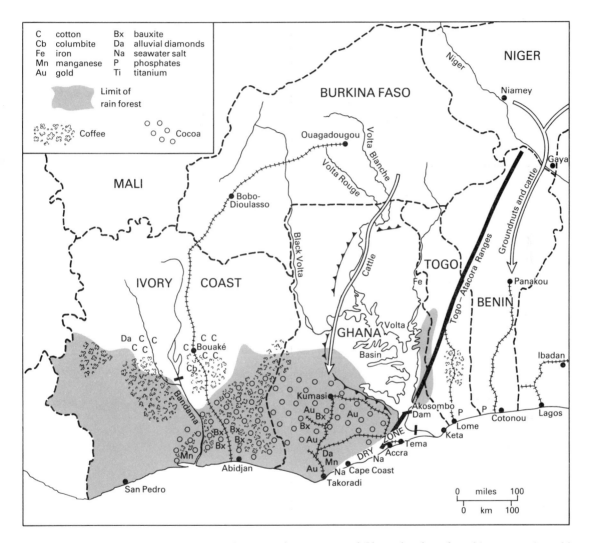

Fig. 11.2. *Ivory Coast, Ghana, Togo, and Benin. The economy of Ghana has been based in part on its gold and timber resources but to a much greater extent on cocoa. Minerals are not important economically to Ivory Coast, where coffee as well as cocoa and timber have been the mainstays of the economy. Togo has benefited from the export of phosphates from its coastal zone. Both Togo and Benin import electricity generated at Akosombo on the lower Volta in Ghana. Industrial development in Ivory Coast and Ghana was based on the processing of local raw materials. The development of local production of substitutes for imported manufactured domestic consumables at Abidjan and Tema has suffered in recent years from a shortage of foreign exchange for purchasing components from overseas. Cotonou in Benin has gained from its nearness to Nigeria, importing goods destined for that country when facilities at Lagos were overstretched and also benefiting at times from Nigerian investment. Workers have been attracted to Nigeria from Ghana and other countries when oil prices have been high.*

11.3.4 *Ivory Coast*

The history of Ivory Coast's development has been out of phase with that of Ghana. Its growth was delayed until after 1950 and then resembled that of Ghana between the Wars. There was plenty of forestland available and production of cocoa, coffee, and timber all expanded. Prices paid to producers were kept quite high and the real value of the money they received was maintained, because Ivory Coast's currency remained tied to the French franc. Cocoa production in Ivory Coast continued to increase after 1965, when not only Ghanaian but also Nigerian production was diminishing.

Industrialization concentrated on the processing and refining of agricultural products and the promotion of the textile industry. In the 1970s agricultural production was still expanding, probably benefiting from cheap immigrant labour from countries to the north which were suffering from drought. The economy profited considerably from a sharp increase in coffee and cocoa prices about 1975–78. Imports of foodstuffs greatly increased and the government was encouraged to borrow large sums for further expansion. But the high prices were short-lived, and in the early 1980s Ivory Coast found itself carrying a heavy debt and with a much reduced income from sales of coffee and cocoa. In consequence there was a severe cutback in the construction and industrial sectors and foreign debt servicing had to be rescheduled.

In the long term, countries like Ghana and Ivory Coast cannot rely on being able to increase in prosperity to any considerable degree simply by increasing production of crops for export. There are limits to the amount of such crops that the world market can absorb, and prices are extremely variable and unpredictable.

12

MODERNIZING AGRICULTURE

Agriculture in Africa has traditionally involved growing crops and raising livestock by making use of soils and fodder much as they exist in nature. Technical progress was not entirely lacking. Crops and livestock were selected for special qualities and to suit local conditions. Farm plots near settlements were enriched by household wastes and dung from domestic animals. Under special circumstances soils were conserved by terracing and crops were irrigated from springs and rivers. But planting, cultivation, weeding, pest control, and harvesting were done, and for the most part are still done, by simple hand tools. Only in the Mediterranean lands and Ethiopia was animal power widely employed; elsewhere in Africa, men, women, and children did the work themselves.

Under favourable conditions, hand farmers can produce enough food to feed themselves and a surplus for sale. But in most parts of the continent there was and still is a hungry season in the rural areas when last year's harvest has been consumed and this year's crops have yet to ripen. Nutritional levels are on the whole low, and in years when the weather is unfavourable malnutrition is widespread, especially amongst women and children. In recent years food production per head has been falling in many African countries; imports of food have been increasing, but mainly to feed the rapidly growing towns.

Modernizing agriculture involves many technological, institutional, and management changes aimed at increasing productivity per unit area, per animal, and per person. The main technical changes in cropping comprise the use of improved plant varieties, optimum spacing of plants and timing of operations, provision of

Terracing on the lower southern slopes of Kilimanjaro, with an artificial channel leading water from the moist upper margins of the forest to villages lower down where it is used for domestic purposes and for irrigating crops.

Water from streams and channels on Kilimanjaro is piped to village houses amongst bananas and coffee.

water, the supply of plant nutrients in the form of artificial fertilizers, weed and pest control by chemical means, and the mechanization of ploughing, sowing, and harvesting. In livestock rearing, improved breeds, rotational grazing, supplementary feeding, supply of water, and control of disease are the key factors. All these changes require capital inputs; they cost money. Institutional and management changes are intended to bring together the inputs and dispose of the outputs in an efficient manner, the efficiency being measurable in terms of yields, profitability, and enhancement of fertility.

Because some people profit and some people may lose from modernization such development has political overtones. This is particularly the case in relation to any changes that may take place in the ownership of and rights to land and water. These changes may be deliberate and brought about by legislation, or may be inadvertent, resulting from the sum total of the responses of individuals and communities to economic and social forces.

Modernization of agriculture in Africa came first in Egypt and the regions of European settlement. In the second half of the nineteenth century European engineers built dams in the Nile delta, ran estates, and provided a market for the long-staple cotton. Most of the land remained in Egyptian hands. In North Africa, French settlers acquired large estates where, employing local labour, they produced wine, wheat, citrus, and early vegetables for the French market. South of the Sahara, European settlers carved out large farms on the high plains of southern and eastern Africa, cropping a limited area and using much of the rest of the land for raising livestock. African labourers on white farms were allowed small plots for their own use in return for working for the Europeans. They were squatters without security of tenure and, as machinery came into use, they were liable to be evicted.

Outside the European farming areas, in colonies of white settlement Africans retained their customary rights in 'native reserves' and in extensive areas of semi-arid grazing land, usually at a distance from the railways and main roads. It was the European farmers who benefited most from government subsidies, agricultural research and marketing facilities. In Kenya, Africans were prohibited from growing certain cash crops on the pretext that they would not control disease or maintain quality standards of coffee, for instance; another reason was that they might effectively compete with European producers. The Europeans were able to obtain bank loans; they had the knowledge, the capital, and the political leverage, and they dominated commercial agriculture in the countries where they were settled. This was the case even in Tanzania and Zambia, where Whites were few in number and where they owned less than 10 per cent of the farming land. Even so, except in Zimbabwe where tobacco was a profitable crop after the Second World War, most European farmers did not acquire great wealth from their farms.

Modernized agriculture on European estates and plantations run by companies usually involved not mixed farming but the production of a limited range of commercial crops often

A household grain store in a remote part of the rift valley of southern Tanzania.

grown to supply the needs of a processing plant—a sugar-extraction, sisal, palm-oil, tea, or coffee factory. Considerable amounts of capital were invested in such estates; they were run by European managers and technicians with African labourers. In some cases African farmers in the neighbourhood were encouraged to produce supplies of raw materials for the processing plant and might receive inputs in one form or another, the costs of which were deducted from the sale price of their produce.

When independence came to Kenya and Tan-zania, arrangements were made by which most of the European farms were acquired by the independent governments, with compensation being paid to their former owners, and the land being allocated to Africans. Fears were expressed that yields and production would decline, but in fact this has not happened. Nevertheless, the newly independent Zimbab-wean government has been slow to take over European farms because of the need to retain the foreign exchange earnings that continue to be derived from the sale of the tobacco and other crops such farms produce. In Kenya, some of the commercial estates continue to be under company control for similar reasons. Generally, Africans who have acquired European farms continue to employ the modern methods that were used by the Europeans, and governments have endeavoured to extend such methods to the farming population at large through extension services, that is by government employees who have been trained in modern farming methods and can explain them to African smallholders. In other cases, foreign firms have operated their own extension services to advise African farmers how to grow tobacco or tea, for instance, of the required quality; they may provide planting material, fertilizers, and other inputs, as well as advice, and may purchase the harvested crop.

In those countries where independence came as a result of bitter conflict the situation is quite different. Europeans left Algeria, Angola, and Mozambique in a hurry, abandoning their land, which was taken over by worker co-operatives or by other state organizations. After the revolution in Ethiopia in 1974 the state nationalized land and established many state farms. Such enterprises have not been markedly successful; civil servants do not seem to adapt readily to the exigencies of managing farming operations.

12.1 Land tenure

The tenurial (land-holding) and management arrangements that have emerged since independence vary from one country to another, depending very much on the political complexion of the government in power. Practice does not always conform with legal provisions, and spatial variation in the way land is held occurs on all scales, so that generalizations are not readily made. Broadly, four kinds of tenure can be distinguished, two of them traditional and two introduced.

12.1.1 Traditional tenure systems

In traditional land-holding systems a distinction may be made between communal and individual tenure. Communal land is available to all the members of a community; individual tenure gives rights of use and disposal to individuals or family groups.

Communal land is generally sparsely settled and is available for grazing, hunting, and the collection of wood and other wild produce. Some restrictions exist on the use of such land, with certain individuals being recognized as having authority for allocating resources. Amongst pastoralists, for instance, a leading individual or group may stipulate the time of year when herds can have access to certain grazing areas. The rights to water from certain wells may be restricted to those individuals who dug them or whose ancestors did so. In operating fisheries, members of certain ethnic groups may be recognized as having special rights and privileges.

The chief of the community is traditionally the protector of the community's rights over communal land. One of his most important powers is to allocate land to members of the community needing it for farming. Usually, the individual or family acquiring such a right and clearing the land for farming retains the right to use it and to pass that right on to his successor. In most groups the transmission is from father to sons, but in some groups inheritance is through the female line—it may be from a man through his sisters' children. People may borrow land, or pay labour, cash, or kind for its use for a certain or indefinite period, or mortgage it. The traditional systems are flexible, allowing for change in family size and age structure. But under systems of this kind, buying and selling of farmland is not recognized and land cannot therefore be readily used as security for a bank loan. However, as increasing areas are planted with commercial crops, land acquires a cash value and sales begin to take place in spite of custom; the traditional system of land-holding tends to break down under the impact of the cash economy.

12.1.2 Introduced tenure systems

12.1.2.1 The development of tenurial mosaics Under colonial rule, 'native law and custom' were generally respected with regard to land matters in African farming areas. In Muslim communities, Islamic land law, which recognizes the sale and purchase of land, was widely accepted, but Islamic qadis or judges, in northern Nigeria for instance, might under some circumstances apply local customary law if it differed from the Koranic law. European tenure systems were applied in townships and also in European farming and mining areas. Large areas of sparsely settled land were set aside as forestry and game reserves administered by the colonial government and later by the independent state. As pressure on land increased and it became a rarer resource, so the frequency of disputes over ownership increased and costs of litigation mounted.

12.1.2.2 The mailo *system in Buganda* In some particular cases, European systems of individual ownership of land were introduced to African farming areas. In the kingdom of Buganda, for instance, according to the Uganda Agreement of 1900 made between the Kabaka, who was the supreme ruler of the Baganda people, and the British government, nearly half the land was divided between 4000 people, made up of the Kabaka, his chiefs, and other notables. Subsequently, the holdings of these individuals were subdivided on inheritance and plots were sold to buy cars or houses. When independence came there were reckoned to be some 130 000 landowners in Buganda, some with large holdings, others merely landed peasants. On the larger holdings, tenants acquired squatters' rights that were carefully protected by law, and consequently few of the *mailo* estates, as they were called, especially the larger ones, were actually at the disposal of their owners. Eventually, under a Land Reform Decree of 1975, Amin, then dictator of Uganda, abolished the *mailo* system by converting the *mailo* titles into long leaseholds.

12.1.2.3 The changing tenurial situation in Nigeria In southern Nigeria, ownership of land according to customary law has been in the hands of the family, lineage, or clan. In the Islamic north, on the other hand, there is little or no concept of lineage or clan land and the practice of buying and selling has become widespread even though, according to the law, farmers have had only rights of occupancy. A Land Use Decree of 1978 imposed on the Federation a uniform system of land tenure according to which the title to land is in the hands of government, disputes are to be settled by State land tribunals, and local authorities have the power to grant use rights to individuals or groups for cultivation or grazing. The number of land transactions that would have to be dealt

with annually by each State government would exceed 10 000 and, not surprisingly, the law and its machinery have yet to be brought into operation. In the mean time, as farming has become more commercialized, the poorer, less successful farmers are selling their land to richer individuals. In the late 1980s, large firms were acquiring tracts of land in Bendel and Kaduna States for farming purposes in spite of the Land Use Decree of 1978 which limited individual customary rights to 500 hectares for agriculture and to 5000 hectares for grazing. The area of cultivable land in Nigeria amounts to less than one hectare per head so there would now seem to be risks of land ownership becoming concentrated in the hands of a smaller section of the population with many individuals landless.

12.1.3 Villagization

Quite commonly colonial governments encouraged African people scattered over the countryside, living on their farmland, to come together into nucleated settlements, where they could more economically be provided with educational, health, and other facilities—and more readily be administered and taxed.

12.1.3.1 Zimbabwe Enormous areas of the best land in Southern Rhodesia were set aside for Europeans. The Native Reserves, or Tribal Trust Lands as they were called after 1925, were becoming congested, eroded, and overstocked. In the course of the 1920s a policy of 'centralization' was introduced which was intended to improve conditions in the reserves by re-arranging the settlement pattern on a rational basis, people being gathered together into nucleated settlements and so villagized. Arable land was demarcated from grazing land and the village buildings were lined up between the two. Attention was paid to water supplies and sanitation when sites were selected. Each householder was allotted a plot of land and there were agricultural demonstrators to advise them. By 1946, almost 4 million hectares (10 million acres) of land had been 'centralized' in this way.

12.1.3.2 Kenya It was argued in the 1950s that African landholding was economically unsatisfactory, especially amongst the Kikuyu. A single Kikuyu holding of, say, 2 to 3 hectares (5 to 7 acres) was usually split into several small parts, it might be seven or eight, and the fragmentation prevented agricultural methods being improved. This situation sprang from the traditional rules of inheritance amongst the Kikuyu. Furthermore, many of the holders had no real security of tenure. For example, a stretch of land over which rights had been acquired from another tribe would be divided amongst close relations and also amongst tenants. The latter could be bought out at will. This resulted in hundreds of costly land cases being brought before the courts.

At the time of the Mau-Mau troubles in the 1950s, the colonial government expelled the Kikuyu for security reasons from the white farming areas. They and other Kikuyu from the scattered farmsteads where they normally lived in the reserves were made to assemble in new villages. At the same time the opportunity was taken to reorganize land tenure. Records were compiled of existing rights to land in the villages, the holdings were surveyed, and then the land was redivided to give each holder a single block of land plus a plot of building land in one of the new villages, the two together being equal in area to all the bits he had previously held. A large part of Kikuyuland was redivided in this way and provision was made for keeping a register of titles to land and changes resulting from sale and inheritance. By 1957 about 5 million hectares had been registered, including almost all the high-potential land.

Such new systems are costly and time-consuming to operate. Some people cling to the customary forms of inheritance and ignore the new laws. Many have moved out of the nucleated villages, preferring to live on their farms. It has been argued that individual tenure of this kind leads to the development of a proper-tied class of people, many of whom live in towns, while a landless class emerges in the rural areas. In Kenya, at about the time that land reform was taking place, over 400 000 hectares (a million acres) of land that had been farmed by Europeans became available for division amongst African farmers, many of whom obtained holdings of 8 to 15 hectares. This helped to prevent the onset of landlessness. Since then the population has doubled, taking up the slack, and there is a growing number of people without land.

12.1.3.3 Algeria During the war of independence against French rule, the French administration followed a policy of bringing the rural people together into nucleated settlements to make surveillance easier and guerrilla activity more difficult. Some of these settlements persisted after independence because the inhabitants found they benefited from the new conditions; others were abandoned.

12.1.3.4 Tanzania A more radical policy of rural development has been followed in Tanzania than in any other African country, with the possible exceptions of Algeria, Ethiopia, Mozambique, and Angola. The last three of these have been so disturbed by internal conflict that the effects of their tenurial policies are difficult to assess.

In Tanzania, rights to land have traditionally been associated with membership of a community. Where crops such as coffee and tea are intensively cultivated, notably amongst the Chagga on the lower slopes of Kilimanjaro, the Haya, and the people living on the plains and slopes rising to the Rungwe volcanic massif at the northern end of Lake Nyasa, land has become scarce. In these areas enclosure of com-

Land intensively cultivated with coffee and bananas by the Chagga people living on the southern slopes of Kilimanjaro in northern Tanzania.

mon land was virtually complete by the time of independence and was beginning even in more remote areas. With a doubling of population over the last quarter of a century, shifting cultivation has been replaced in many parts of the country by semi-permanent and permanent farming. None the less, nucleated villages were typical of only limited areas, and until the 1970s most families continued to live in compounds scattered singly or in small groups through the farmed land.

Largely as a result of spontaneous development by African entrepreneurs and varying resource endowments, increasing disparities were emerging in the prosperity of different regions and different individuals in the 1960s. Land was beginning to accumulate in the hands of a relatively small number of people growing cash crops, hiring labour, and engaged in mechanized cultivation. In the political climate of newly independent Tanzania, incipient capitalism was deprecated both in government and in academic circles.

Village settlement schemes had been inherited from the colonial regime. They had required high capital inputs and had not been particularly successful, but President Nyerere in 1967 saw such villages, if only they could renew the community spirit which he supposed had once existed in African villages and could be more self-reliant, as a means of transforming social attitudes and rural economies. He advocated *ujamaa* ('familyhood') villages as a means of putting socialism into practice, envisaging the rural people coming together to build their own villages and work the adjoining land communally. For the next two years the manpower and financial resources of the Ministry of Food, Agriculture, and Co-operatives were devoted directly or indirectly to this end.

In 1969, following flooding in the lower Rufiji valley, people were removed from the flood-plain and resettled in villages at higher levels; they were not given much choice in the matter and there does not seem to have been a realization of the difficulties they might encounter through farming in a quite different ecological setting. The next year, semi-nomadic people near Dodoma who had been hit by drought were also settled in villages in an operation directed by government. By 1973 about 15 per cent of the population, some 2 million people,

were living in nucleated villages as compared with half a million six years before. The *ujamaa* campaign, it would seem, was having a considerable impact. However, only in 60 of the villages was as much as half the cultivated land being worked collectively. In the majority only between 4 and 60 hectares (10–150 acres) were being farmed in this way and most people worked on the collective farm on no more than a few days in the year.

The Tanzanian government was dissatisfied with the rate of progress and in 1973 ordered that within three years all peasants were to live in villages of at least 250 families; this figure was chosen to conform with the settlement size required to support a primary school and to warrant the provision of water supplies. The next year, 1974, drought afflicted much of Tanzania. Harvests were poor and there was a massive influx of people into the new villages, especially in the least prosperous parts of the country. In the heavily settled areas growing commercial crops, any reorganization was scarcely possible and would certainly have met with resistance; yet, by 1978, about 10 million people were living in nucleated villages.

The new emphasis on villagization rather than on the *ujamaa* kind of communality had a number of practical advantages. It was found to be impossible to coerce people into collective work; on the other hand it was not too difficult to ensure they should live in nucleated settlements. They could then be served with schools and dispensaries, they would be able to exchange ideas with their fellow-villagers, and they might be reached more readily by government officials and by activists of the ruling political party. The new villages took over the activities of Co-operative Unions and sold local produce to Crop Authorities at prices fixed by government. In the villages, Party cells were organized on a basis of 10 households to a cell, the cells coalescing into a hierarchy of successively larger groupings. The local Party chairman was normally chairman of a locally elected Village Development Committee or Council and a civil servant acted as village manager. The Council has the power to confer rights to land on the individual according to local custom.

The majority of the people who have moved into the villages have come from within a radius of 10 km. They usually helped to select

A village school in south-west Tanzania.

village sites and layout. On the whole, more emphasis was placed on siting villages alongside roads than near cultivable land and good water supplies. Small teams of planners visited villages from time to time and on occasion there was confusion as to whose plans were being followed. Houses were arranged on geometrical layouts and in many instances had to be moved when a plan was revised. Problems have been arising in areas where the soils are not inherently fertile and land close to villages has become impoverished and deprived of plant cover as a result of grazing and fuel-wood collection. Under these circumstances, the establishment of satellite villages becomes necessary (Fig. 12.1).

Villagization in Tanzania has clearly been a step of great importance, probably a step that was essential to social betterment, but the environmental consequences have yet to become fully apparent. The success of the whole programme has been undermined by the economic difficulties Tanzania has suffered

since the 1970s as a result of droughts, the oil price rises, an expensive war againt Amin in Uganda, falling commodity prices, and national indebtedness.

12.1.3.5 Ethiopia Since the removal of Haile Selassie as Emperor in 1974 all rural and urban land in Ethiopia has been nationalized and is now owned by the state. Families working the land have been granted rights over a maximum of 10 hectares (25 acres). The reform has been welcomed in the south of the country, where the majority of the farmers were tenants paying rent to Shoan landlords. In the north, where tenure was based on kinship, the reforms have scarcely impinged.

Throughout the country a number of Peasant Associations have been elected, representatives of which liaise with agricultural extension services. They also provide a means by which the government can exert its will and control the movements of people about the country. The eventual aim is to have one Association to

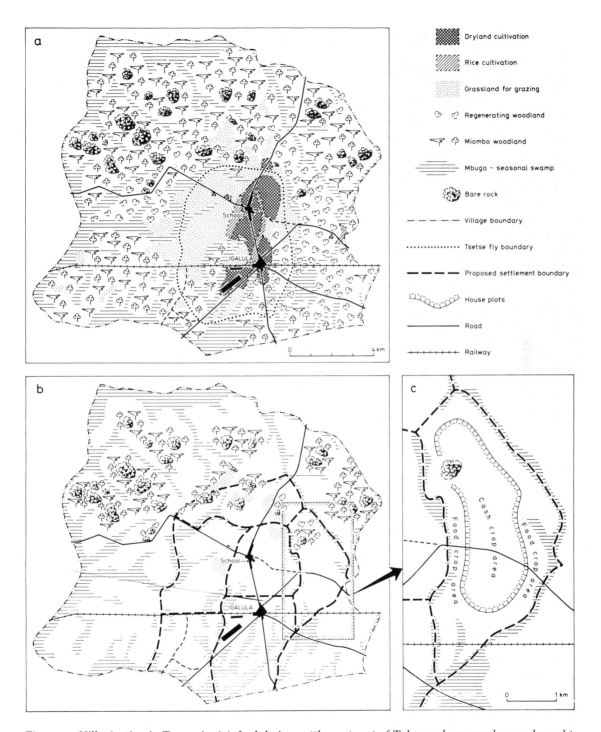

Fig. 12.1. *Villagization in Tanzania. (a). Igalula is a settlement east of Tabora where people were brought together from the surrounding area in the 1970s. They now have to walk long distances to the furthest fields. (b). As a result of an ODA (British Overseas Development Administration) survey it has been suggested that the village area should be divided up and satellite settlements established, (c) for instance, each with its own house plots, food crop and cash crop areas.*

every 800 ha (c.2000 acres) and for such Associations to organize the smallholdings into communal farms. Communal settlement schemes have been started on the lowlands and in the less heavily settled parts of the south-west.

Irrigated estates and commercial farms, which constituted only one per cent of the cultivated land in Ethiopia, were converted into state farms. They were increased in number by bringing more land under cultivation. Eventually they were absorbing three-quarters of the fertilizers and nearly all the improved seed used in the country, but were generating only about 5 per cent of the agricultural output. More intensive measures to collectivize agriculture in 1984 coincided with famine conditions. The peasants, who still farm 97 per cent of the land, have been concentrating on producing enough for their own consumption. Prices paid to producers for grain and coffee have been kept low, and people are not keen on investing in land which is subject to reallocation.

The Ethiopian government, in response to famine and scarcity of land, has tried to bring together people living in scattered homesteads into villages with a view to co-operative production. By 1986 four and a half million people had been villagized, many of them forcibly, and it is visualized that, eventually, 20 million people will have been resettled. Since the revolution, standards of living in urban and rural areas have markedly declined, but it is difficult to determine how much this is to be attributed to villagization, and how much to droughts, continued civil strife, and reorganization.

12.1.3.6 Mozambique

The lower Limpopo valley in southern Mozambique, in spite of massive labour migration to South Africa, was once the most productive area in the country. The cash earned by migrant workers helped to support the local economy and provided inputs to agriculture.

The Portuguese had instituted commercial farming, with both white settlers and African smallholders producing rice for sale. When independence came there was not much enthusiasm in this environment for FRELIMO's plans for communal villages and co-operative working of 100-ha farms. Nevertheless the land abandoned by the Portuguese settlers was incorporated into 25 state farms, each of several thousand hectares, each made up of banana plantations, livestock units, and rice and maize fields. Technical and organizational problems arose when attempts were made to restructure the irrigation network to fit the new large farm units and develop capital-intensive methods; the necessary money, equipment, and experienced staff were lacking.

In 1977 came severe flooding which swept away cattle, trees, and tools, and left many people homeless. The government response was to regroup large numbers of people into new villages high above the floodplain and direct what skilled people there were to repair the irrigation systems of the state farms. The villagers, left to their own devices, had little incentive to work hard on repairs or resume cash cropping, knowing that the money they could earn was worth very little; there was scarcely anything for sale in the markets and shops and so they simply grew enough food for their own needs. For the same reason they were unwilling to work as labourers on the state farms. It was therefore decided to decentralize agriculture planning and administration, dismember the large state farms and distribute land to smallholders.

Mozambique suffered in the early 1980s from drought and later in the decade from the terrorism of RENAMO guerrilla bands. In the severe drought of 1992, the Limpopo was reported to be dry for 250 km upstream from its mouth. Local people dug holes in the riverbed to reach water. Seawater penetrating upstream was used for irrigation and ruined the crops. However, the famine had one beneficial effect, it brought together RENAMO and government in peace negotiations in August 1992.

12.1.4 Changes in land tenure in pastoral areas

Pastoralists in Africa are accustomed to move with their herds over long distances according to the availability of grazing. Commonly families split up for at least part of the year, some members settling down to cultivation in a farming area while the others take the herds to graze far away. Villagization obviously creates problems for such people, as they are not always willing or able to confine their movements within village boundaries.

12.1.4.1 Group ranching in Kenya

In Kenya

since 1962, Masai pastoralists have been able to acquire group ranches each occupying something like 10 000 ha (25 000 acres). However, the Masai are inclined to invite friends and relatives to settle with them and to bring their cattle along as well. On the other hand, in times of drought, such as 1983–84 in Kenya and the Sahel, herds are driven far away in search of grazing, without much regard being paid to ranch boundaries or even international frontiers.

Some pastoralist experts have come to the conclusion that it might be best not to divide up the rangeland into ranches after all but to concentrate on building up authority structures of the traditional kind, capable of organizing herd movements in accordance with needs and natural conditions. But in places like Turkana in northern Kenya and parts of Kordofan in the Sudan Republic individual pastoralists are now taking matters into their own hands and are beginning to enclose land for themselves without paying much attention to government or the experts.

12.1.4.2 Ranching and tribal grazing lands in Botswana Much of Botswana is given over to pastoralism. Until the 1950s both population and livestock were concentrated along the wetter eastern border. Most of the people lived in large villages with cultivated land up to 40 km (24 mls) away and wet-season grazing grounds up to five times as far to the west. People with large herds traditionally put cattle into the hands of clients who would care for the animals and in return would get the milk and make use of the beasts for ploughing. It was called the *mafisa* system. Since the 1950s, thousands of boreholes with diesel pumps to lift the water have been installed by government and by individuals, making the Kalahari thirstland much further west available for livestock. Slaughterhouses at Lobatsi and Francistown provide a market for surplus stock, cattle rearing has become commercialized, and the *mafisa* system no longer operates effectively. Fewer people now have access to cattle than was formerly the case, most of the animals being owned by a limited number of people, mainly chiefs, politicians, and civil servants.

It has been argued that competition for grazing in the heavily settled east would be reduced and farmers there enabled to feed the cattle they need for pulling ploughs, if the owners of the larger herds, who have put down many of the boreholes, were to be allowed to acquire the rights to large tracts of land around the boreholes out in the Kalahari. It was envisaged that about a thousand ranches might eventually be established, each of about 6000 ha (15 000 acres) and capable of supporting 400 head of cattle. However, there are San hunter-gatherers and other people in the areas concerned who have customary rights to the land, and provision would have to be made for their sustenance.

The problems of organizing the use of the tribal grazing lands in the east presents even greater problems. Land devoted to agriculture is mixed with land used for grazing and the two uses are interdependent. In the 1960s the allocation of land in this part of the country was transferred from chiefs to Land Boards mainly consisting of prominent people. It has been argued that decisions about land use should be made at village level, making use of local knowledge and with the weakest members of the community able to protect their rights by being able to speak at public meetings rather than being at the mercy of remote authorities.

12.2 The scale and management of modern farming systems

Modern farming systems differ from one another according to the scale of activities and the kind of management employed. Large operations may involve land units covering hundreds of hectares. It is difficult for a single person, operating under African conditions, to farm more than a hectare at a time, and smallholders usually work something of the order of 5 hectares or less. In between large-scale operators and smallholders there is a relatively small group of what are sometimes called 'progressive farmers', with medium-size holdings.

The intensity of production varies with the nature of the activity. Livestock rearing in semi-arid rangelands, in Botswana for instance, is very extensive, with individual ranches covering tens of thousands of hectares, whereas irrigating fruit and vegetables in the Nile valley is extremely intensive in terms of labour and other inputs per unit area, and running a 50-hectare holding there is a relatively major undertaking.

Management of large operations is usually in

An EEC mechanized agriculture project near Dakar in Senegal.

the hands of either parastatal organizations or commercial companies. Individual white farmers continue to run large farms in South Africa, Zimbabwe, and Zambia. How long they will continue to do so remains to be seen. In Zimbabwe, plans were announced in 1992 to redistribute to black smallholders a half of the 11.5 mn ha, two-thirds of the total arable land, still in the hands of commercial, mainly white farmers. If commercial farmers are displaced from Zimbabwe they are likely to turn their attention to Zambia where land would seem to be available and where an expansion of employment and production from agriculture might help to make up for the decline of copper mining.

The number of such large farm units in any particular country is relatively small. Their managers are accessible, they can be expected to keep accounts, and they can offer security for loans. Such large concerns can be self-contained in the sense that they may be expected to have their own vehicles and machinery, procure their own seed, fertilizers, and pesticides, hire labour, and make their own marketing arrangements.

It is much more difficult to reach the thousands, even millions, of smallholders who work most of the land and grow most of the crops.

They may be a long distance from all-season roads; they may not be literate; the land they farm may not be freehold; they are likely to have no cash reserves and to rely for labour on their immediate family. Furthermore, the social framework in which they live was adapted to the non-competitive existence of a past age when everyone knew his place and there was no desire to increase production. Farming, food storage, and cooking were collective; gift-giving and receiving were obligatory; such a society does not readily readjust to commercial demands and the money market. Smallholders, if they are to modernize, usually have to operate within new institutional frameworks in the form of parastatal projects or co-operatives or, increasingly, as 'outgrowers' attached to 'nuclear estates' run by capitalist commercial organizations. They have to acquire new attitudes to life. Some families are able to do so and thrive; others are less successful, run into debt, lose control of their land, and finish up as landless labourers.

12.2.1 Large-scale farmers

12.2.1.1 Independent farmers Independent farmers in Africa, such as the white farmers in southern Africa, have benefited considerably in recent decades from technological developments which they have been able to adopt successfully. They have seen their yields per acre in crop and animal products increase while at the same time they have been able to reduce their labour requirements at a time when wage rates have been increasing. The surplus labour has been ejected, and sent back to the reserves or homelands.

Many large farmers have been adversely affected by political conditions. Thus the white settlers in Kenya were a target for the Mau-Mau terrorists or freedom fighters—the description depending on which side you were on. Rhodesian tobacco farmers had difficulties coping with guerrilla activity and finding markets for their crops in the UDI period. Until 1992, South African fruit growers found overseas markets for their produce restricted, owing to boycotts in opposition to apartheid. Farms formerly in the hands of white settlers in Tanzania, Kenya, and Algeria were taken over by Africans at about the time those countries became independent. The handover in Kenya was eased by funds provided by the British government and the land was divided up into large and small holdings now owned by Kenyans.

12.2.1.2 State farms

Direct state involvement in agriculture in the colonial period was spectacularly unsuccessful. The Tanganyika Groundnut Scheme in the early post-war period was a costly failure owing to drought, mismanagement, and the high costs of opening up new land. The Mokwa Scheme in the Kontagora area of the Nigerian Middle Belt was another less publicized but more carefully studied scheme. Its failure was the outcome of social as much as environmental problems, with an unsympathetic Emir providing labourers for the scheme who were unsuitable for such a project. Tractor-farming schemes under Nkrumah's government in Ghana were also disastrous, partly owing to the difficulties experienced in keeping the machinery in working order. Sisal plantations taken over by the Tanzanian government just at the time when the market for sisal collapsed have never paid; they have now been returned to the private sector. In more recent times, state farms in Mozambique and Ethiopia have failed to produce efficiently.

12.2.1.3 Commercial companies

Commercial companies seem to have been more successful. Between the wars, a very large company producing soap and margarine, Lever Brothers, not only acquired a monopoly of all the wild oil-palm fruit harvested from enormous areas of the Congo basin but also had an agreement with the Belgian government that enabled it to establish extensive oil-palm plantations.

The American Firestone company began to plant rubber trees in Liberia in the 1930s and by the 1950s they occupied 300 km^2 (115 mls^2). Firestone was not only processing and exporting its own product but also that of about 4700 locally-owned plantations; rubber constituted 85 per cent of the country's exports (Fig. 9.6).

The Gezira scheme, which has provided a model for large irrigation schemes elsewhere in Africa, was for the first forty years of its existence a collaborative three-cornered project involving a British commercial management company called the Sudan Plantations Syndicate, the Anglo-Egyptian government of the Sudan, and Sudanese tenants (Fig. 10.9). The Syndicate stipulated the crops to be grown, provided seed, looked after pest control, and disposed of the harvested crop. The tenants and the government received a share of the proceeds from the sale of the crops, after deductions had been made for the costs of management and other inputs. Since independence the scheme has been under the authority of the Sudanese government and has been extended westwards towards the Blue Nile and now occupies about a million hectares. The chief beneficiaries are the 30 000 tenants and their families. In addition, about 2000 technicians are permanently engaged in supervising the scheme and about 150 000 labourers find employment there. There is now less emphasis on cotton and more on foodstuffs for local consumption. Wad Medani, the commercial centre of the Gezira, continues to profit from the processing and traffic entailed. Khartoum and its merchants benefit from the purchasing power of the large productive community to the south, and the civil servants in the capital depend for their salaries and wages on the taxes paid directly and indirectly by the scheme to the central government.

In recent years TNCs have become heavily involved in sugar-cane production. Lonrho has assisted in the financing of a large integrated sugar scheme to the south of the Gezira, in the Kenana area, where it is intended to irrigate eventually about 400 000 ha (1 million acres), with water stored behind the Roseires dam. A Dutch scheme produced enough sugar-cane on the plains of the Afar depression, downstream of the Koka dam on the Awash river, to supply the Ethiopian market and provide a surplus for export, until it was nationalized. A subsidiary of Tate and Lyle is involved in a new scheme in the upper Benue valley in northern Cameroon. Booker McConnell has a small financial share in the Mumias Sugar Company in Kenya and, much more important, a management contract. The company ploughs and harrows the land, supplies planting stock and fertilizer, organizes harvesting, and provides transport. It is sometimes argued that opportunities for local initiative are removed by such arrangements and that the host country fails to benefit as much as the TNC, but local farmers in this scheme at any rate have increased their income, continue to retain their land, and compete to sign on as participants.

Brooke Bond has long had an agreement with tea growers in east Africa under which it provides access to its sales and finance organization in return for 7.5 per cent of gross sales proceeds. The British American Tobacco Company provides extension and marketing services in several African countries which allow it to direct smallholder tobacco production and integrate it with its manufacture and continent-wide distribution of cigarettes. TNCs have invested in pineapple-growing in Ivory Coast and Kenya, and in the production for the European market of fresh vegetables in Senegal and flowers in Kenya. Nestlés have assisted in the production and adoption of a new coffee variety, Arabusta, which has the physical qualities of Robusta and the aroma of Arabica. The company pays for coffee a price which is fixed a year ahead and so provides some protection for producers against sudden price falls on the world market; it must be added that it also profits when prices suddenly rise. Rice schemes funded by American and Saudi capital have been established on 30 000 hectares in the Casamance area of southern Senegal. Even in countries which have restricted the entry of foreign capital on ideological grounds, tncs are selling their technical expertise and marketing ability; in Tanzania they operate tanneries and

manage pyrethrum extraction plants, and in Bukoba they are responsible for processing coffee.

12.2.2 Smallholder schemes

12.2.2.1 Agricultural improvement schemes in northern Nigeria Initiated by the World Bank in 1974 and funded on a very large scale, these schemes were intended to assist the smallholder without applying pressure on him. Farm service centres were established at intervals of 16 km (10 mls) along existing roads in Gombe, Funtua, Gusau, and Lafia (Fig. 5.4 (b). These areas were all ripe for agricultural development, being not so far north as to suffer severely from drought and, until a few decades ago, having an abundance of land. Additional rural roads were built, though far fewer than was intended; extension workers were based at the roadside centres, where fertilizers, pesticides, and seed were sold at subsidized prices; purchasing agents bought the produce.

Yields of sorghum and maize increased markedly in the Funtua area of southern Katsina in the late 1970s (though this was in part due to better rains). However, it was difficult to find a market for the yellow maize which had been introduced: the taste, or rather the lack of it, was not liked locally, and sorghum continued to dominate the cropped area. Nevertheless, diversity of cropping increased, with rice, sugar, peppers, and tomatoes being grown for sale in local urban markets. Production of groundnuts and cotton, on the other hand, diminished because the prices offered for them were unattractive; it was a time of high oil revenues and rising urban populations, and it was food for the towns that was in demand. The main beneficiaries of the scheme, as so often happens, were the larger farmers, mainly members of the ruling class and farmer-traders with holdings of about 10 to 50 ha (25–125 acres). They were not necessarily the best farmers but they were able to ensure that they got most of the artificial fertilizer that was on sale at subsidized prices. The fertilizer was in short supply and so buyers usually had to pay a supplement—a bribe—to scheme staff if they were to get any; also it was an advantage to have a lorry to carry it away from the store. With their increased incomes the big farmers further enlarged the size of their households and work forces by marrying more wives and employing more labourers; they were also able to purchase and work more land. Rural inequality was thus aggravated by the development, as usually tends to be the case.

Schemes of a similar kind were extended to other parts of the country. In Sokoto and Kano they have been heavily involved in small-scale irrigation, assisting producers with subsidies for tubewells and pumps which have enabled households involved to double their incomes.

12.2.2.2 Cotton in Burkina Faso
A French company for the development of textile fibres assisted the expansion of smallholder cotton cultivation in Upper Volta in the 1950s by providing improved seed and a marketing network. Over the next decade production increased from 3000 to 30 000 tonnes and continued to grow even in the drought years of the early 1970s, when the quantities of cereals harvested were declining. Some would blame the food shortages that developed at that time on the emphasis placed on cotton, which took up land and labour that would otherwise have been devoted to growing cereals. Prices of sorghum rose in the mid-1970s and production shifted away from cotton and towards cereals, but only until granaries had been replenished.

One of the efforts made in the 1970s to relieve the pressure on the land was a move towards settling river valleys which had been abandoned because of river blindness. It was at this time that the UN World Health Organization campaign against onchocerciasis began (see pp. 59, 60). As the threat of the disease recedes, the plan now being pursued is to resettle people on the valley floors and for them to grow irrigated as well as rain-fed crops with modern techniques. Credit is available for the purchase of fertilizers, seeds, and insecticides. Some farmers are prospering and are able to employ labour; others are in debt. However, in relation to the results achieved, the scheme has turned out to be extremely costly for the aid donors.

12.2.2.3 Cotton in Ivory Coast
In Ivory Coast, cotton had been grown traditionally and used by village weavers to make cloth. An improved variety, Allen cotton, was introduced in 1960 to provide long-staple fibres for a textile industry to replace European imports. It was intended that the cotton should be grown by smallholders on plots up to a hectare in size, using chemical fertilizers and pest control. Financial assistance came first from France and then from the European Development Fund.

Cotton production greatly increased in the 1960s, but yields ceased to rise about 1970 and production diminished. In part this could be attributed to drought, but it was also because the cotton was competing for land with food-crops and needed three times the labour traditional cotton had required. Pressure was brought to bear on farmers to cultivate larger acreages and to use animal-drawn implements, finance to assist them being supplied by World Bank loans to the Ivory Coast government. However, prices for rice were increasing, and farmers were finding this a more rewarding crop, so fertilizer prices for cotton were subsidized. The measures taken were successful in the sense that output of cotton in the course of the 1970s increased from 30 000 to 140 000 tonnes and the area under the crop multiplied four times. Families with a large number of young men have benefited from the expansion of cotton-growing but the work load, especially of the women, has greatly increased. Some of the additional labour requirement has been supplied by people escaping from drought and food shortages in Burkina Faso and other countries to the north; they have been glad to take paid work as labourers on the cottonfields in order to survive. The cost to the state, which was effectively subsidizing the local textile industry, has been very considerable, and in the late 1980s it was finding it very difficult to cope with cotton subsidies and at the same time keep up debt repayments to the World Bank and other 'donors'.

12.2.2.4 Privatization in Kenya
In Kenya, privatization is seen as the panacea for the problems of increasing smallholder production. It is now widely recognized that African farmers react positively to economic opportunity and that, within the range of their experience, they are good managers of their resources and ready to respond to changes in the profitability of the crops they grow. But even in Kenya smallholders have difficulty in obtaining the credit they need, whereas large landholders, with their land as security, can obtain bank loans for agricultural development, even when in fact

they intend to use the money for other purposes.

In most parts of Africa, the risks of investing in agriculture are regarded as being high, especially with droughts much in mind and with the uncertainties involved in procuring inputs with a foreign-exchange component. If you have money, the rate of return and the security of your investment is likely to be greater in other sectors of the economy, such as property; the expansion of agricultural production is consequently retarded.

12.3 The indigenous contribution

The failure of many agricultural development schemes in Africa has caused many people to react against the technical innovations involved in modernization and to advocate building on existing indigenous knowledge and methods. A good deal of attention was paid to indigenous systems in the latter years of the colonial period, and it was beginning to be appreciated that African farmers had accumulated a fund of knowledge about the means of coping with the environment in which they operated. In the years following independence both independent governments and visiting experts were inclined to favour centrally-organized, large-scale schemes, and local opinion was neglected. With the occurrence of drought, famine, and foreign currency shortages, confidence in the new ways of doing things has diminished and a greater willingness is being shown to consult the local people and learn from them.

It has been shown that mixing different crops on the same plot of land is advantageous, even though European agriculturalists used to advise against it. Such intercropping ensures that the soil is covered for a longer period of the year, and thereby protected from erosion, and that yields overall are higher. In many areas cultivators practise agro-forestry, planting annual crops under trees as in the oil-palm gardenland of south-east Nigeria, and preserving useful trees like *Acacia albida* in the park savanna farmland of the north. Such conservation methods are not followed everywhere; usually they are confined to areas which have been well settled for many decades or even centuries. There is little doubt that if all farmers were to adopt the methods used by the best,

production would increase very markedly. Spreading information to farmers is not easy. It is necessary to train staff to spread ideas about possible improvements not only to the men but also to the women, who do much of the farm-work. Such staff must be dedicated and well led and these requirements are rarely met.

Very often agricultural developments have taken place without official intervention. Far more areas have been opened up for farming by immigrants using their own initiative than have been affected by official resettlement schemes. African farmers are prepared to adopt

A cow fed on maize leaves and other waste materials and kept in a stall.

Pigs fed on banana stems on a Chagga homestead in the Kilimanjaro area of Tanzania.

Wrecks of farm machines on an agricultural development project in Ghana.

new methods when they are convinced that they will benefit from doing so and will not be taking undue risks. They took up new crops like cassava, maize, and cocoa when they were introduced from overseas. They experiment and select strains of crops which suit local conditions and tastes. When plant geneticists develop new strains which they believe will be improvements on the existing ones they must not only test them carefully on experimental farms but give local farmers the chance to assess them for themselves. The scientists must be prepared to try to understand in what ways their products may prove to be defective as far as the local people are concerned. If more labour is required to grow them, or if they require labour at a time when it is scarce and food crops need all the attention, they may be not be regarded by the local farmers as an improvement on existing, lower-yielding varieties. New strains must be resistant to disease, tolerant of drought, and acceptable as far as flavour and keeping qualities are concerned.

The lessons learnt from the effects of the Green Revolution on rural societies in Asian and South American countries have indicated the problems that may arise and have been emerging in Africa. Total production may increase as a result of modernization but there are dangers that modern farming methods will benefit mainly the more prosperous farmers, while the poorer ones, unable to afford the necessary inputs, find themselves worse off than before. Provision must then be made for the large numbers of rural people who may find they are no longer able to gain a livelihood from the land.

It cannot be denied that modernizing agriculture brings in its wake many problems, and in many areas it may turn out that the best policy is to introduce quite minor improvements to existing systems. At the same time it is becoming evident that unless an agricultural revolution takes place in tropical Africa there will not be enough food grown there to feed the people.

205

13

CRISIS IN AFRICA

More than a century has elapsed since the Congress of Berlin and the carving up of Africa amongst the European powers. A generation has passed since most countries of Africa gained their independence. During the 1980s conditions in much of the continent have deteriorated in ways which have become apparent to the world at large (Figs. 13.1 and 13.2). Africa, it is often stated, is in a state of crisis. Certainly it is in a hazardous situation, conceivably it is at a turning-point; whether decisive action will be taken to cope with the problems remains to be seen.

The most widely known events have been the famines of the early 1970s and the early 1980s. These have been associated with droughts which have been especially damaging in the semi-arid parts of the continent. Concern has been expressed about the part that may have been played in food shortages by 'desertification', a term which has replaced 'desiccation' and 'soil erosion' in the conservationists' vocabulary and is itself being displaced by 'environmental degradation'. It seems quite reasonable to assume that drought has accentuated environmental degradation, and some arguments have been advanced to suggest that changes associated with such degradation might be capable of modifying climate.

Drought and desertification are not by themselves responsible for famines. Certainly they are capable of causing local and regional food shortages. People are likely to go hungry under such circumstances; in Africa most people are hungry for a good deal of the time and many are suffering from malnutrition. Famines occur and people starve if they are unable to acquire food from elsewhere when the sources on which they normally depend fail and they do

not have enough money to buy it, or there is none to buy because the distribution system breaks down. Africa is poor; African countries are amongst the poorest in the world, and when there are famines it is the poor people, especially those in rural areas, who starve. But in many instances food would be available for those who are starving if distribution systems had not failed on account of war or civil disturbance. Famines occur when and where both the environmental and human systems function badly.

13.1 Famine

Famine disasters have occurred from time to time since antiquity, for instance in Egypt in biblical times and at intervals since then when the Nile flood has failed. In modern times millions of people died in the USSR in a famine in the 1920s resulting from policies followed by the Soviet government, eliminating private land ownership and forcing people in rural areas to hand over to the state the crops they had harvested. In India, during the Second World War, famine in Bengal was the outcome of wartime inflation and the inability of a large sector of the population to afford to pay for supplies of food that had been diminished in volume by floods and droughts and by purchases made for British and allied troops in the region.

In the Sahel and Ethiopia in the 1970s, famine was the outcome of drought. Cattle starved for lack of grass and cereal crops failed; the people were too poor to purchase supplies from outside and governments failed to overcome problems of distribution. In the 1980s the same combination of circumstances resulted in famines in the western and eastern parts of the Sudan Republic, their effects being accentuated by the presence of large numbers of refugees— from the west escaping from conflict in the Chad Republic, from the east fleeing from con-

flict and food shortages in northern Ethiopia.

In Ethiopia food shortages and famine in 1984–5 and again in 1987–8 resulted from drought and from the disorganization assoc- iated with the efforts of government troops to

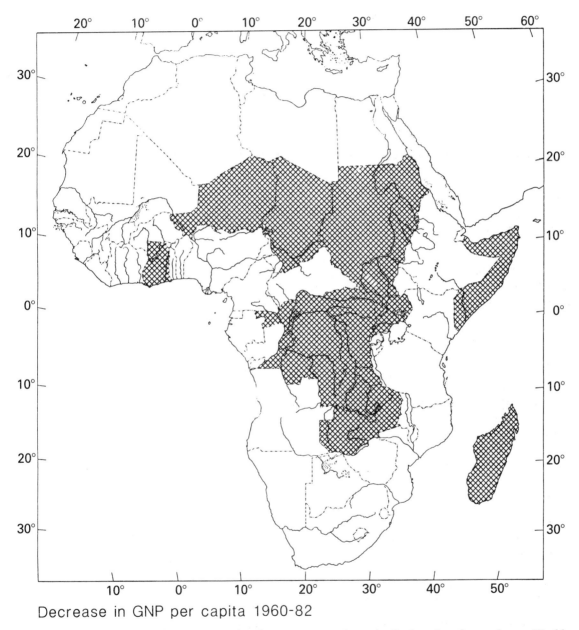

Decrease in GNP per capita 1960-82

Fig. 13.1. *Countries with a decrease in national output per capita 1960–82, based on figures from a World Bank report 'Towards sustained development in sub-Saharan Africa: a joint programme of action' (1984). Since the report appeared Mozambique, Ethiopia, Mauretania, Sierra Leone, and Angola could probably be added to those countries where standards of living in terms of product per head have fallen since 1960.*

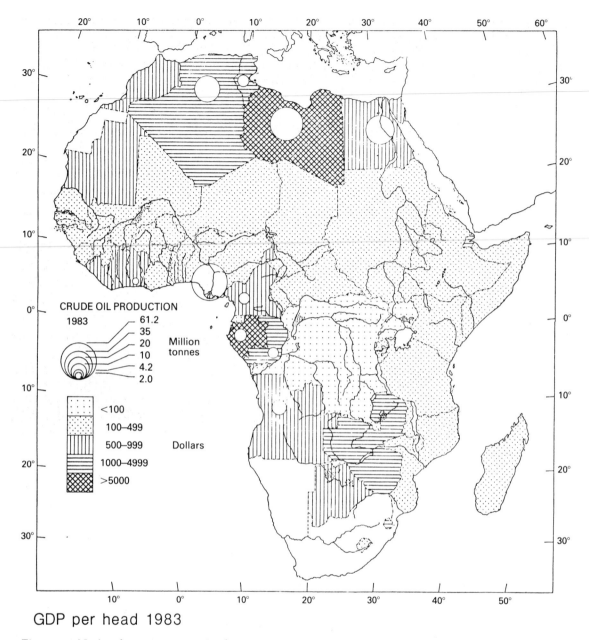

GDP per head 1983

Fig. 13.2. *National output per capita by country, 1983, according to a World Bank report (1984). Oil production is responsible for the high values in Libya and Gabon and it also helps to support those of Algeria and Egypt. In spite of its oil, product per head in Nigeria remains low because of the great size of the population in relation to total production.*

overcome a rebellion against its rule in the Tigraian and Eritrean northern parts of the country. In the Ogaden border region, large numbers of pastoralist refugees added to food-supply problems under drought conditions in both Ethiopia and Somalia. Every famine disaster has its own particular roots and is the outcome of a particular crisis.

In the years around 1990 about 900 000 refugees from strife and famine in Mozambique

Famine refugees in northern Ethiopia.

flowed across the border into Malawi, increasing numbers in that country by 10 per cent. Nearly all the land in Malawi suitable for cultivation was already in use, most rural households in that country having less than a hectare of farmland on which to survive. Fuel wood is scarce, being needed for curing tobacco as well as for domestic use. When the drought came in 1992, the strain on the country's resources was almost unbearable and political stresses, already severe, were accentuated.

In most of these cases the people who suffer are the poor people in remote rural areas. Even under normal conditions they are undernourished, suffering particularly severely in the months before the harvest. When food is scarce for whatever reason, be it drought, flood, pests, or conflict, and prices rise, the poor do not have the money to pay for it. They sell first their animals, then their meagre possessions, and finally they eat the seed for next year's planting (Fig. 13.3). Eventually there is no alternative for

them but to move to places where they think there may be a chance to survive. The old and the very young are most at risk. The rest find their way to towns where food can be scavenged or to camps where food aid from overseas may be available.

13.1.1 Food aid

Food aid cannot be provided rapidly in substantial amounts because of the delays involved in purchasing, shipping, and delivering it to where it is needed. In any case, most African countries have a limited capacity to absorb large amounts of foodstuffs made rapidly available by governments and charities. If people are to use wheat flour, to which they are unaccustomed, they need ovens and must learn to bake bread. For milk powder to provide a safe and nutritious food it has to be mixed with clean water. Food aid does save lives, but it may not be able to prevent the survivors suffer-

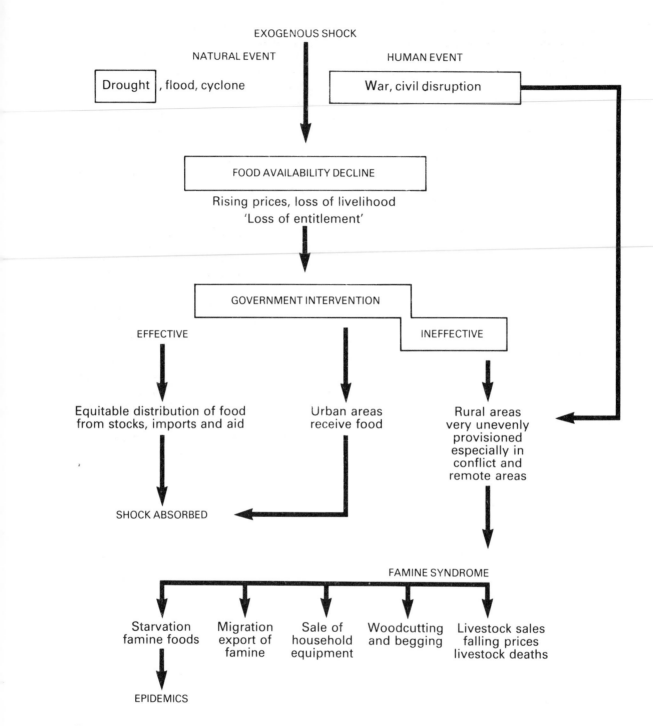

Fig. 13.3. *The development of the famine syndrome. Under African conditions, where a very high proportion of the people are poor and undernourished, the famine syndrome rapidly develops. If they are deprived of food by drought, or conflict, or a combination of these, farmers are forced to sell off their livestock and then their meagre household goods, turn to traditional famine foods, and finally migrate to the cities or relief camps.*

ing in the long term from the effects of hunger and the diseases associated with it. No doubt mortality can be further reduced by improving forecasts of impending disasters through monitoring the climate and, still more important, the social indicators of distress. At the same time it is now accepted that supplying food aid may carry with it risks of upsetting local production and marketing systems in the long term. In order to reduce such risks, 'food for work' campaigns have been advocated, with people making roads and soil conservation terraces in return for food. Above all it is important that attention should be directed towards dealing with the basic causes of famine.

13.1.2 *The geographical distribution of famine hazard and disasters*

In Africa there would seem to be an important geographical dimension to famine. In particular it is possible to distinguish two latitudinal zones where risk is greatest, one near the northern tropic, Cancer, one near the southern tropic, Capricorn (Fig. 13.4). In both zones there are political conflicts as well as serious drought hazard. The northern zone extends across the Sahel and Sudan zones into Ethiopia and Somalia; the southern one stretches across Angola through Botswana, Zambia, and Zimbabwe into Mozambique.

13.2 Drought

Drought can be defined in various ways, most simply as a condition when much less rain is received than might normally be expected. In the semi-arid to sub-humid regions of Africa the rains are normally confined to a few months of the year. On the whole, the lower the mean annual rainfall the less reliable it is, so droughts are experienced more frequently as one approaches the desert margins. People in these areas have adapted their ways of life to the drought hazard by using various coping strategies, but these have not been adequate to prevent disasters in recent years. Why is this so?

First it must be emphasized that famine associated with drought is not a stranger to the Sahel–Sudan zone. At the same time it is apparent from Figs 1.14 and 1.15 that rainfall totals and river discharges were unusually low in the early 1970s and early 1980s. Rainfall totals in

this zone for this period scarcely ever reached what had been regarded as mean values, and in 1984 they were the lowest on record. The Nile flood was lower than it had been since 1913 and the discharge of the Niger at Niamey in the early months of 1985 was lower than it had been in living memory and possibly for hundreds of years. Lake Chad was reduced to a small fraction of its usual extent. This is not to say that the whole of Africa is getting drier; nor is there any certainty that the dry conditions in the Sahel–Sudan zone will persist. Although droughts have been experienced in east Africa and south-central Africa in recent decades, the high levels of Lake Malawi and the high discharge of the Zambezi between 1946 and 1980 point to wetter rather than drier conditions in the region between the equator and the tropic of Capricorn.

It has long been supposed that man can influence the climate by clearing forests and otherwise changing the environment. By reducing the biomass and burning fossil fuel he has been feeding large quantities of carbon dioxide into the atmosphere. Only about a half of this supply is being absorbed into the oceans, and, especially in the latter part of this century, the concentration of carbon dioxide in the air has been steadily rising. There is little doubt that this causes global warming as a result of more of the long-wave reradiation from the earth being trapped in the atmosphere. Such a warming is likely to be more marked in higher latitudes than near the equator, and to be accompanied by modifications of the atmospheric and marine circulation patterns and changes in the regional distribution of rainfall. It is conceivable that the global warming which has been a prominent feature of the changing climatic scene for more than a century is an outcome of increasing carbon dioxide concentrations in the atmosphere, and it is possible that the increased severity of drought in the Sahel–Sudan is to be attributed to man's impact on the constitution of the atmosphere.

Two more ideas are worth mentioning. It has been suggested that man may be causing aridity to increase in the semi-arid lands by the way in which he has been changing conditions in the desert borderlands. It has been argued that clearing the woodland and reducing the plant cover on the southern side of the Sahara

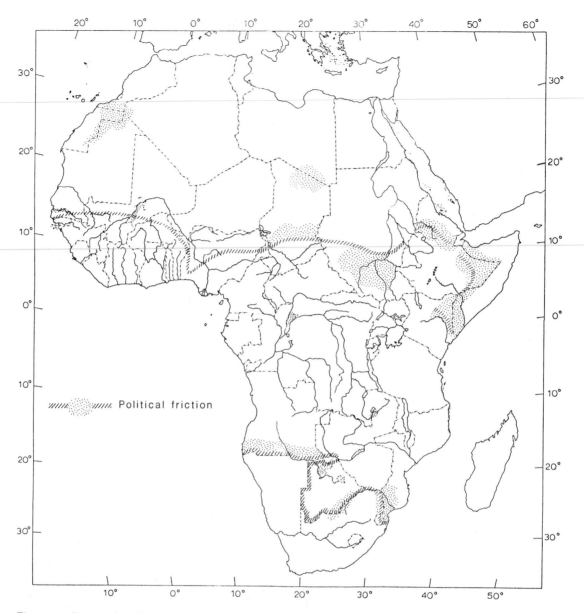

Fig. 13.4. *Zones of political friction in Africa. Many of these are associated with international frontiers which derive from colonial time, such as those of west Sahara and the Aozou strip between Libya and Chad. Chad and the Sudan Republic are pluralist states where Muslim and non-Muslim are in conflict. Somali pastoralists are accustomed to graze regions which extend into Ethiopia and Kenya and resent being subject to the taxes and regulations of those countries. The South African government, under pressure from its neighbours to drop apartheid, supported armed groups opposed to the established governments of Angola and Mozambique so as to destabilize them and thus reduce their effectiveness as opponents. The main zones of political friction happen to coincide with the zones threatened by desertification. (From A. T. Grove, 1986, 'The state of Africa in the 1980s', Geogr J. 152: 193–203.)*

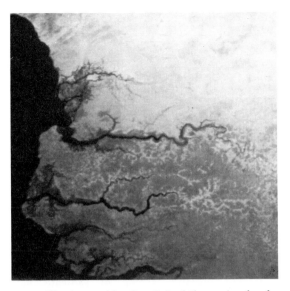

A satellite image (April 1984) of the region bordering the Gambia river in west Africa, indicative of the high reflectivity of the ground surface towards the edge of the desert.

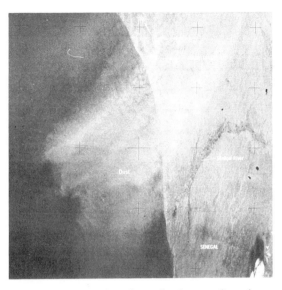

Skylab picture of a dust cloud extending from Mauritania south-south-west over the Atlantic.

A dust cloud driven by east-north-east winds moving across the Inland Niger Delta near Jenne.

has increased the albedo, the reflectivity of the surface, possibly doubling it, thereby causing less of the incoming solar radiation to be absorbed and reradiated and more to be returned into space as short-wave radiation. This could conceivably result in reduced warming of the atmosphere and a greater tendency for subsidence to occur at the margins of the desert, with an associated reduction in rainfall. The desert would consequently expand and might be said to be feeding on itself. It is an ingenious and possibly correct idea, but the extent and intensity of the feedback is uncertain and in dispute amongst climatogolists.

With increased aridity and deterioration of the plant cover as a result of grazing and cultivation, winds at the desert margins generate more dust. The fine material is carried aloft and transported long distances by the easterly winds as a long dust cloud that has been observed from satellites extending out to sea from the west African coast. Some of the dust is blown all the way across the Atlantic and settles out in the Caribbean region. It has been observed during the rainy season, both from aircraft flying at high altitudes and from astronauts on board the Space Shuttle, that cumulus clouds which might normally be expected to grow vertically and produce rain, cease to grow upwards through the dust layer. The dust, heated by the sun, seems to produce a warm layer through which clouds will not grow to reach the freezing level, and so prevents rain falling where otherwise it would have done.

At present there is little that can be done to reduce the incidence of droughts. The production of carbon dioxide by the burning of fossil fuels depends more on the price of the fuel than on consideration of any environmental consequences it may have. Improving the plant cover at the desert margins is desirable for many reasons, quite apart from reducing the albedo, but is a very long-term objective. If the main sources of dust can be identified and if they turn out to be limited in extent then something might conceivably be done to reduce its generation, but no doubt at great cost.

Recent research seems to indicate that drought in the Sahel is associated with high temperatures of the surface waters of the southern ocean. This may or may not be associated with increased concentrations of carbon dioxide in the atmosphere but it would seem that on the south side of the Sahara there has been a southward shift in the climatic belts through about 100 km (60 mls) or more since the first half of the century and that human use of the Sahel may have to adapt to this change.

Gully erosion in a savanna landscape with high relief and deeply weathered material underlying the surface soils. It is often difficult to tell how long such erosion has been in progress, and always costly to stop it.

13.3. Desertification

Desertification is the reduction of the biological productivity of land to low levels, especially as a result of human action in semi-arid areas. The word was originally used by a French forester called Aubreville to include the environmental degradation that accompanies the destruction of forests in humid regions. Instances have been noted where this has occurred, for example on sandy soils in south-east Nigeria where rain forest has been replaced by unproductive open grassland dissected by deep gullies.

Attention was directed to the problem of desertification in the early 1970s at the time of the Sahelian drought and famine. It was suggested that the damaging effects of rainfall deficiencies had been accentuated by long-continued reduction of the plant cover and accompanying deterioration and erosion of the soils. The degradation was often attributed to the production of crops for export at a time when people and domestic animals were increasing in number and subjecting the biological resources of the semi-arid and sub-humid lands to ever greater pressure.

Few studies have been able to provide reliable quantitative information about the rate at which desertification has been taking place. Most concern has been expressed about the deterioration of ecological conditions in the Sahel–Sudan zone (Fig. 13.5). It is particularly difficult in this zone to distinguish between the effects of a climatic shift and the consequences of the ways in which people are using the land. The environmental degradation resulting from human activity is probably best documented and most readily traced in quite different areas in Africa, notably on the islands of St Helena and Mauritius and at the Cape, where European settlers, within a few decades around 1700, are known to have destroyed the original plant cover as well as many animal species with resultant accelerated soil erosion, loss of fertility, and impaired water supplies. In other parts of the continent there is usually less certainty about the timing and the nature of the sequence of events.

Careful use of soils, woodland, and streams can conserve natural resources even in semi-arid environments. Terracing of steep slopes, building check dams across wadis, restricting the felling of trees, firing grass early in the dry season before it burns too strongly, and regulating the movements of flocks and herds so as not to overgraze the rangeland can all be managed by a settled people under a stable government. Some African people employed such measures long before colonial times. The terraces they made survive to this day, especially in those parts of the savannalands where people sought refuge from marauding horsemen by living high up in rocky hills. A chain of such areas can be traced across the Sudan zone, including the lands of the Dogon people of the Bandiagara plateau overlooking the Inland Niger Delta in Mali, the Kabré of northern Togo, the Kofyar and other groups at the margins of the Jos Plateau in Nigeria, and the Mandara on the rocky hills of northern Cameroon. The Fulani of the Niger bend were amongst pastoralist groups who controlled grazing by regulating the seasonal movements of herds between the nutrient-rich grasslands at the desert edge and the less nutritive dry-season grazing lands of the Inland Delta.

Much of Africa has seen great changes in the human condition over the last hundred years. The white man has come as a settler and trader, building roads and railways, excavating mines, and disrupting traditional land-use practices and whole societies. Native peoples were restricted to farming in reserves in the first half of this century in colonies of European settlement. They have increased in number and attempt to grow more crops and raise more cattle in order to purchase manufactured goods from overseas and pay taxes, first to their colonial rulers and now to their own governments. With populations now several times greater than they were at the beginning of the century, much more wood is needed for fuel and for constructional purposes, especially within range of large towns. The effects are being etched ever deeper into the landscape.

The colonial governments recognized that soil erosion was a serious menace and attempted to counter it by enacting laws to prevent people farming steep slopes, and by requiring them to terrace or otherwise protect vulnerable farmland. Remote, thinly settled areas were set aside as game reserves and large areas, especially on watersheds, were proclaimed forest reserves where permission was needed to fell trees. These actions were not much appreciated by the local people, who looked upon them as

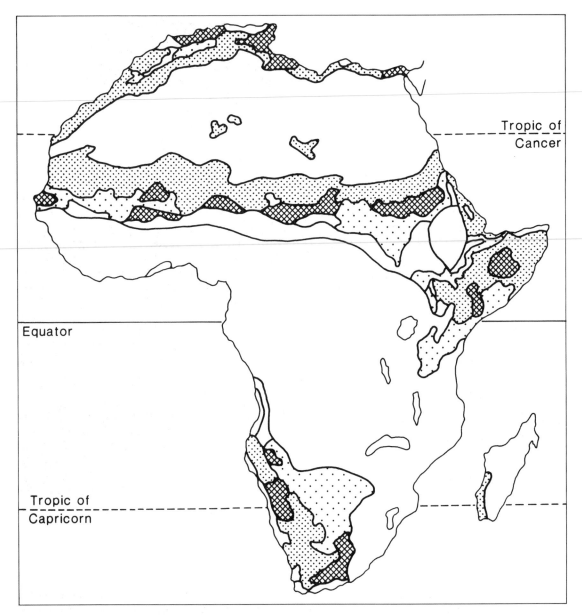

Fig. 13.5. *Desertification risk in arid and semi-arid Africa. Cross-hatching—very high risk; closely spaced dots—high risk; widely spaced dots—medium risk. (From Heathcote,* The Arid Lands: their use and abuse, *Longman 1983.)*

infringements of their traditional rights, and, as independence approached, the rules and regulations were commonly flouted. The newly independent governments showed little concern about enforcing them and many of the terraces and other soil conservation structures fell into disrepair.

Soil erosion and other forms or degradation tend to worsen slowly and then, once a critical stage is reached, they accelerate rapidly. If

Terracing in the Konso area of southern Ethiopia. The area is heavily settled and the local people have long been accustomed to terrace slopes to conserve the soils.

preventive action is taken in good time the situation remains manageable; but once a critical stage is passed, counter-measures become very costly (Fig. 13.6). The situation tends to become serious at times when climatic extremes result in floods and droughts. Desertification itself may accentuate both hazards. Erosion of the absorbent topsoil and removal of the plant cover reduces infiltration of water into the soil and allows rapid storm runoff; the consequence is higher flood-discharge peaks, incision in headwater slopes, and bank erosion downstream. Increased yields of sediment choke river channels and fill reservoirs; mean-dering streams are converted to braided rivers. In the semi-arid regions, wind action becomes more effective as plant protection of the soils diminishes. Both the dust carried aloft and bare land surfaces reflect the incoming solar radiation rather than absorbing it. The air becomes more stable and clouds are prevented from growing by convection to levels at which they might give rain. Desertification in these ways tends to magnify the harmful effects of drought and introduces desert processes of erosion into humid lands where, on account of the frequency of heavy storms, they can operate very effectively.

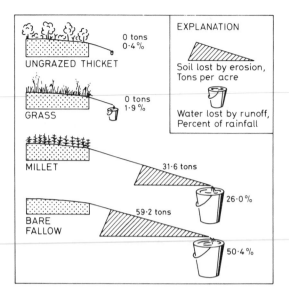

Fig. 13.6. *Accelerated erosion under African conditions. Experimental evidence from east Africa indicates the kinds of annual rates of soil loss under different methods of land use (31.6 tons/acre = 13 tonnes/hectare; 59.2 tons/acre = 24 tonnes/hectare, equivalent to a thickness of 1 or 2 mm of soil lost per year). The figures are merely rough and ready indicators, which will depend very much on rainfall intensity, nature of the soil, angle and length of slope, and preceding history of land use. They indicate that rates of soil loss by erosion when land is cultivated are liable to be considerably greater than rates of soil formation. The increased percentage runoff values under cultivation point to the dangers of reduced infiltration on the uplands and increased flooding downvalley.*

Soil conservation and afforestation entail much labour and expense and are slow to bring returns. People are not easily persuaded that they will profit from their own efforts to protect the environment. Many of them have few resources and are more concerned with ensuring they have enough to eat today and tomorrow than with planning years ahead. But unless the people of rural areas are involved in the planning and implementation of projects, little progress is likely to be made. The current lack of success of many of the projects sponsored by European countries and the USA and designed to combat desertification is largely due to failure to involve local people. Much of the expenditure goes into remote sensing, feasibility studies, and pilot projects rather than on widespread action within the degraded areas themselves.

Some development programmes themselves have been responsible for desertification. Improvement of water supplies can result in livestock remaining for longer periods of the year, with consequent overgrazing, in areas from which they were formerly excluded by lack of water; irrigation can cause water-tables to rise to the point where moisture can ascend to the surface by capillary action and result in soil salinization. Impact assessments are needed to ensure that the long-term costs of development schemes in the form of environmental deterioration do not outweigh the benefits received.

13.3.1 North Africa

The critical zone for desertification in north Africa lies between the 100 mm and 400 mm isohyets. In this zone, where sheep and goats are raised and barley and wheat grown, mechanized cultivation has been encroaching on steppe grasslands and groundwater is being exploited for irrigation and watering stock. Problems are arising of salinization and penetration of sea water into coastal aquifers. The land on either side of the lower Nile valley in Egypt was transformed into desert some four thousand years ago as a result of decreasing rainfall and the clearing of woodland for timber and fuel by the people living at the margins of the floodplain. Roman cities in north Africa, when they prospered two thousand years ago, may well have enjoyed more rain than now, and it is difficult to suppose their surroundings then were as barren as they are today. Woodland, it is suspected, suffered from the demand for fuel by townspeople of those times and by the nomadic herdsmen who succeeded them.

In Algeria the government is concentrating its efforts on holding back the desert by employing a 'Barrage Vert', a Green Belt 1500 km long and 20 km wide, which was started in 1971 and is largely the work of the Algerian army (Fig. 6.4). Running from the Moroccan border to the Tunisian, it has involved planting Mediterranean pine (*Pinus halipensis*) and alfa grass (*Stipa tenacissima*), upgrading rural roads and waterpoints, and improving grazing areas. In recent years a greater variety of trees has been used in order to reduce fire and disease hazards in the planted zone. Associated with the Barrage is a desert species gene bank which is intended to be of value to other north African countries.

In Libya, Centre-Pivot Sprinkler irrigation is a spectacular feature of the Kufra area, clearly visible on satellite imagery; groundwater is available at depth but it is not being recharged, and there are dangers of the water-table falling excessively as a result of the abstraction. In coastal areas, petroleum products sprinkled on the surface have been used to provide a permeable thin black layer that fixes sand dunes for a year or two while trees such as *Prosopis* and *Atriplex* are planted and become established.

In Egypt, sheets of polymer gel, made from petroleum by-products, have been used to stabilize and fertilize soils for agricultural purposes. Field experiments are being carried out to find other ways of improving the management of sandy desert soils. In the Western Desert of Egypt, attempts are being made to develop agriculture in the great desert depressions, using artesian water from the Nubian Sandstone. This has resulted in so much waterlogging and salt accumulation in soils that little overall benefit has so far been gained.

In southern Tunisia the very old technique of building stone dams a metre or two high across waterways and planting fig, olive, and palm trees on the sediments accumulating behind has been successfully applied. Active dunes in Morocco, formed from sediments brought down by storm-water from the eroding slopes of the Atlas mountains, are being fixed by planting tamarisk trees and erecting simple palm-frond fences to reduce the transporting power of the wind. Roads threatened by sand are given an aerofoil profile to speed up the air flowing across them and sweep away the sand that would otherwise accumulate and block them.

13.3.2 Sudan–Sahel region

This was the region which originally attracted international attention to desertification. Numerous non-governmental organizations as well as government departments are now involved in attempting to combat the process.

Many of the projects begun after the drought of the early 1970s suffered severely from renewed and even more intense drought conditions in the early 1980s. It is difficult to assess whether the hundreds of international projects that have been started have had much effect on the situation as a whole; probably not.

In Chad, armed conflict and political instability have resulted in many schemes being abandoned. *Acacia albida* trees, which come into leaf in the dry season, fix nitrogen, and yield a crop of beans useful as cattle fodder, have been established on 3500 ha (86 000 acres) of farmland, and *Acacia senegal*, the tree that provides gum arabic, has been successfully planted over an area of 700 ha. But such areas are minute in comparison with the millions of hectares at risk or already desertified. *Acacia albida* trees, *Borassus aethiopium* groves and acacia windbreaks have been planted in Niger. In Nigeria, where numerous nurseries to produce tree seedlings have been established successfully, afforestation has difficulty in competing for scarce land with agriculture and pastoralism. In Burkina Faso, a green belt is being planted around the capital Ouagadougou to combat encroaching sand and reduce dust pollution in the town. Village wood-lots are being established and more efficient wood-stoves promoted. Major plantation projects have not been very successful because of fires and losses from drought, and the fact that the exotic species commonly planted are not what the local people want; indigenous species are usually better suited to their needs.

In Mauritania, where the rainfall is low and natural conditions harsh, most anti-desertification projects have been failures. This has had a demoralizing effect on local officials and donors. Suggestions have been made that here and elsewhere in the Sudan–Sahel zone greater reliance should be placed on Muslim clerics of the religious brotherhoods when projects are formulated and implemented, because they have the support and confidence of the local people which is so essential for success.

13.3.3 The rift valley region of east Africa

On fertile but steep slopes in Rwanda, south-west Uganda, and several other heavily settled areas careful terracing has been successfully practised since pre-colonial times. Elsewhere soil erosion is a particularly serious threat because of the high relief, erodible soils, heavy rainfall at high levels, and aridity on the rift floors. The rainfall with its two seasonal peaks is very unreliable, occasionally excessive, and commonly deficient, and sediment yields are often remarkably high.

Ethiopia has suffered badly from deforestation of the highlands and resultant water erosion and also from overgrazing of the eastern lowlands. Some action has been taken to introduce soil conservation structures, but effective action in the most degraded areas was prevented until recently by the civil war.

In Kenya the Agricultural Department has long been aware of the dangers of erosion. Government is now renewing its efforts to cope with the problem and numerous non-

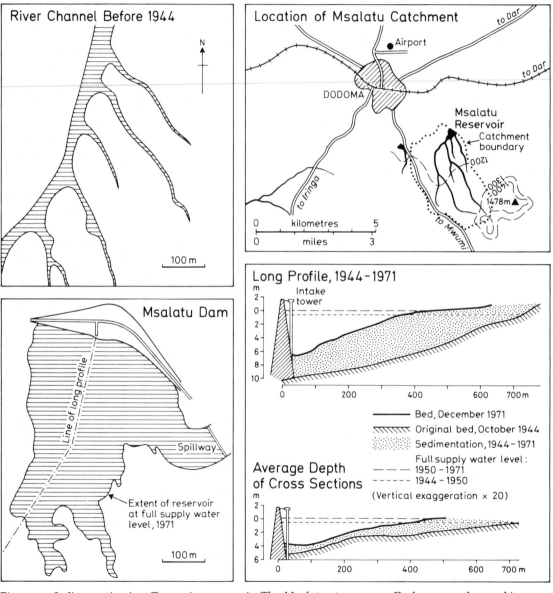

Fig. 13.7. *Sedimentation in a Tanzanian reservoir. The Msalatu stream near Dodoma was dammed in 1944 only about 5 km below its source. By 1971 a layer of sediment about 2 m thick had accumulated on the floor of the reservoir, greatly reducing its capacity and usefulness.*

government organizations are also involved. Turkana in the north of the country has been severely affected by drought and overgrazing. On the highlands particular attention is being paid to agro-forestry techniques which involve planting trees along the contour to hold the soil in place and provide a source of fuel, with cultivation of the intervening strips. Such methods of 'alley cropping' are being adopted in the Machakos area east of Nairobi. Farmers require some assistance for a few years when new land is being brought under cultivation to make up for that under the young trees. Efforts are also being made to promote projects which include both cropping and livestock raising.

A number of soil conservation schemes were started in Tanganyika in colonial times but they were generally unpopular with the local people, and improved methods of land use were widely abandoned at independence. Studies by geographers in the early 1970s showed how rapidly erosion processes were operating (Fig. 13.7). Since then villagization has accentuated the problem, for many of the villages were located without proper consideration of the suitability of the land for crop production and grazing. Current efforts stress the need to gain popular support. It has been demonstrated in the Kondoa area that exclusion of livestock can transform a desolate landscape of bare ground and heavily browsed shrubs to impressive vistas of grass and vigorously sprouting shrubs. But the area involved is small and the costs heavy.

13.3.4 Southern Africa

Conditions vary widely in this region, which includes the Kalahari in Botswana on the west and the forests of northern Madagascar in the east. In many of the countries a high proportion of the young adult males are working abroad and are not available to do the hard work required to conserve the soil. Farming is mainly left to women, and they are the ones who have to be persuaded that action is needed.

The seriousness of the threat of erosion and desiccation, both of which are closely associated with desertification, has long been appreciated in the Republic of South Africa. A good deal of reliance has been placed on conserva-

tion structures, especially in the European farming areas, but the most serious environmental degradation has been in the Homelands, where too many people have attempted to scratch a living from the land without the means to build up its fertility.

Lesotho, though nominally independent, is in many respects like a Homeland, with many of the men working in the Republic. With its high relief it is especially susceptible to gully erosion. In colonial times much effort was expended on constructing contour terraces, planting grass strips, and damming gullies; but the structures deteriorated because of poor maintenance and occasional heavy storms. Several donor agencies have provided technical and financial assistance to a multiplicity of projects in recent years, but a way has yet to be found to persuade farmers that it is to their long-term advantage to maintain the conservation works. In 1979 legislation was enacted which allowed individuals to have title to grazing land, in the belief that landowners would not allow their own land to deteriorate. The most successful schemes have been those concerned with establishing wood-lots throughout the country; both conifers and eucalyptus grow well at the lower levels, but species suited to altitudes above 2000 m are lacking.

In Botswana, a market economy and the production of cattle for sale, together with the sinking of thousands of boreholes, resulted in a rapid increase in livestock numbers between the drought years of the early 1960s and those of the early 1980s. Grazing land policy has been constantly under review and many ranching projects have been attempted but so far without much success. Many of the largest stockowners are wealthy townspeople, some of whom have little knowledge of rangeland requirements.

Some of the most spectacular erosion anywhere in the world has been depicted on Space Shuttle photography of northern Madagascar where marine embayments have silted up over the last few years as a result of massive erosion resulting from deforestation and the high rainfall intensity accompanying tropical cyclones.

13.4. Conflict within states

Food shortages have on occasions developed

into famines in Africa because government authority and administration have not been effective, dangers have not been foreseen, and appropriate arrangements have not been made to deal with them. In other cases the actions of central government have actually accentuated the risks of famine.

Most African states are recent creations, the outcome of late nineteenth-century European colonialism. South of the Sahara nearly every country is made up of several ethnic groups, each group speaking its own language and occupying its own region, with the different groups coming together in the main towns. Little attempt was made by the colonial powers to promote national unity within their colonies; people were encouraged to look towards the imperial metropolis as the political centre. Especially in British colonies, indirect rule employed and supported the authority structures of the individual ethnic components of the population, not deliberately in order to divide and rule but for reasons of economy and convenience. Government of such countries is now rendered difficult because of the absence of a consciousness of common origins and aims amongst the people, and often a lack of respect for the national government's legitimacy.

With class structure weakly developed, political parties tend to reflect ethnic divisions. In the countries along the south side of the Sahara, problems associated with tribal diversity are less apparent than in some others, because many ethnic groups were involved in large state formations in the past. However, religious differences are very apparent in the Sudan, Chad, and Nigeria, the north being dominantly Muslim while the southern peoples are non-Muslim and include many Christians. The differences between northern and southern peoples are cultural as well as religious, involving contrasting attitudes to women, diet, dress, and authority. In such countries it is not easy for both Muslims and non-Muslims to agree to form a single government and to agree on laws relating to voting rights, women's rights, education, land tenure, and other such matters. Each group tends to promote its own beliefs, behaviour patterns, and authority with resultant friction. This is especially the case when religious fundamentalism emerges. Solutions are perhaps to be found in the adoption of federal structures of government that allow a considerable degree of regional autonomy to constituent ethnic groups.

The bureaucracies of the new colonial states were run by European officials and it was many years before locally recruited staff had the opportunity to reach senior levels in the administrative or technical departments of government. By the time independence came, governments everywhere had come to accept that they were responsible not only for keeping the peace but also for health, education, and other social services and for economic affairs. Limited numbers of Africans were professionally qualified as lawyers, doctors, and teachers but few, if any, had gained experience at a high level in banking, business, and financial affairs. Technical, scientific, and commercial institutions of the kind that form the circles of power and influence in industrial countries had scarcely begun to emerge. Infrastructure was poor, industrial development typically belated, limited in scope, and dependent on foreign technology and know-how. African countries still have to rely heavily on expertise from overseas sources, to their own inevitable disadvantage.

The ideologies of the independent states differ. Kenya, Ivory Coast and Nigeria are usually regarded as capitalist countries where private enterprise flourishes. Algeria, Guinea, Ethiopia, Mozambique, and Angola, on the other hand, adopted Marxist-Leninist attitudes and attempted to operate centralized planned economies. They were unsuccessful because of inadequate assistance from outside sources, and in some cases because of civil war. Now Ethiopia's Russian military advisers have gone home; Cuban troops have left Angola; Tanzania is moving towards a market economy.

Within most African countries, capitalist as well as socialist, governments attempt to operate through centralized bureaucracies and endeavour to promote development through state and parastatal organizations. Because state structures are generally weak, governments have difficulty in implementing crucial policies. Insufficient attention has been paid to agriculture, and scarce resources have been allocated inefficiently. Urban populations have been placated with cheap food while producers have been paid low prices for their export crops. Concessions of various kinds have been granted to locally powerful individuals and groups to purchase their support. Licences to import have been misused; contracts and dubious loans have been granted to favoured individuals.

In many if not most countries the military have intervened to rid the country of the politicians they consider to be corrupt. They are then tempted to remain in power, and about one-third of the countries and one-third of the people in Africa now live under military regimes. Some are no worse than the civilian regimes they have displaced, others, notably in Uganda under Amin, have become a byword for misgovernment.

One of the longest-lasting military regimes has been that of General Mobutu in Zaire. Since he assumed full power in 1965 he has governed the country through a political aristocracy, using administrative and financial means and the police to maintain power over his subjects. Economic management does not really exist, the government apparently perceiving no relationship between savings, investment, and production as the source of wealth and economic growth. The money which has held the regime together for over 20 years has come from the sale of mineral ores and other commodities and from overseas borrowing on a large scale. Western countries appear to be prepared to lend money to Zaire because of its wealth of resources and because its government is seen as being counter-revolutionary.

In states such as this, conflicts are liable to arise between factions. Administrative structures break down, transport systems are inadequate to cope with the demands created by regional food shortages, and famine may be used as a weapon. Such strategies are not confined to Africa; attempts have often been made to apply them in Europe in times of war.

13.5 Relations between African states

Friction between individual states was minimized by the general acceptance of the Organization of African Unity that frontiers inherited from colonial times should be respected. However, since the 1970s the consensus has been fading. Morocco attempted to incorporate the Spanish Sahara in a Greater Morocco and as a result has become involved in a struggle with local 'Polisario' forces supported by Algeria

and Libya. Senegal took the opportunity provided by a coup against the government of Gambia to intervene forcibly in the affairs of that country. The Somalis tried to extend their rule westwards over neighbouring parts of the Ogaden, where Somali pastoralists have been accustomed to nomadize, and were repelled by Ethiopian forces backed by the USSR. Libya has invaded northern Chad in an effort to acquire parts of the Tibesti mountain region which are reputed to have valuable mineral resources and where the frontier between the two countries has been disputed since colonial times. Tanzania reacted to Ugandan troops infringing its frontiers by invading Uganda and driving out the corrupt government of Idi Amin, an operation it could ill afford. Shaba in southern Zaire has twice been invaded by forces from bases in Angola.

All such conflicts disrupt people's lives; they are unable to plant and harvest their crops, refugees seek shelter in towns or neighbouring countries and find themselves stranded without resources. The countries where the religious divide between Muslims and non-Muslims is most marked are also countries liable to suffer from drought and desertification. South of the equator, four of the countries sharing a common frontier with the Republic of South Africa and Namibia border the Kalahari thirst-lands.

For many years, the most serious and persistent threat to peace and prosperity on the continent appeared to be white minority rule in South Africa and the reaction of the states lying to the north. Angola and Mozambique had fought for and obtained their independence from Portugal in the late 1970s. At the same time, a white minority government in Rhodesia was unsuccessfully attempting to maintain itself in power. When newly independent Mozambique, with a Marxist government, attempted to apply sanctions against Rhodesia, the white Rhodesian government supported guerrilla forces of the Mozambique National Resistance (RENAMO) against the government of Mozambique. Eventually the black majority came to power in Rhodesia and all three newly independent countries, Angola, Mozambique, and Zimbabwe, plus Tanzania, Zambia, Malawi, and Botswana formed an organization called SADCC (Southern African Development Co-ordination Conference) to press for black majority rule in South Africa and Namibia. Malawi was lukewarm in its support and Botswana recognized its own relative impotence. Nevertheless SADCC gained support from the United Nations, the EEC, the USA, and other countries for trade and other sanctions against South Africa. In the early 1990s, with the abandonment of apartheid and the apparent willingness of the South African government to negotiate with black majority leaders, sanctions began to be lifted and it seemed possible that SADCC would cease to be an effective organization.

The effects of the conflict in South Africa continue to be felt in neighbouring countries. South Africa had supported rebel forces against both the Angola and the Mozambique governments. In Angola it has backed UNITA rebel forces and in Mozambique the RENAMO guerrillas. Mozambique was already suffering from the effects of drought and from disorganization associated with the departure of the Portuguese and the attempts of the Marxist government to introduce large-scale state farming. Disruption of the state by RENAMO has resulted in many districts within the country suffering from famine and terror.

Amongst other consequences of the fighting in Mozambique has been the destruction of the power transmission lines from Cabora Bassa to South Africa and, more important, the cutting of rail links from the interior of southern and south-central Africa to the coast at Benguela and Beira. The railway from Zambia through Tanzania to Dar es Salaam has remained open and has been carrying much of Zambia's copper to the coast. Traffic through Dar es Salaam doubled in the course of the 1980s. The line across southern Mozambique to Maputo, running very close to the South African border, has been open to attacks from guerrillas and traffic through Maputo halved in the 1980s. The trade of SADCC countries to the outside world and even that of Shaba in southern Zaire have remained to a large degree dependent on South Africa and the railways running south to the ports of Durban, Port Elizabeth and Cape Town. Mining and manufacturing activity in Zimbabwe and Zambia rely on South Africa for investment, materials and markets. The future of the whole of southern Africa, not merely that of the Republic, depends on a successful outcome of the negotiations to create a multi-ethnic state. The course of such negotiations is quite unpredictable and it would be optimistic to suppose that they will be completed peacefully and within a short time.

13.5.1 Regional groupings.

The colonial powers recognized the advantages of grouping together their colonies into larger blocks for certain purposes. The French West African territories were administered from Dakar and those of Equatorial Africa from Brazzaville. Their currencies were tied to the French franc, while those of the British territories were tied to sterling. The three British east African colonies formed a free trade area with a common tariff barrier and with common postal, railway, research, and other services. Such groupings encouraged intra-African trading by providing larger market areas and reduced administrative costs. Now there are 52 independent African countries, 24 of them with fewer than 5 million people; market areas have shrunk and administrative costs have greatly increased.

Collaboration between the independent states has not been remarkably successful. Though the Organization of African Unity succeeded in its early years in defusing some potentially explosive situations, of recent years it has become increasingly ineffective.

An East African Community which took over the operation of the common services in 1967 soon ran into difficulties, largely because of the differences in the ideologies of the three states and also because it was felt by Tanzania and Uganda that Kenya was profiting at their expense. In spite of negotiations intended to result in more industries being located outside Kenya, disagreements reached such a pitch that for several years after 1977 the frontier between Kenya and Tanzania was closed, and flights between the two countries had to be routed through a third.

An Economic Community of West African States, ECOWAS, established in 1975, was based first in Lagos and latterly in Abuja, Nigeria. In its first 17 years, it failed to make much impression. However, in the early 1990s it did help towards restoring peace in Liberia. Some tariff barriers have been reduced but the main concern is with non-tariff barriers between and within the various states. Numerous check-points have been set up in west African countries, not only by immigration and customs officials at international boundaries but by soldiers and police along main roads. These state employees are not being properly paid and they use the check-points to extract money for themselves.

A new treaty was signed in 1992 with a view towards greater economic co-operation. It is intended that ECOWAS shall procure funds from international aid sources for improving rural water supplies and for building bridges and roads to link together the West African countries. Telephone communications between the capitals have already been improved and there is now a single West African health organization. Preparations have been made to set up regional cattle breeding and seed production centres. Floating weeds in coastal lagoons have been especially troublesome since 1985 and a project to control them has been started. It is intended to create a single monetary zone with a common currency by the year 2000. It is now becoming recognized in West Africa that bureaucrats who have been used to running state control systems that put checks on the private sector must learn to create an environment favourable to private sector initiative. Corruption and mismanagement have to be eliminated. But until the check-points are removed, extortion ceases, and internal security for travellers and goods in transit improves, little real progress can be expected.

Perhaps the most effective unifying theme has been the association of most African countries with the European Economic Community under the Lomé agreements. These give duty-free access of 66 developing countries in Africa, the Caribbean, and the Pacific (ACP) to the European market. They also provide for preferential access for European Community manufactures to African countries. At the same time, various forms of financial assistance for development policies are provided by the Community. The third Lomé Convention, which came into force in March 1985, includes proposals to work out ways of making EEC food surpluses available to the ACP countries. Assistance is to be given in developing farming and fisheries and in doing so to involve the local people. A system has also been provided for helping to stabilize ACP export earnings by providing subsidies to producers when prices of commodities fall below critical levels. Lomé IV places

new emphasis on the reform of economic policies and provides funds for structural readjustment. It sets the environment at the centre of EC/ACP cooperation, with a view towards conserving natural resources, protecting ecosystems, and controlling desertification and deforestation. It promises that environmental assessments shall precede all large-scale projects and aims to prohibit the export of toxic wastes to ACP states.

13.6 Aid and indebtedness

There are some similarities between personal and state borrowing. If an individual borrows money from a bank or other financial institution, interest has to be paid on the sum borrowed, either at an agreed fixed rate or, more usually, one that varies from time to time according to the economic climate. In addition, arrangements are made for repayment of the capital sum borrowed over a certain period, it may be a few, it may be many years. Loans may be made to meet a borrower's short-term cash needs, perhaps resulting from an unforeseen mishap of some kind. On the other hand, they

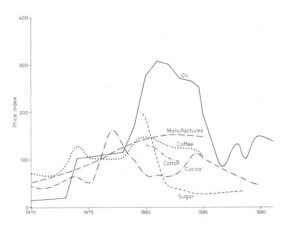

Fig. 13.8. *While the price of oil rose steeply in the 1970s and that of manufactured goods also increased, prices of the commodities most African countries export fluctuated and on the whole fell. In other words, unless they were oil exporters, the terms of trade turned against them. In the 1980s, the price of oil and of commodities generally declined in relation to the price of manufactures.*

225

may be designed to provide equipment and other requirements for undertakings designed to increase production and earn a larger income. National governments relying on their power bases can raise money by taxing imports, exports, incomes, sales, and purchases. They can borrow from individuals or institutions by issuing savings bonds of one kind or another; they can also borrow from commercial banks, local, foreign or international. Most if not all states are in debt to their own citizens. Some countries are in debt to the rest of the world; other countries are net creditors, being owed more than they have borrowed abroad themselves.

Most African countries have had difficulties in raising funds locally for development purposes unless they have valuable minerals to export and local communities in privileged positions prepared to invest their savings locally. In some countries, government marketing boards provided a source of funding in the 1950s and 1960s by purchasing crops at a low price and selling them on the world market at a higher price, but this source proved inadequate in the 1970s, when commodity prices fell in relation to the imported inputs required (Fig. 13.8). At the same time, advanced countries were prepared to make loans or gifts to underdeveloped countries in order to exert political influence or to further economic expansion.

The newly independent African states came to rely on borrowing from overseas sources, at first on a modest scale but in the late 1970s on a scale which far exceeded their capacity to service the loans—that is, to pay the interest charges and repay the original loans by instalments. In part this came about because of natural disasters such as droughts and the need to import food from overseas; in part it was the result of the rise in the price of oil. This price rise greatly increased the cost of imports, of which oil constituted a high proportion; at the same time foreign banks were anxious to lend funds which had been accumulated by the oil-producing countries, especially those in the Middle East.

There are various reasons why African governments have been unable to live within their incomes. Colonial administrations had been very careful not to run into debt; they were required by metropolitan governments to avoid deficit financing. With independence, the colonial institutional restraints on expenditure disappeared. Government ministers were anxious to spend money; there were so many needs and opportunities. The governors of Central Banks were appointed by the government and could be bent to its requirements. The President had to comply with the desire to spend in order to maintain his popularity. No individual seemed to benefit from restraint, in the short term. There were in addition more deep-seated reasons for states becoming bankrupt; some simply did not have the productive capacity to provide for the essential needs of their people.

Africa's external debts grew from about $6 billion in 1970 to about $82 billion in 1985 and $200 billion in 1987. The sum, though huge, is less than a tenth of the total amount owed by the Third World as a whole and is no greater than that owed by individual countries in Latin America, notably Mexico and Brazil. However, in relation to their national outputs, the level of indebtedness is higher in Africa than in Latin America. In 1984 the money owed by African countries was more than three times the value of that year's exports. By the late 1980s, interest payments due annually on foreign loans amounted to about 40 per cent of the total value of Africa's exports. Even countries like Nigeria, Algeria, Morocco, and Ivory Coast were in difficulties. Because their economies had appeared to be healthy they had been able to obtain larger loans, especially from commercial banks, than had other countries that were clearly in a precarious position. Nigeria's debt in 1986 constituted about one-fifth of the continent's total. With the low prices they were receiving for their exports in the late 1980s, Nigeria and others of the more prosperous African countries were in serious financial trouble.

The situation was relieved to some extent, in the years around 1990, by the lower price of oil and the reduced value of the American dollar. Some countries were relieved of their debts, in part, by creditors who could see no hope of being paid back what they had lent. In the circumstances, commercial banks were reluctant to provide more money and the flow of funds from private sources into Africa greatly diminished, putting a brake on further development. African countries had to rely increasingly on assistance from international institutions such as the International Monetary Fund and the World Bank. These institutions have laid down strict conditions for providing loans. They have required governments to take measures to stabilize their economies by reducing public spending and abolishing food subsidies. Such measures are unpopular in the towns and have provoked rioting in Cairo and Lusaka. Other conditions have included devaluation of currencies, with accompanying risks of inflation and shortages of vital imports, and reductions of controls on imports and exports. Such intervention by the IMF, which itself is very dependent on USA funding, seems to be comparable to that of Britain and France in Egyptian affairs in the 1870s.

13.7 The way ahead

It is now generally recognized both outside and inside Africa that the continent is faced by very severe problems of which famine is a symptom. It may not be possible to do very much to counter drought effectively; ways have to be found to live with it. Rehabilitating degraded land is a very costly and lengthy process that has hardly begun. Altogether, the environmental situation is not one that offers good grounds for optimism. On the other hand there is a great deal of land that is still underused, especially in the southern parts of the continent.

Food supply must have high priority. It is true that cereal production in all African countries was rising in the 1960s and 1970s; in Kenya, Tanzania, Malawi, Zimbabwe, and Ivory Coast it more than doubled over a period of about two decades. But there are still shortages in certain countries in individual years, and it is important to note that in many countries populations have been increasing faster than food production. The question arises as whether food production can keep pace with the demographic expansion in the future. It would seem that there are many opportunities to expand agricultural output by the application of existing techniques and, with the general realization of the need for action, it may reasonably be hoped that adequate food supplies will become available before the end of the century.

Even if the food supply problem is solved, Africans and their governments will still be poor and life will be hard for them unless they can raise productivity in other sectors of their economies as well as in agriculture. Such developments are very dependent on political stability, without which government administration cannot be efficient and investment cannot be fruitful. In particular it would seem to be essential that manufacturing industry should expand much more rapidly than at present. If this is to be achieved, African states will have to be prepared to collaborate much more fully with each other and will need to receive much more assistance from the rest of the world than is at present generally visualized.

In Africa we can see old societies crumbling and new ones emerging. The process is a slow and painful one, and for many people, in Africa and outside, such changes are unwanted and are opposed. A whole sector of human culture is being transformed. Over the whole scene looms the spectre of AIDS. We seem to be witnessing processes that involve the disappearance for ever of much that is of value and interest in the geography of mankind.

GUIDE TO FURTHER READING

In the 1980s, African studies were affected by the deterioration in conditions in many African countries. Government departmental reports and statistical information have become more difficult to obtain. Foreign scholars have experienced delays in obtaining research permission. African universities have been disturbed by strikes and closures, and shortage of foreign exchange has limited their purchases of journals and equipment. As a result, academic research has suffered and several locally published journals have ceased to appear. The situation is not a new one. In *The Book Hunger*, (eds. R. Barker and R. Escarpit, Paris: UNESCO, 1973); it was noted that some African nations were becoming virtually bookless societies (Crisis in Third World Publishing, *The African Book Publishing Record XVII*, Hans Zell, Oxford, 1991, p. 7). A UK-registered charity, The Ranfurly Library Service (2 Coldharbour Place, 39–41 Coldharbour Lane, Camberwell, London SE5 9NR0) provides international book aid, including a service for sending suitable donated books to places in Africa where they are needed.

Outside Africa, studies of the continent have also suffered setbacks. Funding of higher education has ceased to expand at the rate of the 1960s and 1970s and some Area Study Centres have disappeared from the scene.

Articles on African geography

These continue to appear in a large number of journals. The main ones in Great Britain are the *Geographical Journal*, the *Transactions of the Institute of British Geographers*, and the *Scottish Geographical Magazine*. In America, mention may be made of *Economic Geography*, the *Annals of the Association of American Geographers*, and the *Geographical Review*. The Ahmadu Bello University, Zaria, periodical *Savanna* has been revived. Popular articles with many illustrations appear in the monthlies, the *National Geographic* and the *Geographical Magazine*.

Non-geographical quarterlies which commonly have articles of interest to geographers include the *Journal of Modern African Studies, Journal of Southern African Studies, Journal of Developing Areas, Journal of Development Studies, Journal of Peasant Studies, Journal of African History. Paleoecology of Africa*, published by Balkema, Cape Town, appears annually. The Royal African Society produces *African Affairs*, which provides in each number a select list of articles on Africa, including a large number appearing in non-Africanist periodicals. Many African issues are discussed in *Oxford Development Project Reports*. Recent news and views on Africa appear in the monthlies *New African* and *African Events*, and in the weekly *West Africa*. Reports are published from time to time by *News from Africa Watch* (90 Borough High Street, London and 485 Fifth Avenue, New York). The Economist Intelligence Unit produces regular country reports. The UN Economic Commission for Africa surveys economic and social conditions.

The African Studies Association of the United Kingdom, which has been in existence since 1963, co-ordinates activities between persons and institutions concerned with the study of Africa. R. Hodder-Williams of the Department of Politics, University of Bristol has edited (1986) for the Association a directory of Africanists in Britain.

African studies Centres

Those established at universities in the United Kingdom are listed in the SCOLMA (Standing Conference on Library Materials in Africa) *Directory of Libraries and Special Collections on Africa*, compiled by R. Collison and revised by H. Hannam, 4th edn. (London, 1983). SCOLMA produces *African Research and Documentation* and other publications useful to librarians which can be obtained from the Main Library of Birmingham University UK (PO Box 363). Centres include the School of Oriental and African Studies and the Institute of Commonwealth Studies, London University; Rhodes House and the Institute of Commonwealth Studies, Oxford University; African Studies Unit, Leeds University; School of African and

Asian Studies, Sussex University; Centre of West African Studies, Birmingham University. The Centre of African Studies, Edinburgh University, publishes Occasional Papers. The African Studies Centre, Cambridge University, publishes a Monograph Series and Occasional Papers as paperbacks, and collaborates with Cambridge University Press in the African Studies Series.

Of Centres in North America the following are important:

Africa Collection, Hoover Institution, Stanford University, which publishes various series including a Bibliographical Series.
African Department, Northwestern University, which publishes a joint acquisitions list of Africana of 19 libraries in Evanston, Illinois, Canada and UK.
African Collection, Yale University.
African Studies Centre, Boston University.
Committee on African Studies, University of Chicago.
African Studies Centre, University of California, Los Angeles.
Programme of East African Studies, Syracuse University.
Committee on African Studies in Canada, University of Alberta.

Centres in other countries include the following:

Scandinavian Institute of African Studies, University of Uppsala, Sweden.
Geneva Africa Institute, Switzerland produces a quarterly *Genéve Afrique* with papers in English as well as French.
Afrika-Studiecentrum, Leyden, Netherlands publishes in English a quarterly *Abstracts Journal*.
Institutionen der Afrika-Forschung und Afrika-Information in der Bundesrepublik Deutschland und Berlin
Afrika-studien, IFO Institute for Economic Research, Munich, West Germany.
Centre of African Studies, Universytet Warszawski, Poland.

Comprehensive information on libraries, publishers, magazines, periodicals, major newspapers and the retail book trade is contained in *The African Book World and Press: a Directory*, Hans Zell 1988.

Hannam, H., Librarian of the Foreign and Commonwealth Office, edits *African Research and Documentation*, which appears twice a year. The subscriptions manager is Tom French at the Main Library, Birmingham University.

Bibliographies

BLACKHURST, H. (ed.) in association with the International African Institute, *Africa Bibliography*, Manchester University Press. Appears annually.
HALL, D. (compiler and editor) *Quarterly International African Bibliography* (listing articles and monographs). Centre of African Studies, SOAS, London University.
D'HERTEFELT, M. & BOUTTIAUX, A.–M. *Bibliographie de l'Afrique sud-Saharienne: Sciences, humaines et sociales*. Agence de Cooperation culturelle et technique, Musée Royale de l'Afrique centrale, Tervuren, Belgium. Appears annually or biennially.
LIBRARY OF CONGRESS (Office in Nairobi) *Quarterly Index to Periodical Literature, Eastern and Southern Africa*.
RUMNEY, T. A. *Africa South of the Sahara; a Selected Bibliography of Geographical Writings*. Montibello, IL, Vance Bibliographies, 1989.
SCHEVEN, Y. (ed.) *Bibliographies for African Studies, 1970–86*. Munich: Hans Zell, 1988.

Atlases

ADE AJAYI, J. F. A. & CROWDER, M. *Historical Atlas of Africa*. Harlow: Longman, 1985.
DAVIES, H. R. J. *Tropical Africa: an Atlas for Rural Development*. Cardiff, 1973.
International Atlas of West Africa, Organization of African Unity.
FREEMAN-GRENVILLE, G. S. P. *The New Atlas of African History*. London: Macmillan, 1991.
GRIFFITHS, I. *Africa, an Atlas of African Affairs*. London: Methuen, 1984.
PRIDE, D. H. *Atlas of World Cultures: a geographical guide to ethnographic literature*. Newbury Park, California: Sage Publication, 1989,

General

Africa South of the Sahara, 17th edn. London: Europa, 1987. This is a survey and reference book of all the countries south of the Sahara. It includes a who's who of major personalities in the region.
AKE, C. *A political Economy of Africa*. Harlow: Longman, 1981.
BROWNLIE, I. with BURNS, I. R. *African Boundaries: a Legal and Diplomatic Encyclopaedia*. London: Hurst, 1979.
Cambridge History of Africa, in several volumes. Cambridge University Press.
CROWDER, M. & AJAYI, J. F. A. (eds.) *A History of West Africa*. Harlow: Longman, 1987.
DAVIDSON, B. *Africa in History: Themes and Outlines*. London: Paladin, 1984.

LORD HAILEY, *African Survey*, revised 1956. London: Oxford University Press, 1957.

ILIFFE, J. *The African Poor: a History*. Cambridge University Press, 1988.

LEGUM, C. *Africa Contemporary Record*. London: Africana, appears annually.

LEWIS, L. A. & BERRY, L. *African Environments and Resources*. Boston: Unwin Hyman, 1988.

MABOGUNJE, A. L. *The Development Process: a Spatial Perspective*. London: Hutchinson, 1980.

MAZRUI, A. *The Africans: a Triple Heritage*. London: BBC Publications, 1986.

MILLINGTON, A. C., BINNS, A., & MUTISO, S. *African Resources: Appraisal, Monitoring and Management*. Reading University: Reading Geographical Papers Series (in press).

MOOREHEAD, A. *The White Nile*. Harmondsworth: Penguin, 1983.

The Blue Nile. Harmondsworth; Penguin, 1983.

MOUNTJOY, A. B. & HILLING, D. *Africa: geography and development*. London, Hutchinson, 1988.

NAFGIZER, E. W. *Inequality in Africa: political elites, proletariat and the poor*. Cambridge University Press, 1991.

NELSON, N. (ed.) *African Women in the Development Process*. London: Cass, 1981.

O'CONNOR, A. M. *The Geography of Tropical African Development: a Study of Spatial Patterns of Economic Change since Independence*. Oxford: Pergamon, 1978.

Poverty in Africa: a geographical approach. London: Bellhaven, 1991.

RIMMER, D. (ed.) *Africa 30 Years On*. London: Currey, 1991.

SENDER, J. & SMITH'S. *The Development of Capitalism in Africa*. London: Methuen, 1986.

UNESCO. *General History of Africa*, appearing in several volumes. London: Heinemann Educational: Berkeley: University of California Press.

For many individual countries the US Army Area Handbooks are useful compilations.

1. Physical environment

BISHOP, W. W. (ed.) *Geological Background to Fossil Man: Recent Research in the Gregory Rift Valley, East Africa*. Edinburgh: Scottish Academic Press, 1978.

BROWN, M. *Where Giants Trod: the saga of Kenya's desert lake* (Turkana). London: Quiller Press, 1989.

CAHEN, L. *The Geochronology and Evolution of Africa*. Oxford: Clarendon Press, 1984.

DARDIS, G. F. & MOON, B. P. (eds.) *Geomorphological Studies in Southern Africa*. Rotterdam: Balkema, 1988.

DEACON, J. & LANCASTER, N. *Late Quaternary Environments of Southern Africa*. Oxford: CLarendon Press, 1988.

DESSAUVAGIE, T. F. J. & WHITEMAN, X. (eds.) *African Geology*. Ibadan University Press, 1972.

FROSTICK, L. E., RENAUT, R. W., REID, I. & J.–J. TIERCELIN (eds.) *Sedimentation in the African Rifts, Geological Society Special Publication No. 25*. Oxford: Blackwell, 1986.

GOUDIE, A. S. *Duricrusts in Tropical and Subtropical Landscapes*. Oxford Research Studies in Geography, 1973.

HAMILTON, A. C. *Environmental History of East Africa: a Study of the Quaternry*. London: Academic Press, 1982.

HAYWARD, D. & OGUNTOYINBO, J. S. *The Climatology of West Africa*. London: Hutchinson, 1987.

HOWELL, P. P., LOCK, M. & COBB, S. (eds.) *The Jonglei Canal: impact and opportunity*. Cambridge University Press, 1988.

HOWELL, P. P. (ed.) *The Nile: resource evaluation, resource management, hydropolitics and legal issues*. SOAS, University of London and Royal Geographical Society, 1922.

KLEIN, R. G. (ed.) *Southern African Prehistory and Paleoenvironments*. Rotterdam: Balkema, 1984.

LANCASTER, N. *The Namib Sand Sea: dune form processes and sediments*. Rotterdam: Balkema, 1989.

STEWART, S. *Old Serpent Nile: a journey to the source*. London: John Murray, 1991.

THOMAS, S. G. & SHAW, P. A. *The Kalahari Environment*. Cambridge University Press, 1991.

TRUSWELL, J. F. *The Geological Evolution of South Africa*. London: Purnell, 1977.

TYSON, P. D. *Climatic Change and Variability in Southern Africa*. Oxford University Press, 1986.

WILLIAMS, M. A. J. & FAURE, H. (eds.) *The Sahara and the Nile*. Rotterdam: Balkema, 1980.

WRIGHT, J. B. (ed.) *Geology and Mineral Resources of West Africa*. London: Allen & Unwin, 1985.

2. Ecology

BEADLE, L. C. *The Inland Waters of Tropical Africa*, 2nd. edn. London: Longman, 1981.

COE, M. & COLLINS, N. M. *Kora: an ecological inventory of the Kora National Reserve, Kenya*. London: Royal Geographical Society, 1987.

EPSTEIN, H. *The Origins of the Domestic Animals of Africa*. New York: Africana Publishing Company, 1971.

HOWELL, F. C. & BOURLIERE, F. (eds.) *African Ecology and Human Evolution*. London: Viking Fund Publication in Anthropology, 1964.

HUNTLEY, B. J. (ed.) *Biotic Diversity in Southern Africa: concepts and conservation*. Cape Town: OUP, 1989.

JAMES, V. U. *Africa's Ecological and Economic Problems*. New York, Westport & London: Bergin & Garvey, 1991.

KOWAL, J. M. & KASSAN, A. H. *Agricultural Ecology of Savanna: a Study of West Africa.* Oxford: Clarendon Press, 1978.

LAWSON, G. W. *Plant Ecology in West Africa: systems and processes.* London: Wiley, 1986.

McMAHON, I. & FRASER, M. *A Fynbos Year* (The Cape). Cape Town: David Philip, 1988.

MOREAU, R. E. *The Bird Faunas of Africa and its Islands.* London: Academic Press, 1966.

The Palearctic-African Bird Migration Systems. London: Academic Press, 1972.

NYE, P. H. & GREENLAND, D. J. *The Soil under Shifting Cultivation.* Technical Communication No. 51. London: Commonwealth Bureau of Soils, 1960.

OWEN, D. F. *Animal Ecology in Tropical Africa,* 2nd. edn. London: Longman, 1976.

OWEN-SMITH, R. N. (ed). *Management of Large Mammals in African Conservation Areas.* Pretoria: Haum, 1983.

PRATT, D. & GWYNNE, M. *Rangeland Management and Ecology in East Africa.* London: Hodder & Stoughton, 1977.

ROGERS, D. J. *A Bibliography of African Ecology: a Geographically and Topically Classified List of Books and Articles.* London; Greenwood Press, 1979.

RZOSKA, J. (Ed.) *The Nile: Biology of an Ancient River.* Junk: The Hague, 1976.

SCHOLZ, C. H. & HOLM, E. *Insects of Southern Africa.* Durban: Butterworth, 1985.

SINCLAIR, A. R. E. & NORTON-GRIFFITHS, M. (eds.) *Serengeti: dynamics of an ecosystem.* University of Chicago Press, 1984.

WELCOMME, R. L. *Fisheries Ecology of Floodplain Rivers.* Longman: London, 1979.

YEOMAN, G. *Africa's mountains of the Moon* (Ruwenzori), London: Elm Tree Books (Penguin), 1989.

The United Nations Sudanian Sahelian Office (UNSO, One United Nations Plaza, New York 10017), established by the U.N. in 1973 to assist in the drought-stricken countries of Africa, produces Technical Publications, for example:

Lakes of Grass: regenerating Borgou in the Inner Delta of the Niger River, 1990.

Ecological Monitoring: the Senegal model, 1990.

The One Humped Camel: an analytical and annotated bibliography 1980–89, 1990.

Reforestation: the Ethiopian Experience 1984–9, 1991.

Sand Encroachment Control in Mauritania, 1991.

3. Pests and diseases

FORDE, J. *The Role of Trypanosomiases in African Ecology.* Oxford University Press, 1971.

HARTWIG, G. W. & PATTERSON, K. D. *Disease in African history.* Durham, NC: Duke University Press, 1978.

JORDAN, A. M. *Trypanosomiasis Control: an African Rural Development.* Harlow: Longman, 1986.

4. Ethnicity

ASIWAJU, A. I. (ed.) *Partitioned Africa: Ethnic Relations across Africa's International Boundaries, 1884–1984.* London: Hurst, 1985.

AYISI, A. O. *An Introduction to the Study of African Culture.* London: Heinemann Educational, 1979.

BAXTER, P. T. W. & ALGIAGOR, U. (eds.) *Age, Generation and Time: Some Features of East African Age Organisations.* London: Hurst, 1978.

BELL, M. *Contemporary Africa: Development, Culture and the State.* London: Longman, 1986.

EVANS-PRITCHARD, Sir E. *The Nuer: a Description of the Modes of Livelihood and Political Institutions of a Nilotic People.* Oxford University Press, 1969.

GIBBS, J. L. *Peoples of Africa.* New York: Holt, Reinhart, and Winston, 1978.

GOODY, J. *Technology, Tradition and the State in Africa.* Cambridge University Press, 1980.

HELLAND, J. *Five Essays on the Study of Pastoralists and the Development of Pastoralism.* Bergen: Universitetit i Bergen, Sosial antropologisk institutt, No. 20, 1980.

ISMAGILOVA, R. N. *Ethnic Problems of Tropical Africa: Can They Be Solved?* Moscow: Progress Publishers, 1978.

KESBY, J. D. *The Cultural Regions of East Africa.* London: Academic Press, 1977.

MAIR, L. *African Kingdoms.* Oxford: Clarendon Press, 1977.

OCHOLLA-AYAYO, A. B. C. *The Luo Culture: a Reconstruction of the Material Culture Patterns of a Traditional African Society.* Wiesbaden: Steiner, 1980.

OLE SAIBULL, S. *Herd and Spear: the Maasai of East Africa.* London: Collins & Harvill, 1981.

OPPONG, C. *Marriage among a Matrilineal Elite: Middle-class African Marriage: a Family Study of Ghanaian Senior Civil Servants.* London: Allen & Unwin, 1981.

ROBERTSON, C. & BERGER, I. (eds.) *Women and Class in Africa.* London: Africana, 1986.

SCHNEIDER, H. K. *The Africans: an Ethnological Account.* London: Prentice-Hall, 1981.

TURNBULL, C. M. *Man in Africa.* Harmondsworth: Penguin, 1978.

VINNICOMBE, P. *People of the Eland: Rock Paintings of the Drakensberg Bushmen as a Reflection of Their Life and Thought.* Pietermaritzburg: University of Natal Press, 1976.

5. Traditional Activities

ALLAN, W. *The African Husbandman.* London: Oliver and Boyd, 1965.

BATES, R. H. & HINRICHS, R. *Essays on the Political Economy of Rural Africa*. Cambridge University Press, 1983.

FOOD AND AGRICULTURE ORGANIZATION. *Changes in Shifting Cultivation in Africa: Seven Case Studies*, 1986.

GROVE, A. T. & KLEIN, F. M. G. *Rural Africa*. Cambridge University Press, 1977.

LAWSON, S. M. *Farming Systems in Africa: a Working Bibliography*. Boston: G. K. Hall, 1979.

RICHARDS, P. *Coping with Hunger: hazard and experiment in an African rice-farming system* (Sierra Leone). London: Allen & Unwin, 1986.

RUTHENBERG, H. *Farming Systems in the Tropics*. Oxford University Press, 1980.

STONE, J. C. (ed.) *Pastoral Economies in Africa and Long-term Response to Drought*. Aberdeen University African Studies Group, 1991.

6. *Africa before the colonial period*

ANDERSON, R. & FAWZY, A. *Egypt Revealed: Scenes from Napoleon's Description de l'Égypte*. American university in Cairo Press, 1987.

CONNAH, G. *African Civilizations*. Cambridge University Press, 1987.

CURTIN, P., FEIERMAN, S., THOMPSON, L., & HIBBERT, C. *Africa Explored: Europeans in the Dark Continent, 1769–1889*. London: Allen Lane, 1982.

LOVEJOY, P. E. *Caravans of Kola: the Hausa Kola Trade, 1700–1900*. Zaria, Nigeria: Ahmadu Bello University Press, 1980.

OLIVER, R. & FAGE, J. D. *A Short History of Africa*. London: Penguin, 1988.

PHILLIPSON, D. W. *African Archaeology*. Cambridge University Press, 1984.

ROBERTSHAW, P. (ed.) *A History of African Archaeology*. London: James Currey, 1988.

SUTTON, J. A. *Thousand Years of East Africa*. Nairobi: British Institute in East Africa, 1990.

VANSINA, J. *African History*. London: Longman, 1981.

Oral Tradition as History. London: James Currey, 1985.

WICKENS, P. L. *An Economic History of Africa from the Earliest Times to Partition*. Oxford University Press, 1981.

7. *The colonial era and the coming of independence*

AMIN MOHAMMED, WILLETTS, D. & MATTHESON, A. *Railway Across the Equator: the story of the East Africa lines*. London: Bodley Head, 1987.

BARBOUR, K. M. (ed.) *The First Ascent of Mount Kenya: by H. J. Mackinder*. London: Hurst, 1991.

BOAHEN, A. A. (ed.) *Africa under Colonial Domination*. Vol. 7 UNESCO History of Africa. London: James Currey (54B Thornhill Square, Islington, London N1 1BE), 1990.

BOATENG, E. A. *A Political Geography of Africa*. Cambridge University Press, 1978.

CHABAL, P. *Political Domination in Africa: Reflections on the Limitations of Power*. Cambridge University Press, 1986.

CHRISTOPHER, A. J. *The Crown Lands of British South Africa 1853–1914*. Kingston, Ontario: Limestone Press. 1984.

HOYLE, B. S. *Gillman of Tanganyika 1882–1946: the Life and Work of a Pioneer Geographer*. Aldershot: Avebury, 1987.

Transport and Development in Tropical Africa. London: Murray, 1988.

KINGSLEY, M. *Travels in West Africa*, edited and introduced by Elspeth Huxley. London: Folio Society, 1976.

MAZRUI, A. *The African Condition: a Political Diagnosis*. Cambridge University Press, 1980.

MAZZEO, D. (ed.) *African Regional Organizations*. Cambridge University Press, 1984.

ROBINSON, R., GALAGHER, J. with DENNING, A. *Africa and the Victorians: the Official Mind of Imperialism*. London: Macmillan, 1981.

RODNEY, W. *How Europe Underdeveloped Africa*. Washington, DC: Howard University Press, 1982.

WRIGHT, J. *Libya, Chad and the central Sudan*. London: Hurst, 1989.

8. *Population, migration, and urbanization*

CENTRE OF AFRICAN STUDIES, EDINBURGH. *African Historical Demography*, 1977.

CLARKE, J. I. & KOSINSKI, L. A. (eds.) *Redistribution of Population in Africa*. London: Heinemann, 1982.

CLARKE, J. I., KHOGALI, M., & KOSINSKI, L. A. *Population and Development Projects in Africa*. Cambridge University Press, 1985.

DRAKAKIS-SMITH, D. (ed.) *Urban and Regional Change in Southern Africa*. New York: Routledge, 1992.

GOYER, D. S. & DOMSCHKE, E. M. *Handbook of National Population Censuses: Africa and Asia*. Westwood, Conn.: Greenwood Press, 1987.

INIKORI, J. E. *Forced Migration*. London: Hutchinson, 1982.

LINDSAY, B. (ed.) *African Migration and National Development*. Pennsylvania University Press, 1986.

MARKAKIS, J. National and Class Conflict in the Horn of Africa. Cambridge University Press, 1987.

MASSER, T. & GOULD, W. T. S. *Inter-regional Migration in Tropical Africa.* Institute of British Geographers Special Publication No. 8, 1975.

O'CONNOR, A. *The African City.* London: Hutchinson, 1983.

OMINDE, S. H. & EJEUGU, C. N. *Population Growth and Economic Development in Africa.* London: Heinemann, 1987.

OLUSANYA, P. O. & EBIGBOLA, J. A. 1991 *Nigeria's Population Dynamics, Problems and Perspectives.* Ile-Ife, Rewaju House Press.

STREN, R. & WHITE, R. *African Cities in Crisis: Managing Rapid Urban Growth.* Boulder, Colorado: Westview Press, 1988.

WILLIAMS, G. J. (ed.) *Lusaka and its environs: a geograpahical study of a planned capital city in tropical Africa.* Lusaka: the Zambia Geographical Association, 1986.

9. Mining

GREENHALGH, P. *West African Diamonds 1919–1983: an Economic History.* Manchester University Press, 1985.

HERBERT, E. W. *Red Gold of Africa: Copper in precolonial History and Culture.* Madison: University of Wisconsin Press, 1984,

DE KUN, N. *Mineral Economics of Africa.* Amsterdam: Elsevier, 1987.

LANG, J. *Johannesburg: Men, Mines and the Challenge of Conflict.* Johannesburg: Jonathon Ball, 1986.

LANNING, G. with MUELLER, M. *Africa Undermined: Mining Companies and the Underdevelopment of Africa.* Harmondsworth: Penguin, 1979.

KUBIECK, R. V. *Economic Imperialism in Theory and Practice: the Case of South African Gold Mining Finance, 1886–1914.* Durham, NC: Duke University Press, 1979.

OGUNBADEJO, O. *The International Politics of Africa's Strategic Minerals.* London: Francis Pinter, 1985.

10. Water resource development

ADAMS, W. M. & GROVE, A. T. *Irrigation and Tropical Africa: Problems and Problem Solving.* African Monographs 3: Cambridge University African Studies Centre, 1984.

BARNETT, T. *The Gezira Scheme: an Illusion of Development.* London: Cass 1977.

BELL, M., FAULKNER, R., HOTCHKISS, P. LAMBERT, R., ROBERTS, N. & WINDRAM, A. *The Use of Dambos in Rural Development with Reference to Zimbabwe.* Loughborough University Press, 1987.

HART, D. *The Volta River Project: a Case Study in Politics and Technology.* Edinburgh University Press, 1980.

MORIS, J. R. E. & THOM, D. J. *Irrigation development in Africa; lessons of experience.* Boulder and London: Westview, 1990.

OLSEN, M. M. & LENSELINK, K. J. *Annotated Bibliography on Irrigation and Drainage in Kenya.* University of Nairobi: Department of Agricultural Engineering, 1988.

RYDZEWSKI, J. R. *Workshop on Irrigation Development Planning.* Southampton University, 1977.

11. Industrialization in Africa

COUGHLIN, P. & GERRISHON IKIARA (eds.) *Industrialization in Kenya: in search of a strategy.* Nairobi: Heinemann, 1988.

ONYEMELUKE, J. O. C. *Industrialization in West Africa.* London: Croom Helm, 1984.

PEAT, R. *Manufacturing, Industry and Economic Development in the SADCC countries.* Uppsala: Scandinavian Institute of African Studies, 1984.

12. Modernizing agriculture

AGROFORESTRY LITERATURE: *A selected bibliography on Subsaharan Africa.* The International Council for Research in Agroforestry, Nairobi.

AURET, D. *A Decade of Development: Zimbabwe 1980–1900* (especially Tribal Trust Lands). Gweru: Mambo Press, 1989

DINHAM, B. & HINES, C. *Agribusiness in Africa.* London: Earth Resources Research, 1983.

HART, K. *The Political Economy of West African Agriculture.* Cambridge University Press, 1982.

HEYER, J., ROBERTS, P., & WILLIAMS, G. (eds.) *Rural Development in Tropical Africa.* London: Macmillan, 1981.

HILL, P. *Development Economics on Trial: the Anthropological Case for a Prosecution.* Cambridge University Press, 1986.

IKPI, A. E. & HAHN, N. D. *Cassava: Lifeline for the Rural Household.* Ibadan: Book Builders, 1989.

LEVI, J. & HAVINDEN, M. *Economics of African agriculture.* Harlow: Longman, 1982.

LIVINGSTONE, I. & ORD, H. W. *Agricultural Economics for Tropical Africa.* London: Heinemann, 1981.

LOWE, R. G. *Agricultural Revolution in Africa.* London: Macmillan 1986.

MELLOR, J. W. *et al.* (eds.) *Accelerating Food Production in Sub-Saharan Africa.* Baltimore, MD: Johns Hopkins University Press, 1987.

MORTIMORE, M., OLOFIN, E. A., CLINE COLE, R. A. & ABDUL KADIR (eds.) *Perspectives on Land Administration and Development in Northern Nigeria.* Kano, Bayero University, Department of Geography.

NORCLIFFE, G. & PINFOLD, T. *Planning African Development* (Kenya). Boulder: Westview & London: Croom Helm, 1991.

RICHARDS, P. *Indigenous Agricultural Revolution: Ecology and Food Crops in West Africa.* Hutchinson: London, 1985.

RIMMER, D. (ed.) *Rural Transformation in Tropical Africa.* London: Bellhaven, 1988.

SANDFORD, S. *Management of Pastoral Development in the Third World.* Chichester: Wiley, 1983.

SIMPSON, J. R. & EVANGELOU, J. *Livestock Development in SubSaharan Africa: Constraints, Prospects and Policy.* Epping, UK: Bowker, 1983.

WATERS, G. & ODERO, J. *Geography of Kenya and the East African Region.* London: Macmillan, 1986.

WATTS, M. (ed.) *State, Oil and Agriculture in Nigeria.* University of California at Berkeley: Institute of International Studies, 1987.

13. *Crisis in Africa*

ADEBAYO ADEDEJI, SADIG RASHID, MELODY MORRISON (eds.) *The Human Dimension of Africa's Persistent Economic Crisis.* For ECA, London: Hans Zell, 1990.

ALTERNATIVE DEVELOPMENT STRATEGIES FOR AFRICA, I. *Coalition for Change*, 1990; II, *Environment and Women* (ed. Mohammed Suliman), 1991; III. *Debt and Democracy* (ed. Ben Turok) 1991. Institute for African Alternatives, 23 Bevenden Street, London N16BH.

ANDERSON, D. & GROVE, R. H. *Conservation in Africa: Peoples, Policies and Practice.* Cambridge University Press, 1987.

CHAZAN, N. & SHAW, T. H. (eds.) *Coping with Africa's Food Crisis.* Boulder, Colorado: Lynne Rienner, 1988.

FRAZER TAYLOR, D. R. & MACKENZIE, F. (ed.) *Development from Within: survival in rural Africa.* London: Routledge, 1992.

FRIEDLAND, E. *A Guide to African International Organizations.* Oxford: Hans Zell, 1990.

GLANTZ, M. H. (ed.) *Drought and Hunger in Africa: denying famine a future.* Cambridge University Press, 1987.

HARRISON, P. *The Greening of Africa: Breaking Through in the Battle for Land and Water.* London: Paladin, 1987.

HINCHEY, M. T. (ed.) *Symposium on Drought in Botswana.* Gaberone: National Museum of Botswana, 1979.

IHONVBERE, J. (ed.) *The Political Economy of Crisis and Underdevelopment in Africa: selected works of Claud Ake.* Lagos: JAD publishers.

ILIFFE, J. *Famine in Zimbabwe, 1890–1960.* Gweru: Mambo Press, 1990.

LEGUM, C. & LEE, B. *Conflict in the Horn of Africa.* London: Rex Collings, 1977.

JOHNSON, D. H. & ANDERSON, D. M. (eds.) *The Ecology of Survival: Case Studies from Northeast African History.* London: Crook Academic Press, 1987.

LAWRENCE, P. (ed.) *World Recession and the Food Crisis in Africa.* London: James Currey, 1986.

MARTIN, M. The crumbling Façade of African Debt Negotiation. Basingstoke: Macmillan, 1991.

MORTIMORE, M. *Adapting to Drought: farmers, famines and desertification in West Africa.* Cambridge University Press, 1989.

NATRASS, N. & ARDINGTON, E. *The Political Economy of South Africa.* Cape Town: OUP 1990.

NIGERIAN ENVIRONMENTAL STUDY TEAM. *Nigeria's Threatened Environment.* Ibadan, PMB 5297: NEST, 1991.

RAPP, A., BERRY, L., & TEMPLE, P. (eds.) *Studies of Soil Erosion and Sedimentation in Tanzania.* Dept. of Physical Geography: University of Uppsala.

RAVENHILL, J. *Africa in Economic Crisis.* New York: Columbia University Press, 1986.

ROSENBLUM, M. & WILLIAMSON, D. *Squandering Eden: Africa at the Edge.* Oxford: Bodley Head, 1988.

SANDBROOK, R. & BARKER, J. *Politics of Africa's Economic Stagnation.* Cambridge University Press, 1985.

SHAW, T. M. & OLAJIDE ALUKU. *Africa Projected: from Recession to Renaissance by the Year 2000?* London: Macmillan, 1985.

TIMBERLAKE, L. *Africa in Crisis: the Causes, the Cures of Environmental Bankruptcy.* London: Earthscan, 1985.

VAUGHAN, M. *The Story of an African Famine: gender and famine in twentieth-century Malawi.* Cambridge University Press, 1987.

WILSON, F. & RAMPHELE, M. *Uprooting Poverty: the South African challenge.* Claremont (P.O. Box 23408, 7735 South Africa): David Philip.

WORLD BANK. *Towards Sustained Development in Sub-Saharan Africa: a Joint Programme for Action.* Washington, DC: World Bank, 1984.

STATISTICAL TABLE

	Area in km² (thousands)	Population 1989 (thousands)	Annual rate of increase 1985–89 (%)	Number of people per km² 1989	Aid received in US$ per head 1988	External debt in millions US$ 1988	Fish landed 1987 (thousands metric tonnes)	Head of cattle 1987 (thousands)	Motor vehicles in use (thousands 1985)	Imports CIF 1987 (millions US$)	Exports FOB 1987 (millions US$)	GDP per head 1990/91 (US$)
Algeria	2 382	24 579	3.0	10	14.0	23 229	70	1 523		7 029	8 186	2 124
Angola	1 247	9 747	2.7	8	15.2		81	3 390				
Benin	113	4 591	3.2	41	31.4	904	42	896	37			356
Botswana	582	1 256	3.7	2	164.4	494	2	2 300	37			1 970
Burkina Faso	274	8 763	3.3	32	34.1	805	7	2 784	24	434	155	330
Burundi	28	5 302	2.9	190	37.0	749	5	479	16	212	90	204
Cameroon	475	11 540	3.2	24	26.6	2 939	83	4 362	1 360	1 749	829	1 185
Cape Verde Is.	4	369	2.5	91	240.0	126	7	12	4	110	4	830
Central African Rep.	623	2 841	2.1	5	61.6	585	13	2 224		252	131	369
Chad	1 264	5 538	2.5	4	37.6	300	110	4 002	14	366	111	264
Comorro Is.	2	503	3.1	228	112.5	188	5	25		32	12	432
Congo	342	1 941	2.7	6	100.8	4 098	31	70	45	529	673	1 500
Djibouti Rep.	23	395	2.6	17	219.7	157		70	25	188	20	
Egypt	1 001	53 080	2.3	83	35.5	42 128	250	1 900	1 217	11 941	4 352	1 250
Equatorial Guinea	28	341	2.6	12	101.9	176	4	5				363
Ethiopia	1 222	49 513	3.3	41	13.6	2 790	4	30 000	59	1 101	371	117
Gabon	268	1 138	3.5	4	90.8	2 128	21	9	27	866	1 271	3 450
Gambia	11	838	2.8	74	129.9	271	14	300	7	127	40	244
Ghana	239	14 566	3.4	61	29.8	2 238	372	1 248		919	909	383
Guinea	246	6 906	2.5	27	38.8	2 312	30	1 800	43			460
Guinea-Bissau	36	966	2.7	27	109.4	389	4	340	7			180
Ivory Coast	322	12 098	4.2	38	53.2	8 088	103	925	236	2 241	3 110	1 142
Kenya	580	24 872	5.0	43	23.1	4 241	131	9 500	217	1 756	961	340
Lesotho	30	1 700	2.7	56	67.6	270		520	21			320
Liberia	111	2 508	3.4	23	33.4	1 101		42	20	308	382	380
Libya	1 760	4 385	3.7	2	8.5		8	212		4 723	8 766	4 600
Madagascar	587	11 603	3.8	20	32.1	3 317	64	10 565		302	332	242
Malawi	118	8 022	3.2	68	38.2	1 190	89	940	29	298	278	235
Mali	1 240	7 960	3.0	6	41.0	1 928	56	4 889	22	493	260	300
Mauritania	1 025	1 970	2.7	2	100.2	1 823	99	1 200	16	235	428	516
Mauritius	2	1 090	1.7	535	76.3	652	18	32	43	1 013	901	2 600
Morocco	447	24 522	2.6	55	33.7	18 567	491	3 178	748	4 230	2 827	1 012
Mozambique	802	15 326	2.6	19	44.7	3 801	36	1 350	43			
Namibia	824	1 818	3.2	2	9.8		520	2 040				502
Niger	1 267	6 895	3.0	5	52.8	1 286	2	3 400	44			300
Nigeria	924	109 178	3.3	118	3.4	28 630	249	12 700	384	3 917	7 383	280
Réunion	3	586	1.7	233	1 025.4		2	19	183	1 465	148	
Rwanda	26	6 989	3.4	265	36.2	5 846	2	650	15	357	130	310
São Tomé and Principi	1	116	1.7	120	179.0	91	3		3			340
Senegal	197	7 172	2.3	36	87.8	2 985	299	1 543	37	1 023	606	590
Seychelles	0.3	67	0.7	239	422.9	123	4		5	114	22	4 167
Sierra Leone	72	4 047	2.5	56	16.8	510	53	330	34	137	132	200
Somalia	638	7 339	3.4	12	829.0	1 784	17	4 770		132	104	170
South Africa	1 221	34 492	2.2	28			902	11 799	4 202			2 591
Sudan	2 506	24 485	2.9	10	29.8	8 044	24	22 400	93	929	504	330
Swaziland	17	763	4.5	44	58.6	255		641	40			850
Tanzania	945	24 802	3.3	26	37.0	4 091	314	13 000		976	310	93
Togo	57	349	3.1	39	37.2	1 067	15	290	29	424	244	460
Tunisia	164	7 990	2.4	49	52.6	5 886	99	610	326	3 047	2 171	1 522
Uganda	236	17 804	3.5	75	17.4	1 438	200	3 905	16			247
W. Sahara	266	174	2.7	1								
Zaire	2 345	34 491	2.7	15	20.2	7 013	166	1 379	133	756	970	
Zambia	753	7 804	3.7	10	57.7	4 194	68	2 850	107	739	873	408
Zimbabwe	391	9 122	2.1	23	41.7	2 231	18	5 567	278	1 046	14 190	660

Source: United Nations Demographic Yearbook 1989 (New York 1991); *United Nations Statistics Yearbook 1987* (New Year 1990).

INDEX

ACP, 225
AIDS, 53, 152, 227
Abidjan, 105, 142
Abuja, 140
Acacia albida, 204, 219
Acacia senegal, 219
Acacia seyal, 48
Accra, 80, 105, 140, 142
Acioa barteri, 76
Addis Ababa, 137
Adowa, 96
Aedes aegyptica, 57
Afar depression, 202
Afrikaners, *see also* Boers, 94, 178
agriculture, 21 30, **73–82**, *73*, *77*, 120,
   122, 127, *133*, 177, 178, 189–205
Agulhas Bank, 181
Ahaggar mountains, 2, 81
aid, **225–6**
Air mountains, 25
Ajaokuta, 184
Akosombo dam, 12, **159–62**, 186
Akwapim, 159
Aladja, 183
Alexandria, 87, 91, 96, 97, 130
alfa grass, 218
Alger, *101*
Algeria, 63, 71, 89, 102, 113, 114, 120,
   122, 136, 137, 152, 153, 154, 155,
   175, 177, **182–3**, 192, **194**, 201, 212,
   222, 223, 226
Algiers, 92, 136, 153
alumina, 9
aluminium, 159, 160, 162, 177, 180
Angola, 2, 14, 63, 64, 83, 93, 114, 127,
   136, 152, 159, 192, 194, 222, 223, 224
Annaba, 182
Anopheles gambia, **56–7**
antelope, 51, 58, 61
antimony, 148
ants, 58
apartheid, 178
Arabian Sea, 92
Arabs, 63–4, 82, 89, 90, 96, 97, 134
Armenoid, 62–4
Arusha, 184
Arzew, 153, 182

asbestos, 3, 148, 149, 152, 182
Ashanti, 93, 102, 145
Asians, 64, 136, 142, 176, 184
Assyrians, 87
Aswan, High Dam, 12, 30, 115, 130,
   170, 171, 182
Asyut, 130
Atbara river, 31, 171
Atlas Mountains, 2, 7, 30, **101**, 219
Atriplex, 219
Australopithecus, 86
Awash river, 27, 80
Axum, 88, 96

Baganda, 135, 193
Bahr el Yusuf, 87, 130
Bakolori scheme, **165–7**
Balfour, 148
bananas, 73, 74, 89, 131, 195
Bandama river, 162
Bandiagara, 215
Bankeveld, 148
Bantu, 66, 88–9, 94–6, 136, 148, 181
Barbary States, 102
barley, 73, 218
Baro, 109, 110
Basement Complex, 150
Bathurst, 105
bauxite, 4, 120, 152, 159
beans, 78, 81, 131
Beaufort West, 181
Bechuanaland, 106, 108
beer, 76, 178, 183
Beira, 224
Belgian Congo, 63, 65, 108
Belgians, 63, 106, 114
Bemba, 76, 93
Bendel, 183, 193
Benguela, 224
Benguela current, 16
Benin (formerly Dahomey), 84, 92,
   93, 130, 160, *187*
Benue river, 25, 30, 31, *33*, 101, 105,
   110, 202
Berbers, 89, 90, 91, 113
Berlin Conference, 105, 106, 117, 206

beryl, 3, 95
Biafra, 117
bicycles, 176
bilharzia, *see also schistosomiasis*, 174
biomes, **35–46**, 44
Biomphalaria, **60–1**
Bira, 74
birds, **51–2**
Birom, 145
Black Homelands, 136
Bloemfontein, 178
Blue Nile, 30, 96, 97, 127, 170, 173
Boers, 94–5, 106
Bonny, 140, 153, 183
Borassus palm, 48, 219
Border Industries, 178
Borno, 100
Boteti river, 34
Botswana, 95, 124, 127, 130, 150, 152,
   178, 199, 221, 224
Bozo, 84
Brachystegia woodland, 55
brandy, 181
Brazzaville, 106, 224
breadfruit, 73, 89
British, 63, 92, 94, 97, 101–2, 104–23,
   145, 201, 224
British South Africa Company, 106
Broken Hill (now Kabwe), 108
buffalo, 58
Buganda, 99, 193
Bukoba, 202
Bulawayo, 108, 113
Bulinus, **60–1**
Burkina-Faso (formerly Upper
   Volta), 135, 136, **203**, 219
Burundi, 131, *131*
Bushmen, *see also* San, 94, 127
Bushveld, 148
Byzantine Empire, 89

Cabinda, 120, 154
Cabora Bassa Dam, 159, 224
cadmium, 152
Cairo, 91, 96, *130*, 137, 226
calcrete, 10, *10*, 47

camels, 70, 89
Cameroon Republic, 2, 34, 63, 65, 120, 202, 215
Canaries current, 16
Cape Agulhas, 1
Cape Coloureds, 63, 64
Cape hake, 52
Cape of Good Hope, 1, 92
Cape Province, 127
Cape Town, 5, 64, 93, 93, 94, 106, 108, 150, 178, **180–1**, 224
Carthage, 88–9
Casamance, 202
cassava, 73, 74, 76, 205
catena, *see* soil catena
cattle, 51, 58, 61, **69–72**, 76, 77, 85, 94, 172, 198, 204
Caucasoid, 62–4
cement, 183
Central African Federation, 181
Central African Republic, 117
centuriation, 89
Chad basin, *28*, 63
Chad Republic, 63, 65, 117, 170, 207, 219, 222, 223
Chad river, *30*, 52
Chagga, 80, 194
charcoal, 35, 145
Chari river, 34, 80, 168
chemicals, 177, 178
Chew Bahir, 29
Christianity, 64, 68, 76, 86, 89, 96, 222
chrome, 148, 149
chromium, 3
cigarettes, 181, 183, 184
Ciskei, 94
Citharinus citharus, 52
citimine, 76
citrus, 73, 190
climate, 1, **15–29**
cloves, 97
coal, *4*, 95, 120, 148, 150, 186
coastlines, **11–14**
cobalt, 3, 152
cocoa, 41, 107, 110, 120, 122, 130, 135, 138, 175, 186–8, 205
coco-yams, 73
coffee, 120, 131, 171, 175, 188, 191, 194, 198, 202
coffee-cleaning, 176
Conakry, 105
Congo, 92, 107, 120, 154
Congo basin, *see* Zaire basin
Congo Free State, 102, 106
Congo river, *see* Zaire river
Congress of Berlin, *see* Berlin Conference
confectionery, 180
copper, 3, 4, 87, 90, 92, 95, 108, 114, 123, 143, 145, 148, 150–2, 175, 182, 224
Copperbelt, 76, 120, 140, 150–1, *150*, *151*
Copts, 68, 89

corn, 89
cotton, 43, 104, 120, 131, 135, 164, 171, 173, 175, 181, 183, 190, 202, 203
cowpeas, 168
craftworkers, 78
crocodiles, 50
Cuando river, 34
Cubango river, 34
Cunene river, 63
cyclones, *see* hurricanes
Cyrenaica, 15, 111

Dagomba, 105
Dahomey, 93
Dakar, 110, 224
Dar es Salaam, *11*, 140, *141*, 142, 184, 186, 224
Darfur, 97
date palms, 73, 80–1, *82*
Delagoa Bay, 94
dengue fever, 57
desertification, 35, 206, **215–221**, *216*
deserts, 1, 35, 43–4, 47, 73, 74, 127
Diama, 169
diamonds, 3, 4, *4*, *95*, 106, 114, 145–6, 152
Dinka, 97, 172
Dodoma, 140, 195
Dogou, 215
Douala, 162
Drakensberg, *30*, 94
drought, 21, 22, 42, 43, 84, 87, 107, 123, 157, 159, 162, 168, 184, 186, 195, 198, 201, 202, 203, 204, 205, 206, **211–14**, 215, 217, 219, 221, 224, 225
duiker, 58
dunes and dunefields, 24, 25
Durban, 64, 95, 107, *143*, 180, 181
Durban-Pinetown, 178, **179–80**
dust, *213*, *214*, 217
Dutch, 63, 93, 94, 181, 202

EEC, 224, 225
East London, 94, 178, 181
Ede, 138
Edea, 162
Egypt, 31, 63, 64, 68, 80, 86, 87, 91, 92, 96–7, 104, 105, 107, 113–16, 120, 124, *125*, 127, 130, 136, 152, 154, 155, 170–2, 176, **182**, 190, 218, 219
Eldoret, 184
eleusine millet, 74
elephants, 50, 51
Elmina, 92
Emir, 201
Ensete, 131
Enugu, 138, 140
Eritrea, 171
erosion, 9, 10, 12, 13, 43, 48, 204, *214*, 215, 216, *218*, 220, 221
ethanol, 182

Ethiopia, 2, 3, 68, 71, 73, 80, 87, 88, 96, 97, 107, 114, 116, 124, 131, **131–4**, 171, 173, 175, 176, 177, 192, 194, **196–8**, 201, 206, 207, 208, 217, 220, 222
Etosha Pan, *118*
Europeans, 63–5, **92–103**, 104–123, 106, 114, 115, 116, 119, 122, 135, 142, 145, 151, 154, 175, 178, 181, 184, 192
evaporation, **18–20**, 29, 173
Ewe, 83, 105
explosives, 177

FAO, *see* United Nations
fadamaland, 79
Faiyoum, 87, 130
famine, 134, 198, 204, 206–11, 215, 222
fauna, **50–2**
ferricrete, 9, 11, 47
fertilizers, 182, 184, 190, 200, 202
figs, 81, 219
filariae, 57
fires, 35, 42
fish, **52**, 175
fishing and fisheries, 52, 72, **82–5**, *83*, *84*, 159, 181, 192, 225
floods and flooding, 21, 22, 84, 198, 217
flour-milling, 183
forest, 35, 43, 55, 74–6, 211, 221
Freetown, 93, 100
French, 93, *101–2*, 103, 104–23, 136, 137, 182, 190, 194, 224
French Congo, 117
French Equatorial Africa, 117
French Guinea, 105
French Soudan, 117
French Union, 113–14, 116
fruit-processing, 180
Fulani, 85, 100, 138, 216
Fung, 97
Funtua, 202
furniture, 176, 184

GDP, *208*
GNP, *207*
Gabon, 117, 122, 126, 154
Galla, 96
Galula, *99*
Gambia, 126, 223
Gambia river, 96, 105, *213*
game reserves, *see* national parks
Gao, 90, 137
Gatooma, 181
Gedaref, 127
geological table, 6
germanium, 152
Germans, 63, 93, 105, 106
Gezira, 170, 201

Gezira scheme, 163, **171–3**, *171*
Ghana, 65, 84, 90, 92, 120, 122, 124,
    130, 135, 136, 140, 143, 152, 159,
    160, 162, **186–8**, 201
Ghardaia, 88
giraffes, 50, 51
glaciation and glaciers, 25, 39
goats, 76, 218
gold, 3, *4*, 5, 90, 92, 93, 106, 114, 120,
    145–9, 152, 175, 178, 181, 182
Gold Coast, *see also* Ghana, 92, 102,
    105, 107, 112, 114, 116
Gombe, 202
Gondwanaland, 3, 6–7, 29
gourds, 74
grassland, 35
Great Dyke, 149
Great Fish river, 94, 173
Great Lakes, 31, 102, 134
Great North Road, 76
Greeks, 89, 176
groundnuts and groundnut oil, 43,
    47, 73, 74, 107, 110, 120, 122, 131,
    135, 175, 183, 202
Guinea, Republic of, 90, 116, 120,
    145, 222
Guinea Bissau, 126
guinea corn, 165
Guinea Highlands, 2
Gulf of Aden, 88
Gulf of Gabes, 89, 153
Gulf of Guinea, 12, **130**
Gulf of Syrte, 153
gum arabic, 43, 219
Gusau, 202
Gwembe Tonga, 174
Gwembe valley, 150
gypsum, 186

hake, 83
Harare, 150
Hassi Messaoud, 153
Hassi R'mel, 153
Hausa, 85, 91, 100, 188
Hausaland, 76, 78, 100, 131
Haya, 194
heavy engineering, 179
henna, 81
herring, 52
High Africa, 2
Hindus, 64
hippopotamus, 50
hoe, 73
Hopetown, 106
Horn of Africa, *132*
horses, 58
Hottentots, *see also* Khoi-Khoi, 94
humidity, *18*, 19
hunting, **69**
hurricanes, 16, *16*, **16–18**
Hutu, 135
hydroelectricity, 157–63, *158*

IMF, 226
Ibadan, 137, 138
Ibibio, 130
Ibo, 75, *75*, 76, 117, 130
Iboland, 75
Ife, 93, 138
Ifriqiya, 89
Igbo, 75, 93
Ik, 69
Ikrun, 138
Ile-Ife, 137
Ilesha, 138
Ilobu, 138
Imperial British East Africa
    Company, 107
independence, 113, **114–18**, 222
Indian Ocean, 11, 15, 68, 89
Indians, 96
Indonesians, 62, 64, 89–90
industry, 175–8
Inga, 162
inselbergs, 10, *11*
Intertropical Convergence Zone
    (ITCZ) 15, 16
iron ore, 4, 9, 91, 95, 120, 123, 145,
    148, 150, 152, 177, 178, 184
irrigation, 78, 80, 82, 157, **163–9**,
    170–4, 181, 219
Islam, 63, 64, 68, 77, 86, 89, 90, 91, 96,
    113, 116, 134, 137, 173, 192, 193,
    219, 222, 223
Itakpe, 184
Italians, 107, 114, 116, 176
Ituri forest, 74
ivory, 92, 93, 97
Ivory Coast, 63, 84, 114, 162, 177, *187*,
    188, 202, **203**, 222, 226
Iwo, 138

Jebba, 109, 162
Jebel Aulia dam, 170
Jebel Marra, 2, 34
Jenne, 145
Jinja, 171
Johannesburg, 120, 130, 138, 145,
    146, 147, 148, 177, 179, *179*
Jonglei Scheme, **172–3**
Jos Plateau, 110, 120, 145, 157, 183,
    215
Juba, 173

Kabara, 111
Kabré, 215
Kabwe (formerly Broken Hill), 150
Kaduna, 183, 193
Kaduna river, 162
Kafue, 159
Kainji dam, 162
Kairouan, 91
Kalahari, 2, 15, 34, 127, 199, 221, 223
Kamerun, 112

Kampala, 137
Kanem, 91
Kano, 76, 78, 91, 109, 110, 137, 165
Kano river, 137, 162, **165**
Kanuri, 100, **165**
Karoo system of rocks, 5–6, 7, 147,
    148, 150
Kasai, 152
Kashm el Girba, 171
Katanga (now Shaba), 106, 108, 109,
    114
Katsina, 76, 91, 100, 137, 183
Kenana, 202
Kenya, 63, 64, 80, 111, 113, 116, 117,
    117, 124, 134, 176, **184**, 190, 191,
    192, **193–4**, 198–9, 201, 202, **203–4**,
    220, 222, 224, 226
Keta, 12
Khoi-Khoi, 63, 64
Khartoum, 97, 173, 201
Kigoma, 110
Kikuyu, 116, 131, 135, 193, 194
Kilimanjaro, Mount, 7, 8, 37, 79, 80,
    99, 110, 131, *189*, 190
Kilwa, 186
Kimberley, 106, 109, 145, 146, 150,
    178
kimberlite, 145
Kinshasa, 109, 163
Kisumu, 110
Kipushi, 152
Kitale, 186
Kitwe, 151
Klerksdorp, 147
Kofyar, 216
Kola nuts, 39, 130
Kolwezi, 152
Konda, 221
Kordofan, 199
Kontagora, 201
Kossou dam, 162
Kossou lake, 162
Koumbi Saleh, 90
Kpong dam, 162
Kruger National Park, 148
Kufra, 219
Kumasi, 110, 137
Kwa Zulu, 180
Kwara, 184

Lagos, 13 102, 109, 110, 138, 140, 224
    Lagos/Apapa, 183
Lake Abiyata, 27
    Albert (Mbotu), 8
    Bangweulu, 84
    Chad, 24, 31, 32, 34, *34*, 84, 91,
        100, 105, **167–8**, 169, 211
    Debo, 85
    Edward, 8
    George, 83
    Kariba, 158–9, 174
    Kainji, 162
    Kivu, 8, 83

Malawi (Nyasa), 8, 52, 61, 107, 116, 134, 194, 211
Manyara, 186
Mweru, 54
Naivasha, 83
Nasser, 130
Ngami, 34
Rukwa, 54
Tanganyika, 8, 52, 54, 84, 97, 99, 110
Turkana, 27, 87
Victoria, 2, 25, 32, 55, 58, 102, 107, 110, 131, *131*, 138, 170–1
lakes, 1, 27, **29–34**, 85, 157–73
language,
  Afrikaans, 63, 94
  Arabic, 63, 65, 89
  Bantu, 62, 63, 65, 94, 134
  Berber, 63
  Dutch, 94
  English, 65, 142
  Flemish, 65
  French, 65, 142
  Hausa, 65
  Khoisan, 62
  Nigritic, 63
  Nilotic, 62
  Portuguese, 142
  Sudanic, 63
  Swahili, 65, 142
  Tamazight, 88
  West African, 63
languages, 62–4, **65**, *65*, 66, 91, 99–100
Lates niloticus (Nile perch), 52
lead, 3, 91, 95, 108, 150, 152
Lebanese, 176
Leopoldville (now Kinshasa), 108
leprosy, 53
Lesotho, 135, 148, 170, 178, 221
Liberia, 93, 107, 114, 120, 183, 201
Libya, 89, 107, 111, 114, 116, 120, 122, 124, 152, 154, *154*, 155, 219, 223
Likasi, 152
Limpopo river, 90, 94, 130, 148, 198
linen, 91
lion, 50
livestock, 189, 190, 198, 199, 221
Lobatsi, 199
locusts, **53–4**
Logone river, 34, 80, 170
Lomé, 105
Lomé agreements, 225
Lourenço Marques (now Maputo), 107
Low Africa, 2
Lualaba, 157
Lualaba river, 102
Luanda, 93
Luba, 93
Lubumbashi, 152
Lufira, 157
Lunda, 93

Machakos, 221
machine tools, 176
machinery, 178
mackerel, 181
Madagascar, 1, 12, 62, 73, 89, 106, 221
mafisa system, 199
Maghreb, 2, 15, 45, 88, 91, 92, 102, *102*, 103, 134, 136, 155
Mahdists, 106,
maize, 73, 74, 76, 130, 131, 165, 168, 171, 178, 202, 205
Makgadikgadi Depression, 34
Malagarasi swamps, 84
Malakal, 32, 173
malaria, 53, **56–7**, 101
Malawi, 119, 130, 134, 135, 178, 224, 226
Mali, 85, 90, 92, 105, 164, 168, 216
Mali Federation, 117
malnutrition, 189, 206
Mamluks, 96
mammals, **50–1**
Manantali dam, 168
Mandara, 215
manganese, 4, *95*, 123, 152
mangoes 73, 74
manioc, *see* cassava
Maputo, 107, 142, 178, 206
Masai, 198
masakwa, 168
Matabele, 106
Matadi, 31, 108
Mau-Mau, 116, 194, 201
Mauritania, 16, 120, 219
Mauritius, 1, 215
Mayo Kebbi, 25
Mbala (formerly Abercorn), 55
Mbeya, 186
Mbuti, 74
measles, 107
meat-packing, 176
Mediterranean pine, 218
melons, 81
Meroe, 88
Meru, 110
Mesopotamia, 89, 91
metal-working, 176, 178, 182
migration, **134–6**, *134*, 144
milk, 71–2
millet, 47, 73, 76, 80, 81, *82* 131
minerals, 3–5, 77, 95, 120, **145–52**, *146*, *147*, *149*, 153, 155–6, 175
modern farming, **199–204**
Mokwa scheme, 201
Molepolole, 150
molluscs, 52
Mombasa, 97, 110, 138, 184, 186
Mongalla, 34
monkeys, 51, 53, 57
Monrovia, 93
montane forests and vegetation, *26*, *27*, *37*, **38–9**, *38*, 44–5.
Moors, 91
Mopti, 34, 84

Morocco, 63, 90, 107, 111, 113, 116, 120, 124, 134, 137, 152, 155, 175, 219, 223
Moshi, 136
mosquito, **56–7**
motor vehicles, 178, 183, 184
Mount Kenya, 8, 45, 99, 131
Mozambique, 14, 63, 64, 130, 135, 136, 137, 148, 152, 159, 178, 192, 194, **198**, 201, 222, 223, 224, 226
Mozambique Channel, 2, 89, 114

nagana, *see* trypanosomiasis
Nairobi, 132, 138, *140*, 162, 174, 184, 221
Nakuru, 184
Namibia, 16, 117, 130, 152, 178, 223, 224
Natal, Province of, 64, 94, 95, 96, 107, 180
national parks, 50–1
national unity, 62
natural gas, 120, 122, 152, 153, 154, 182, 183
Ndebele (Matabele), 95
Ndola, 151
Negroes, 62–4
Newcastle, 180
Nguni, 94–5
Ngwato, 95
Niamey, 211
nickel, 4, *95*, 150, 182
Niger delta, 39, 153, *164*, 164, 182
Niger Republic, 34, 84, 85, 219
Niger river, 2, 30, *31*, *33*, 52, 80, 84, *85*, 90, 100, 101, 105, 109, 110, 120, 124, 145, 162, 211, 216
Nigeria, 34, 63, 65, 68, 75, 76, 77, 78, 85, 93, 109, 116, 117, 120, 123, 130, 131, 135, 136, 137, 138, *138*, 140, 144, 145, 152, 153, 155, *155*, 157, 162, 163, 165, *165*, 170, 174, 175, **183–4**, 188, 192, 193, 199, **202–3**, 204, 215, 219, 222, 226
Nile and Nile valley, 12, 22–4, 29, *30*, *31*, *32*, 52, 68, 80, 84, 87, 89, 91, 96, 97, *98*, 128, **130**, 136, 170–2, 190, 199, 206, 211, 218
niobium-tantalite ores, 3
Northern Rhodesia, *see also* Zambia, 108, 111, 116, 158
Nuba mountains, 97
Nubia, 89, 97
Nubians, 88, 97, 171
Nuer, 97, 172
Nyanza, 131
Nyasaland, *see also* Malawi, 116, 181

oases, 73, **80–2**
Oba, 92, 138
Odendaalsrus, 147
Ogaden, 223

Ogbomosho, 138
oil, 3, 4, 82, 120, 130, **152–6**, 175, 177, 179, 182, 183, 186, 202, 225, *225*, 226
oil-palm, *see* palm-oil
Oil Rivers, 100, 101
Okavango delta, 34
olive trees, 219
olives, 89
Onchocerca volvulus, 59
onchocerciasis, *see also* river blindness, **59–60**, 203
onions, 81
Onne, 184
Oran, 153
Orange Free State, 94, 147, 148, 178
Orange river, 94, 157, 170, **173**, *174*
Orapa, 152
orchards, 181
Organization of African Unity, 223, 224
Oshogbo, 138, 183
ostrich, 50
Ottoman Turks, *see* Turks
Ouagadougou, 219
Oubangui-Chari, 117
Ouémé river, 84
Owen Falls dam, 170
oxen, 73
Oyo State, 93, 137

paint and roofing materials, 183, 184
palm-oil, 39, 40, 41, 47, 73, 74, 101, 107, 120, 122, 130, 134, 175, 183, 191, 201, 204
papaya, 73
paper, 183
parasitic worms, **59**
pastoralists, 29, 58, **69–72**, *70*, 77, 78, 82, 88, 91, 96, 97, 172, 173, 174, 192, **198–9**, 216, 223
pawpaw, *see* papaya
peanuts, *see* groundnuts
peas, 81
pepper, 92
peppers, 202
Phoenicians, 88
phosphates, 3, 4, 120, 130, 148, 152, 155, 175, 186
Pietermaritzburg, 178, 179, 180, 181
Pietersburg, 148
pigs, 204
pilchards, 83
pineapple, 202
plantains, 73, 130, 131
Plasmodium falciparum, 56
plastic products, 176, 177
platinum, 148
plough, 73, *73*
political friction, *212*, 213
polygamy, 67
Pool Malebo, 31, 102
population, **124–34**, 140, *142*, 143, 194, 195

Port Elizabeth, 94, 107, 178, 224
Port Harcourt, 140, 183
Porto Novo, 105
Portuguese, 63–4, 69, 73, 89, 92, 94, 114, 136, 145, 198, 224
Portuguese East Africa, 107
precipitation, *see also* rainfall, *17, 20*
Pretoria, 117, 148, 179, 181
Prosopis, 219
pumpkins, 74
Pygmies, 62–4, 74, 127
pyrethrum, 202

qanat, 81
qasrs, 89
Que Que, 150, 181

RENAMO, 224
race, **62–5**, *62*
radios, 176, 184
raffia, 76
railways, 106, **107–110**, *108, 109, 119*, 178, 215
rain and rainfall, 1, **15–29**, 35, 36, 39, 43, 80, 130, 131, 134, 159, 211, 220
rain forest, 1, 15, 26, 35, 38–9, *39*, 74
Rand, 106, 107, 130, 135, 138, 145, 146, 148, *148*, 152, 173, 177, 178, 179
reafforestation, 40
Red Sea, 1, 11, 15, 68, 88, 89, 97
reedbuck, 58
reg, 47
regolith, 8–9, 10, 18, 47
religions, *see also* Christianity and Islam, 62, **68**
Réunion, 1
rhinoceros, 51, *51*
Rhodesia (formerly Southern Rhodesia), *see also* Zimbabwe, 108, 111, 113, 114, 116, 117, 134, 158, 159, 181, 223
rice, 73, 85, 130, 198, 202
Rift Valley, east Africa, 1, 2, 3, 8, 63, 86, 130, **219–21**
rinderpest, **61**, 107, 112
Rio de Oro, 113
river blindness, *see also* onchocerciasis, 43, 134
river transport, 108–110, 111
rivers, 27, **29–34**, 85, 157–73
Rivers State, 184
roads, 111, 215
rock paintings, 62, 87
rock weathering, **8–12**
Roda Gauge, 24–25
Roman Empire, 68, 89
Roseires, 171, 173, 202
Rossing, 152
Ruanda-Urundi, *see also* Rwanda and Burundi, 112
rubber and rubber trees, 47, 120, 130, 135, 177, 201

Rufiji river, 195
Rungwe volcanic massif, 194
Ruwenzori, 25, *25*
Rwanda, 131, 135, 219

SADCC, 224
St Helena, 215
St Louis, 110, *110*
Sahara, 1, 2, *2*, 15, 29, 54, 62, 63, 71, 80, 87, 91, 116, 127, 145, 152, 155, 170, 211, 214
Sahel, 1, 43, *43*, 63, 68, 87, 122, 163, 198, 206, 211, 214, 215, 219
Salisbury (now Harare), 113
salt, 90, 95, 145
San, 62–4, 69, 199
Sanaga river, 162
sanctions, 178, 182, 224
Sansanding, 164
São Jorge da Mina, 92
saqiya, 87
sardines, 52, 83
Sasolburg, 179
savanna, 35, **41–3**, 47, 55, 58, 73, 74, 76–80
schistosomiasis, **60–1**, *60*
schools, 195
Segu, 34
Selibe-Pikwe, 150
Senegal, 14, 63, 65, 90, 110, 114, 120, 135, 155, 202, 223
Senegal river, 29, 30, 52, 80, 96, 100, **168–9**
Sennar dam, 170
Seven-Forks Hydroelectric complex, 162
Seychelles, 1
Shaba, 135, 152, 162–3, 223, 224
shadufs, 79, 82, 87, 174
shallots, 78, 80, 174
share-croppers, 82, 135, 178
shea-butter, 42
sheep, 51, 76, 94, 218
shoes, 176, 180, 184
Shilluk, 97, 172
Sidamo, 131
sickle-cell anaemia, 57
Sierra Leone, 93, 105, 126, 152
silica, 9
silcrete, 9, 47
silver, 152
Simulium damnosum, 59, *59*
Sinai peninsula, 1
sisal, 120, 191, 201
Skikda, 153, 182
slaves and slavery, 69, 82, 90, **92–3**, 97, 100–1, 107
sleeping sickness, *see also* trypanosomiasis, 43, **57–8**, 107
smallpox, 107
snakes, 51
soap-making, 176, 183, 184, 201
Sobat river, 31, 32

society, **65–8**
Sofala, 90
soil catena, 48, *49*
soils, 8, 9, 10, 21, **46–9**, *95*, 189
Sokoto, 105, 135, 165
Somali current, 17
Somalia, 2, 17, 208
Somaliland, 107
Somalis, 96, 223
Songhai, 85, 90, 91
sorghum, 47, 73, 76, 131, 202, 203
Soudan, 90
South Africa, Republic of (formerly Union of), 63, 64, 76, 93–6, *95*, 112–17, 119, 124, 127, 134, 135, 136, 143, **145–9**, 155, 156, 159, 170, 175, **177–9**, 181, 198, 199, 201, 221, 223, 224
Southern Rhodesia, *see* Rhodesia and Zimbabwe
Spaniards, 92
Stanley Pool, *see* Pool Malebo
steel, 150, 152, 177, 178, 179, 183, 184
steppe, 35, **43–4**
Sterkfontein dam, 173
stockfish, 52
Straits of Gibraltar, 67
Sudd, 32, 89, 97, 172, 173
Sudan Republic, 2, 65, 80, 88, 97, 117, 127, 134, 135, 136, 143, 163, 170, *170*, 171, 172, 173, 176, 199, 201, 207
Sudan zone, **90–1**, *98*, 100, 116, 211, 215, 219, 222
Suez Canal, 1, 104–5, 113–15, 134, 152, 182
sugar and sugar cane, 73, 78, 91, 120, 174, 175, 177, 180, 182, 202
sugar-refining, 176
Sukuma, 131
Sukumaland, 131
sulphuric acid, 152, 186
swamplands, 35, 84–5
Swazi, 95
Swaziland, 135
sweet potatoes, 73, 74, 131

Table Bay, 181
Table Mountain, 5, 181
Tabora, 97, 110
Tana, *162*, *163*, 184
Tanga, 110, *110*, 186
Tanganyika, 111, 112, 116, 184, 221
Groundnut Scheme, 201
Tanganyika plateau, 97
tanning, 180
Tanzania, 64, 65, 80, 84, 89, 99, 117, 131, 134, 140, 143, 176, **184–6**, 190, 191, *191*, **194–6**, 197, 201, 202, 220, 222, 223, 224, 226
Tarkwa, 110
taxation, 111
tea, 120, 175, 177, 191, 202

teak forest, 41
tenure systems, **192–3**
Tema, 140, 159, 160
temperature, *20, 21*
termites, **55–6**, *55, 56*
Tete, 152
textiles and clothing, 176, 178, 181, 182, 183, 184, 188
Thabazimbi, 148
Thika, 162, 184
thunderstorms, 16, *16*
Tibesti mountains, 2, 81, 223
Tibu, 82
Tigrai, 131
Tilapia galilaea, 52, 84
timber, 130, 175, 188
Timbuktu, 34, 91, 100, *112*, 137, 145
tin, *3, 4, 95*, 110, 114, 120, 145, 148, 152, 157
titanium 152
tobacco, 74, 80, 120, 181, 190, 191, 202
Togoland, 105, 112, 120, 130, 155, 160, *187*, 215
toiches, 172
tomatoes, 81, 202
Tombouctu, *see* Timbuktu
Tongo, 67
toposequence, *see* soil catena
Touareg, 82
tourism, *186*
towns, 120, **136–44**, 189
tractors, 176
Transkei, 94
Transnational companies (TNCs), 176, 201, 202
Transvaal, 94, 106, 107, 108, 113, 120, 127, 128, 130, 145, 147, 149, 173, 178, **179**
Tribal Trust Lands (formerly Native Reserves), 193
tribes and tribalism, *65, 67–8*, 91, 114, 136
Tripoli, 92
Tripolitania, 111
trypanosomiasis, *see also* sleeping sickness, 51, **57–8**, 61, 76
tsetse fly, 51, **57–8**, 61, 71, 76, 134
Tsumeb, 152
Tshikapa, 152
Tugela river, 173
tuna, 52, 83
tungsten, *3, 95*
Tunis, 1, 92, 113
Tunisia, 63, 89, 91, 114, 116, 117, 120, 137, 153, 154, 219
Turkana, 199, 221
Turks, 91, 92, 96, 104
tyres, 176, 184

UNITA, 224
Udi plateau, 76
Udi escarpment, 138–40
Uélé basin, 106

Uganda, 64, 116, 117, 131, 135, 136, 176, 184, 186, 193, 196, 219, 223, 224
Ughelli, 183
ujamaa, 195
Ujiji, 97
Umgeni river, 180
Umlaas river, 180
Unilateral Declaration of Independence (UDI), 182, 201
United Nations, 115, 120, 224
Food and Agricultural Organisation (FAO), 54, 167, 174
Upper Volta, *see* Burkina-Faso
uranium, *4, 5, 95*, 148, 152

Vaal river, *129, 130, 173*, 179
Vandals, 89
vegetables, 78
vegetation, 35, *36, 37*
Vereeniging, 148, 173, 178, 179
Victoria Falls, 159
Victoria Island, *13*
villagization, **193–8**, 221
vines, 81, 181
volcanoes, 8
Volta dam, 140
Volta delta, 79, *79*, 174
Volta Lake, 159–62, *161*
Volta river, *12*, 60, 159

Wad Medani, 201
Wankie, 108, 150
Warri, 153, 183
warthog, 58
waterholes, *19*
wattle, 180
Welkom, 147, 148
West Nicholson, 150
Western Desert, Egypt, 219
wheat, 73, 78, 165, 168, 171, 173, 181, 190, 218
White Nile, 25, 29, 31, 97, 102, 170, 172
Windhoek, 152
wine, 76, 190
winter rainfall zone, 74
wire ropes, 177
Witbank, 148, 179
Witwitersrand, *see* Rand
wool, 91, 181
World Bank, 202, 203
World Health Organisation, 60, 203
World War, First, *106*, **111–12**
World War, Second, **114–16**, 121, 178, 181, 182

Xhosa, 94

yams, 73, 89
yellow fever, 53, 57

Yemen, 96
Yoruba, 130, 137, 138, 139, 142

Zaire, 63, 65, 74, 117, 120, 122, 127,
    131, 143, 149, 150, **152**, 162, 175,
    222, 223, 224
Zaire basin, 1, 38, 39, 52, 63, 102, 137,
    201

Zaire river, *30, 31, 97, 102, 157*
Zambezi river, *31, 31, 34, 52, 61, 90,
    92, 152,* **158–9**
Zambia, *see also* Northern Rhodesia,
    76, 84, 116, 120, 127, 134, 135, 140,
    143, 149, **150–2**, 159, 181, 190, 199,
    224
Zande, 74, 75, 97

Zanzibar, 97, 99
Zaria, 76, 174
zebra, *50*
zinc, 3, 95, 108, 150, 152
Zimbabwe, *see also* Rhodesia, 63, 92,
    95, 124, 135, *145, 149–50,* 151, 159,
    175, 177, **181–2, 193,** 199, 223–4, 226
Zulu, 94–6, 134